Essentials of the U.S. Health Care System

Third Edition

Leiyu Shi, DrPH, MBA, MPA
Professor
Department of Health Policy and Management
Bloomberg School of Public Health
Johns Hopkins University
Baltimore, Maryland

Douglas A. Singh, PhD, MBA
Associate Professor Emeritus of Management
School of Business and Economics
Indiana University–South Bend
South Bend, Indiana

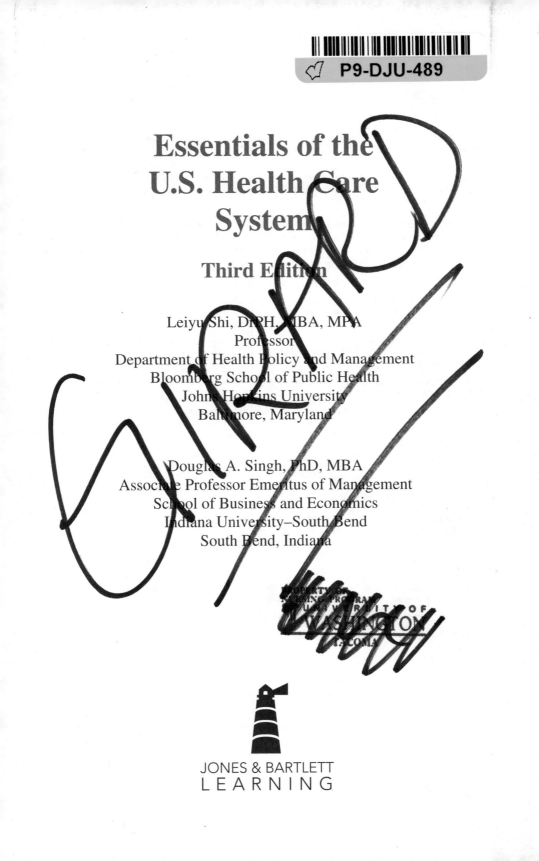

JONES & BARTLETT
LEARNING

World Headquarters
Jones & Bartlett Learning
5 Wall Street
Burlington, MA 01803
978-443-5000
info@jblearning.com
www.jblearning.com

Jones & Bartlett Learning books and products are available through most bookstores and online booksellers. To contact Jones & Bartlett Learning directly, call 800-832-0034, fax 978-443-8000, or visit our website, www.jblearning.com.

Substantial discounts on bulk quantities of Jones & Bartlett Learning publications are available to corporations, professional associations, and other qualified organizations. For details and specific discount information, contact the special sales department at Jones & Bartlett Learning via the above contact information or send an email to specialsales@jblearning.com.

Production Credits
Publisher: Michael Brown
Managing Editor: Maro Gartside
Editorial Assistant: Kayla Dos Santos
Editorial Assistant: Chloe Falivene
Associate Production Editor: Rebekah Linga
Senior Marketing Manager: Sophie Fleck Teague
Manufacturing and Inventory Control Supervisor: Amy Bacus
Composition: Cenveo Publisher Services
Cover Design: Scott Moden
Cover Image: © iStockphoto/Thinkstock
Printing and Binding: Edwards Brothers Malloy
Cover Printing: Edwards Brothers Malloy

To order this product, use ISBN: 978-1-284-03542-1

Library of Congress Cataloging-in-Publication Data
Shi, Leiyu.
  Essentials of the U.S. health care system / Leiyu Shi and Douglas A. Singh. — 3rd ed.
    p. ; cm.
  Essentials of the United States health care system
  Includes bibliographical references and index.
  ISBN 978-1-4496-5261-6 (paper) — ISBN 1-4496-5261-1
  I. Singh, Douglas A., 1946- II. Title. III. Title: Essentials of the United States health care system.
  [DNLM: 1. Delivery of Health Care—United States. 2. Health Policy—United States. W 84 AA1]

  362.10973—dc23
                                                                            2012010584
6048

Printed in the United States of America
17 16 15 14 13   10 9 8 7 6 5 4

Contents

Preface

This book is a condensed and simplified version of our standard text-book on the U.S. health care system, *Delivering Health Care in America: A Systems Approach, Fifth Edition*, which has been widely used for teaching both undergraduate and graduate courses. While retaining the main themes of the larger book, this version covers the essential elements of U.S. health care but leaves out much of the data and technical details found in the expanded version. It has an easier-to-read format that is intended for two main audiences: junior college students taking a basic course in U.S. health care, and students who need a condensed text to supplement materials in another course, such as an advanced course in health policy or various courses taught in allied health settings in which a section of a course is devoted to the health care delivery system.

This book retains the systems model to organize the major themes of U.S. health care delivery. The first three chapters lay the foundation that is necessary for understanding the U.S. health care delivery system, which is distinct from any other system in the world. "Major Characteristics of U.S. Health Care Delivery" (Chapter 1) gives an overview of U.S. health care and contrasts the American system with the three most commonly used models of health care delivery in other advanced nations, such as Canada, the United Kingdom, and Germany. "Foundation of U.S. Health Care Delivery" (Chapter 2) explains the different models for understanding health and its determinants. In the context of American beliefs and values, this chapter also discusses the issue of equity using the concepts of market justice and social justice, and explains how health services are rationed in both market justice- and social justice-based systems. "Historical Overview of U.S. Health Care Delivery" (Chapter 3) traces the history of U.S. health care from colonial times to the present. The key to understanding the nature of the current health care system and its likely future direction is to understand its evolutionary past. This chapter also includes current trends in corporatization, information revolution, and globalization as they pertain to health care delivery.

The next three chapters are about the resources—both human and non-human—employed in delivering health care. "Health Care Providers and Professionals" (Chapter 4) addresses the roles played by some of the major types of personnel in health care delivery. It also discusses some key issues pertaining to the number and distribution of physicians and the effect these factors have on the delivery of health care. "Technology and Its Effects" (Chapter 5) discusses medical technology and the various issues related to its development and dissemination. "Financing and Reimbursement Methods" (Chapter 6) explains the concept of health insurance, the major private and public health insurance programs in the United States, and methods of reimbursing providers.

The next group of chapters describe the system processes, beginning with outpatient and primary care services (discussed in Chapter 7). Hospitals are the focus of the next chapter. "Managed Care and Integrated Systems" (Chapter 9) examines managed care, which has revolutionized health care delivery in the United States, as well as the different types of arrangements found in integrated organizations. "Long-term Care Services" (Chapter 10) explores the meaning and scope of long-term care and provides an overview of community-based and institution-based long-term care services. "Populations with Special Health Needs" (Chapter 11) highlights vulnerable populations and their special health care needs. This chapter also includes a section on mental health.

The next two chapters deal with the main outcomes of the health care system and the ways in which those outcomes are addressed through health policy. The main outcomes associated with health care are presented in (Chapter 12), "Cost, Access, and Quality." "Health Policy" (Chapter 13) gives an overview of health policy, including the major participants in its development and the process by which it is created, in the United States. "The Future of Health Services Delivery" (Chapter 14) explores the future of health care in the United States in the context of health reform, conflicting issues of cost and access, implications of global occurrences for public health, and technological innovations.

NEW IN THE THIRD EDITION

This third edition has been updated with the latest health statistics and pertinent information available at the time the manuscript was prepared. Some key additions to the text include the following:

- Integrated delivery systems, long-term care delivery systems, public health systems, and updated health care systems of selected countries ("Major Characteristics of U.S. Health Care Delivery")
- *Healthy People 2020* and examples of policy, community, and health care interventions ("Foundation of U.S. Health Care Delivery")
- Delivery of mental health in asylums and national health care in the context of the Patient Protection and Affordable Care Act of 2010 (ACA of 2010) ("Historical Overview of U.S. Health Care Delivery")
- Public health professionals ("Health Care Providers and Professionals")
- Promotion of electronic health records under the American Recovery and Reinvestment Act of 2009 and expanded information on remote health services ("Technology and Its Effects")
- Summary of the ACA of 2010 as it pertains to health insurance, expanded information on employer-based health insurance, expanded information on Medicare Advantage (Part C), and an overview of the Outpatient Prospective Payment System (OPPS) for freestanding clinics ("Financing and Reimbursement Methods")
- Updated community health center information, alternative medicine, and the medical home concept ("Outpatient Services and Primary Care")
- Information on critical access hospitals, academic medical centers, and the Magnet Recognition Program of the American Nurses Association ("Hospitals")
- The Centers for Medicare and Medicaid Services (CMS) star rating system for Medicare Advantage plans and an introduction to accountable care organizations ("Managed Care and Integrated Systems")
- New census data on racial/ethnic minorities, and the relationship between the uninsured and the ACA of 2010 ("Populations with Special Health Needs")
- Access to care and the ACA of 2010, and new quality initiatives ("Cost, Access, and Quality")

- Health policy and the ACA of 2010, smoking and tobacco use, cost-containment strategies, and comparative international health policies ("Health Policy")
- Health care reform and its future; the changing needs of the U.S. population and the challenges posed by cost, access, care delivery, and workforce issues; and global threats and the imperative of international cooperation ("The Future of Health Services Delivery")

About the Authors

Leiyu Shi, DrPH, MBA, MPA is Professor of Health Policy and Health Services Research at Johns Hopkins University, Bloomberg School of Public Health, Department of Health Policy and Management. He is also Director of Johns Hopkins Primary Care Policy Center. He received his doctoral education from University of California, Berkeley, majoring in health policy and services research. He also has a master's degree in business administration focusing on finance. Dr. Shi's research focuses on primary care, health disparities, and vulnerable populations. He has conducted extensive studies on the association between primary care and health outcomes, particularly on the role of primary care in mediating the adverse effects of income inequality on health outcomes. Dr. Shi is also well known for his extensive research on vulnerable populations in the United States—in particular, community health centers that serve vulnerable populations, including their sustainability, provider recruitment and retention experiences, financial performance, experience under managed care, and quality of care. Dr. Shi is the author of seven textbooks and more than 140 scientific journal articles.

Douglas Singh, PhD, MBA retired from Indiana University–South Bend, where he taught graduate and undergraduate courses in health care delivery, policy, finance, and management in the School of Business and Economics and in the Department of Political Science. He also taught in the School of Business at Andrews University. Dr. Singh's background includes health services research, publishing, business consulting, and 14 years in senior management positions in the U.S. health care industry.

Acknowledgments

We gratefully acknowledge Sylvia Shi for creating the cartoons for this book. We are also grateful for the valuable assistance of Sarika Rane, Kyle Callahan, Eun hee Cho, and Hannah Sintek from Johns Hopkins University. Of course, all errors and omissions remain the responsibility of the authors.

Leiyu Shi
Douglas A. Singh

List of Exhibits

List of Tables

List of Figures

List of Abbreviations

ACA of 2010	Patient Protection and Affordable Care Act of 2010
ACO	Accountable care organization
ADLs	Activities of daily living
AHA	American Hospital Association
AHRQ	Agency for Healthcare Research and Quality
AIDS	Acquired immunodeficiency syndrome
ALOS	Average length of stay
AMA	American Medical Association
AMC	Academic medical center
AOA	American Osteopathic Association
APC	Ambulatory payment classification
CAH	Critical access hospital
CBO	Congressional Budget Office
CCRC	Continuing-care retirement community
CDC	Centers for Disease Control and Prevention
CEO	Chief executive officer
CHIP	Children's Health Insurance Program
CMS	Centers for Medicare and Medicaid Services
CPI	Consumer price index
CPOE	Computerized physician-order entry
CPT	Current procedural terminology
DHHS	Department of Health and Human Services
DME	Durable medical equipment
DRG	Diagnosis-related group
EBM	Evidence-based medicine

EHR	Electronic health record
ESRD	End-stage renal disease
FDA	Food and Drug Administration
FPL	Federal poverty level
GDP	Gross domestic product
HDHP	High-deductible health plan
HEDIS	Healthcare Effectiveness Data and Information Set
HHRG	Home health resource group
HI	Hospital insurance (in Medicare)
HIPAA	Health Insurance Portability and Accountability Act
HIV	Human immunodeficiency virus
HMO	Health maintenance organization
HRA	Health reimbursement arrangement
HSA	Health savings account
HTA	Health technology assessment
IADLs	Instrumental activities of daily living
ICF/MR	Intermediate care facility for the mentally retarded
IDS	Integrated delivery system
IHR	International Health Regulations
IPA	Independent practice association
IT	Information technology
JCAHO	Joint Commission on Accreditation of Healthcare Organizations; now known as The Joint Commission
LPN	Licensed practical nurse
LTC	Long-term care
LTCH	Long-term care hospital
LVN	Licensed vocational nurse
MA-PD	Medicare Advantage Prescription Drug Plan
MCO	Managed care organization
MMA	Medicare Prescription Drug, Improvement, and Modernization Act
MRI	Magnetic resonance imaging
MSA	Metropolitan statistical area
NCQA	National Committee for Quality Assurance
NF	Nursing facility (certification)
NIH	National Institutes of Health
OASIS	Outcomes and Assessment Information Set
OPPS	Outpatient prospective payment system

PDP	Stand-alone prescription drug plan
PERS	Personal emergency response system
PHO	Physician–hospital organization
PMPM	Per member per month
POS	Point-of-service (plan)
PPO	Preferred provider organization
PPS	Prospective payment system
R&D	Research and development
RBRVS	Resource-based relative value scale
RHS	Remote health services
RN	Registered nurse
RUG	Resource utilization group
SARS	Severe acute respiratory syndrome
SMI	Supplementary medical insurance (in Medicare)
SNF	Skilled nursing facility
SSI	Supplemental Security Income
UCR	Usual, customary, and reasonable (charges)
VA	Department of Veterans Affairs

Chapter 1

Major Characteristics of U.S. Health Care Delivery

INTRODUCTION

The United States has a unique system of health care delivery compared with other developed countries around the world. Almost all other developed countries have universal health insurance programs in which the government plays a dominant role. Almost all of the citizens in these countries are entitled to receive health care services that include routine and basic health care. In contrast, only insured Americans have been able to obtain routine and basic health care services on a continuous basis. The passage of the Patient Protection and Affordable Care Act in 2010 (ACA of 2010) holds the promise of universal coverage under government mandates. However, expansion of health insurance at an affordable cost will likely remain a major challenge. Expanding access to health care while containing overall costs and maintaining expected levels of quality continues to confound academics, policy makers, and politicians alike.

To facilitate understanding of the structural and conceptual bases for the delivery of health services, this book is organized according to the systems framework presented at the end of this chapter. One of the main objectives of this chapter is to provide a broad understanding of how health care is delivered in the United States.

The overview presented here introduces the reader to several concepts that are discussed more extensively in later chapters. As this discussion will make clear, the U.S. health care delivery system is both complex and massive. Interestingly, it is not actually a "system" in the true sense because the components illustrated in Figure 1.2 are only loosely coordinated. Yet it is called a system when its various features, components, and services are referenced. Although it may be somewhat misleading to talk about the American health care delivery "system" (Wolinsky, 1988, p. 54), for the sake of simplicity, this term will nevertheless be used throughout this book.

Organizations and individuals involved in health care range from educational and research institutions, medical suppliers, insurers, payers, and claims processors, to health care providers. There are nearly 16.4 million people employed in various health delivery settings, including professionally active doctors of medicine (MDs), doctors of osteopathy (DOs), nurses, dentists, pharmacists, and administrators. Approximately 410,000 physical, occupational, and speech therapists provide rehabilitation services. The vast array of institutions includes 5,815 hospitals, 16,000 nursing homes, almost 2,900 inpatient mental health facilities, and 11,000 home health agencies and hospices. Nearly 1,200 programs support basic health services for migrant workers and the homeless, community health centers, black lung clinics, human immunodeficiency virus (HIV) early intervention services, and integrated primary care and substance abuse treatment programs. Various types of health care professionals are trained in 151 medical and osteopathic schools, 56 dental schools, 102 schools of pharmacy, and more than 1,500 nursing programs located throughout the country (Bureau of Labor Statistics, 2011; Bureau of Primary Health Care, 2011).

There are 195 million Americans with private health insurance coverage. An additional 105 million are covered under two major public health insurance programs—Medicare and Medicaid—financed by the U.S. government. Private health insurance can be purchased from approximately 1,000 health insurance companies and 70 Blue Cross/Blue Shield plans. The private managed care sector includes approximately 452 licensed health maintenance organizations (HMOs) and 925 preferred provider organizations (PPOs). A multitude of government agencies are involved with the financing of health care, medical and health services research, and regulatory oversight of the various aspects of the health care delivery system (Aventis Pharmaceuticals, 2002; Bureau of Primary Health Care, 2011; Healthleaders, 2011; National Center for Health Statistics, 2007; Urban Institute, 2011; U.S. Bureau of the Census, 1998; U.S. Census Bureau, 2007).

SUBSYSTEMS OF U.S. HEALTH CARE DELIVERY

In the United States, multiple subsystems of health care delivery have developed, either through market forces or as a result of the need to take care of certain population segments often referred to as special populations. Discussion of the major subsystems follows.

Managed Care

Managed care is a system of health care delivery that (1) seeks to achieve efficiency by integrating the basic functions of health care delivery, (2) employs mechanisms to control (manage) utilization of medical services, and (3) determines the price at which the services are purchased and, consequently, how much the providers get paid. Managed care is the dominant health care delivery system in the United States today and covers most Americans in both private and public health insurance programs.

The employer or government is the primary financier of the managed care system. The financier contracts with a managed care organization (MCO), such as an HMO or a PPO, to offer a selected health plan to employees, and, in case of public health insurance, to Medicare and Medicaid beneficiaries. The MCO functions like an insurance company and promises to provide health care services, contracted under the health plan, to the enrollees of the plan.

The term *enrollee* (member) refers to the individual covered under the plan. The contractual arrangement between the MCO and the enrollee—including the collective array of covered health services to which the enrollee is entitled—is referred to as the *health plan* (or "plan" for short). The health plan designates selected providers from whom the enrollees can choose to receive routine services. Primary care providers or general practitioners typically deliver routine medical services and make decisions about referrals for higher-level or specialty services. Hence, primary care physicians are often referred to as "gatekeepers." The choice of major service providers, such as hospitals, is also limited under health plans. Some services may be delivered through the plans' own hired physicians, but most are delivered through contracts with providers such as physicians, hospitals, and diagnostic clinics.

Although the employer finances the care by purchasing a plan from an MCO, the MCO is responsible for negotiating with providers. Providers are typically paid either through a capitation (per head) arrangement, in which providers receive a fixed payment for each patient or employee under their care, or via a discounted fee arrangement. Providers are willing to discount their services for MCO patients in exchange for being included in the MCO network and being guaranteed a patient population. As part of their planning process, health plans rely on the expected cost of health care utilization, which always runs the risk of costing more than the premiums collected. By underwriting this risk, the plan assumes the role of insurer.

As of 2009, there were 66.21 million people enrolled in health maintenance organizations (HMO), 53.20 million people enrolled in preferred provider organizations (PPO), 8.87 million people enrolled in point-of-service (POS) plans, and 7.09 million people enrolled in high-deductible health plans (Kaiser Family Foundation and Health Research & Educational Trust, 2009; U.S. Department of Labor 2009).

Figure 1.1 illustrates the basic functions and mechanisms that are necessary for the delivery of health services within a managed care environment. The four key functions of financing, insurance, delivery, and payment make up the quad-function model. Managed care integrates the four functions to varying degrees.

Military

The military medical care system is available free of charge to active-duty military personnel of the U.S. Army, Navy, Air Force, and Coast Guard, as well as to members of certain uniformed nonmilitary services such as the Public Health Service and the National Oceanographic and Atmospheric Association (NOAA). It is a well-organized, highly integrated system that provides comprehensive services. It covers both preventive and treatment services, which are provided by salaried health care personnel, many of whom are themselves in the military or uniformed services. This system combines public health with medical care. Routine ambulatory care

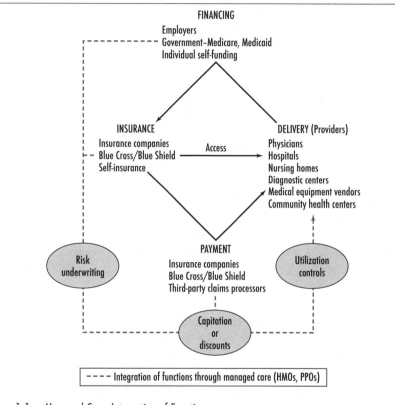

FINANCING
Employers
Government–Medicare, Medicaid
Individual self-funding

INSURANCE
Insurance companies
Blue Cross/Blue Shield
Self-insurance

Access

DELIVERY (Providers)
Physicians
Hospitals
Nursing homes
Diagnostic centers
Medical equipment vendors
Community health centers

Risk underwriting

PAYMENT
Insurance companies
Blue Cross/Blue Shield
Third-party claims processors

Utilization controls

Capitation or discounts

---- Integration of functions through managed care (HMOs, PPOs)

Figure 1.1   Managed Care: Integration of Functions

is provided close to the military personnel's place of work at the dispensary, sick bay, first aid station, or medical station. Routine medical services are provided at base dispensaries, in sick bays aboard ship, and at base hospitals. Advanced hospital services are provided in regional military hospitals. Although patients have little choice regarding how services are provided, the military medical care system generally provides high-quality health care.

Families and dependents of active-duty or retired career military personnel are either treated at the hospitals or dispensaries or are covered by *TriCare*, a program that is financed by the U.S. Department of Defense.

This insurance plan permits the beneficiaries to receive care from both private and military medical care facilities.

The Veterans Administration (VA) health care system is available to retired veterans who have previously served in the military, with priority given to those who are disabled. The VA system focuses on hospital care, mental health services, and long-term care. It is one of the largest and oldest (dating back to 1930s) formally organized health care systems in the world. Its mission is to provide medical care, education and training, research, contingency support, and emergency management for the U.S. Department of Defense medical care system. It provides health care to more than 5.5 million persons at over 1,100 sites, including 153 hospitals, 807 ambulatory and community-based clinics, 135 nursing homes, 209 counseling centers, 47 domiciliaries (residential care facilities), 73 home health care programs, and various contract care programs. The VA budget exceeds $40 billion, and it employed a staff of nearly 280,000 as of 2010 (Department of Veterans Affairs, 2011; National Center for Veterans Analysis and Statistics, 2007).

The entire VA system is organized into 23 geographically distributed *Veterans Integrated Service Networks (VISNs)*. Each VISN is responsible for coordinating the activities of the hospitals, outpatient clinics, nursing homes, and other facilities located within its jurisdiction. Each VISN receives an allocation of federal funds and is responsible for equitable distribution of those funds among its hospitals and other providers. VISNs are also responsible for improving efficiency by reducing duplicative services, emphasizing preventive services, and shifting services from costly inpatient care to less costly outpatient care.

Subsystem for Special Populations

Special populations, also called vulnerable populations, refer to those with health needs but inadequate resources to address those needs. For example, they include individuals who are poor and uninsured, those belonging to certain minority groups or immigrant status, or those living in geographically or economically disadvantaged communities. They typically receive care through the nation's "safety net," which includes public health insurance programs such as Medicare and Medicaid, and providers such as community health centers, migrant health centers, free clinics, and hospital emergency departments. Many safety net providers offer comprehensive medical and enabling services (e.g., language translation, transportation, outreach, nutrition and health education, social support services, case management, and child care) targeted to the unique needs of vulnerable populations.

As an example, federally funded health centers have provided primary and preventive health services to rural and urban underserved populations for more than 30 years. The Bureau of Primary Health Care (BPHC), located within the Health Resources and Services Administration in the Department of Health and Human Services (DHHS), provides federal support for community-based health centers that include programs for migrant and seasonal farm workers and their families, homeless persons, public housing residents, and school-aged children. These services facilitate regular access to care for patients who are predominantly minority, low income, uninsured, or enrolled in Medicaid, the public insurance program for the poor. In 2010, the nationwide network of 1,124 community health organizations served 19.5 million people across 8,100 service sites, and handled a total of 77 million patient visits. Approximately 93 percent of this population was living on incomes that were less than 200% of the poverty level, and 38% were uninsured (Bureau of Primary Health Care, 2011). Health centers have contributed to significant improvements in health outcomes for the uninsured and Medicaid populations and have reduced disparities in health care and health status across socioeconomic and racial/ethnic groups (Politzer et al., 2003; Shi et al., 2001).

Medicare is one of the largest sources of public health insurance in the United States, serving the elderly, the disabled, and those with end-stage renal disease. Managed by the Centers for Medicare and Medicaid Services (CMS), another division within the DHHS, Medicare offers coverage for hospital care, post-discharge nursing care, hospice care, outpatient services, and prescription drugs.

Medicaid, the third largest source of health insurance in the country, covering approximately 16% of the U.S. population, provides coverage for low-income adults, children, the elderly, and individuals with disabilities. This program is also the largest provider of long-term care to older Americans and individuals with disabilities.

In 1997, the U.S. government created the Children's Health Insurance Program (CHIP) to provide insurance to children in uninsured families. The program expanded coverage to children in families who have modest incomes but do not qualify for Medicaid. In 2009, the CHIP program spent $10 billion to cover approximately 7.7 million children (Centers for Medicare and Medicaid Services [CMS], 2011b). At little or no cost to the patient, CHIP pays for children's physician visits, immunizations, hospitalizations, and emergency room visits.

Despite the availability of government-funded health insurance, the United States' safety net is by no means secure. The availability of safety net services varies from community to community. Vulnerable populations residing in communities without safety net providers must often forego care or seek services from hospital emergency departments if available nearby. Safety net providers, in turn, face enormous pressure from the increasing number of uninsured and poor in their communities. The inability to shift costs for uncompensated care onto private insurance has become a significant problem as revenues from Medicaid—the primary source of financing for core safety net providers—have been declining because of limitations in public budgets.

Integrated Delivery

Over the last decade, the hallmark of the U.S. health care industry has been organizational integration to form *integrated delivery systems (IDSs)*, or health networks. An IDS represents various forms of ownership and other strategic linkages among hospitals, physicians, and insurers. Its objective is to have one health care organization deliver a range of services. An IDS can be defined as a network of organizations that provides or arranges to provide a coordinated continuum of services to a defined population, and that is willing to be held clinically and fiscally accountable for the outcomes and health status of that population. From the standpoint of integration, the major participants or players in the health care delivery system are physicians, hospitals, and insurers. The key strategic position that physicians, hospitals, and insurers hold has given rise to many different forms of health networks.

As quality improvement and cost control receive increasing emphasis, integrated delivery is becoming more important to the delivery of health care in the United States. Integrated delivery is increasingly seen as a way to enhance efficiency by having one health delivery organization provide a wide variety of health care services to its surrounding community. Recent studies of highly integrated health delivery systems in the United States have shown that hospitals within such systems provide a higher quality of care compared to nonintegrated hospitals (Leibert, 2011). Although the difference between the two delivery systems in terms of cost-effectiveness is negligible, clinical quality performance improves significantly in the highly integrated hospitals. Integration of communication among providers within a highly integrated system may be one reason that such systems can deliver high-quality services.

Long Term Care Delivery

Long-term care (LTC) consists of medical and nonmedical care that is provided to individuals who are chronically ill or who have a disability. LTC includes not only health care but also support services for daily living, and is delivered across a wide variety of venues, including patients' homes, assisted living facilities, and nursing homes. In addition, family members and friends provide the majority of LTC services without getting paid for them. Medicare does not cover LTC; thus, costs associated with this form of care can impose a major burden on families. Medicaid covers several different levels of LTC services, but a person must be an indigent to qualify for Medicaid. LTC insurance is offered separately by insurance companies, but most people do not purchase these plans because premiums can be unaffordable. By 2020, more than 12 million Americans are projected to require LTC, which will impose a severe strain on the nation's financial resources (CMS, 2011a).

Public Health System

The mission of the *public health system* is to improve and protect community health. The Institute of Medicine's *Future of Public Health in the 21st Century* has outlined the need for a more robust public health infrastructure and a population-based health approach for a healthier U.S. population (Centers for Disease Control and Prevention [CDC], 2011). The National Public Health Performance Standards Program identifies ten essential public health services that a system needs to deliver:

1. Monitoring health status to identify and solve community health problems
2. Diagnosing and investigating health problems and hazards
3. Informing and educating people about health problems and hazards
4. Mobilizing the community to solve health problems
5. Developing policies to support individual and community health efforts

6. Enforcing laws and regulations to support health safety
7. Providing people with access to necessary care
8. Assuring a competent and professional health workforce
9. Evaluating the effectiveness, accessibility, and quality of personal and population-based health services
10. Performing research to discover innovative solutions to health problems

CHARACTERISTICS OF THE U.S. HEALTH CARE SYSTEM

The health care system of a nation is influenced by external factors, including the political climate, level of economic development, technologic progress, social and cultural values, the physical environment, and population characteristics such as demographic and health trends. It follows, then, that the combined interaction of these environmental forces has influenced the course of health care delivery in the United States. This section summarizes the basic characteristics that differentiate the U.S. health care delivery system from that of other countries. There are ten main areas of distinction (see **Exhibit 1.1**).

Exhibit 1.1   Main Characteristics of the U.S. Health Care System

- No central governing agency and little integration and coordination
- Technology-driven delivery system focusing on acute care
- High in cost, unequal in access, and average in outcome
- Delivery of health care under imperfect market conditions
- Government as subsidiary to the private sector

- Fusion of market justice and social justice
- Multiple players and balance of power
- Quest for integration and accountability
- Access to health care services selectively based on insurance coverage
- Legal risks influence practice behaviors

No Central Governing Agency; Little Integration and Coordination

The U.S. health care system stands in conspicuous contrast to the health care systems of other developed countries. Most developed countries have centrally controlled universal health care systems that authorize the financing, payment, and delivery of health care to all residents. In contrast, the U.S. system is not centrally controlled; it is financed both publicly and privately and, therefore, features a variety of payment, insurance, and delivery mechanisms. Private financing, predominantly through employers, accounts for approximately 54% of total health care expenditures; the government finances the remaining 46% (National Center for Health Statistics, 2009).

Centrally controlled health care systems are less complex than the U.S. health care system. They are also less costly because they can manage total expenditures through global budgets and can govern the availability and utilization of services. The United States has a large private system of financing and delivery; thus the majority of hospitals and physician clinics are private businesses that are independent of the government. Nevertheless, the federal and state governments in the United States play an important role in health care delivery. They determine public-sector expenditures and reimbursement rates for services provided to Medicaid and Medicare patients. The government also formulates standards of participation through health policy and regulation, which means that providers must comply with the standards established by the government to deliver care to Medicaid and Medicare patients. Certification standards are also regarded as minimum standards of quality in most sectors of the health care industry.

Technology Driven and Focusing on Acute Care

The United States is a hotbed of research and innovation in new medical technology. Growth in science and technology often creates a demand for new services despite shrinking resources to finance sophisticated care. Other factors contribute to increased demand for expensive technological care. For example, patients often assume that the latest innovations represent the best care, and many physicians want to try the latest gadgets. Even hospitals compete on the basis of having the most modern equipment and are often under pressure to recoup capital investments made in technology. Legal risks for providers and health plans alike may also play a role in the reluctance to deny new technology.

Although technology has ushered in a new generation of successful interventions, the negative outcomes resulting from its overuse are many. For example, the use of high technology adds to the rising costs of health care, making it more difficult for employers to extend insurance to part-time workers or for insurance companies to lower their premiums. It is essential to think twice before assuming that the best solution always involves technology, given that there are limited resources to invest in the American health care system. Considering the broad benefits of primary care in preventing acute conditions that ultimately require technological intervention, it seems essential to strive for a balanced investment in both high- and low-technology medicine.

High in Cost, Unequal in Access, and Average in Outcome

The United States spends more than any other developed country on health care (primarily medical care), and costs continue to rise at an alarming rate. Despite spending such a high percentage of the nation's gross domestic product (16% in 2008 and 17.6% in 2009) on health care, many U.S. residents have limited access to even the most basic care (Anderson et al., 2003) (see **Figure 1.2**).

Access refers to the ability of an individual to obtain health care services when needed. In the United States, access is restricted to those who (1) have health insurance through their employers, (2) are covered under a government health care program, (3) can afford to buy insurance out of their own private funds, (4) are able to pay for services privately, or (5) can obtain services through safety net providers. Health insurance is the primary means for ensuring access. In 2010, the number of uninsured Americans—those without private or public health insurance coverage—was estimated to be 48.2 million, representing 18.2% of the U.S. population (National Center for Health Statistics, 2011). For consistent basic and routine care, commonly referred to as primary care, the uninsured are unable to see a physician unless they can pay on an out-of-pocket basis. Those who cannot afford to pay generally wait until health problems develop, at which point they may be able to receive services in a hospital emergency department. It is well acknowledged that the absence of insurance inhibits a patient's ability to receive well-directed, coordinated, and continuous health care through access to primary care services and, when needed, referral to specialty services. Experts generally believe that inadequate access to basic and routine primary care services is the main reason that the United States lags behind

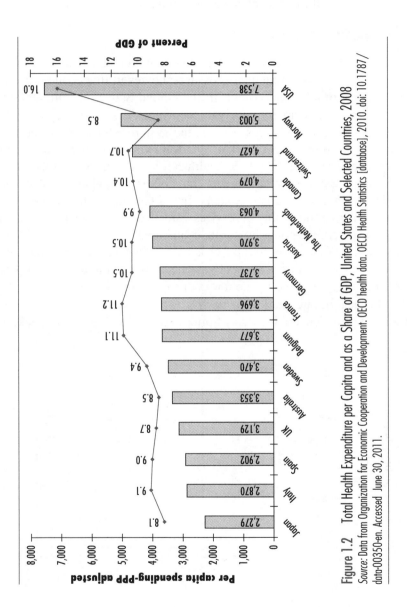

Figure 1.2 Total Health Expenditure per Capita and as a Share of GDP, United States and Selected Countries, 2008

Source: Data from Organization for Economic Cooperation and Development. OECD health data. OECD Health Statistics [database], 2010. doi: 10.1787/data-00350-en. Accessed June 30, 2011.

other developed nations in measures of population health, such as infant mortality and overall life expectancy (see **Figure 1.3** and **Figure 1.4**).

Imperfect Market Conditions

Under national health care programs, patients may have varying degrees of choice in selecting their providers; however, true economic market forces are virtually nonexistent. In the United States, even though the delivery of services is largely in private hands, health care is only partially governed by free market forces. Hence, the system is best described as a quasi-market or an imperfect market. The following key characteristics of free markets help explain why U.S. health care is not a true free market.

In a free market, multiple patients (buyers) and providers (sellers) act independently. In a free market, patients should be able to choose their provider based on price and quality of services. If matters were this simple, patient choice would determine prices by the unencumbered interaction of supply and demand. In reality, however, the payer is an MCO, Medicare, or Medicaid, rather than the patient. Prices are set by agencies external to the market; thus they are not freely governed by the forces of supply and demand.

For the health care market to be free, unrestrained competition must occur among providers on the basis of price and quality. Generally speaking,

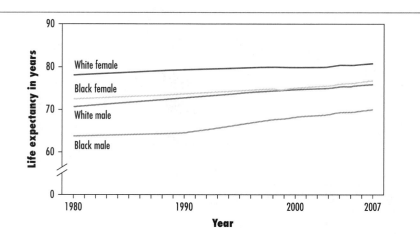

Figure 1.3   Life Expectancy at Birth

Source: Centers for Disease Control and Prevention, National Center for Health Statistics. *Health, United States, 2010,* Figure 1. Data from the National Vital Statistics Systems.

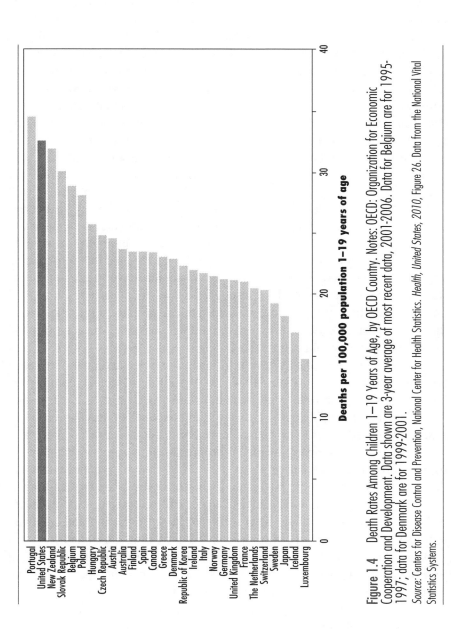

Figure 1.4   Death Rates Among Children 1–19 Years of Age, by OECD Country. *Notes:* OECD: Organization for Economic Cooperation and Development. Data shown are 3-year average of most recent data, 2001-2006. Data for Belgium are for 1995-1997; data for Denmark are for 1999-2001.

Source: Centers for Disease Control and Prevention, National Center for Health Statistics. *Health, United States, 2010*, Figure 26. Data from the National Vital Statistics Systems.

free competition exists among health care providers in the United States. The consolidation of buying power into the hands of private health plans, however, is forcing providers to form alliances and IDSs on the supply side. As explained earlier, IDSs are networks that offer a range of health care services. In certain geographic locations of the country, a single giant medical system has taken over as the sole provider of major health care services, restricting competition. As the health care system continues to move in this direction, it appears that only in large metropolitan areas will there be more than one large integrated system competing for the business of the health plans.

A free market requires that patients have information about the availability of various services. Free markets operate best when consumers are educated about the products they are using, but patients are not always well informed about the decisions that need to be made regarding their care. Choices involving sophisticated technology, diagnostic methods, interventions, and pharmaceuticals can be difficult and often require physician input. Acting as an advocate, primary care providers can reduce this information gap for patients. Increasingly, health care consumers have begun to take the initiative to educate themselves through the use of Internet resources for gathering medical information. Pharmaceutical product advertising (i.e., direct-to-consumer advertising) also has altered consumer expectations and increased awareness of available medications.

In a free market, patients have information on price and quality for each provider. In the United States, however, the current pricing methods for health care services further confound free market mechanisms. Hidden costs make it difficult for patients to gauge the full expense of services ahead of time. *Item-based pricing*, for example, refers to the costs of ancillary services that often accompany major procedures such as surgery. Patients are usually informed of the surgery's cost ahead of time but cannot anticipate the cost of anesthesiologists and pathologists or hospital supplies and facilities, thus making it extremely difficult for them to ascertain the total price before services have actually been received. Package pricing and capitated fees can help overcome these drawbacks by providing a bundled fee for a package of related services. *Package pricing* covers services that are bundled together for one episode of care, which is less encompassing than capitation. *Capitation* covers all services an enrollee may need during an entire year.

In a free market, patients must directly bear the cost of services received. The fundamental purpose of insurance is to cover major expenses when unlikely events occur; but health insurance covers even basic and routine services, which undermines this fundamental principle. Health insurance coverage for minor services such as colds, coughs, and earaches amounts to pre-payment for such services. A moral hazard exists, in that after enrollees have purchased health insurance, they typically use health care services to a greater extent than they would without health insurance.

In a free market for health care, patients as consumers make decisions about the purchase of health care services. The main factors that severely limit the patient's ability to make health care purchasing decisions have already been discussed, but at least two additional factors limit this ability to make decisions. First, decisions about the utilization of health care are often determined by need rather than by price-based demand. *Need* has generally been defined as the amount of medical care that medical experts believe a person should have to remain or become healthy. Second, the delivery of health care can result in creation of demand. This outcome follows from self-assessed need that, coupled with moral hazard, leads to greater utilization. The result is a creation of an artificial demand because prices are not taken into consideration. Practitioners who have a financial interest in additional treatments may also create artificial demand, commonly referred to as "provider-induced demand."

Government as Subsidiary to the Private Sector

In most other developed countries, the government plays a central role in delivering health care. In the United States, the private sector plays the dominant role. This arrangement can partially be explained by the American tradition of reliance on individual responsibility and a commitment to limiting the power of the national government. As a result, government spending for health care has been largely confined to filling in the gaps left open by the private sector. These gaps include environmental protection, support for research and training, and care of vulnerable populations.

Fusion of Market Justice and Social Justice

Market justice and social justice are two contrasting theories that govern the production and distribution of health care services. The principle of *market justice* places the responsibility for fair distribution of health care on market forces in a free economy. In such a system, medical care and its benefits are distributed on the basis of people's willingness and ability to pay (Santerre & Neun, 1996, p. 7). In contrast, *social justice* emphasizes the well-being of the community over that of the individual; thus the inability to obtain medical services because of a lack of financial resources is considered unjust. In a system that blends public and private resources, the two theories often work well together, contributing ideals from both theories. As an example, employed individuals with middle-class incomes obtain employer-sponsored health insurance, whereas the most needy members of society depend on government-sponsored programs. On the other hand, the two principles of justice also create conflicts. For example, many of the small employers in the United States do not offer health insurance or, if it is offered, many employees cannot afford the cost. Yet, these individuals do not qualify for government-sponsored health insurance which is available mainly to the elderly, the disabled, and the poor. Such uninsured individuals and their families may have difficulty obtaining health care when needed because safety net services are also not widely available throughout the nation.

Multiple Players and Balance of Power

The U.S. health services system involves multiple players such as physicians, administrators of health service institutions, insurance companies, large employers, and the government. Big business, labor, insurance companies, physicians, and hospitals make up a set of powerful and politically active special-interest groups represented before lawmakers by high-priced lobbyists. Each player has a different economic interest to protect; however, problems frequently arise because the self-interests of the various players are often at odds. For example, providers seek to maximize government reimbursement for services delivered to Medicare and Medicaid patients, but the government wants to contain cost increases. The fragmented self-interests of the various players produce counteracting forces within the system. One positive effect of these opposing forces is that they prevent any single entity from dominating the system. In an environment that is rife with motivations to protect conflicting self-interests, achieving comprehensive, system-wide health care reforms is next to impossible, and cost containment remains a major challenge. Consequently, the approach to health care reform in the United States is best characterized as incremental or piecemeal and can sometimes be regressive when presidential administrations change. (Note: the health care reform under the ACA of 2010 is really an example of incremental health care financing reform.)

Quest for Integration and Accountability

Currently in the United States, there is a drive to use primary care as the organizing hub for continuous and coordinated health services. Although this

model gained popularity with the expansion of managed care, its development stalled before reaching its full potential. The ideal role for primary care
would include integrated health care in the form of comprehensive, coordinated, and continuous services offered with a seamless delivery (also termed
medical home or health home for patients). Furthermore, this model emphasizes the importance of the patient–provider relationship and considers how it
can best function to improve the health of each individual, thereby strengthening the population as a whole. Integral to this relationship is the concept
of accountability. Accountability on the provider's behalf means providing
quality health care in an efficient manner; on the patient's behalf, it means
safeguarding one's own health and using available resources sensibly.

Access to Health Care Services Selectively Based on Insurance Coverage

Unlike in countries with national health plans providing universal coverage, access to health care services in the United States is limited. Although
the United States offers some of the best medical care in the world, this
care is often available only to individuals who have health insurance plans
that provide adequate coverage or who have sufficient resources to pay for
the procedures themselves.

In addition, as mentioned earlier, there is a relatively large population of
uninsured in the country. The uninsured have limited options when seeking
medical care. They can either (1) pay physicians out of pocket at rates that are
typically higher than those paid by insurance plans, (2) seek care from safety
net providers, or (3) obtain treatment for acute illnesses at a hospital emergency department for which hospitals do not receive direct payments unless
patients have the ability to pay. The Emergency Medical Treatment and Labor
Act of 1986 requires screening and evaluation of every patient, provision
of necessary stabilizing treatment, and hospital admission when necessary,
regardless of ability to pay. Unfortunately, the inappropriate use of emergency
departments results in cost-shifting, whereby patients able to pay for services,
privately insured individuals, employers, and the government ultimately cover
the costs of medical care provided to the uninsured in emergency rooms.

Legal Risks Influence Practice Behaviors

Americans as a society are quick to engage in lawsuits. Motivated by
the prospects of enormous jury awards, many people are easily persuaded
to drag alleged offenders into the courtroom at the slightest perception of
incurred harm. Private health care providers are increasingly becoming

more susceptible to litigation, and the risk of malpractice lawsuits is a serious consideration in the practice of medicine. As a form of protection, most providers engage in what is known as *defensive medicine* by prescribing additional diagnostic tests, scheduling checkup appointments, and maintaining abundant documentation on cases. Many of these efforts may be unnecessary, and simply drive up costs and promote inefficiency.

HEALTH CARE SYSTEMS OF OTHER DEVELOPED COUNTRIES

Three basic models for structuring national health care systems prevail in Western European countries and Canada. In Canada, the government finances health care through general taxes, but the actual care is delivered by private providers. In the context of the quad-function model (see Figure 1.1), the Canadian system requires a tighter consolidation of financing, insurance, and payment functions, which are coordinated by the government; delivery is characterized by detached private arrangements.

In Great Britain, the government manages the infrastructure for the delivery of medical care, in addition to financing a tax-supported national health insurance program. Under such a system, most of the medical institutions are operated by the government. Most health care providers, such as physicians, are either government employees or are tightly organized in a publicly managed infrastructure. In the context of the quad-function model, the British system requires a tighter consolidation of all four functions, typically by the government.

In Germany, health care is financed through government-mandated contributions by employers and employees. Health care is delivered by private providers. Private not-for-profit insurance companies, called sickness funds, are responsible for collecting the contributions and paying physicians and hospitals (Santerre & Neun, 1996, p. 134). In this kind of socialized health insurance system, insurance and payment functions are closely integrated, and the financing function is better coordinated with the insurance and payment functions than it is in the United States. Delivery is characterized by independent private arrangements. The government exercises overall control.

Canada

Canada's national health insurance system, referred to as Medicare, was initially established by the Medical Care Act of 1966, providing 50/50 cost sharing for provincial or territorial medical insurance plans. The system provides universal coverage with free care at the point of contact and is publicly funded through taxes, although it is privately run. Most doctors are private practitioners who are paid on a fee-for-service basis and submit service claims directly to the health insurance plan for payment. The federal government determines how health care is run, whereas provincial and territorial governments administer and deliver heath care services and health insurance plans.

To receive full funding for health insurance, the provincial governments in Canada must meet five criteria. Care must be (1) available to all eligible residents of Canada, (2) comprehensive in coverage, (3) accessible without financial and other barriers, (4) portable within the country and while traveling abroad, and (5) publicly administered.

Canada's health care system relies heavily on primary care physicians, who account for 51 percent of all active physicians in the country. These physicians serve two key functions. First, they provide first-contact health care services, and second, they coordinate patient health care services across the system to ensure continuity. Primary physicians arrange patient access to specialists, hospital admissions, and diagnostic testing and prescription drug therapy.

Canada has recently established wait time guarantees in an effort to decrease the wait times for patients. It is also putting an emphasis on improving health information technology to improve efficiency. In 2005, the Supreme Court of Canada ruled that provinces cannot prohibit private health insurance being offered for medically necessary services. Because of the long waiting lists, a significant increase in private health insurance is likely in the future of Canadian health care.

Great Britain

In Great Britain, universal health coverage is provided by the National Health Service (NHS), which is publicly funded and run, and whose operation reflects the principle that every citizen is entitled to health care. Additionally, the purchase of private health insurance is a choice for individuals, with 7 million people (12% of the population) being covered by these plans.

The NHS has been plagued by serious problems that vary in severity across the country involving funding, service, and staff. One of the largest concerns plaguing the NHS is referred to as "health tourism," which occurs when individuals travel into the country to get treated, escaping monetary fees and costing the agency almost £200 million (or US$300 million) each year. There are also long wait times for care, especially elective procedures, with 41.2% of patients reporting a wait period of 12 or more weeks to see a specialist or receive surgical care. Finally, much of the medical equipment used is outdated, as there is little funding directed toward technological innovation.

Due to rising fiscal constraints, Great Britain may see a major shift in the way in which health care is delivered in coming years. The plan is to shift care from the bureaucracy of the central government to doctors on a more local level. In this way, the British government hopes to reduce administrative costs by as much as 45% and to deliver care more efficiently. The NHS also hopes that by shifting decision making to the local level, more power will be given to patients in the health decision-making process (Department of Health, 2010).

Germany

Under government mandates, German employees and employers are required to provide 50/50 contributions if the employed individual earns less than a specific level of income (€40,500 per year in 2004 or US$55,000). The health plan also covers the employee's spouse and children (up to a certain age). If the employee's income exceeds the statutory limit, the individual is given a choice between paying for private health insurance or the state insurance. More than 90 percent of the population is covered by national health insurance, while the remainder is privately insured. Although this system prevents the growth of an uninsured population, it has met with mixed results. In 2003, the German health ministry concluded that the system suffers from a lack of competition, superfluous, insufficient, or inappropriate care, shrinking revenue, and an aging population.

Recently, Germany has been trying to move toward a system with more integrated delivery of health care, particularly because of the rising levels of chronic disease in an aging population. In addition, the implementation of integrated care may help combat the growing perceptions of low quality of care by the German people and lower the cost of delivering care (Amelung & Wolf, 2011).

Table 1.1 presents selected features of the national health care programs and health outcomes in Canada, Germany, and Great Britain and compares them with those in the United States.

Table 1.1 Health Care Systems of Selected Industrialized Countries

	United States	Canada	United Kingdom	Germany
Type	Pluralistic	National health insurance	National health system	Socialized health insurance
Ownership	Private	Public/private	Public	Private
Financing	Voluntary, multipayer system (premiums or general taxes)	Single-payer (general taxes)	Single-payer (general taxes)	Employer–employee (mandated payroll contributions and general taxes)
Reimbursement (hospital)	Varies (DRGs, negotiated fee-for-service, per diem, capitation)	Global budgets	Global budgets	Per diem payments
Reimbursement (physicians)	RBRVS, fee-for-service	Negotiated fee-for-service	Salaries and capitation payments	Negotiated fee-for-service
Consumer copayment	Small to significant	Negligible	Negligible	Negligible
Life expectancy for women	83	82.7	81.8	80.4
Infant mortality per 1,000 live births	5.1	3.9	4.7	6.8
Expenditures as a percentage of GDP	16.0	10.0	8.4	10.5

Note: DRGs, diagnosis-related groups; RBRVS, resource-based relative value scale.
Data from Organization for Economic Cooperation and Development. OECD health data. OECD Health Statistics [database], 2010. doi: 10.1787/data-00350-en. Accessed June 30, 2011.

SYSTEMS FRAMEWORK

A system consists of a set of interrelated and interdependent components designed to achieve some common goals. The components are logically coordinated. Even though the various functional components of the health services delivery structure in the United States are at best only loosely coordinated, the main components can be identified with a systems model. The systems framework used here helps understand that the structure of health care services in the United States is based on some basic principles, provides a logical arrangement of the various components, and demonstrates a progression from inputs to outputs. The main elements of this arrangement are system inputs (resources), system structure, system processes, and system outputs (outcomes). In addition, system outlook (future directions) is a necessary element of a dynamic system. This framework has been used as the conceptual base for organizing later chapters in this book (see **Figure 1.5**).

System Foundations

The structure of the current health care system is not an accident—historical, cultural, social, and economic factors explain its current structure. As discussed later in this book, these factors also affect forces that shape new trends and developments and those that impede change.

System Resources

No mechanism for the delivery of health services can fulfill its primary objective without the necessary human and nonhuman resources. Human resources consist of the various types and categories of workers directly engaged in the delivery of health services to patients. Such personnel—including physicians, nurses, dentists, pharmacists, other professionals trained at the doctoral level, and numerous categories of allied health professionals—usually have direct contact with patients. Numerous ancillary workers, such as those involved in billing and collection, marketing and public relations, and building maintenance, often play important but indirect supportive roles in the delivery of health care. Health care managers are needed to manage and coordinate various types of health care services.

System Processes

The system resources influence the development and change in physical structures, such as hospitals, clinics, and nursing homes. These structures

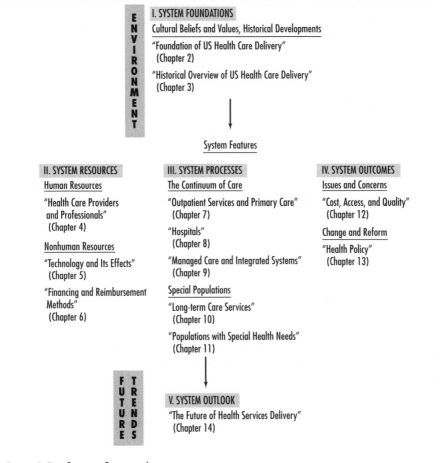

Figure 1.5   Systems Framework

are associated with distinct processes of health services delivery, and the processes are associated with distinct health conditions. Most health care services are delivered in noninstitutional settings, which are mainly associated with processes referred to as outpatient care. Institutional health services (inpatient care) are predominantly associated with acute care hospitals. Managed care and integrated systems represent a fundamental change in the financing (including payment and insurance) and delivery of health care. Even though managed care represents an integration of the resource and process elements of the systems model, it is discussed as a process for the sake of clarity and continuity of the discussions. Special institutional and community-based settings have been developed for long-term care and mental health.

System Outcomes

System outcomes refer to the critical issues and concerns surrounding what the health services system has been able to accomplish—or not accomplish—in terms of its primary objective. The primary objective of any health care delivery system is to provide cost-effective health services that meet certain established standards of quality to an entire nation. The previous three elements of the systems model (foundations, resources, and processes) play a critical role in fulfilling this objective. Access, cost, and quality are the main outcome criteria for evaluating the success of a health care delivery system. Issues and concerns regarding these criteria trigger broad initiatives for reforming the system through health policy.

System Outlook

A dynamic health care system must look forward. In essence, it must project into the future the accomplishment of desired system outcomes in view of anticipated social, cultural, and economic changes.

CONCLUSION

The United States has a unique system of health care delivery, but this system lacks universal access; therefore, continuous and comprehensive health care is not enjoyed by all Americans. Health care delivery in the United States is characterized by a patchwork of subsystems developed either through market forces or the need to take care of certain population segments. These components include managed care, the military and VA systems, the system for vulnerable populations, and the emerging IDSs. No country in the world has a perfect system. Most nations with a national health care program have a private sector that varies in size. The systems framework provides an organized approach to an understanding of the various components of the United States health care delivery system.

REFERENCES

Amelung V, Wolf S. [Health care system facing change : Physician networks: driving force for integrated care?] *Urologe A.* November 24, 2011.

Anderson GF, et al. It's the prices, stupid: Why the United States is so different from other countries. *Health Affairs.* 2003;22(3):89–105.

Aventis Pharmaceuticals. *HMO-PPO Digest: Managed Care Digest Series.* Bridgewater, NJ: Aventis Pharmaceuticals; 2002.

Bureau of Labor Statistics. Occupational employment and wages: Healthcare practitioners and technical occupations. 2011. http://www.bls.gov. Accessed December 1, 2011.

Bureau of Primary Health Care. *BPHC-UDS Annual Report.* Rockville, MD: Bureau of Primary Health Care, Health Resources and Services Administration; 2011.

Centers for Disease Control and Prevention (CDC). National Public Health Performance Standards Program. 2011. www.cdc.gov/nphpsp. Accessed December 1, 2011.

Centers for Medicare and Medicaid Services (CMS). Long term care. 2011a. http://www.medicare.gov/longtermcare/static/home.asp. Accessed December 1, 2011.

Centers for Medicare and Medicaid Services (CMS). *Net Reported Medicaid and CHIP Expenditures, FY1998–FY 2009.* 2011b.

Department of Health. *Equity and Excellence: Liberating the NHS.* United Kingdom: Department of Health; 2010.

Department of Veterans Affairs. Quick facts. 2011. www.va.gov/vetdata. Accessed December 1, 2011.

Healthleaders. Special data request via Kaiser. 2011. statehealthfacts.org.

Kaiser Family Foundation and Health Research & Educational Trust. Employer health benefits 2009 annual survey. Exhibit 5.1. 2009. www.kff.org.

Leibert M. Performance of integrated delivery systems: quality, service and cost implications. *Leadership Health Serv.* 2011;24(3):196–206.

National Center for Health Statistics. *Health, United States, 2007.* Hyattsville, MD: Department of Health and Human Services; 2007.

National Center for Health Statistics. *Health, United States, 2009.* Hyattsville, MD: Department of Health and Human Services; 2009.

National Center for Health Statistics. *Health, United States, 2010.* Hyattsville, MD: Department of Health and Human Services; 2011.

National Center for Veterans Analysis and Statistics. *FY07 VA Information Pamphlet*. Washington, DC: Department of Veterans Affairs; 2007.

Politzer RM, et al. The future role of health centers in improving national health. *J Public Health Policy* 2003;24(3):296–306.

Santerre RE, Neun SP. *Health Economics: Theories, Insights, and Industry Studies*. Chicago: Irwin; 1996.

Shi L, et al. The impact of managed care on vulnerable populations served by community health centers. *J Ambul Care Manage* 2001;24(1):51–66.

Urban Institute. *The Urban Institute and Kaiser Commission on Medicaid and the Uninsured Estimates Based on Data from Medicaid Statistical Information System (MSIS) Reports from the Centers for Medicare and Medicaid Services (CMS)*. 2011.

U.S. Bureau of the Census. *Statistical Abstract of the United States: 1998*. 118th ed. Washington, DC: Bureau of the Census; 1998.

U.S. Census Bureau. Current populations report. In: *Income, Poverty, and Health Insurance Coverage in the United States: 2006*. Washington, DC: Government Printing Office; 2007:60–233.

U.S. Department of Labor. National compensation survey: Employee benefits in the United States, March 2009. Table 9. September 2009. http://www.bls .gov/ncs/ebs/benefits/2009/ebbl0044.pdf.

Wolinsky FD. *The Sociology of Health: Principles, Practitioners, and Issues*. 2nd ed. Belmont, CA: Wadsworth; 1988.

Chapter 2

Foundation of U.S. Health Care Delivery

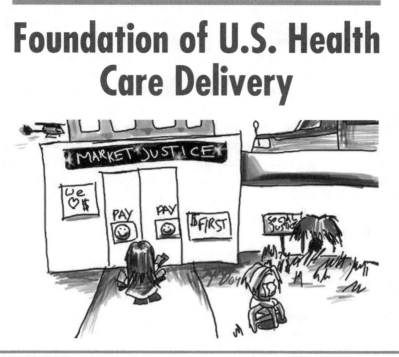

INTRODUCTION

From an economic perspective, curative medicine seems to yield decreasing returns on health improvement while health care expenditures increase (Saward & Sorensen, 1980). There is increasing recognition of the benefits to society that can result from the promotion of health and the prevention of disease, disability, and premature death. Although the financing of health care has primarily focused on curative medicine, slow progress continues toward an emphasis on health promotion and disease prevention. The progress has been slow due to the insurance system, cultural values, and medical practice that emphasize disease rather than health. The common definitions of health, as well as measures for evaluating health status, reflect similar inclinations.

Demographic and health trends and initiatives focused on reducing disease and disability must govern the planning of health services. In addition, the concepts of health and its determinants should be used to design appropriate educational, preventive, and therapeutic initiatives. This chapter proposes a comprehensive approach to health, although this model may be an ideal that the health care delivery system is simply not able to achieve under present conditions.

This chapter also explores the contrasting theories of market justice and social justice as they apply to health care. Beliefs and values ingrained in the American culture have also been influential in laying the foundations of a system that has remained predominantly private, as opposed to a tax-financed national health care program. In recent years, however, societal values have slowly shifted toward a social justice mindset, and the expectations of many Americans suggest that a gradual departure from traditional American values of self-reliance may be giving way to greater dependence on the government. Passage of the Patient Protection and Affordable Care Act (ACA) of 2010 presages a gradual shift from market justice to social justice in the U.S. health care system.

WHAT IS HEALTH?

In the United States, the concepts of health and health care have largely been governed by the medical model or, more specifically, the biomedical model. The *medical model* presupposes the existence of illness or disease, thereby emphasizing clinical diagnosis and medical intervention in the treatment of disease or its symptoms. Under the medical model, health is defined as the absence of illness or disease. The implication is that optimal health exists when a person is free of symptoms and does not require medical treatment; however, this reasoning does not actually provide a definition of health in the true sense, but rather a definition of what is not ill health (Wolinsky, 1988, p. 76). Accordingly, prevention of disease and health promotion are relegated to a secondary status; thus, when the term "health care delivery" is used, it actually refers to the delivery of medical care or illness care. A measure that is often used to indicate lack of health in a population is mortality or death (see **Figure 2.1** for death rates by age and cause in the United States).

Medical sociologists have gone a step further by defining health as the state of optimal capacity of an individual to perform his or her expected social roles and tasks, such as work, school, and household chores

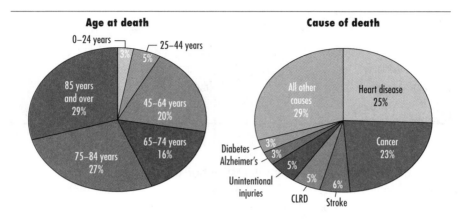

Figure 2.1   Deaths for All Ages, 2007. Note: CLRD: chronic lower respiratory diseases.
Source: Centers for Disease Control and Prevention, National Center for Health Statistics. Health, United States, 2010, Figure 24. Data from the National Vital Statistics Systems.

(Parsons, 1972). A person who is unable (as opposed to unwilling) to perform his or her social roles in society is considered sick even though many people continue to engage in their social obligations despite suffering from pain, cough, colds, and other types of temporary disabilities, including mental distress. Hence, a person's engagement in social roles does not necessarily signify that the individual is in a state of optimal health.

An emphasis on both the physical and mental dimensions of health is found in the definition of health proposed by the Society for Academic Emergency Medicine (SAEM). This organization defines health as "a state of physical and mental well-being that facilitates the achievement of individual and societal goals" (SAEM, 1992).

The World Health Organization's (WHO) definition of health is most often cited as the ideal that health care delivery systems should try to achieve. The WHO (1948) defines *health* as "a complete state of physical, mental, and social well-being, and not merely the absence of disease or infirmity." This definition includes physical, mental, and social dimensions, which constitute the biopsychosocial model of health. The WHO has also defined a "*health care system*" as all of the activities aimed at promoting, restoring, or maintaining health (McKee, 2001). As this chapter points out, health care should include much more than medical care.

Exhibit 2.1   Indicators of Health

- Self-reported health status
- Life expectancy
- Morbidity (disease)
- Mental well-being

- Social functioning
- Functional limitations
- Disability
- Spiritual well-being

There has been a growing interest in holistic or comprehensive health, which emphasizes the well-being of every aspect of what makes a person whole and complete. *Holistic medicine* seeks to treat the individual as a whole person (Ward, 1995). Holistic health incorporates the spiritual dimension as a fourth element in addition to the physical, mental, and social aspects necessary for optimal health. Hence, the holistic model provides the most complete understanding of what health is (see **Exhibit 2.1** for some key examples of health indicators). A growing volume of medical literature now points to the healing effects of a person's religion and spirituality on morbidity and mortality (Levin, 1994). Numerous studies have identified an inverse association between religious involvement and all-cause mortality (McCullough et al., 2000). Religious and spiritual beliefs and practices have been shown to positively influence a person's physical, mental, and social well-being—they may affect the incidences, experiences, and outcomes of several common medical problems (Maugans, 1996).

The spiritual dimension is often tied to one's religious beliefs, values, morals, and practices. More broadly, it is described as meaning, purpose, and fulfillment in life; hope and will to live; faith; and a person's relationship with God (Marwick, 1995; Ross, 1995; Swanson, 1995). The holistic approach to health also alludes to the need for incorporating alternative therapies into the predominant medical model.

Illness and Disease

The terms *illness* and *disease* are not synonymous, although they are often used interchangeably, as they are throughout this book. Illness is recognized by means of a person's own perceptions and evaluation of how he or she feels. For example, an individual may feel pain, discomfort, weakness, depression, or anxiety, but a disease may or may not be present; however, the ultimate determination that disease is present is based on a medical professional's evaluation rather than the patient's assessment. It reflects the highest state of professional knowledge, particularly that of the physician, and it requires therapeutic intervention (May, 1993). Certain diseases, such as hypertension (high blood pressure), are asymptomatic and are not always manifested through illness. A hypertensive person has a disease but may not know it. Thus it is possible to be diseased without feeling ill. Likewise, a person may feel ill, yet not have a disease.

Disease can be classified as acute, subacute, or chronic. An *acute condition* is relatively severe, episodic (of short duration), and often treatable (Timmreck, 1994, p. 26). It is subject to recovery, and treatment is generally provided in a hospital. Examples of acute conditions include a sudden interruption of kidney function or a myocardial infarction (heart attack). A *subacute condition* lies between the acute and chronic extremes on the disease continuum, but has some acute features. Subacute conditions can be post-acute, requiring further treatment after a brief stay in the hospital. Examples include ventilator and head trauma care. A *chronic condition* is less severe but of long and continuous duration (Timmreck, 1994, p. 26). The patient may not fully recover from such a condition. The disease may be kept under control through appropriate medical treatment, but if left untreated, it may lead to severe and life-threatening health problems. Examples include asthma, diabetes, and hypertension.

Quality of Life

The term *quality of life* is used in a denotative sense to capture the essence of overall satisfaction with life during and after a person's encounter with the health care delivery system. Thus the term is used in two different ways. First, it is an indicator of how satisfied a person was with his or her experiences while receiving health care services. Specific life domains such as comfort factors, dignity, privacy, security, degree of independence, decision-making autonomy, and attention to personal preferences are significant to most people. These factors are now regarded as rights that patients can demand during any type of health care encounter. Second, quality of life can refer to a person's overall satisfaction with life and with self-perceptions of health, particularly after some medical intervention. The implication is that desirable processes during medical treatment and successful outcomes would subsequently have a positive effect on an individual's ability to function and carry out social roles and obligations. It can also enhance a sense of fulfillment and self-worth.

DETERMINANTS OF HEALTH

The *determinants of health* have made a major contribution to the understanding that a singular focus on medical care delivery is unlikely to improve the health status of any given population. Multiple factors determine health and well-being. Hence, a more balanced approach must emphasize health determinants at an individual level as well as broad policy interventions at the population level (**Figure 2.2**).

The leading determinants of health (see examples in **Exhibit 2.2**) can be classified into four main categories:

- Environment
- Behavior and lifestyle
- Heredity
- Medical care

Environment

Environmental factors encompass the physical, socioeconomic, sociopolitical, and sociocultural dimensions of life. Physical environmental factors such as air pollution, food and water contaminants, radiation, and toxic chemicals are easily identified as factors that can significantly influence health; however, the relationship of other environmental factors to health may not always be so obvious. For example, socioeconomic status is related to health and well-being. People who have higher incomes often live in

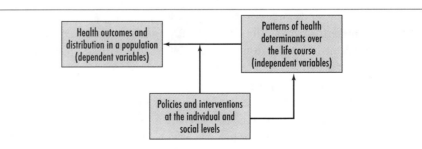

Figure 2.2   Schematic Definition of Population Health
Source: Adapted from Kindig D, Stoddart G. What is population health? *Am J Public Health.* 2003;93(3):380–833.

Exhibit 2.2   Examples of Health Determinants

• Physical activity	• Mental health
• Overweight/obesity	• Injury and violence
• Tobacco use	• Environmental quality
• Substance abuse	• Immunization
• Responsible sexual behavior	• Access to health care

areas where they are less exposed to environmental risks and have better access to health care. The association of income inequality with a variety of health indicators such as life expectancy, age-adjusted mortality rates, and leading causes of death is well documented (Kaplan et al., 1996; Kawachi et al., 1997; Kennedy et al., 1996; Mackenbach et al., 1997). The greater the economic gap between the rich and poor in a given geographic area, the worse the overall health status of the population in that area will be. Moreover, wide income gaps may produce less social cohesion and greater psychosocial stress and, consequently, poorer health (Wilkinson, 1997).

The relationship between education and health status is also well established. Less-educated Americans die younger than their better-educated counterparts. One possible explanation for this relationship is that better-educated people are more likely to avoid risky behaviors such as smoking and drug abuse.

The environment can also have a significant influence on developmental health. Neuroscientists have found that good nurturing and stimulation during the first three years of life—a key period for brain development—activate the brain's neural pathways and may even permanently increase the number of brain cells. Hence, the quality of child care provided in the first three years of life is of monumental importance (Shellenbarger, 1997). Early childhood development has an enormous influence on a person's future health.

Behavior and Lifestyle

Individual lifestyles or *behavioral factors* are also a key determinant of health. For example, diet, exercise, a stress-free lifestyle, risky or unhealthy behaviors, and other individual choices have been found to play a major role in most of the significant health problems of today. Heart disease, diabetes, stroke, sexually transmitted diseases, and cancer are just some of the ailments with direct links to individual choices and lifestyles.

Heredity

Heredity is a key determinant of health because genetic factors predispose individuals to certain diseases. There is little anyone can do about the genetic makeup he or she has already inherited, but engaging in a healthy lifestyle and health-promoting behaviors can significantly influence the development and severity of inherited disease in those predisposed to it, as well as the risk for future generations.

Medical Care

Although environment, behavior and lifestyle, and heredity are more important in the determination of health, well-being, and susceptibility to premature death, access to medical care is nevertheless a key factor influencing health. Both individual health and population health are closely related to access to adequate preventive and curative health care services. The health care delivery system and the way that care is delivered can have a major effect on a person's health. In the United States, most health care expenditures are allocated to the treatment of medical conditions, and not to the prevention or control of factors that contribute to these medical conditions. This misallocation can be attributed to many factors, including the insurance system, cultural beliefs, and traditional medical training and practice.

CULTURAL BELIEFS AND VALUES

A value system orients members of a society toward defining what is desirable for that society. It has been observed that even a society as complex and highly differentiated as the United States can be said to have a relatively well-integrated system of institutionalized common values at the societal level (Parsons, 1972). Although such a view may still prevail, the current American society now incorporates several different subcultures that have grown in size because of a steady influx of immigrants from different parts of the world. Such diversity promotes sociocultural variations in how people view their health and, more importantly, how such differences influence people's attitudes and behaviors concerning health, illness, and death (Wolinsky, 1988, p. 39). Historically, cultural beliefs and values have been strong forces against attempts to initiate fundamental changes in the financing and delivery of health care.

STRATEGIES TO IMPROVE HEALTH

Healthy People Initiatives

Since 1980, the United States has undertaken a series of 10-year plans outlining certain key national health objectives to be accomplished during each of the 10-year time frames. These initiatives have been founded on the integration of medical care with preventive services, health promotion, and education; integration of personal and community health care; and increased access to integrated services. The *Healthy People 2010: Healthy People in Healthy Communities* initiative was launched in January 2000. Its objectives were defined in the context of changing demographics in the United States, reflecting an older and more racially diverse population. The *Healthy People 2010* objectives also defined new relationships between public health departments and health care delivery organizations (U.S. Department of Health and Human Services [DHHS], 1998). *Healthy People 2010* specifically emphasized the role of community partners such as businesses, local governments, and civic, professional, and religious organizations as effective agents for improving health in their local communities. The objectives had a particular focus on determinants of health, discussed earlier in this chapter.

The current initiative, *Healthy People 2020*, was launched in December 2010. *Healthy People 2020* takes into account some of the achievements made over the last decade, such as increased life expectancy and a decreased death rate from coronary heart disease and stroke, and identifies other areas for improvement over the next decade. *Healthy People 2020*'s objectives include identifying nationwide health improvement priorities; increasing public awareness and understanding of the determinants of health, disability, and disease; providing measurable objectives and goals that are applicable at all levels; engaging multiple sectors to take action to strengthen policies and improve practices that are driven by the best scientific evidence and knowledge; and identifying critical research, evaluation, and data collection methods. *Healthy People 2020* will assess progress through measures of general health status, health-related quality of life and well-being, determinants of health, and disparities (DHHS, 2011).

The overarching goals of *Healthy People 2020* include the following:

- Attaining high-quality, longer lives free of preventable disease, injury, and premature death
- Achieving health equity, eliminating disparities, and improving the health of all groups
- Creating social and physical environments that promote good health for all
- Promoting quality of life, healthy development, and health behaviors across all life stages

The graphic framework for *Healthy People 2020* is presented in **Figure 2.3**.

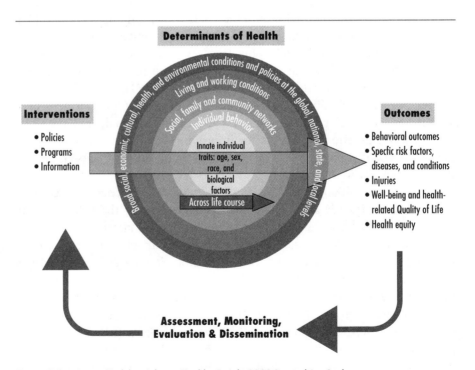

Figure 2.3   Action Model to Achieve *Healthy People 2020* Overarching Goals
Source: Secretary's Advisory Committee on Health Promotion and Disease Prevention Objectives for 2020. Phase I report recommendations for the framework and format of *Healthy People 2010*, p. 8, Exhibit A. http://www.healthypeople.gov /2010/hp2020/Advisory/PhaseI/PhaseI.pdf.

Distribution of Health Care

In a perfect world, the production, distribution, and subsequent consumption of health care would be perceived as equitable. Unfortunately, no society has found a perfectly equitable method to distribute limited economic resources; in fact, any method of resource distribution leaves some inequalities. Societies, therefore, try to allocate resources according to some guiding principles acceptable to each society. Such principles are ingrained in a society's values and belief systems. It is generally recognized that not everyone can receive everything that medical science has to offer. The fundamental question that deals with distributive justice or equity is who should receive the medical goods and services that society produces (Santerre & Neun, 1996, p. 7). By extension, this basic question about equity encompasses not only who should receive medical care, but also which types of services and in what quantity. Even though various ethical principles can be used to guide decisions pertaining to just and fair allocation of health care in individual circumstances, the broad concern about equitable access to health care services is addressed by theories referred to as *market justice* and *social justice*. These two contrasting theories govern the production and distribution of health care services.

Market Justice

The principle of market justice proposes that market forces in a free economy can best achieve a fair distribution of health care. Within such a system, medical care and its benefits are distributed on the basis of people's willingness and ability to pay (Santerre & Neun, 1996, p. 7). In other words, people are entitled to purchase a share of the available goods and services that they value. They must purchase these valued goods and services by using the financial resources acquired through their own legitimate efforts. This is how most goods and services are distributed in a free market. The free market implies that giving people something they have not earned would be morally and economically wrong. The principle of market justice is based on the following key assumptions:

- Health care is like any other economic good or service and, therefore, can be governed by the free market forces of supply and demand.
- Individuals are responsible for their own achievements. When individuals pursue their own best interests, the interests of society as a whole are best served (Ferguson & Maurice, 1970).

- People make rational choices in their decisions to purchase health care products and services to rectify their health problems and restore their health.
- People, in consultation with their physicians, know what is best for themselves. This assumption implies that people place a certain degree of trust in their physicians and that an ongoing physician–patient relationship exists.
- The marketplace works best with minimum interference from the government. In other words, the market, rather than the government, can allocate health care resources in the most efficient and equitable manner.

Under market justice, the production of health care is determined by how much consumers are willing and able to purchase at prevailing market prices. It follows that in a free market system, individuals without sufficient income or who are uninsured face a financial barrier to obtaining health care (Santerre & Neun, 1996, p. 7). Thus prices and ability to pay combine to ration the quantity and type of health care services people consume. Such limitations to obtaining health care are referred to as *demand-side rationing* or price rationing. The key characteristics of market justice and their implications are summarized in **Table 2.1**.

Market justice emphasizes individual, rather than collective, responsibility for health. It proposes private, rather than government, solutions to the social problems of health.

The principles of market justice work well in the allocation of economic goods when their unequal distribution does not affect the larger society. For example, based on their individual success, people live in different sizes and styles of homes, drive different types of automobiles, and spend their money on different things; however, market justice principles generally fail to rectify critical human concerns such as crime, illiteracy, and homelessness, which can significantly weaken the fabric of a society. Many Americans believe that health care is also a social concern.

Social Justice

The idea of social justice is at odds with the principles of capitalism and market justice. According to the principle of social justice, the equitable distribution of health care is a societal responsibility. This goal can best be achieved by letting a central agency—generally the government—take

Table 2.1 Comparison of Market Justice and Social Justice

Market Justice	Social Justice

Characteristics

Market Justice	Social Justice
• Views health care as an economic good	• Views health care as a social resource
• Assumes free market conditions for health services delivery	• Requires active government involvement in health services delivery
• Assumes that markets are more efficient in allocating health resources equitably	• Assumes that the government is more efficient in allocating health resources equitably
• Production and distribution of health care are determined by market-based demand	• Medical resource allocation is determined by central planning
• Medical care distribution is based on people's ability to pay	• Ability to pay is inconsequential for receiving medical care
• Access to medical care is viewed as an economic reward of personal effort and achievement	• Equal access to medical services is viewed as a basic right

Implications

Market Justice	Social Justice
• Individual responsibility for health	• Collective responsibility for health
• Benefits are based on individual purchasing power	• Everyone is entitled to a basic package of benefits
• Limited obligation to the collective good	• Strong obligation to the collective good
• Emphasis on individual well-being	• Community well-being supersedes that of the individual
• Private solutions to social problems	• Public solutions to social problems
• Rationing based on ability to pay	• Planned rationing of health care

over the production and distribution functions. Social justice regards health care as a social good—as opposed to an economic good—that should be collectively financed and available to all citizens regardless of the individual recipient's ability to pay for that care. Most industrialized countries long ago reached a broad social consensus that health care was a social good (Reinhardt, 1994). Public health also has a social justice orientation

(Turnock, 1997). Under the social justice system, an inability to obtain medical services because of a lack of financial resources is considered unjust. The principle of social justice is based on the following assumptions:

- Health care is different from most other goods and services. Health-seeking behavior is governed primarily by need rather than by cost.
- Responsibility for health is shared. Individuals are not held totally responsible for their condition because factors outside their control may have brought on the condition. Society feels responsible for a lack of control over certain environmental factors such as economic inequalities, unemployment, unsanitary conditions, or air pollution.
- Society has an obligation to the collective good. The well-being of the community is held to be superior to that of the individual. An unhealthy individual is a burden on society; a person carrying a deadly infection, for example, poses a threat to society. Society is obligated to eliminate (cure) the problem by providing health care to the individual because doing so benefits the society as a whole.
- The government, rather than the market, can better decide through rational planning how much health care to produce and how to distribute it among all citizens.

Under a system based on social justice, the amount of health care produced is determined by the government. Of course, no country can afford to provide unlimited amounts of health care to all of its citizens (Feldstein, 1994, p. 44). Thus the government must find ways to limit the availability of certain health care services by deciding, for instance, how technology will be dispersed and who will be allowed access to certain types of high-tech services, even though basic services may be available to all. This concept is referred to as *planned rationing* or *supply-side rationing*. The government makes deliberate attempts, often referred to as "health planning," to limit the supply of health care services, particularly those beyond the basic level of care. The main characteristics and implications of social justice are summarized in Table 2.1.

Justice in the U.S. Health Care System

It is important to recognize that the current U.S. health care system is not a market-justice based system because American health care delivery does not follow free-market principles. A significant shift away from market justice began in 1965 with the creation of Medicare and Medicaid. Since then the move toward social justice has been gradual and ongoing. Currently, a little less than half of the financing for health care services in the United States comes from the government. The government also plays a major role in exercising a significant degree of control over the system through various policies governing insurance, payment to providers, availability of new drugs and procedures, use of information systems, funding for medical research, and quality initiatives, to name a few.

In the United States, the principles of market justice and social justice complement each other. Private, employer-based health insurance—mainly for middle-income Americans—is driven by market justice. Publicly financed Medicaid and Medicare coverage for certain disadvantaged groups and workers' compensation programs for those injured at work are based on social justice. The two principles collide, however, regarding the large number of uninsured who cannot afford to purchase private health insurance and do not meet the eligibility criteria for Medicaid, Medicare, or other public programs.

With the passing of the ACA of 2010, the question of how insurance can be provided to all Americans was, for the first time, addressed in a major way (details are furnished in subsequent chapters). The Act's major changes are scheduled to take effect in 2014, with the goal being that all Americans have health insurance in the near future. This is an example of a major step in moving the U.S. health care system toward the goals of social justice.

Public Health System

Public health is a reflection of society's desire and effort to improve the health and well-being of the total population, and relies on the role of government, the private sector, and the public in addition to focusing on the determinants of population health. The *public health system* reflects an organized effort to deliver public health services within a jurisdiction with the goal of improving health and well-being of the population.

Research evidence indicates that public health contributes positively to population health. Indicators at the national, state, and local levels should be developed to measure public health performance along with a national surveillance system to consistently track indicators so as to gain a better understanding of the system's effectiveness. In addition, innovative efforts by states to improve their public health systems' infrastructure, practices, and performance should be encouraged and evaluated, given that most significant reforms take place at this level than at the federal or municipal level.

Turning Point

Turning Point is an initiative of the Robert Wood Johnson Foundation to transform and strengthen the public health system, in which 21 states currently participate. As part of this initiative, multisector partnerships to produce public health improvement plans employ strategies that include institutionalization within government, establishing "third-sector" institutions, cultivating relationships with significant allies, and enhancing communication and visibility among multiple communities (Shi and Stevens, 2010).

Focusing on Determinants

To improve the nation's health and minimize disparities among its vulnerable populations, development of a framework embodying social and medical determinants is warranted. This framework, presented in **Figure 2.4**, puts a balanced emphasis on both social and medical care determinants because it is the combination of these factors that ultimately shapes health and well-being. This model synthesizes multiple health influences and highlights points for intervention. "Health" in this model is not just a state of being free of disease and injury, but also includes the positive concept of well-being and encompasses the physical, mental, social, and spiritual aspects of health.

Social Determinants of Health

The framework acknowledges the effects of demographics, socioeconomic status, personal behavior, and community-level inequalities and their defining influence on health. Personal demographics (e.g., race/ethnicity or age) directly contribute to vulnerability levels. Whether socioeconomic status is defined by education, employment, or income, both individual- and community-level socioeconomic status have independent effects on health. The health impact of personal behaviors (e.g., smoking or exercise) is well documented, but such behavior is rarely isolated from the social and environmental contexts in which choices are made.

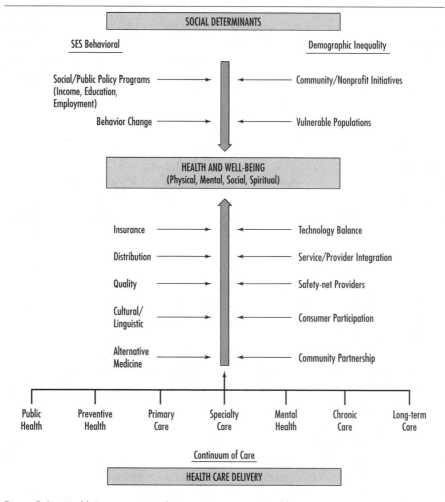

Figure 2.4 Health Determinants and Strategies to Improve Health

Social and income inequalities have also been shown to contribute to disparities in health. Underinvestment in human capital, erosion of social cohesion, and the consequences of relative deprivation are mechanisms by which income inequalities can lead to poorer health outcomes. For example, *discrimination*—the difference in one's actions toward an individual or group based on the innate personal characteristics of that group, such as race and/or ethnicity— has direct consequences for individual health. Many of the social factors of health care are also the root causes of poor health; thus addressing them is vital to the improvement of population health and health disparities.

Medical Care Determinants of Health

Although social determinants influence people's health status, the medical care system primarily focuses on treating illness or poor health. Preventive care is an exception to this rule, but understanding the influences of medical care on health should also take into consideration disparities that exist in basic health care access and quality. The framework includes a broad spectrum of medical care services and interventions to improve health. Whereas some services (preventive and primary care) contribute to general health status, others are more influential in end-of-life situations (specialty and long-term care). As patients move across the spectrum, they are likely to contend with issues of fragmentation, poor continuity of care, and insufficient coordination of care for multiple health needs.

The relative value of each health service in the spectrum should be evaluated in determining health policy. For example, should equal investments be made in each service, or are some investments better than others (e.g., primary versus specialty care)? How can we optimize the medical system's potential for eliminating disparities with limited resources (e.g., focusing on primary care for all versus higher levels of technology care for certain populations)? Other health care factors, such as the quality of care, access to alternative therapies, and technology, will further affect a patient's health care experience and health outcomes.

Social and Medical Points of Intervention

Considering that social and medical determinants are responsive to numerous outside forces, the framework highlights important points for intervention. Dramatic reductions in health disparities are obtainable through interventions in both the social and medical domains and are grouped according to four main strategies: (1) social or medical care policy interventions, (2) community-based interventions, (3) health care interventions, and (4) individual interventions. The following sections elaborate on these strategies.

Policy Interventions Social or public policy affects the health of the population in many ways. Product safety regulations, screening food and water sources, and enforcing safe work environments are just a few of the ways in which public policy directly guards the welfare of the nation. With fewer resources at their disposal, however, vulnerable populations are uniquely dependent on social and public policy to develop and implement programs that address basic nutritional, safety, social, and health care needs. Many of the mechanisms relating vulnerable status to poor health are amenable to policy intervention, and policy initiatives can be primary prevention strategies to alter the fundamental dynamics linking social factors to poor health.

As an example, in 1970, the Occupation Safety and Health Act was passed, which created the Occupational Safety and Health Administration (OSHA). The goal of OSHA is to protect employees of companies from the potential dangers of an unsafe environment that may exist at the workplace. For example, OSHA established the Injury and Illness Prevention Program that requires employers to implement a system that would ensure employees' compliance with a safe and healthy work environment. This is part of an overall effort to more effectively identify hazards in the workplace to protect employees who otherwise may be working in dangerous work environments (U.S. Department of Labor, 2011).

Community-Based Interventions Many of the sources of health disparities may be addressed at the community or local level. Neighborhood poverty, the presence of local health and social welfare resources, and societal cohesion and support are all likely to contribute to inequalities in a community. An understanding of the multidimensional risks and needs in a particular community can better equip local agencies responsible for designing interventions to successfully address health disparities in their communities (see the examples in **Exhibit 2.3**). Because community partnerships reflect the priorities of a local population and are often managed by members of the community, they minimize cultural barriers and improve community buy-in to the program.

Addressing disparities using community approaches has several other advantages. For example, the use of resources that directly help needy

Exhibit 2.3   Strategies to Improve Health and Reduce Disparities

- Nutrition programs
- Work/environment safety efforts
- Community-based partnerships
- Culturally appropriate care
- Patient safety/medical error reduction
- Prevention-oriented effort
- Coordinated care for chronically ill persons

members of the community can provide businesses and other local partners with greater incentive to contribute to local health causes. Communities should be seen as action centers for development, progress, and change, with local members and leaders playing a central role in planning and managing strategies for health improvement. Community solutions also benefit from participatory decision making. Local researchers, health practitioners, social services, businesses, and community members can be invited to contribute to the process of designing, implementing, evaluating, and sustaining programs. Moreover, many community programs are run by nonprofit organizations, and in exchange for providing services, these organizations are subsidized through federal, state, or local funds and receive tax exemptions. Thus they are able to offer services at lower cost than private health organizations that are obligated to their shareholders to price their services competitively.

As an example, in an effort to counteract the recent rise in childhood obesity rates, many schools are beginning classroom-conducted nutritional programs. These multicomponent nutritional interventions involve administrators, food services staff, teachers, parents, and students. The goal is to reach multiple levels of the community in an effort to increase community-wide participation and expand the program's effectiveness. Teaching students about proper nutrition in the classroom while concurrently educating parents increases the possibility of the program's success in fighting childhood obesity (DeMattia & Denney, 2008).

Health Care Interventions   Although social policy and community-level interventions are designed to address social disparities in health, billions of public and private dollars are spent annually to monitor and improve facets of the U.S. health care system. For example, interventions such as integrated electronic medical records systems have been designed to potentially improve patient care while also reducing waste in the health care system (Dorman & Miller, 2011; Hillestad et al. 2005; Sperl-Hillen et al., 2011). It is estimated that if integrated electronic medical records are used by 90% of providers in the United States, it could potentially save $77 billion per year by improving the health care system's efficiency. Electronic health records also hold the promise of improved quality through better coordination and integration of care among various providers. Coordinated and integrated care is particularly important in light of the increasing burden of chronic disease. For example, coordination of care and counseling for type 2 diabetes has been shown to improve blood glucose management in patients.

Individual-Level Interventions Where policy and community-level interventions are unable to reduce either the occurrence of compromising social determinants or their consequences, individual-level initiatives can attempt to intervene and minimize the effects of negative social determinants on health status. Altering individual behaviors that influence health (e.g., reducing smoking and increasing exercise) is often the focus of these individual-targeted interventions, and numerous theories have been promulgated to identify the complex pathways and barriers to eliciting changes or improvements in behavior. The integration of behavioral science into the public health field has been a valuable contribution, providing a toolbox of health-related behavior-changing strategies.

CONCLUSION

Health and its determinants are multifactorial. Although important, medical care is only one factor that contributes to health and well-being. Factors such as physical, social, cultural, and economic environments; behaviors and lifestyles; and heredity play a greater role in determining health and well-being for both individuals and populations. The delivery of health care is primarily driven by the medical model, which emphasizes illness rather than wellness. Even though major efforts and expenditures have been directed toward the delivery of medical care, they have failed to produce a proportionate impact on the improvement of health status. Holistic concepts of health care, along with integration of medical care with preventive and health promotional efforts, should be adopted to significantly improve the health of Americans; but such an approach would require a fundamental change in how Americans view health. It would also require taking individual responsibility for one's own health-oriented behaviors, as well as forging community partnerships to improve both personal and community health. An understanding of the determinants of health, health education, community health assessment, and national initiatives such as *Healthy People 2020* are essential for accomplishing such goals. Over the years, the U.S. health care system has been gradually transitioning toward social justice, yet all Americans still do not have equal access to health care services. To improve the nation's health and resolve disparities among its vulnerable populations, it is critical to address both the social and medical determinants of health.

REFERENCES

DeMattia L, Denney SL. Childhood obesity prevention: Successful community-based efforts. *Ann Am Acad Politic Soc Sci.* 2008;615:83.

Dorman T, Miller BM. Continuing medical education: The link between physician learning and health care outcomes. *Acad Med.* 2011;86(11):1339.

Feldstein PJ. *Health Policy Issues: An Economic Perspective on Health Reform.* Ann Arbor, MI: Association of University Programs in Health Administration/Health Administration Press; 1994.

Ferguson CE, Maurice SC. *Economic Analysis.* Homewood, IL: Richard D. Irwin; 1970.

Hillestad R, Bigelow J, Bower A, et al. Can electronic medical record systems transform health care? Potential health benefits, savings, and costs. *Health Affairs.* 2005;24(5):1103–1117.

Kaplan GA, et al. Income inequality and mortality in the United States. *Br Med J.* 1996;312(7037):999–1003.

Kawachi I, et al. Social capital, income inequality, and mortality. *Am J Publ Health.* 1997;87:1491–1498.

Kennedy BP, et al. Income distribution and mortality: Cross sectional ecological study of the Robin Hood Index in the United States. *Br Med J.* 1996;312(7037):1004–1007.

Levin JS. Religion and health: Is there an association, is it valid, and is it causal? *Soc Sci Med.* 1994;38(11):1475–1482.

Mackenbach JP. Socioeconomic inequalities in morbidity and mortality in Western Europe. *Lancet.* 1997;349:1655–1660.

Marwick C. Should physicians prescribe prayer for health? Spiritual aspects of well-being considered. *JAMA*. 1995;273(20):1561–1562.

Maugans TA. The SPIRITual history. *Arch Family Med*. 1996;5(1):11–16.

May, LA. The physiologic and psychological bases of health, disease, and care seeking. In Williams SJ, Torrens PR, eds. *Introduction to Health Services*. 4th ed. New York: Delmar; 1993:31–45.

McCullough ME, et al. Religious involvement and mortality: A meta-analytic review. *Health Psychol*. 2000;19(3):211–222.

McKee M. Measuring the efficiency of health systems. *Br Med J*. 2001;323(7308):295–296.

Parsons T. Definitions of health and illness in the light of American values and social structure. In Jaco EG, ed. *Patients, Physicians and Illness: A Sourcebook in Behavioral Science and Health*. 2nd ed. New York: Free Press; 1972.

Reinhardt UE. Providing access to health care and controlling costs: The universal dilemma. In Lee PR, Estes CL, eds. *The Nation's Health*. 4th ed. Sudbury, MA: Jones and Bartlett; 1994:263–278.

Ross L. The spiritual dimension: Its importance to patients' health, well-being and quality of life and its implications for nursing practice. *Intl J Nurs Stud*. 1995;32(5):457–468.

Santerre RE, Neun SP. *Health Economics: Theories, Insights, and Industry Studies*. Chicago: Irwin; 1996.

Saward E, Sorensen A. The current emphasis on preventive medicine. In Williams SJ, ed. *Issues in Health Services*. New York: John Wiley & Sons; 1980:17–29.

Shellenbarger S. Good, early care has a huge impact on kids, studies say. *Wall Street Journal*, April 9, 1997, p. B1.

Shi L, Stevens G. *Vulnerable Populations in the United States*. Jossey-Bass Publishers, Inc., San Francisco, CA, 2nd edition, 2010.

Society for Academic Emergency Medicine (SAEM), Ethics Committee. An ethical foundation for health care: An emergency medicine perspective. *Ann Emerg Med*. 1992;21:1381–1387.

Sperl-Hillen J, Beaton S, Fernandes O, et al. Comparative effectiveness of patient education methods for type 2 diabetes: A randomized controlled trial. *Arch Intern Med*. 2011;171(22):2001–2010.

Swanson CS. A spirit-focused conceptual model of nursing for the advanced practice nurse. *Issues Comprehen Pediatr Nurs*. 1995;18(4):267–275.

Timmreck TC. *An Introduction to Epidemiology*. Sudbury, MA: Jones and Bartlett; 1994.

Turnock BJ. *Public Health: What It Is and How It Works*. Gaithersburg, MD: Aspen; 1997.

U.S. Department of Health and Human Services (DHHS). Objectives: Draft for public comment. In *Healthy People 2010: Healthy People in Healthy Communities*. Washington, DC: Department of Health and Human Services; 1998.

U.S. Department of Health and Human Services (DHHS). *Healthy People 2010: Understanding and Improving Health*. 2nd ed. Washington, DC: U.S. Government Printing Office; 2000.

U.S. Department of Health and Human Services (DHHS). About *Healthy People*. 2011. http://www.healthypeople.gov/2020/about/default.aspx. Accessed December 10, 2011.

U.S. Department of Labor. Injury and illness prevention programs. 2011. http://www.osha.gov/dsg/topics/safetyhealth/. Accessed December 10, 2011.

Ward B. Holistic medicine. *Austral Family Phys*. 1995;24(5):761–762, 765.

Wilkinson RG. Comment: Income, inequality, and social cohesion. *Am J Public Health*. 1997;87:1504–1506.

Wolinsky F. *The Sociology of Health: Principles, Practitioners, and Issues*. 2nd ed. Belmont, CA: Wadsworth; 1998.

World Health Organization (WHO). *Preamble to the Constitution*. Geneva, Switzerland: World Health Organization; 1948.

Chapter 3

Historical Overview of U.S. Health Care Delivery

INTRODUCTION

Knowledge of the history of health care is essential for understanding the main characteristics of the medical delivery system as it exists today. For example, the system's historical foundations explain why Americans have resisted universal health insurance, which has been adopted by most industrialized nations.

Traditionally held American cultural beliefs and values, social changes, technological advances, economic constraints, and political opportunism are the main historical factors that have shaped U.S. health care delivery (see examples in **Exhibit 3.1**). As a result, health care in the United States is mainly a private industry, yet it also receives a fairly substantial amount of financing from the government. Inspite of the dual sources of financing, those who cannot afford the price of premiums and do not qualify for government insurance programs are left without any health insurance, as explained in previous chapters.

Exhibit 3.1   Major Forces of Change in Health Care Delivery

- **Cultural beliefs and values**
  - Self-reliance
  - Welfare assistance only for the most needy
- **Social changes**
  - Demographic shifts
  - Immigration
  - Health status
  - Urbanization
- **Technological advances**
  - New treatments
  - Training of health professionals
  - Facilities and equipment
- **Economic constraints**
  - Health care costs
  - Health insurance
  - Family incomes
- **Political opportunism**
  - President's agenda
  - Domestic and foreign priorities
  - Party politics
  - Power of interest groups
  - Laws and regulations

Changes driven by cultural, social, technological, economic, and political forces have shaped the delivery of medical services in the past and will continue to shape its future direction. These forces interact in a complex manner. For example, President Barack Obama's political agenda trumped economic constraints and led to the enactment of the Patient Protection and Affordable Care Act in 2010 (ACA of 2010). Historically, the beliefs and values espoused by the majority of Americans have been primarily responsible for shielding the U.S. health care system from a major overhaul. For example, most experts have agreed that traditional American beliefs in capitalism and limited government, which promote self-reliance, have been the main reason why past proposals for universal health insurance have failed in the United States. Conversely, social, political, and economic forces led to certain compromises, as seen in the creation of Medicare and Medicaid and other public programs to extend health insurance to certain defined groups of needy people. Could the U.S. health care system eventually achieve universal health care coverage? It is anyone's guess, but the ACA of 2010 would certainly seem to steer U.S. health care in that direction.

Advancements in science and technology have played a major role in shaping the U.S. health care delivery system. As a result, medical practice in the United States is highly specialized, while basic and routine care is given only secondary importance. Emphasis on the latest treatments and the frequency of their use have led to ever-increasing health care costs that experts do not think can be sustained in the longer term. Extending access to health care to a larger segment of the American population will necessitate containment of these costs.

This chapter traces the evolution of health care delivery through three major historical periods, each demarcating a major change in the structure of the medical delivery system. The first phase is the *preindustrial* era, which lasted from the middle of the 18th century until the latter part of the 19th century. The second phase is the *postindustrial era*, which began in the late 19th century. The third, but by no means the final phase, which we call the *corporate era*, covers developments that started around 1970 and continue into the 21st century.

MEDICAL SERVICES IN PREINDUSTRIAL AMERICA

From colonial times to the late 1800s, medical education and practice were far more advanced in Great Britain, France, and Germany than they were in the United States. The practice of medicine in the United States had a strong domestic—rather than professional—character because medical procedures were rather primitive. As medical education was not grounded in science, medical practice was more a trade than a profession. The nation had only a handful of hospitals. There was no health insurance, private or public. Health care had to be purchased using personal funds, and health care was delivered in a free market. The main characteristics of health care delivery during this period are summarized in **Exhibit 3.2**.

Medical Training

Until around 1870, medical training was largely received through individual apprenticeship with a practicing physician rather than through university education. The irony is that many of the preceptors under whom medical students apprenticed were themselves poorly trained (Rothstein, 1972, p. 86). Only a small number of medical schools existed at that time. To train a larger number of students than was possible through apprenticeship, American physicians began opening medical schools, albeit mainly to supplement their incomes by collecting student fees that were paid directly to the physicians.

Exhibit 3.2   Health Care Delivery in Preindustrial America

- Medical training and education were not grounded in science.
- Primitive medical procedures were practiced.
- Intense competition existed because any tradesman could practice medicine.
- People relied on family members, neighbors, and publications for domestic remedies.
- Physicians' fees were paid out of personal funds.
- Health care was delivered in a free market.
- Hospitals were few and located only in big cities.
- Hospitals had poor sanitation and unskilled staff.
- Almshouses served the destitute and disruptive elements of society and provided some basic nursing care.
- State governments operated asylums for patients with untreatable, chronic mental illness.
- Pesthouses quarantined people with contagious diseases.
- Dispensaries delivered outpatient charity care in urban areas.

These physicians did not have classroom facilities at their disposal, however, nor did they have the authority to confer the doctor of medicine (MD) degree. Hence, they had to affiliate with local colleges to use their facilities and confer degrees. As part of this approach, four or more physicians would get together to form a faculty. Medical schools were inexpensive to operate and often quite profitable. It is estimated that 42 such schools were in operation in the United States in 1850 (Rothstein, 1972, p. 91).

Medical education at this point was still seriously lacking in science. The 2-year MD degree required attending courses for 3 to 4 months during the first year and then essentially repeating the same coursework during the second year. Because fees were paid only as the student passed each course, low standards and a less-than-rigorous curriculum were necessary to attract and retain students. Even the best medical schools admitted students without a high school diploma. Training in the biological sciences was considered useful but not essential. Laboratories were nonexistent. Library facilities were inadequate, and clinical observation and practice were not part of the curriculum (Starr, 1982).

Medical Practice

As noted previously, the early practice of medicine was regarded more as a trade than a profession, and it most assuredly lacked the prestige it has today. First, it did not require the rigorous course of study, clinical practice, residency training, board exams, and licensing, without all of which it is impossible to practice medicine today. Second, medical procedures were primitive because medical science was still in its infancy. Bleeding, use of emetics, and purging with enemas and purgatives were popular forms of clinical therapy in early medicine. Surgery was limited because anesthesia had not yet been developed, and antiseptic techniques were not known. The stethoscope and x-rays had not been discovered. The clinical thermometer was not in use, and the microscope was not available for medical diagnosis. Physicians mainly relied on their five senses and experience to diagnose and treat medical problems. Hence, in most cases, physicians did not possess technical expertise any greater than that possessed by family members at home and experienced neighbors in the local community.

One of the main consequences of nonprofessional medicine was that anyone—trained or untrained—could practice as a physician. The clergy, for example, often combined medical services and religious duties. The generally well-educated clergymen and government officials were actually more learned in medicine than many physicians (Shryock, 1966, p. 252). Tradesmen such as tailors, barbers, commodity merchants, and those engaged in numerous other trades also practiced the healing arts by selling herbal prescriptions, nostrums, elixirs, and cathartics. The red-and-white striped poles (symbolizing blood and bandages) outside barber shops today are reminders that barbers also functioned as surgeons at one time, using the same blade to cut hair, shave beards, and perform bloodletting.

This system of free entry into medical practice created intense competition. Physicians did not enjoy the status, influence, and income that they do today. Indeed, many physicians found it necessary to engage in a second occupation because income from their medical practice alone was inadequate to support a family. It is estimated that most physicians' incomes in the mid-1800s put them in the lower echelon of the middle class (Starr, 1982, p. 84).

In the small communities of rural America, a spirit of strong self-reliance prevailed. Families and communities treated the sick using folk remedies that were passed on from one generation to the next. It was common for people to consult published books and pamphlets on home remedies (Rosen, 1983, p. 2). The market for physicians' services was also limited by affordability. Most families simply could not afford the cost because they had to pay for services out of pocket, without the help of health insurance. Also, most Americans resided in small rural communities, and summoning a physician could require traveling for several hours, and sometimes an entire day, which resulted in loss of work and income.

Medical Institutions

Before the 1880s, the United States had only a few isolated hospitals, which were found in large cities such as New York, Boston, New Orleans, St. Louis, and Philadelphia. In France and Great Britain, in contrast, general hospital expansion began long before the 1800s (Stevens, 1971, pp. 9–10). In Europe, medical professionals were closely associated with hospitals and readily adopted new advances in medical science. The situation was much different in the United States, where hospitals were characterized by deplorable sanitation conditions and poor ventilation. Unhygienic practices prevailed because nurses were generally unskilled and untrained. It was far more dangerous to receive care in a hospital than at home. Hospitals had a popular image as houses of death and institutions of welfare. People went to hospitals only because of dire circumstances, not by personal choice.

The forerunner of today's hospitals and nursing homes in the United States was the *almshouse* (also called a *poorhouse*). Almshouses existed in almost all cities of moderate size and were run by the local government. The almshouse was not a health care institution in the true sense, but rather a place where the destitute and disruptive elements of society were confined. The inmates, as they were called, included many of the elderly, the homeless, orphans, the ill, and the disabled. They were given food, shelter, and some basic nursing care if needed. In many ways, the almshouse was an infirmary, old-age facility, mental asylum, homeless shelter, and orphanage all rolled into one institution. Living conditions in these institutions were squalid, and they were a far cry from today's health care facilities. Thus the early health care institutions emerged mainly to take care of indigent people who could not be cared for by their own families.

An *asylum* was the forerunner of today's inpatient psychiatric facilities. Although almshouses were used to accommodate some mental patients, asylums were built by state governments for patients with untreatable, chronic mental illness. Attendants in these asylums employed physical and psychological techniques in an effort to return patients to some level of rational thinking. Techniques such as bleeding, forced vomiting, and hot and ice-cold baths were also used in these facilities (U.S. Surgeon General, 1999).

Another type of institution, the *pesthouse,* was operated by local governments to isolate people who had contracted a contagious disease such as cholera, smallpox, typhoid, or yellow fever. Their main function was to contain the spread of communicable disease and protect the inhabitants of a city.

Dispensaries were established as outpatient clinics to provide free care to those who could not afford to pay. They provided basic medical care and dispensed drugs to ambulatory patients (Raffel, 1980, p. 239). Around 1900 in the United States, approximately 100 dispensaries were located in large cities (Madison, 1990). Generally, young physicians and medical students desiring clinical experience staffed the dispensaries (as well as hospital wards) on a part-time basis for little or no income (Martensen, 1996). The dispensary can be regarded as the forerunner of today's more than 1,200 free clinics where services are delivered mainly by trained volunteer staff to the poor, the homeless, and the uninsured.

MEDICAL SERVICES IN POSTINDUSTRIAL AMERICA

The postindustrial era was marked by the growth and development of a medical profession that benefited from urbanization, new scientific discoveries, and reforms in medical education. American physicians formed professional organizations which acted as a powerful force in resisting proposals for a national health care program. The private practice of medicine, free from employment by hospitals and corporations, became firmly entrenched as physicians organized into a cohesive profession, opted for specialization, and gained power and prestige. The hospital emerged as a repository for high-tech facilities and equipment. Private and public health insurance took roots. Notable developments of this era are summarized in **Exhibit 3.3**. Changes that revolutionized health care delivery are discussed in subsequent sections.

Medical Profession

Notably, much of the transformation in U.S. medicine occurred in the aftermath of the American Civil War (1861–1865), as the country transitioned from a rural agricultural economy to a system of industrial capitalism. Urban development attracted increasingly more Americans to the growing towns and cities. In 1840, only 11% of the U.S. population lived in urban areas; by 1900, that share had increased to 40% (Stevens, 1971, p. 34).

Urbanization created increased reliance on the specialized skills of paid professionals, as this trend distanced people from their families and

Exhibit 3.3   Notable Developments During the Postindustrial Era

- Urbanization
- Scientific discoveries and their applications in medicine
  - Advanced science-based treatments
  - Increased health care costs
  - Growing imbalance between specialists and generalists
- Medical education reform
- Power and prestige of physicians
- Organized medicine
  - Control over medical training
  - Powerful political interest group
- Support of licensing laws
- Opposition to national health insurance proposals
- Support of private entrepreneurship in medical practice
- Hospitals became true medical care institutions
- Growth of private health insurance
- Creation of Medicare and Medicaid

neighborhood surroundings where family-based care had traditionally been given. At the same time, urbanization led to the concentration of medical practice in cities and towns where office-based practice began to replace house calls. Closer geographic proximity to their patients enabled physicians to see more patients in a given amount of time. Greater productivity, in turn, produced higher incomes for the physicians.

As medicine became increasingly driven by science and technology, lay people could no longer deliver legitimate medical care. Science-based medicine also created an increased demand for the advanced services that were no longer available through family and neighbors. Developments in bacteriology, antiseptic surgery, anesthesia, immunology, and diagnostic techniques, along with a growing array of new drugs, helped bring medical practice into the category of a legitimate profession. **Exhibit 3.4** summarizes some of the groundbreaking early scientific discoveries in medicine made during this era.

A preoccupation with science and technology in the American culture brought numerous benefits, but also produced some undesirable effects. For example, an overemphasis on the use of technology in medical care delivery created a bias toward specialization in medical training, which

Exhibit 3.4   Groundbreaking Medical Discoveries

- The discovery of anesthesia was instrumental in advancing the practice of surgery. Nitrous oxide (laughing gas) was first employed as an anesthetic around 1846 for tooth extraction by Horace Wells, a dentist. Later, ether and chloroform were used as anesthetics. Before the anesthetic properties of certain gases were discovered, strong doses of alcohol were used to dull the sensations. A surgeon who could do procedures, such as limb amputations, in the shortest length of time was held in high regard.

- Around 1847, Ignaz Semmelweis, a Hungarian physician practicing in a hospital in Vienna, implemented the policy of hand washing. Thus an aseptic technique was born. Semmelweis was concerned about the high death rate from puerperal fever among women after childbirth. Even though the germ theory of disease was unknown at this time, Semmelweis surmised that there might be a connection between puerperal fever and the common practice by medical students of not washing their hands before delivering babies and right after doing dissections. Semmelweis's hunch was right.

- Louis Pasteur is generally credited with pioneering the germ theory of disease and microbiology around 1860. Pasteur demonstrated sterilization techniques, such as boiling to kill microorganisms and withholding exposure to air to prevent contamination.

- Joseph Lister is often referred to as the father of antiseptic surgery. Around 1865, he used carbolic acid to wash wounds and popularized the chemical inhibition of infection (antisepsis) during surgery.

- Advances in diagnostics and imaging can be traced to the discovery of x-rays in 1895 by Wilhelm Roentgen, a German professor of physics. Radiology became the first machine-based medical specialty. Some of the first training schools in x-ray therapy and radiography in the United States attracted photographers and electricians to become doctors in roentgenology (a term from the inventor's name).

- Alexander Fleming discovered the antibacterial properties of penicillin in 1929.

ultimately ended up creating far too many specialists in relation to generalists. Technology and specialization also increased the cost of medical care, but without significantly improving the health status of Americans. In contrast, other developed nations emphasized primary care in which, apart from delivering routine and basic care, a primary care physician and trained nurses ensured the continuity, coordination, and appropriateness of medical services received by a patient.

The American Medical Association

The American Medical Association (AMA) has historically played a critical role in galvanizing the profession and in protecting the interests of physicians. The concerted activities of physicians through the AMA have been collectively referred to as *organized medicine* to distinguish them from the uncoordinated actions of individual physicians competing in the marketplace (Goodman & Musgrave, 1992, pp. 137, 139). Although it was founded in 1847, the AMA did not attain real strength until it delegated regional control by organizing its members into county and state medical societies. It first consolidated its power by controlling medical education. The AMA also vigorously pursued its objectives by supporting states in the establishment of medical licensing laws.

Employment of physicians by hospitals and insurance companies was frowned upon. Physicians who attempted to seek salaried employment in a corporate setting were chastised by the medical profession and pressured into abandoning such practices. Independence from corporate control promoted private entrepreneurship and put American physicians in an envious strategic position in relation to organizations such as hospitals and insurance companies.

Thanks to the AMA's concerted activities, physicians' incomes grew sharply, and their supremacy as a profession finally emerged. The sphere of their influence expanded into nearly all aspects of health care delivery. For example, laws were passed that prohibited individuals from obtaining certain classes of drugs without a physician's prescription. Health insurance paid for treatments only when they were rendered or prescribed by physicians.

Educational Reform

Advances in medical science necessitated the reform of medical education, which began around 1870 when medical schools began affiliating with universities. In 1871, Harvard Medical School completely revolutionized the system of medical education. The academic year was extended from 4 to 9 months, and the length of medical education was increased from 2 to 3 years. Following the European model, laboratory instruction and clinical courses such as chemistry, physiology, anatomy, and pathology were added to the curriculum. Johns Hopkins University took the lead in further reforming medical education when it opened its medical school in Baltimore, Maryland, in 1893. For the first time, medical education became a graduate training program requiring a college degree, not a high school diploma, as an entrance requirement. Johns Hopkins also pioneered the practice of complementing classroom education with residency training in its own teaching hospital. Standards at Johns Hopkins became the model of medical education in other leading institutions around the country. Even so, in the early 1900s, fewer than half of the medical schools provided acceptable levels of training.

In 1910, a widely acclaimed report was published by Abraham Flexner under the auspices of the Carnegie Foundation for the Advancement of Teaching. The Flexner Report, as it came to be known, was based on an inspection of medical schools. It found widespread inconsistencies in medical education. By this time, the AMA had gained a firm foothold in medical training by creating the Council on Medical Education. It pushed for state laws that required graduation from a medical school accredited by the AMA as the basis for a license to practice medicine (Haglund & Dowling, 1993). Educational standards were formalized, and schools that did not meet the proposed standards were forced to close. As a note of interest, Howard University School of Medicine (1869) and the Meharry Medical College (1876) were established at the end of the American Civil War specifically to prepare black physicians to practice medicine.

Development of Hospitals

As had already occurred in Europe, the growth of hospitals in the United States came to symbolize the institutionalization of health care (Torrens, 1993). The hospital became the center around which other medical services were organized.

Advancements in medical science created the need to centralize expensive facilities and equipment in a medical institution, reflecting the reality that physicians could no longer afford to have the needed equipment and facilities in their own offices. The hospital became the center for advanced technology used in medical diagnosis and treatment, and for the training of various types of health care personnel. The expansion of surgery, in particular, had profound implications for hospitals, physicians, and the public. Alongside these developments came remarkable progress in sanitation practices. The professionalization of nursing promoted healing and improved patient recovery. As a result of these changes, the growing appeal of hospital services in communities, sick patients' increasing need for hospital care, and the increasing professionalization of medical practice became closely intertwined.

Hospitals, for their part, depended on physicians to refer patients to keep their beds filled. These conditions created the need for informal alliances between hospitals and physicians. Physicians began to play a dominant role in hospital affairs even though they were not employees of the hospitals. As hospitals grew in number, physicians' ability to decide where to hospitalize their patients gave them enormous influence over hospital policy.

HISTORY OF HEALTH INSURANCE

There are several reasons why private health insurance (also called *voluntary health insurance*) took root and expanded in the United States. Later, the struggle to meet the medical needs of the elderly and the poor in an environment of rising health care costs prompted the U.S. Congress to create the publicly financed Medicare and Medicaid programs.

Worker's Compensation

The first broad-coverage health insurance in the United States emerged in the form of workers' compensation. It was originally designed to make cash payments to workers for wages lost because of job-related injuries and disease. Later, compensation for medical expenses and death benefits for survivors were added.

Between 1910 and 1915, workers' compensation laws made rapid progress in the United States (Stevens, 1971, p. 136). Looking at the trend, some reformers believed that because Americans had been persuaded to adopt compulsory insurance against industrial accidents, they could also be persuaded to adopt compulsory insurance against sickness. Workers' compensation served as a trial balloon for the idea of government-sponsored health insurance. However, the growth of private health insurance, along with other key factors discussed later, prevented any proposals for a national health care program from taking hold in the United States.

Emergence and Rise of Private Health Insurance

Private health insurance began in the form of disability coverage that provided income during temporary disability due to bodily injury or sickness. During the early 1900s, medical treatments and hospital care became a more entrenched part of American life. At the same time, they also became increasingly more expensive, and people could not predict their future needs for medical care or its costs. These developments pointed to the need for some kind of insurance to spread an individual's financial risk over a large number of people. Between 1916 and 1918, 16 state legislatures, including those in New York and California, attempted to enact legislation compelling employers to provide health insurance, but the efforts were unsuccessful (Davis, 1996).

First Hospital Plan and the Birth of Blue Cross

The dire economic conditions of the Great Depression set the stage for innovation in health insurance to cover hospitalization costs. Hospitals faced economic instability when they relied too much on philanthropic donations. On the other hand, individual patients faced not only loss of income from illness but also burdensome debt from medical care costs. In 1929, the blueprint for modern health insurance was conceived when Justin F. Kimball began a hospital insurance plan for teachers at the Baylor University Hospital in Dallas, Texas. Within a few years, it became the model for Blue Cross plans around the country (Raffel, 1980, p. 394). At first, other independent hospitals copied Baylor and started to offer single-hospital plans. Within a few years, plans sponsored by groups of hospitals became more popular because they offered consumers a choice of hospitals. The American Hospital Association (AHA) supported these hospital plans and became the coordinating agency that united the plans into the Blue Cross network. The Blue Cross plans were nonprofit; that is, they had no shareholders to receive profit distributions. Later, control of the plans was transferred to a completely independent body, the Blue Cross Commission, which subsequently became the Blue Cross Association (Raffel, 1980, p. 395).

Hospital insurance quickly grew in popularity. In 1946, Blue Cross plans in 43 states served 20 million members. Within a few years, lured by the success of the Blue Cross plans, commercial insurance companies also started offering hospital insurance. Between 1940 and 1950 alone, the proportion of the U.S. population covered by hospital insurance increased from 9% to 57% (Anderson, 1990, p. 128). Private health insurance had received the AMA's endorsement, but the AMA had also made it clear that health insurance plans should include only hospital care.

First Physician Plan and the Birth of Blue Shield

In 1939, the California Medical Association started the first Blue Shield plan, which was designed to pay physician fees. By endorsing hospital insurance and by actively developing the first plans that covered physicians' services, the medical profession protected its own financial interests. The AMA ensured that private health insurance would be preserved, but remained opposed to government-run national health insurance.

Starting in 1974, Blue Cross and Blue Shield plans began to merge. Now, in nearly every state, Blue Cross and Blue Shield plans are joint corporations or have close working relationships (Davis, 1996).

Employer-Based Health Insurance

Three main factors explain how health insurance in the United States became employer based:

- During the World War II period, the U.S. Congress imposed wage freezes in an attempt to control wartime inflation. Employees accepted employer-paid health insurance to compensate for the loss of raises in their salaries.
- In 1948, the U.S. Supreme Court ruled that employee benefits were a legitimate part of union–management negotiations. Health insurance thus became an important component of collective bargaining between unions and employers.
- In 1954, Congress amended the Internal Revenue Code to make employer-paid health coverage nontaxable. In economic value, employer-paid health insurance was equivalent to getting additional salary without having to pay taxes on it, which provided an incentive to obtain health insurance as an employer-furnished benefit.

In subsequent years, employment-based health insurance expanded rapidly, and private health insurance became the primary vehicle for the delivery of health care services in the United States.

Failure of National Health Insurance in the United States

In some Western European countries, national health insurance initiatives were closely associated with labor movements and worker sentiments. Notably in Germany and England, labor unrest threatened political stability. Universal health insurance for all citizens was seen as a means to obtain workers' loyalty and thwart any labor uprisings. By around 1912, national health insurance had spread throughout Europe, but political conditions in the United States were quite different. Unlike the situation in European countries, the American government was highly decentralized and engaged in little direct regulation of social welfare. Despite this fact, Theodore Roosevelt ran for the U.S. presidency in 1912 on a platform of social reform. Not surprisingly, Roosevelt was defeated by Woodrow Wilson. Even so, the Progressive movement favoring national health insurance remained alive for several more years.

The entry of the United States into World War I in 1917 dealt a political blow to the national health care movement as anti-German feelings were aroused and the U.S. government denounced German social insurance. Opponents of national health care called it a "Prussian menace" inconsistent with American values (Starr, 1982, pp. 240, 253). Any subsequent attempts to introduce national health insurance were met with the stigmatizing label of *socialized medicine*, a term that has since become synonymous with any large-scale government-sponsored expansion of health insurance. The traditional American values based on capitalism, self-determination, distrust of big government, and reliance on the private sector to address social concerns stood as a bulwark against broad-based government interventions. Conversely, during times of national distress, such as the Great Depression, pure necessity may have legitimized the advancement of social programs, such as Social Security and unemployment compensation.

The AMA played a leading role in opposing national health care, seeing it as a potential threat to the private practice of medicine. For example, the AMA was instrumental in the demise of several bills related to national health insurance that were introduced in Congress in the early 1940s during Franklin Roosevelt's presidency. In 1946, Harry Truman became the first president to make a direct appeal for a national health care program (Anderson, 1990, p. 119). Initial public reaction to Truman's plan was positive. However, when a government-controlled medical plan was compared with privately obtained insurance, polls showed a drastic decline in public support. The AMA was once again vehement in denouncing the plan. Other powerful health care interest groups, such as the American Hospital Association, also opposed the proposal. In 1948, Truman was reelected while promising national health insurance, which actually came as a surprise to many political observers. This time the AMA launched what was to become one of the most expensive lobbying efforts in U.S. history. The campaign directly linked national health insurance with communism until the idea of socialized medicine was firmly implanted in the public's minds. By 1950, national health insurance was a dead issue, and it remained so for decades.

After taking office in 1993, President Bill Clinton made health reform one of his top priorities, but his proposal was largely rejected by the American people. Defeat of the Clinton plan furnished another lesson on the power of beliefs and values prevalent in the United States. As a matter of principle, Americans have endorsed tax-supported health insurance to help needy citizens, but they also have been unwilling to pay, in the form of higher taxes, for what a universal health insurance program could realistically cost. Moreover, Americans have been uneasy about more government regulation and interference with employer-based private health insurance. In a 1999 national poll, half of the respondents—regardless of gender, race, age, or working status—indicated that employers were their preferred source of health insurance. Only 18% said they would prefer to rely on the government (Commonwealth Fund, 2000). Most people did not wish to have a negative effect on their own access to care or the quality of care they were receiving (Altman & Reinhardt, 1996). **Exhibit 3.5** provides a summary of the main historical reasons for the failure of national health care in the United States.

Exhibit 3.5   Reasons Why National Health Care Has Historically Failed in America

- Unlike in Europe, national health care failed to get an early footing because of labor and political stability in the United States.
- A decentralized American system gave the U.S. federal government little direct control over social policy.
- The German social insurance system was denounced during World War I. Since then, the term "socialized medicine" has been used as a synonym for national health insurance.
- The AMA opposed national health care initiatives.
- Middle-class Americans have traditionally espoused beliefs and values that are consistent with capitalism, self-determination, and distrust of big government.
- Middle-class Americans have been averse to higher taxes to pay for the increased cost of a national health care program.

Creation of Medicaid and Medicare

Before 1965, private health insurance was the only widely available source of payment for health care, and it was available primarily to middle-class working people and their families. The elderly, the unemployed, and the poor had to rely on their own resources, on limited public programs, or on charity from hospitals and individual physicians.

The earlier debates over national health insurance had made one thing clear: Most Americans did not desire government intervention in how they received health care, with one exception—they would be less opposed to reform initiatives for the underprivileged classes. In principle, the poor were considered a special class who could be served through a government-sponsored program. The elderly—those 65 years of age and older—were another group that started to receive increased attention in the 1950s. On their own, most of the poor and the elderly could not afford the increasing cost of health care. Also, because the health status of these population groups was significantly worse than that of the general population, their medical needs were more critical. The elderly, in particular, had a higher incidence and prevalence of disease than did younger age groups. Despite their greater need for health care, fewer than half of all elderly persons were covered by private health insurance. Many of them could not obtain private health insurance because of poor health status. Also, the growing elderly middle class was becoming a politically active force.

A bill introduced in Congress by Aime Forand in 1957 started the momentum for including necessary hospital and nursing home care as an extension of Social Security benefits (Stevens, 1971, p. 434). The AMA, however, undertook a massive campaign to portray a government insurance plan as a threat to the physician–patient relationship. The bill stalled initially, but public hearings around the country, which were packed by the elderly, produced an intense grassroots support to push the issue onto the national agenda (Starr, 1982, p. 368). A compromise reform, the Medical Assistance Act, also known as the Kerr-Mills Act, went into effect in 1960. Under the act, federal grants were given to the states so they could extend health services under their welfare programs to low-income elderly persons. However, enrolling the elderly in a welfare program became controversial, as liberal congressional representatives regarded it as a source of humiliation to the elderly (Starr, 1982, p. 369). Within 3 years, the program was declared ineffective because many states did not even implement it (Stevens, 1971, p. 438). In 1964, health insurance for the aged and the poor became a top priority of President Lyndon Johnson's Great Society programs.

After considering several different proposals, a three-part program was adopted. Part A and Part B of Medicare (also known as *Title 18* of the Social Security amendment of 1965) became the first two layers. Medicare provided publicly financed health insurance to all elderly individuals, regardless of their income. *Part A* of Medicare was designed to use Social Security funds to finance hospital insurance and short-term nursing home coverage after discharge from a hospital. *Part B* of Medicare was designed to cover physicians' bills through government-subsidized insurance, in which the elderly would pay a small portion of the premiums. The *Medicaid* program (*Title 19* of the Social Security amendment of 1965) was the third layer. It covered the eligible poor and was based on the earlier Kerr-Mills program. It would be financed through federal matching funds to the states in accordance with each state's per capita income.

Although adopted together, Medicare and Medicaid reflected sharply different traditions. Medicare enjoyed broad grassroots support and, being attached to Social Security, had no class distinction. Medicaid, in contrast, carried the stigma of public welfare. As a federal program, Medicare had uniform national standards for eligibility and benefits. State-administered Medicaid programs varied across states in terms of eligibility and benefits. Medicare covered anyone at or older than the age of 65, whereas Medicaid became a *means-tested program*, which confined eligibility to people below a predetermined income level. Consequently, many of the poor did not qualify because their incomes exceeded the means-test limits.

Initially created to cover only the elderly, the Medicare program was expanded in 1973 when Congress extended coverage to two other categories of people: (1) nonelderly disabled people receiving Social Security for at least 24 months, and (2) people with end-stage renal disease (ESRD) who needed dialysis or a kidney transplant. In 1997, Medicare added coverage options under Part C, and in 2003 a prescription drug benefit (Part D) was added. The main characteristics of Medicare and Medicaid are summarized in **Exhibit 3.6**.

These two major public health insurance programs were instrumental in covering millions of Americans. By 1970, 20.4 million individuals received health care through Medicare and another 17.6 million through Medicaid. The increased access, however, came at a high price

Exhibit 3.6   Comparisons Between Medicare and Medicaid

Medicare	Medicaid
• Covers all elderly persons, nonelderly disabled persons on Social Security, and nonelderly persons with end-stage renal disease	• Covers only the very poor
• No income/means test	• Income criteria established by states (means test)
• No class distinction	• Public welfare
• Part A for hospitalization and short-term nursing home stay	• All services are covered under one program
• Part B for physician and other outpatient services	
• Nationally uniform program	• Program varies from state to state
• Title 18 of the Social Security Act	• Title 19 of the Social Security Act
• Part A financed through Social Security taxes	• Financed by the states, with matching funds from the federal government according to each state's per capita income
• Part B subsidized through general taxes, but the participants pay part of the premium cost	

in the form of unrelenting government regulations and uncontrolled public expenditures.

The Medicare and Medicaid programs are financed by the government, but the *beneficiaries* generally receive health care services from private hospitals, physicians, and other providers. As a major payer of health care services, the government has implemented numerous regulations that govern the delivery of services and reimbursement to providers. As a result, the regulatory powers of government have increasingly encroached on the private sector. In 1977, the Health Care Financing Administration (now called the Centers for Medicare and Medicaid Services) was created to manage Medicare and Medicaid separately from the Social Security Administration.

The creation of Medicare and Medicaid had a drastic impact on both federal and state budgets, but the federal government bore the brunt of this burden. As shown in **Table 3.1**, the gross domestic product

Table 3.1 Average Annual Percent Increase in Gross Domestic Product and Federal and State Expenditures Between 1965 and 1970

	Total (%)	Health Care (%)
Gross domestic product	7.6	—
Federal government expenditures	11.3	30.0
State and local government expenditures	13.6	12.5

National Center for Health Statistics. *Health, United States, 1995,* p. 235.

(GDP)—representing total economic consumption—grew at an average annual rate of 7.6% between 1965 and 1970. By comparison, total state and local government expenditures grew at an average annual rate of 13.6%, but health care expenditures grew at a somewhat slower rate of 12.5%. In the case of the federal government, however, health care expenditures increased at an average annual rate of 30%, whereas total federal expenditures increased at a rate of only 11.3%.

Is National Health Care on the Horizon?

Despite the obstacles that have historically kept national health insurance from taking root in the United States, the U.S. Senate passed the Patient Protection and Affordable Care Act on December 24, 2009, and on March 21, 2010, Democrats in the House of Representatives successfully passed (by a 219 to 212 vote) the same bill, which was signed into law 2 days later by President Obama. Not a single Republican voted in favor of the legislation. Although a small number of provisions in the ACA of 2010 have gone into effect, the main provisions dealing with the expansion of health insurance will be implemented beginning in 2014.

Passage of the ACA of 2010 is a classic example of political opportunism. Obama took advantage of the Democrat majority in both houses of Congress to push his health care agenda without public disclosure of the details contained in this massive piece of legislation. Surprisingly, this time the AMA caved in and supported the legislation. Since its heyday in political activism, the AMA has become a much weakened organization, supported by only 17% of U.S. doctors (Scherz, 2010).

After this legislation's enactment, more than half of the states and some private parties filed lawsuits challenging the constitutionality of the ACA of 2010. Also in 2010, the Republican party gained control of the House of Representatives, while the Democrats held their majority in the Senate. The Republican presidential hopefuls have all declared war on the ACA of 2010, vowing to repeal it if elected to the presidency. In November 2011, the U.S. Supreme Court decided to hear the constitutional challenges; it was expected to render a verdict in mid-2012. Hence, the national elections in 2012, along with the legal challenges to be decided by the U.S. Supreme Court, will determine the final fate of the ACA of 2010.

MEDICAL SERVICES IN THE CORPORATE ERA

The latter part of the 20th century and the beginning of the 21st century have been marked by the growth and consolidation of large business corporations and tremendous advances in global communications, transportation, and trade. These developments are changing the way health care is delivered in the United States and, indeed, around the world. The rise of multinational corporations, the information revolution, and globalization have been interdependent phenomena.

Corporatization of Health Care Delivery

Corporatization here refers to the ways in which health care delivery in the United States has become the domain of large organizations. Since the 1990s, managed care has become the primary source for health insurance and the delivery of medical services to the majority of Americans. The rise of managed care organizations (MCOs) consolidated immense purchasing power and applied it to obtain health care services at discounted prices and to implement various types of controls to reduce the rising costs of health care. To counteract this imbalance, providers began to consolidate as well, and larger, integrated health care organizations began forming. Large *integrated delivery systems* (IDSs) can provide a full array of health care services that include hospital inpatient care, surgical services in both inpatient and outpatient settings, primary care and multispecialty outpatient services, home health care, long-term care, and specialized rehabilitation services. Together, MCOs and IDSs have corporatized the delivery of health care in the United States. At the same time, they have made the health care system extremely complex.

In a health care landscape increasingly dominated by corporations, individual physicians have struggled to preserve their autonomy. As a matter of survival, many physicians had to consolidate into larger group practices, form strategic partnerships with hospitals, or start their own specialty hospitals. A growing number of physicians have become employees of large medical corporations.

Information Revolution

The delivery of health care is being transformed in unprecedented and irreversible ways by telecommunications. For example, telemedicine and e-health have been on the rise. *Telemedicine* came to the forefront in the 1990s with technological advances in the distant transmission of image data. This technology has made it possible to provide health care at a distance, such as real-time transmission of video examinations as well as telesurgery. *E-health* refers to health care information and services offered over the Internet by professionals and nonprofessionals alike (Maheu et al., 2001). These services include medical information from reliable sources such as the prestigious National Institutes of Health and the world-renowned Mayo Clinic through their websites, online purchase of health care products, online consultations with physicians, and online interaction with other consumers about health-related matters. The Internet has created a new revolution that is increasingly characterized by patient empowerment. Access to expert information is no longer strictly confined to the physician's domain, which in some ways has led to a dilution of the dependent role of the patient.

Globalization

Globalization refers to various forms of cross-border economic activities. It is driven by the global exchange of information, the production of goods and services more economically in developing countries, and the increased interdependence of mature and emerging world economies. It confers many advantages, but also has some downsides.

From the standpoint of cross-border trade in health services, Mutchnick and colleagues (2005) identified four different modes of economic interrelationships:

- Cross-country telemedicine and outsourcing of certain medical services have been made possible by advanced telecommunications technology. For example, teleradiology (the electronic transmission of radiological images over a distance) now enables physicians in the United States to transmit radiological images to Australia, where they are interpreted and reported back the next day (McDonnell, 2006).

- Consumers travel abroad to receive medical care (sometimes referred to as medical tourism). For example, countries such as India and Thailand offer surgeries in state-of-the-art medical facilities to foreigners at a fraction of what it would cost to have the same procedures done in the United States or Europe.

- Foreign direct investment in health services enterprises has become common. For example, Chindex International, a U.S. corporation, provides medical equipment, supplies, and clinical care in China. American providers such as Johns Hopkins Hospital, the Cleveland Clinic, the Mayo Clinic, Duke University, and several others are now delivering medical services in a variety of developing countries and emerging economies.

- Health professionals are choosing to move to other countries that offer high demand for their services and better economic opportunities than their native countries. Migration of physicians from developing countries helps alleviate at least some of the shortage in underserved locations in the developed world. On the downside, the developing world pays a price when emigration leaves these countries with shortages of trained professionals.

Globalization has also presented some new threats—for instance, the threat of diseases that were previously unknown in the United States, and the threat of bioterrorism that diverts resources from other needed health care services. Infectious diseases appearing in one country can spread rapidly to other countries. Human immunodeficiency virus (HIV)/acquired immunodeficiency syndrome (AIDS), hepatitis B, and hepatitis C infections have spread worldwide. New viral infections such as avian flu and severe acute respiratory syndrome (SARS) have at times threatened to create worldwide pandemics.

CONCLUSION

In a little more than 100 years, health care delivery has come a long way in the United States, evolving from a primitive and family-oriented craft to a technology-driven service and the largest industry in the country. In the process, many medical procedures and services have become increasingly unaffordable. Both private and public health insurance have become firmly entrenched mechanisms to pay for costly health care, yet public insurance programs cover only those individuals who meet established criteria for eligibility. Previous efforts to create a national health insurance program had repeatedly failed until a massive piece of legislation, the Patient Protection and Affordable Care Act of 2010, was passed. Scheduled to go into effect in 2014, the new law faces both political and legal challenges.

The 21st century has been characterized as the corporate era in the delivery of medical care. Corporatization has put the delivery of health care into the hands of large managed care and integrated health care organizations, and it has turned the delivery of health care into a complex enterprise. The information revolution has created advanced telecommunication technologies, whose application in health care has made the distant delivery of certain health care services possible. E-health has given consumers access to health care information over the Internet. Globalization has added a worldwide dimension to the delivery of medical care through telemedicine and outsourcing, availability of advanced services in foreign countries at reduced costs, foreign direct investment in health care enterprises, and migration of health care professionals from underdeveloped to developed countries. Globalization has conferred many advantages, but it has not been without its disadvantages. Spread of infectious diseases from one country to another and the threat of bioterrorism are some of the main adverse consequences of globalization.

REFERENCES

Altman SH, Reinhardt UE, eds. *Strategic Choices for a Changing Health Care System.* Chicago: Health Administration Press; 1996.

Anderson OW. *Health Services as a Growth Enterprise in the United States Since 1875.* Ann Arbor, MI: Health Administration Press; 1990.

Commonwealth Fund. *1999 National Survey of Workers' Health Insurance.* New York: Commonwealth Fund; 2000.

Davis P. The fate of Blue Shield and the new Blues. *S Dakota J Med.* 1996;49(9):323–330.

Goodman JC, Musgrave, GL. *Patient Power: Solving America's Health Care Crisis.* Washington, DC: CATO Institute; 1992.

Haglund CL, Dowling WL. The hospital. In: Williams SJ, Torrens PR, eds. *Introduction to Health Services.* 4th ed. New York: Delmar; 1993:133–176.

Madison DL. Notes on the history of group practice: The tradition of the dispensary. *Med Group Manage J.* 1990;37(5):52–54, 56–60, 86–93.

Maheu MM, et al. *E-Health, Telehealth, and Telemedicine: A Guide to Start-up and Success.* San Francisco: Jossey-Bass; 2001.

Martensen RL. Hospital hotels and the care of the "worthy rich." *JAMA.* 1996;275(4):325.

McDonnell J. Is the medical world flattening? *Ophthalmol Times.* 2006;31(19):4.

Mutchnick IS, et al. Trading health services across borders: GATS, markets, and caveats. *Health Affairs: Web Exclusive.* 2005;24(suppl 1):W5-42 – W5-51.

Raffel MW. *The U.S. Health System: Origins and Functions.* New York: John Wiley & Sons; 1980.

Rosen G. *The Structure of American Medical Practice 1875–1941.* Philadelphia: University of Pennsylvania Press; 1983.

Rothstein WG. *American Physicians in the Nineteenth Century: From Sect to Science.* Baltimore, MD: Johns Hopkins University Press; 1972.

Scherz H. Why the AMA wants to muzzle your doctor. *Wall Street Journal.* 2010. http://online.wsj.com/article/SB1000142405274870396110457522632390 9364054.html. Accessed October 2011.

Shryock RH. *Medicine in America: Historical Essays.* Baltimore, MD: Johns Hopkins University Press; 1966.

Starr P. *The Social Transformation of American Medicine.* Cambridge, MA: Basic Books; 1982.

Stevens R. *American Medicine and the Public Interest.* New Haven, CT: Yale University Press; 1971.

Torrens PR. Historical evolution and overview of health services in the United States. In: Williams SJ, Torrens PR, eds. *Introduction to Health Services.* 4th ed. New York: Delmar; 1993.

U.S. Surgeon General. Mental health: A report of the Surgeon General. Overview of mental health services. 1999. http://www.surgeongeneral.gov/library /mentalhealth/chapter2/sec7.html#history. Accessed September 2011.

Chapter 4

Health Care Providers and Professionals

INTRODUCTION

The U.S. health care industry is the largest employer in the nation. It employs at least 13% of the total labor force in the United States (U.S. Department of Labor, 2010). In terms of total economic output, in 2010, the health care sector contributed 18% to the gross domestic product. The health care sector of the U.S. economy will continue to grow for two main reasons: (1) growth in population, mainly due to immigration, and (2) aging of the population, especially as the baby boom generation hits retirement age in the year 2011 and beyond.

Health services professionals include physicians, nurses, dentists, pharmacists, optometrists, psychologists, podiatrists, chiropractors, nonphysician practitioners (NPPs), health services administrators, and allied health professionals. Therapists, laboratory and radiology technicians, social workers, and health educators are referred to as allied health professionals.

Health professionals are among the most well-educated and diverse of all labor groups. Almost all of these practitioner groups are now represented by professional associations.

Health services professionals work in a variety of health care settings, including hospitals, managed care organizations (MCOs), nursing care facilities, mental health centers, insurance firms, pharmaceutical companies, outpatient facilities, community health centers, migrant health centers, school clinics, physicians' offices, laboratories, voluntary health agencies, professional health associations, colleges of medicine and allied health professions, and research institutions. According to 2009 data (**Table 4.1**), the majority of health professionals are employed by hospitals (40.5%), followed by nursing care facilities (12.1%), and physicians' offices and clinics (10.0%).

The growth of health care services is closely linked to the demand for health services professionals. The expansion of the number and type of health services professionals closely follows population trends, advances in research and technology, disease and illness trends, and changes in health care financing and the delivery of services. Both population growth and the aging of the population enhance the demand for health services. Advances in scientific research contribute to new methods of preventing, diagnosing, and treating illness. New and complex medical techniques and machines are constantly introduced, and health services professionals must then learn how to use them. Specialization in medicine has contributed to the proliferation of different types of medical technicians. In addition, the changing pattern of disease, from acute to chronic, has created a greater need for health services professionals who are formally prepared to address health risks, their consequences, and their prevention. The widespread availability of insurance from both the public and private sectors has contributed to the increase in medical care utilization, which in turn has created a greater demand for health services professionals. Finally, delivery of health care through managed care has put greater emphasis on the role of primary care providers.

This chapter provides an overview of the large array of health services professionals who are employed in a vast assortment of health delivery settings. It summarizes the training and practice requirements for various health professionals, their major roles, the practice settings in which they are generally employed, and some critical issues concerning their professions. Emphasis is placed on physicians because they play a leading role

Table 4.1 Persons Employed at Health Services Sites

Site	1994		2001		2009	
	Number of Persons (in thousands)	Percentage Distribution	Number of Persons (in thousands)	Percentage Distribution	Number of Persons (in thousands)	Percentage Distribution
All health services sites	10,587	100.0	12,211	100.0	15,478	100.0
Offices and clinics of physicians	1,404	13.3	1,387	11.4	1,555	10.0
Offices and clinics of dentists	596	5.6	672	5.5	801	5.2
Offices and clinics of chiropractors	105	1.0	120	1.0	136	0.09
Hospitals	5,009	47.3	5,202	42.6	6,265	40.5
Nursing care facilities	1,692	16.0	1,593	13.0	1,869	12.1
Other health services sites	1,781	16.8	3,273	26.5	4,852	31.3

Sources: Data are from the National Center for Health Statistics. 1999. *Health, United States* (p. 265); 2006. *Health, United States* (p. 353). Hyattsville, MD: U.S. Department of Health and Human Services.
Data are from U.S. Department of Labor, Bureau of Labor Statistics, Current Population Survey: Employment and Earnings, January 2010. http://www.bls.gov/cps /cpsa2009.pdf.

in the delivery of health care. The role of NPPs (e.g., nurse practitioners [NPs], physician assistants, certified nurse–midwives [CNMs]) continues to increase in the delivery of primary care services. As a group, they have taken over some basic medical functions that were traditionally performed by physicians only.

The U.S. health care delivery system is characterized by an imbalance between primary and specialty care services, which has contributed to an imbalance in the ratio of generalists to specialists. There is also a maldistribution of practitioners and an aggregate oversupply of physicians. This chapter describes these imbalances and explores their main causes. In addition, it highlights some of the main differences between primary and specialty care.

PHYSICIANS

Physicians play a central role by evaluating a patient's health condition, diagnosing abnormalities, and prescribing treatment. Some physicians are engaged in medical education and research to find new and better ways to control and cure health problems. A growing number are involved in the prevention of illness.

All states require physicians to be licensed before they can practice medicine. The licensure requirements include graduation from an accredited medical school that awards a doctor of medicine (MD) or doctor of osteopathic medicine (DO) degree, successful completion of a licensing examination administered by either the National Board of Medical Examiners or the National Board of Osteopathic Medical Examiners, and completion of a supervised internship/residency program (Stanfield, 1995, pp. 102–104). *Residency* is graduate medical education in a specialty that takes the form of paid on-the-job training, usually in a hospital. Most physicians serve a 1-year rotating internship after graduation before entering a residency, which may last 2 to 6 years.

The number of active physicians, both MDs and DOs, has steadily increased in the United States, rising from 14.1 physicians per 10,000 population in 1950 to 27.7 physicians per 10,000 population in 2009 (**Table 4.2**). Of the 151 medical schools in this country, 129 teach allopathic medicine (see the next section for its definition) and award the MD degree, and 28 teach osteopathic medicine and award the DO degree.

Table 4.2 Active Physicians: Type and Number per 10,000 Population

Year	All Active Physicians	Doctors of Medicine	Doctors of Osteopathy	Active Physicians per 10,000 Population
1950	219,900	209,000	10,900	14.1
1960	259,500	247,300	12,200	14.0
1970	326,500	314,200	12,300	15.6
1980	457,500	440,400	17,100	19.7
1990	589,500	561,400	28,100	23.4
1995	672,859	637,192	35,667	25.6
2000	772,296	727,573	44,723	27.8
2009	785,326	731,875	53,451	27.7

Data are from the National Center for Health Statistics 1995. *Health, United States* (p. 220); 2002. *Health, United States* (p. 274); 2006. *Health, United States* (p. 358). Hyattsville, MD: U.S. Department of Health and Human Services. * July 1, 2009, population estimates are from the U.S. Census Bureau (December 2009). Physician data are from the AMA Physician Masterfile (Release date: December 31, 2009).

Similarities and Differences Between MDs and DOs

Both MDs and DOs use traditionally accepted methods of treatment, including drugs and surgery. The two differ mainly in their philosophies and approaches to medical treatment. *Osteopathic medicine*, practiced by DOs, emphasizes the musculoskeletal system of the body (e.g., the correction of joints or tissues). In their treatment plans, DOs stress preventive medicine such as diet and the environment as factors that might influence natural resistance. They take a holistic approach to patient care. In contrast, MDs are trained in *allopathic medicine*, which views medical treatment as an active intervention to produce a counteracting reaction in an attempt to neutralize the effects of disease. MDs, particularly generalists, may also use preventive medicine along with allopathic treatments. Approximately one-third of MDs and more than one-half of DOs are generalists (U.S. Bureau of Labor Statistics, 2002a).

Generalists and Specialists

Whereas most DOs are generalists, most MDs are specialists. In the United States, physicians trained in family medicine/general practice, general internal medicine, and general pediatrics are considered primary care physicians or *generalists* (Rich et al., 1994). For the most part, primary care physicians provide preventive services (e.g., health examinations, immunizations, mammograms, Pap smears) and treat frequently occurring and less severe problems. Referrals are often made to specialists for problems that occur less frequently or that require complex diagnostic or therapeutic approaches.

Physicians in nonprimary care specialties dealing with particular diseases or organ systems are referred to as *specialists*. Specialists must seek certification in an area of medical specialization, which commonly requires additional years of advanced residency training followed by several years of practice in the specialty. A specialty board examination is often required as the final step for becoming a board-certified specialist. The common medical specialties include anesthesiology, cardiology, dermatology, specialized internal medicine, neurology, obstetrics and gynecology, ophthalmology, pathology, pediatrics, psychiatry, radiology, and surgery. These specialties can be divided into six major functional groups: (1) the subspecialties of internal medicine; (2) a broad group of medical specialties; (3) obstetrics and gynecology; (4) surgery of all types; (5) hospital-based radiology, anesthesiology, and pathology; and (6) psychiatry (Cooper, 1994).

Hospitalists

One type of specialty not categorized by a specific organ, disease, or age is that of a *hospitalist*, whose specialty is organized around the site of care, the hospital. Hospitalists are involved in inpatient medicine, and their roles parallel those of primary care physicians in an outpatient setting, in that they manage the care of hospitalized patients. Although this specialty has long served a significant role in urban hospitals in Canada and the United Kingdom, it surfaced in the U.S. health care system to a significant extent only in the last decade when managed care began to dominate the health care system. Working in a system built around the idea of cost-efficiency, hospitalists seek to decrease overall cost and length of stay for patients, yet still maintain referring-physician satisfaction and the readmission rates of subspecialist colleagues. Most practicing hospitalists train under various primary care concentrations such as general internal medicine, family practice, or general pediatrics.

Differences Between Primary and Specialty Care

Primary care can be distinguished from specialty care by the time, focus, and scope of services provided to patients. The five main areas of distinction are as follows:

1. In linear time sequence, primary care is first-contact care and is regarded as the portal to the health care system (Kahn et al., 1994). Specialty care, when needed, generally follows primary care.

2. In a managed care environment where health services functions are integrated, primary care physicians serve as gatekeepers—an important role in controlling costs, utilization rates, and the rational allocation of resources. In the gatekeeping model, specialty care requires referral from a primary care physician.

3. Primary care is longitudinal (Starfield & Simpson, 1993). In other words, primary care providers follow a patient through the course of treatment and coordinate various activities, including initial diagnosis, treatment, referral, consultation, monitoring, and follow-up. Specialty care is episodic and, therefore, more focused and intense.

4. Primary care focuses on the person as a whole, whereas specialty care deals with particular diseases or organ systems of the body. Primary care is holistic in nature and serves an integrating function. Patients often have multiple problems, a condition referred to as comorbidity. Primary care seeks to balance the multiple requirements that a patient's condition may call for and refers patients to appropriate specialty care when needed. In contrast, specialty care tends to be limited to episodes of illness, specific organ systems, or the disease process involved. Specialty care is also associated with secondary and tertiary levels of services.

5. The difference in scope is reflected in how primary and specialty care providers are trained. Primary care medical students spend a significant amount of time in ambulatory care settings, familiarizing themselves with a variety of patient conditions and problems. Students in medical subspecialties spend significant time in inpatient hospitals, where they are exposed to state-of-the-art medical technology to diagnose and treat diseases and perform surgeries.

Work Settings and Practice Patterns

Physicians practice in a variety of settings and arrangements. Some work in hospitals as medical residents or staff physicians. Others work in the public sector, such as federal government agencies, public health clinics, community and migrant health centers, schools, and prisons. Most physicians, however, are office-based practitioners, and most physician contact with patients occurs in offices. An increasing number of physicians are partners or salaried employees under contractual arrangements—working in various outpatient settings such as group practices, freestanding ambulatory care clinics, diagnostic imaging centers, and MCOs.

Figure 4.1 shows that in 2005, physicians in general/family practice accounted for the greatest proportion of ambulatory care visits in the United States (22.4%), followed by those in internal medicine (17.4%) and pediatrics (13.4%).

Imbalance and Maldistribution of Physicians

Aggregate Physician Oversupply

Aided by tax-financed subsidies, the United States has experienced a sharp increase in its physician labor force. Current numbers far surpass the estimated 145 to 185 physicians per 100,000 population that the country actually needs, according to the Council on Graduate Medical Education (COGME).

Obstetrics/gynecology	6.7%
Pediatrics	13.4%
Internal medicine	17.4%
General/family practice	22.4%
Specialists	40.1%
Total	100.0%

Figure 4.1   Ambulatory Visits by Generalists and Specialists in the United States, 2005
Source: Cherry DK, Woodwell DA, Rechtsteiner EA. *National Ambulatory Medical Care Survey: 2005 Summary.* Advance data from Vital and Health Statistics, No. 387. Hyattsville, MD: National Center for Health Statistics; 2007.

Current physician supply also exceeds previous projections and future growth projections, at least through the first decade of the 21st century.

A surplus of physicians leads to unnecessary increases in health care expenditures. A shortage, in contrast, adversely affects the delivery of health services. The irony is that despite sharp increases in the aggregate surplus of physicians, physician shortages still exist in certain parts of the country. These shortages are caused by a maldistribution of physicians in terms of both geography and specialty. *Maldistribution* refers to either a surplus or a shortage of the type of physicians needed to maintain the health status of a given population at an optimal level.

Geographic Maldistribution

Physicians often choose to concentrate in metropolitan and suburban areas rather than in rural and inner-city areas, because the former generally offer greater prospects for better living standards, professional interaction, access to modern facilities and technology, continuing education, and professional growth.

The need for additional physicians is primarily determined by the population's health care needs. Medical services, however, are delivered in a market that links delivery of services to people's ability to pay for them, mainly through health insurance. The need-based model assumes an even distribution of physicians in the projection of labor force requirements, whereas the market-oriented model is based on consumer demand factors. The inconsistency between the two models significantly contributes to provider surpluses in metropolitan and suburban areas and provider shortages in rural areas and inner cities. Low rates of health insurance coverage among rural and inner city populations hampers the economic capacity of such areas to support additional physicians.

Specialty Maldistribution

Besides geographic maldistribution of physicians, a considerable imbalance exists between primary and specialty care in the United States. From 1965 to 1992, the number of primary care physicians increased by only 13%, whereas the number of specialists increased by 121% (Rivo & Kindig, 1996). The supply of primary care physicians sharply dropped between 1949 and 1970, and has slowly declined since then. The number of positions filled in family practice residency programs showed an increase during the first few years of the 1990s, but has experienced a slow decline since 1998 (Pugno et al., 2001). Other areas in primary care training show similar trends. The trends portray a declining interest in primary care among medical graduates.

In the United States, approximately 34.5% of physicians are generalists, and the remaining 65.5% are specialists (U.S. Bureau of Labor Statistics, 2002a). In other industrialized countries, only 25% to 50% of physicians are specialists (Schroeder, 1992).

Specialty maldistribution has become ingrained in the U.S. health care delivery system for three main reasons: medical technology, reimbursement methods and remuneration, and specialty-oriented medical education. By comparison, the need for primary care physicians is determined mainly by the demographics of the general population.

The major driving force behind the increasing number of specialists is the development of medical technology. The rapid advances in medical technology have continuously expanded the diagnostic and therapeutic options at the disposal of physician specialists. Because the population grows at a significantly slower rate than technological advancements, the gap between primary and specialty care physician workforces continues to expand.

The higher incomes earned by specialists relative to primary care physicians have also contributed to an oversupply of specialists. Payment reforms undertaken during the 1990s were intended to increase payments to primary care physicians. Still, significant disparities in reimbursement continue.

Specialists not only earn higher incomes, but also have more predictable work hours and enjoy higher prestige, both among their colleagues and from the public at large (Rosenblatt & Lishner, 1991; Samuels & Shi, 1993). High status and prestige are accorded to tertiary care and specialties employing high technology. Perhaps not surprisingly, these considerations have influenced the career decisions of many medical students. Other factors affecting medical students' career choices are society's perception of value, intellectual challenge, and future financial rewards.

The imbalance between generalists and specialists has several undesirable consequences. Having too many specialists has contributed to the high volume of intensive, expensive, and invasive medical services as well as to the rise in health care costs (Greenfield & Nelson, 1992; Rosenblatt, 1992; Schroeder & Sandy, 1993; Wennberg et al., 1993). A greater supply of surgeons increases the demand for initial contacts with surgeons. In fact, the rate of surgery in the United States grew at twice the rate of the population from 1979 to 1986 (Kramon, 1991). Seeking care directly from specialists is often less effective than using primary care physicians who often provide early intervention before complications develop (Starfield, 1992; Starfield & Simpson, 1993). Having higher numbers of primary care professionals is associated with lower overall mortality and lower death rates resulting from cardiovascular disease and cancer (Shi, 1992, 1994). Primary care physicians have also been the major providers of care to minorities, the poor, and people living in underserved areas (Ginzberg, 1994; Starr, 1982). Hence, the underserved populations suffer the most from shortages of primary care physicians.

DENTISTS

Dentists are the major providers of dental care. Their main role is to diagnose and treat problems related to the teeth, gums, and tissues of the mouth. All dentists must be licensed to practice. Licensure requirements include graduation from an accredited dental school that awards a doctor of dental surgery (DDS) or doctor of dental medicine (DMD) degree and successful completion of both written and practical examinations. The median annual income of salaried dentists in the United States was $129,030 in 2000 (U.S. Bureau of Labor Statistics, 2002b).

Some states require dentists to obtain a specialty license before practicing as a specialist in that state (Stanfield, 1995, pp. 110–113). Eight specialty areas are recognized by the American Dental Association: orthodontics (straightening teeth), oral and maxillofacial surgery (operating on the mouth and jaws), pediatric dentistry (dental care for children), periodontics (treating gums), prosthodontics (making artificial teeth or dentures), endodontics (root canal therapy), public health dentistry (community dental health), and oral pathology (diseases of the mouth) (see **Table 4.3** for frequency distribution). The growth of dental specialties is influenced by technologic advances, such as implant dentistry, laser-guided surgery, orthognathic surgery for the restoration of facial form and function, new metal combinations for use in prosthetic devices, new bone graft materials in "tissue-guided regeneration" techniques, and new materials and instruments.

Many dentists are involved in the prevention of dental decay and gum disease. Dental prevention includes regular cleaning of teeth and educating patients on proper dental hygiene. Water fluoridation programs have

· ·

Table 4.3 Specialties for Dentists, 2008

Dentists	120,200
Orthodontists	7,700
Oral surgeons	6,700
Dentists, all other	7,400
Total	142,000

Source: Occupational Employment and Wages: National Employment Matrix. www.bls.gov. Accessed December 1, 2011.

· ·

significantly reduced the rate of dental caries in children. Dentists also spot symptoms that require treatment by a physician. As part of their practices, they employ dental hygienists and assistants to perform many of the preventive and routine care services.

Most dentists practice in private offices, either alone or in groups. As such, dental offices are operated as private businesses, and dentists often perform business tasks such as staffing, financing, purchasing, leasing, and work scheduling. Some dentists work within dental clinics in private companies, retail stores, franchised dental outlets, or MCOs. Group dental practices—which typically offer lower overhead and increased productivity—have slowly grown. The federal government also employs dentists, mainly in the hospitals and clinics of the Department of Veterans Affairs and the U.S. Public Health Service.

The emergence of employer-sponsored dental insurance caused an increased demand for dental care because it enabled a greater segment of the population to afford it. The demand for dentists will continue to increase with the increase in populations having high dental needs, such as the elderly, the handicapped, the homebound, and patients with HIV. Other factors contributing to the increased demand for dentists include greater public awareness of the importance of dental care to general health status, the fairly widespread appeal of cosmetic and aesthetic dentistry, and the inclusion of dental care as part of many publicly funded programs (i.e., Head Start, Medicaid, community and migrant health centers, maternal and infant care).

PHARMACISTS

The traditional role of pharmacists has been to dispense medicines prescribed by physicians, dentists, and podiatrists and to provide consultation on the proper selection and use of medicines. All states require a license to practice pharmacy. In the past, the licensure requirements included graduation from an accredited pharmacy program that awarded a bachelor of pharmacy or doctor of pharmacy (PharmD) degree, successful completion of a state board examination, and practical experience or completion of a supervised internship (Stanfield, 1995, pp. 142–147). After 2005, however, the bachelor's degree provision was phased out, and a PharmD requiring 6 years of postsecondary education is now the standard. The 2011 annual salary range of pharmacists was between $51,000 and $130,000.

Although most pharmacists are generalists—dispensing drugs and advising providers and patients—some become specialists. Pharmacotherapists specialize in drug therapy and work closely with physicians. Nutrition-support pharmacists determine and prepare drugs needed for nutritional therapy. Radiopharmacists or nuclear pharmacists produce radioactive drugs used for patient diagnosis and therapy.

Most pharmacists hold salaried positions and work in community pharmacies that are independently owned or are part of a national drugstore, supermarket, or department store chain. Pharmacists are also employed by hospitals, MCOs, home health agencies, clinics, government health services organizations, and pharmaceutical manufacturers (see **Table 4.4** for sites of employment for pharmacists).

Table 4.4 Sites of Employment for Pharmacists, 2008

Retail	175,435
Hospitals	59,478
Internet pharmacists, wholesalers, physician offices	34,987
Total	269,900

Source: Occupational Employment and Wages: National Employment Matrix. www.bls.gov. Accessed December 1, 2011.

The role of pharmacists has expanded over the last two decades from the preparation and dispensing of prescriptions to include drug product education and serving as experts on specific drugs, drug interactions, and generic drug substitution. Pharmacists play a critical role in promoting rational drug use and effective drug management (Passmore & Kailis, 1994). Since 1990, pharmacists have been required to give consumers information about drugs and their potential misuse. This educating and counseling role of pharmacists is broadly referred to as *pharmaceutical care*. Pharmacists inform physicians of patient compliance, achievement of therapeutic outcome, and potential drug interactions (Marcrom et al., 1992, p. 50), as well as identify, prevent, and resolve drug-related problems (Morley & Strand, 1989, p. 328). In about half of all states, pharmacists have the authority to initiate or modify drug treatment, as long as they have collaborative agreements with physicians.

OTHER DOCTORAL-LEVEL HEALTH PROFESSIONALS

In addition to physicians, dentists, and some pharmacists, some other health professionals have doctoral education, including optometrists, psychologists, podiatrists, and chiropractors (see **Table 4.5** for numbers of these professionals).

Optometrists provide vision care such as examination, diagnosis, and correction of vision problems. They must be licensed to practice. The licensure

Table 4.5 Employment Levels of Doctoral-Level Health Professionals in the United States, 2008

Optometrists	34,800
Psychologists	170,200
Podiatrists	12,200
Chiropractors	49,100

Source: Occupational Employment and Wages: National Employment Matrix. www.bls.gov. Accessed December 1, 2011.

requirements include the possession of a doctor of optometry (OD) degree and completion of a written and clinical state board examination. Most optometrists work in solo or group practices. Others work for the government, MCOs, optical stores, or vision care centers as salaried employees.

Psychologists provide patients with mental health care. They must be licensed or certified to practice. The ultimate recognition is the diplomate in psychology, which requires a doctor of philosophy (PhD) or doctor of psychology (PsyD) degree, a minimum of 5 years of postdoctoral experience, and the successful completion of an examination administered by the American Board of Examiners in professional psychology. Psychologists may specialize in several areas, such as clinical, counseling, developmental, educational, engineering, personnel, experimental, industrial, psychometric, rehabilitation, school, and social domains (Stanfield, 1995, pp. 280–282).

Podiatrists treat patients with diseases or deformities of the feet, by performing surgical operations, prescribing medications and corrective devices, and administering physiotherapy. They must be licensed. Requirements for licensure include completion of an accredited program that awards a doctor of podiatric medicine (DPM) degree and completion of a national examination administered by the National Board of Podiatry. Most podiatrists work in private practice, although some are salaried employees of health services organizations.

Chiropractors provide treatment to patients through chiropractic (Greek for "done by hand") manipulation, physiotherapy, and dietary counseling. They typically help patients with neurologic, muscular, and vascular disturbances. Chiropractic care is based on the belief that the body is a self-healing organism; thus chiropractors do not prescribe drugs or perform surgery. Chiropractors must be licensed to practice. Requirements for licensure include completion of a 4-year accredited program that awards a doctor of chiropractic (DC) degree and an examination by the state chiropractic board. Most chiropractors work in a private solo or group practice.

NURSES

Nurses constitute the largest group of health care professionals. The nursing profession developed around hospitals after World War I, and it primarily attracted women. Before World War I, more than 70 percent of nurses worked in private duty, either in patients' homes or for private-pay patients in hospitals. Hospital-based nursing flourished after the war as the effectiveness of nursing care became apparent. Federal support of nursing education increased after World War II, in the form of the Nursing Training Act of 1964, the Health Manpower Act of 1968, and the Nursing Training Act of 1971, but state funding remains the primary source of financial support for nursing schools.

Nurses are the major caregivers of sick and injured patients, addressing their physical, mental, and emotional needs. All states require that nurses be licensed to practice. The licensure requirements include graduation from an approved nursing program and successful completion of a national examination. Educational preparation distinguishes between two levels of nurses. Registered nurses (RNs) must complete an associate's degree (ADN), a diploma program, or a bachelor of science in nursing (BSN) degree. ADN programs take about 2 to 3 years and are offered by community and junior colleges. Diploma programs take 2 to 3 years and are offered by hospitals. BSN programs take 4 to 5 years and are offered by colleges and universities (Stanfield, 1995, pp. 126–199). Licensed practical nurses (LPNs)—called licensed vocational nurses (LVNs) in some states—must complete a state-approved program in practical nursing and take a national written examination. Most practical nursing programs last about 1 year and include both classroom study and supervised clinical practice.

Nurses work in a variety of settings, including hospitals, nursing homes, private practice, ambulatory care centers, community and migrant health centers, emergency medical centers, MCOs, work sites, government and private agencies, clinics, schools, retirement communities, rehabilitation centers, and as private-duty nurses in patients' homes. They are often classified according to the settings in which they work—for example, hospital nurses, long-term care nurses, public health nurses, private-duty nurses, office nurses, and occupational health or industrial nurses. Head nurses act as supervisors of other nurses; for example, RNs supervise LPNs.

Because hospitals now treat much sicker patients than in the past, more nurses are needed per unit, and their work has become more intensive. In addition, the remarkable growth in alternative settings has created new opportunities for nursing employment. The growing opportunities for RNs in supportive roles such as case management, utilization review, quality assurance, and prevention counseling have also expanded the demand for their services. Estimates show a current national shortfall of nurses, which is projected to increase (Sochalski, 2002). Sluggish wages, low levels of job satisfaction, and inadequate career mobility pose some major impediments to attracting and retaining nurses (Sochalski, 2002). Many U.S. hospitals turn to developing countries (such as the Philippines and China) for their nursing supply and this trend is likely to continue.

Advanced-Practice Nurses

The term *advanced-practice nurse* (APN) is a general name for nurses who have education and clinical experience beyond that required of an RN. Four areas of specialization for APNs exist (Cooper et al., 1998): clinical nurse specialists (CNSs), certified registered nurse anesthetists (CRNAs), nurse practitioners (NPs), and certified nurse–midwives (CNMs). NPs and CNMs are also categorized as NPPs; they are discussed in the next section. Besides being direct caregivers, APNs perform other professional activities such as collaborating and consulting with other health care professionals, educating patients and other nurses, collecting data for clinical research projects, and participating in the development and implementation of total quality management programs, critical pathways, case management, and standards of care (Grossman, 1995). According to the 2008 National Sample Survey of Registered Nurses, there are 251,000 APNs in the United States.

The main difference between CNSs and NPs is that CNSs work in hospitals, whereas NPs mainly work in primary care settings. CNSs can specialize in specific fields such as oncology, neonatal health, cardiac care, or psychiatric care.

NONPHYSICIAN PRACTITIONERS

The term *nonphysician practitioner* (NPP) (also called nonphysician clinician, and mid-level provider) refer to clinical professionals who practice in many of the areas in which physicians practice but who do not have an MD or a DO degree. NPPs receive less advanced training than physicians, but more training than RNs. They are also referred to as physician extenders because in the delivery of primary care they can, in many instances, substitute for physicians. They do not, however, engage in the entire range of primary care or deal with complex cases requiring the expertise of a physician (Cooper et al., 1998). Hence, NPPs often work in close consultation with physicians. NPPs typically include physician assistants (PAs), NPs, and CNMs.

NPs work predominantly in primary care, whereas PAs are evenly divided between primary care and specialty care. According to the 2008 National Sample Survey of Registered Nurses, there are 158,348 NPs, 70,383 PAs, and 8,000 CNMs in the United States (Bureau of Labor Statistics, 2011).

The American Academy of Physician Assistants (AAPA, 1986, p. 3) defines PAs as "part of the healthcare team . . . [who] work in a dependent relationship with a supervising physician to provide comprehensive care." PAs are licensed to perform medical procedures only under the supervision of a physician. PAs assist physicians in the provision of care to patients; the supervising physician may be either onsite or offsite. The major services provided by PAs include evaluation, monitoring, diagnostics, therapeutics, counseling, and referral (Fizgerald et al., 1995). These providers practice in offices, hospitals, MCOs, clinics, nursing homes, mental health facilities, rehabilitation centers, community and migrant health centers, and government institutions. As of 2010, there were 142 accredited PA training programs in the United States, which were experiencing a steady growth in enrollment (Bureau of Labor Statistics, 2010). PA programs award bachelor's degrees, certificates, associate degrees, or master's degrees. In most states, PAs have the authority to prescribe medications.

The American Nurses Association defines NPs as individuals who have completed a program of study leading to competence as RNs in an expanded role. NPs constitute the largest group of NPPs and have also experienced the most growth (Cooper et al., 1998); since 1997, however, enrollments in NP preparatory programs have gradually dropped. The training of NPs may be a certificate program (at least 9 months in duration) or a master's degree program (2 years of full-time study). States vary with regard to their licensure and accreditation requirements for NPs. Most of these providers are now trained in master's- or postmaster's-level nursing programs. In addition, NPs must complete clinical training in direct patient care. The primary function of NPs is to promote wellness and good health through patient education. NPs spend extra time with patients to help them understand the need to take responsibility for their own health. NPs are particularly valuable in outpatient settings where, for many patients, they serve as the first point of contact with the health care system. Another area where they provide service is nursing homes (Brody et al., 1976). NPs have statutory prescribing authority in almost all states.

CNMs are RNs with additional training from a nurse–midwifery program in areas such as maternal and fetal procedures, maternal and child nursing, and patient assessment (Endicott, 1976). CNMs deliver babies, provide family planning education, and manage gynecologic and obstetric care. They often substitute for obstetricians/gynecologists in prenatal and postnatal care, but refer abnormal or high-risk patients to obstetricians or jointly manage the care of such patients. Patients cared for by CNMs are less likely to have continuous electronic monitoring, induced labor, or anesthesia. These differences are associated with lower cesarean section rates and less resource use in areas such as length of hospital stay, operating room costs, and use of anesthesia staff (Rosenblatt et al., 1997).

Value of NPP Services

Efforts to formally establish the roles of NPs, PAs, and CNMs as nonphysician health care providers began in the late 1960s, when it was widely recognized that they could improve access to primary care, especially in rural areas. Studies have confirmed the efficacy of NPPs as health care providers. Many studies have demonstrated that NPPs can provide both high-quality and cost-effective medical care because they show greater personal interest in patients and their services cost significantly less than physician-provided services. Moreover, NPs have been noted to have better communication and interviewing skills than physicians. These skills are considered particularly important in community and migrant health centers in assessing patients who are predominantly of minority origin and often have little education (Brody et al., 1976). Clients are more satisfied with NPs than with physicians because NPs are more likely to do comprehensive examinations. NPPs are also more likely to be employed in rural and medically underserved areas than in urban areas (Moscovice & Rosenblatt, 1979), which alleviates some of the problems created by the geographic maldistribution of physicians. CNMs are considered effective in providing access to obstetrical and prenatal services in rural and poor communities.

Among the issues that remain to be resolved before NPPs can be used to their full potential are legal restrictions on practice, reimbursement policies, and relationships with physicians. The lack of autonomy to practice is a great legislative barrier facing mid-level providers as many states require physician supervision as a condition for practice. In some states, mid-level providers lack prescriptive authority. NPPs also face financial barriers related to reimbursement. Reimbursement for their services is generally indirect; that is, payments are made to the physicians with whom they practice. Also, the opinions of NPPs are not actively sought in making medical policies and decisions.

ALLIED HEALTH PROFESSIONALS

In the early part of the 20th century, the health care provider workforce consisted of physicians, nurses, pharmacists, and optometrists. The growth in technology and specialized interventions subsequently placed greater demands on the time physicians and nurses spent with their patients. Such time constraints as well as limitations in learning new skills created a need to train other professionals who could serve as adjuncts to or as substitutes for physicians and nurses. These professionals received specialized training, and their clinical interventions were meant to complement the work of physicians and nurses. Thus physicians and nurses were relieved of time pressures so that they could attend to functions that they had the expertise to perform. The extra time also allowed them to keep abreast of the latest advances in their disciplines.

Allied health includes many health-related areas, and constitutes approximately 60% of the U.S. health care work force. As noted in Section 701 of the Public Health Service Act, an *allied health professional* is someone who has received a certificate; associate's, bachelor's, or master's degree; doctoral-level preparation; or postbaccalaureate training in a science related to health care and has responsibility for the delivery of health or related services. These services may include those associated with the identification, evaluation, and prevention of diseases and disorders; dietary and nutritional services; rehabilitation; or health system management. Furthermore, these professionals differ from those who have received a degree in medicine (MD or DO), dentistry, optometry, podiatry, chiropractic, or pharmacy; a graduate degree in health administration; a degree in clinical psychology; or a degree equivalent to one of these. Allied health professionals can be divided into two broad categories: technicians and/or assistants and therapists and/or technologists.

Technicians and Assistants

Typically, technicians and assistants receive less than 2 years of postsecondary education and are trained to perform procedures. These individuals require supervision from therapists or technologists to ensure that care plan evaluation occurs as part of the treatment process. This group includes physical therapy assistants, certified occupational therapy assistants, medical laboratory technicians, radiological technicians, and respiratory therapy technicians.

Technologists and Therapists

Technologists and therapists receive more advanced training, including education in how to evaluate patients, diagnose problems, and develop treatment plans. They must also have training that enables them to evaluate the appropriateness and the potential side effects of therapy treatments, and to teach procedural skills to technicians.

Some key allied health professionals are graduates of programs accredited by their respective professional bodies. For example, such programs train physical therapists (PTs), whose role is to provide care for patients with movement dysfunction. The earlier bachelor's degree has been phased out, and those pursuing this profession now enter master's degree (MPT or MSPT) or doctoral degree (DPT) programs in physical therapy. Passing a licensure examination administered by the American Physical Therapy Association is also required for licensure. Occupational therapists (OTs) help people of all ages improve their ability to perform tasks in their daily living and working environments. They work with individuals who have conditions that are mentally, physically, developmentally, or emotionally disabling. Patients requiring occupational therapy services need specialized assistance to lead independent, productive, and satisfying lives. A bachelor's or master's degree in occupational therapy and passing a certification examination administered by the National Board for Certification in Occupational Therapy constitute the minimum requirements for entering the OT profession.

Dietitians, or nutritionists and dietetic technicians, ensure that institutional foods and diets are prepared in accordance with acceptable nutritional standards. Dietitians are registered by the Commission on Dietetic Registration of the American Dietetic Association.

Dispensing opticians fit eyeglasses and contact lenses. They are certified by the American Board of Opticianry and the National Contact Lens Examiners.

Speech–language pathologists treat patients with speech and language problems, whereas audiologists treat patients with hearing problems. The American Speech–Language–Hearing Association is the credentialing association for audiologists and speech–language pathologists.

Social workers help patients and families cope with problems resulting from long-term illness, injury, and rehabilitation, to name a few. The Council on Social Work Education accredits bachelor's and master's degree programs in social work in the United States.

PUBLIC HEALTH PROFESSIONALS

The growing field of public health is another area that employs many health professionals. Public health professionals focus on the community as a whole, rather than on treating the individual, and deal with issues such as access to health care, infectious diseases control, environmental issues, and violence and injury issues. Public health professionals include people working in a wide variety of professions, including physicians, researchers, administrators, lawyers, environmentalists, and social scientists. Most people employed in public health have acquired a graduate degree from a school of public health. As of 2012, there are 49 accredited schools of public health in the United States. Five core disciplines of academic public health have been identified: biostatistics, epidemiology, health services administration, health education/behavioral science, and environmental health (Association of School of Public Health [ASPH], 2011).

HEALTH SERVICES ADMINISTRATORS

Health services administrators are employed at the top, middle, and entry levels of various types of organizations that deliver health services. Top-level administrators provide leadership and strategic direction, work closely with governing boards, and are responsible for an organization's long-term success. They are responsible for the operational, clinical, and financial outcomes of the entire organization. Middle-level administrators may have leadership roles in major service centers such as outpatient, surgical services, or nursing services, or they may be departmental managers in charge of single departments such as diagnostics, dietary, rehabilitation, social services, environmental services, or medical records. Their jobs involve major planning and coordinating functions, organizing human and physical resources, direction and supervision of other employees, operational and financial controls, and decision making. They often have direct responsibility for implementing changes, enhancing efficiency, and developing new procedures with respect to changes in the health care delivery system. Entry-level administrators may function as assistants to mid-level managers, and may supervise a small number of operatives. Their main function may be to oversee and assist with operations critical to the efficient operation of a departmental unit.

Health services administration is taught at the bachelor's and master's levels in a variety of settings, and the programs lead to several different degrees. The settings for such academic programs include schools of medicine, public health, public administration, business administration, and allied health sciences. Bachelor's degrees prepare students for entry-level positions. Mid- and senior-level positions require a graduate degree. The most common degrees held by health services administrators are the master of health administration (MHA) or master of health services administration (MHSA), master of business administration (MBA, with a health care management emphasis), master of public health (MPH), or master of public administration (or affairs; MPA) (Pew Health Professions Commission, 1998). The U.S. graduate schools of public health that are accredited by the Council on Education for Public Health play a key role in training health services administrators in their MHA/MHSA and MPH programs.

Growth of the elderly population, along with a current shortage of qualified administrators, is creating attractive opportunities in long-term care management. The training of nursing home administrators has been influenced to a great extent by government licensing regulations. Passing a national examination administered by the National Association of Boards of Examiners of Long-Term Care Administrators (NAB) is a standard requirement; however, educational qualifications needed to obtain a license vary significantly from one state to another. Although the basic academic qualification required by most states is a bachelor's degree, acquiring adequate skills in nursing home administration requires a degree that specializes in long-term care administration or health care management (Singh, 2005).

CONCLUSION

Health services professionals in the United States constitute the largest proportion of the labor force. The growth and development of these professions are influenced by demographic trends, advances in research and technology, disease and illness trends, and the changing environment of health care financing and delivery. Physicians play a leading role in the delivery of health services. In the United States, there is currently an overall surplus of physicians and a maldistribution of physicians by both specialty and geography. The basic problem with the physician labor force stems from the fact that the supply of physicians is largely determined by population need, yet medical services are actually delivered according to ability to pay either out-of-pocket or through insurance. This inconsistency between supply and demand significantly contributes to the provider surplus found in certain metropolitan and suburban areas, and to shortages noted in rural and inner-city areas. In addition to physicians, many other health services professionals contribute significantly to the delivery of health care, including nurses, dentists, pharmacists, optometrists, psychologists, podiatrists, chiropractors, nonphysician providers, and various allied health professionals. These professionals require different levels of training and work in a variety of health care settings.

REFERENCES

American Academy of Physician Assistants (AAPA). *PA Fact Sheet*. Arlington, VA: AAPA; 1986.

Association of School of Public Health (ASPH). About ASPH. 2011. www.asph.org.

Brody SJ, et al. The geriatric nurse practitioner: A new medical resource in the skilled nursing home. *J Chronic Dis*. 1976;29(8):537–543.

Bureau of Labor Statistics. Occupational employment statistics surveys. 2010. www.bls.gov.

Bureau of Labor Statistics. 2008 national sample survey of registered nurses. 2011. www.bls.gov Occupational Employment Statistics surveys. Accessed December 1, 2011.

Cooper RA. Seeking a balanced physician workforce for the 21st century. *JAMA*. 1994;272(9):680–687.

Cooper RA. Current and projected workforce of nonphysician clinicians. *JAMA*. 1998;280(9):788–794.

Endicott KM. In: Health Resources Administration, U.S. Public Health Service, *Health in America: 1776–1976*. DHEW Pub. No. 76616. Washington, DC: U.S. Department of Health, Education, and Welfare; 1976:138–165.

Fizgerald MA. The midlevel provider: Colleague or competitor? *Patient Care*. 1995;29(1):20.

Ginzberg E. 1994. Improving health care for the poor. *Journal of the American Medical Association* 271 (6):464–467.

Greenfield S, Nelson EC. Recent developments and future issues in the use of health status assessment measures in clinical settings. *Med Care.* 1992; 30(5 suppl):MS23–MS41.

Grossman D. APNs: Pioneers in patient care. *Am J Nurs.* 1995;95(8):54–56.

Kahn NB, et al. AAFP constructs definitions related to primary care. *Am Fam Physician.* 1994;50(6):1211–1215.

Kramon G. Medical second-guessing: In advance. *New York Times*, February 24, 1991, p. 12.

Marcrom R, et al. Create value-added services to meet patient needs. *Am Pharm.* 1992;S32(7):48–57.

Morley P, Strand L. Critical reflections of therapeutic drug monitoring. *J Clin Pharm.* 1989;2(3):327–334.

Moscovice I, Rosenblatt R. The viability of midlevel practitioners in isolated rural areas. *Am J Public Health.* 1979;69(5):503–505.

Passmore P, Kailis S. In pursuit of rational drug use and effective drug management: Clinic and public health viewpoint. *Asia-Pacific J Public Health.* 1994;7(4):236–241.

Pew Health Professions Commission. Pew Commission urges increased action to cut U.S. physician supply. *PT Bulletin*, November 10, 1998, p. 10.

Pugno PA, et al. Results of the 2001 national resident matching program: Family practice. *Fam Med.* 2001;33:594–601.

Rich EC, et al. Preparing generalist physicians: The organizational and policy context. *J Gen Intern Med.* 1994;9(1 suppl):S115–S122.

Rivo ML, Kindig D. A report on the physician work force in the United States. *New Engl J Med.* 1996;334(13):892–896.

Rosenblatt RA. Specialists or generalists: On whom should we base the American health care system? *JAMA.* 1992;267(12):1665–1666.

Rosenblatt RA, Lishner DM. Surplus or shortage? Unraveling the physician supply conundrum. *Western J Med.* 1991;154(1):43–50.

Rosenblatt RA, et al. Interspecialty differences in the obstetric care of low-risk women. *Am J Public Health.* 1997;87(3):344–351.

Samuels ME, Shi L. *Physician Recruitment and Retention: A Guide for Rural Medical Group Practice.* Englewood, CO: Medical Group Management Press; 1993.

Schroeder SA. Physician supply and the U.S. medical marketplace. *Health Affairs.* 1992;(Spring):235–243.

Schroeder S, Sandy LG. Specialty distribution of U.S. physicians: The invisible driver of health care costs. *New Engl J Med.* 1993;328(13):961–963.

Shi L. The relation between primary care and life chances. *J Health Care Poor Underserved.* 1992;3(2):321–335.

Shi L. Primary care, specialty care, and life chances. *Intl J Health Serv.* 1994;24(3):431–458.

Singh DA. *Effective Management of Long-Term Care Facilities.* Sudbury, MA: Jones and Bartlett; 2005.

Sochalski J. Nursing shortage redux: Turning the corner on an enduring problem. *Health Affairs.* 2002;21(5):157–164.

Stanfield PS. *Introduction to the Health Professions.* Sudbury, MA: Jones and Bartlett; 1995.

Starfield B. *Primary Care: Concepts, Evaluation, and Policy.* New York: Oxford University Press; 1992.

Starfield B, Simpson L. Primary care as part of US health services reform. *JAMA.* 1993;269:3136–3139.

Starr P. *The Social Transformation of American Medicine: The Rise of a Sovereign Profession and the Making of a Vast Industry.* New York: Basic Books; 1982.

U.S. Bureau of Labor Statistics. 2002a. http://www.bls.gov/oco/text/ocos074.txt/. Accessed January 18, 2002.

U.S. Bureau of Labor Statistics. 2002b. http://www.bls.gov/oco/content/ocos072 .stm/. Accessed September 23, 2002.

U.S. Department of Labor, Bureau of Labor Statistics. Current population survey: Employment and earnings, January 2010. 2010. http://www.bls.gov/cps /cpsa2009.pdf.

Wennberg JE, et al. Finding equilibrium in U.S. physician supply. *Health Affairs.* 1993;(Summer):89–103.

Chapter 5

Technology and Its Effects

INTRODUCTION

Medical technology has brought numerous benefits to modern civilization. These benefits, however, have come at a price that society has to pay. Research and development (R&D) and the production of new technology are costly. To be sure, sophisticated advanced diagnostic procedures have reduced health complications and disability. New medical cures have increased longevity, and new drugs have helped stabilize chronic conditions and have given an improved quality of life to many. The fact that life expectancy almost doubled from 1900 to 1965 was as a result of advances in social conditions—improved sanitation, nutrition, and living conditions—rather than advances in medical treatment. The continuing increase in longevity since then, however, has been largely attributed to advances in medical technology as well as continued improvement in living conditions.

With the rising cost of medical care, at some point society will have to face the conflict between a commitment to medical innovation and the growth of new technology on the one hand and cost containment on the other hand. One reason why the United States has not been able to afford universal health insurance for all Americans is the tremendous cost of health care and the demands placed by Americans on the use of all available technology.

Canadians and residents of other advanced nations in Europe, who have enjoyed universal health insurance for several decades, have been able to place limits on the availability and use of costly technology through supply-side rationing. In contrast, the notion of medical rationing has not been palatable to Americans. Hence, the idea of extending basic health care to all Americans presents a major predicament. Access to only basic health care for some and availability of technologically advanced services for others are impractical in the United States.

During the postindustrial era, developments in science and technology were instrumental in drastically changing the nature of health care delivery. Since then, the ever-increasing proliferation of new technology has continued to profoundly alter many facets of health care delivery. Following are some of the major changes triggered by technology:

- New technology has raised consumer expectations about what may be possible. Patients' expectations have considerable influence on their health care–seeking behavior, leading to greater demand for and utilization of the latest and best that technology can offer.

- Technology influences the organization and financing of medical services. Specialized services that previously could be offered only in hospitals are now available in outpatient and community settings.

- The introduction of advanced technology has influenced the scope and content of medical training and shaped the practice of medicine, fueling a trend toward specialization in medicine at the expense of public health, preventive medicine, and primary care.

- Although some medical technology may reduce costs, as a whole technology has contributed to health care cost escalation. For both the consumer and the provider, the cost of excessive treatment has generally been of little concern as long as a third party—either an insurance plan or the government—pays for it.

- Technology has raised complex moral and ethical dilemmas in medical research and decision making. For example, when critically ill patients are put on life support with little hope of full recovery, health care resources may be wasteful.

Economic globalization has also enveloped biomedical knowledge and technology. This is particularly true for the developed and developing nations where leading physicians have access to the same scientific knowledge through medical journals and the Internet. Most drugs and medical devices available in the United States are also available in many other parts of the world.

WHAT IS MEDICAL TECHNOLOGY?

Medical technology refers to the practical application of the scientific body of knowledge to improve the delivery of medical care. Medical science has benefited from developments in other applied sciences, such as chemistry, physics, engineering, and pharmacology. For example, advances in organic chemistry made it possible to identify and extract the active ingredients found in natural plants to produce drugs and anesthetics. Developments in electrical and mechanical engineering led to such medical advances as radiology, cardiology, and encephalography (Bronzino et al., 1990, p. 11). Magnetic resonance imaging (MRI), a technology that had its origins in basic research on the structure of the atom, later was transformed into a major diagnostic tool (Gelijns & Rosenberg, 1994). The disciplines of computer science and communication systems have found their application in information technology and telemedicine (Tan, 1995, p. 4).

In its narrow sense, medical technology includes sophisticated machines, pharmaceuticals, and biological therapies. In a broader sense, however, it also covers medical and surgical procedures used in rendering medical care, ultramodern facilities and settings of care delivery, computer-supported information systems, and management and operational systems that make health care delivery more efficient (**Exhibit 5.1**).

INFORMATION TECHNOLOGY

Information technology (IT) has become an integral part of health care delivery. IT involves computer applications that transform massive amounts of data into useful information. IT is indispensable for managing the vast array of information that is used in patient care delivery, quality improvement, cost containment, billing and collections, and other aspects of operating health care organizations. Most large health care organizations

Exhibit 5.1   Examples of Medical Technology

- **Diagnostic equipment**
  - CT (computed tomography) scanner
  - MRI (magnetic resonance imaging)
- **Equipment and devices to render treatment**
  - Lithotripter
  - Heart and lung machine
  - Kidney dialysis machine
  - Pacemaker
- **Pharmaceuticals**
- **Medical procedures**
  - Open-heart surgery
  - Tissue transplants
  - Hip and knee replacements

- **Facilities and organizational systems**
  - Medical centers and systems
  - Laboratories
  - Managed care networks
  - Information systems
  - Patient care management
  - Internet
  - E-health
  - Telemedicine
  - Distance education
  - Electronic medical records

have information systems departments and managers who are charged with maintaining and improving the flow of information. In addition, IT applications are increasingly being used to link health care organizations to agencies outside those organizations. For example, it is a common practice to electronically transmit billing information to payers.

Major Categories

Specific IT system applications in health services delivery fall into four main areas:

1. *Clinical information systems* are IT applications that support patient care delivery. Electronic medical records, for example, can quickly provide reliable information necessary to guide clinical decision making and to produce timely reports on the quality of care delivered. Computerized physician-order entry (CPOE) enables physicians to transmit orders electronically from the patient's bedside. Telemedicine is based on integrated applications of telecommunications and information technologies. *Medical informatics* (or health

informatics) is the term now used for IT applications that are designed to improve clinical efficiency, accuracy, and reliability.

2. *Administrative information systems* are designed to assist in carrying out financial and administrative support activities such as payroll, patient accounting, staff scheduling, materials management, budgeting and cost control, and office automation.

3. *Decision support systems* provide information and analytical tools to support managerial decision making. Such tools are used to forecast patient volume, project staffing requirements, evaluate financial performance, analyze utilization, conduct clinical research, and improve quality and productivity.

4. Internet and e-health applications enable patients and practitioners to access information, facilitate interaction between consumers or between patients and providers, add certain conveniences for both physicians and patients, and enable the possibility of *virtual visits* online between a patient and physician.

Electronic Health Records

Electronic health records (EHRs) are in the process of replacing the traditional paper medical records. In the United States, hospitals and physicians' clinics have been converting their medical records to EHRs, but little progress has been made in the development of information-sharing networks.

EHR networks make it possible to access individual records online from many separate, interoperable automated systems within an electronic network. According to the Institute of Medicine (2003), a fully developed EHR system includes four key components:

- Collection and storage of health information on individual patients over time, where health information is defined as information pertaining to the health of an individual or health care provided to an individual.

- Immediate electronic access to individual and population level information by authorized users.

- Provision of knowledge and decision support that enhance the quality, safety, and efficiency of patient care (medical informatics).

- Support of efficient processes for health care delivery.

To alleviate concerns about the confidentiality of patient information, the Health Insurance Portability and Accountability Act (HIPAA) of 1996 restricted the legal use of personal medical information for three main purposes: health care delivery to the patient, operation of the health care organization, and reimbursement. The HIPAA legislation mandated strict controls on the transfer of personally identifiable health data between two entities, provisions for disclosure of protected information, and criminal penalties for violation (Clayton, 2001). It also established certain patient rights, such as the right of patients to inspect and have copies of their protected health information, to request corrections to the records, and to restrict the use of the information.

It is generally believed that widespread adoption of EHRs will lead to major savings in health care costs, reduced medical errors, and improved health (Hillestad et al., 2005). The American Recovery and Reinvestment Act of 2009, commonly known as the economic stimulus program enacted under the Obama administration, earmarked approximately $19 billion to promote the adoption of EHRs in hospitals and physicians' clinics.

The Internet and E-Health

The Internet has continued to revolutionize certain aspects of health care delivery. "E-health refers to all forms of electronic health care delivered over the Internet, ranging from informational, educational, and commercial 'products' to direct services offered by professionals, nonprofessionals, businesses, or consumers themselves" (Maheu et al., 2001). An increasing number of Americans have reported going online to look for health care information, and approximately half indicated that the information they obtained in this way affected their decisions about treatment and care (Blumenthal, 2002). According to a survey by the American Medical Association, 86% of U.S. physicians use the Internet to obtain medical and prescription drug information (Dolan, 2010).

By accessing information from the Internet, patients have become more active participants in their own health care. Of course, while information empowers patients, it also has the potential to create conflict between patients and their physicians. Using the right source can provide valid and up-to-date information to both consumers and practitioners. For instance, departments of the U.S. government offer a wealth of research-based information.

The Internet is not merely a source of information; it also offers new ways to create efficiency. In practice settings, the Internet is being used to register patients, direct them to alternative care sites, transmit diagnostic results, and order pharmaceuticals and other products. In addition, by accessing patient information through the Internet from their homes or hospital lounges, physicians can get a head start on their hospital rounds (Morrissey, 2002).

Telemedicine and Remote Health Services

Telemedicine, or distance medicine, employs telecommunications technology for medical diagnosis and patient care when the provider and client are separated by distance. It also enables a generalist to consult a specialist when a patient's illness and diagnosis are complex. General adoption of telemedicine has been slow, however. Some of the main barriers have been licensure of physicians and other providers across state lines, concerns about legal liability, and lack of reimbursement for services provided via telemedicine. Also, the cost-effectiveness of most telemedicine applications remains unsubstantiated. Diagnostic and consultative teleradiology, in contrast, is almost universally reimbursed and has proven to be cost-effective (Field & Grigsby, 2002).

Remote health services (RHS) involve patient care interactions that are geographically disparate and enabled by telecommunications, information technology, and sensor technology. Key players involved in such a system are physicians and nonphysician clinicians, sick or healthy individuals, and their family or friends. Despite the obstacles, several new applications are being studied. Remote in-home patient monitoring programs that monitor vital signs, blood pressure, and blood glucose levels, for example, are proving to be cost-effective (Haselkorn et al., 2007).

UTILIZATION OF MEDICAL TECHNOLOGY

High-tech procedures are more readily available in the United States than they are in most other countries, and little is done to limit the expansion of new medical technology. For example, compared with most hospitals in industrialized countries, American hospitals perform a far greater number of catheterizations, angioplasties, and heart bypass surgeries. The United States also has more high-tech equipment such as MRI and computed tomography (CT) scanners available for its population than most countries do (Kim et al., 2001). To control medical costs, almost all other nations have tried to limit—mainly through central planning (supply-side rationing)—the distribution and utilization of high-tech procedures. For instance, compared with the United States, Canada has 76% fewer MRI machines and performs 72% fewer coronary bypass procedures per 100,000 population; the United Kingdom has 55% fewer MRI machines and performs 82% fewer coronary bypass surgeries (Anderson & Hussey, 2001). Only Japan and Switzerland are estimated to have more MRI machines per 100,000 population than the United States. The rationing of medical technology through central planning curtails costs, but it also restricts access to care. For example, Canadians have to wait an average of 9 weeks to obtain specialty treatments, 4.3 weeks for a CT scan, and 10.3 weeks for an MRI (Esmail & Walker, 2006).

Spending on R&D drives innovation, which results in the development of new technology. Once technology has been developed, its use is almost ensured. In 2007, the United States spent approximately $101.1 billion on biomedical research, of which 62% was spent by the private sector, such as the pharmaceutical and biotechnology industry; the remaining 38% came from the government (Dorsey et al., 2010). R&D spending in the United States exceeds that in any other country both on a per capita basis and as a percentage of total health care expenditures.

The major reasons that the United States leads all other nations in the development and use of technology are (1) cultural beliefs and values, (2) medical training and practice, (3) insurance coverage, and (4) competition among providers. These factors are discussed in subsequent sections. **Exhibit 5.2** lists some interventions that the United States might potentially undertake to curtail the growth of technology. Implementing these

Exhibit 5.2   Mechanisms to Control the Growth of Technology

• Implement central planning to determine how much technology will be made available and where • Withdraw federal funding for R&D • Change the patterns of medical training, placing greater emphasis on primary care practice	• Reduce the number of specialty residency slots for medical graduates • Curtail insurance payments for expensive medical treatments • Impose controls on pharmaceutical prices, which in turn will make less money available for R&D and development of new drugs

measures, however, would go against the fundamental beliefs and values of Americans and would generate much controversy.

Cultural Beliefs and Values

American beliefs and values have been instrumental in determining the nature of health care delivery in the United States. Capitalism and limitations on government intervention promote innovation. An economic and political environment in which innovation thrives creates opportunities for scientists and manufacturers to develop new technology. Americans have high expectations of finding cures through science and technology. Consequently, compared to Europeans, for example, Americans demand more medical research and the development and use of new technology (Kim et al., 2001). Americans also equate use of advanced medical technology with high-quality care. In one survey, 91% of Americans indicated that the ability to get the most advanced tests, drugs, medical equipment, and procedures was very important for improving the quality of health care (Schur & Berk, 2008). The desire to have state-of-the-art technology available, accompanied by the desire to use it despite its cost, is called the *technological imperative*.

Medical Training and Practice

The emphasis on specialty care over primary care and preventive services predominates in U.S. medical culture. This emphasis is reflected in the training of physicians. American medical graduates consistently choose to specialize rather than go into primary care practice. For example, between 1995 and 2006, the number of U.S. medical graduates entering primary care residencies dropped by 7%, compared with a 5% increase in those who opted to train as specialists (Evans, 2008). An oversupply of specialists has had important consequences for the development and use of new technology because primary care physicians use less technology than specialists, even for similar medical conditions.

Insurance Coverage

In the United States, financing of health care through insurance has largely insulated both patients and providers from personal accountability for the utilization of high-cost services. Because out-of-pocket costs are of limited concern, patients expect their physicians to provide all that medical technology has to offer. Knowing that the services demanded by their patients are largely covered by insurance, providers have shown little hesitation in delivering the services. Traditionally, the U.S. health care delivery system has lacked internal checks and balances to determine when high-cost services are really appropriate.

Evidence from several countries suggests that fixed provider payments (such as paying physicians a salary) and strong limits on payments to hospitals curtail the incentive to use high-tech procedures. Such payment arrangements, in turn, place limitations on how quickly new technology will be developed and how widely it will become available (McClellan & Kessler, 1999). Countries such as Canada have also implemented direct price controls over pharmaceuticals to keep their costs down.

Competition Among Providers

Specialization has been used by the medical establishment as an enticement to attract insured patients. State-of-the-art technology also plays a role in the ability of a hospital or clinic to recruit specialists. When hospitals develop new services and invest heavily in modernization programs, other hospitals in the area are generally forced to do the same, for competitive reasons. Such practices have resulted in a tremendous amount of duplication of services and equipment and have further contributed to medical specialization.

ROLE OF THE GOVERNMENT IN TECHNOLOGY DIFFUSION

The development and dissemination of technology is called *technology diffusion*. This factor determines which new technology will be developed, when it will be made available for use, and where it can be accessed. Insurance coverage promotes the diffusion and utilization of technology.

Technology diffusion has been accompanied by issues of cost, safety, benefit, and risk. Federal legislation, in turn, has attempted to address these concerns. The government also plays a significant role in carrying out research and providing funding for research to various organizations.

Regulation of Drugs and Devices

The Food and Drug Administration (FDA) is an agency of the U.S. Department of Health and Human Services (DHHS) that is responsible for ensuring that drugs and medical devices are safe and effective for their intended use. The FDA also controls access to drugs by deciding whether a certain drug will be available by prescription only or as an over-the-counter purchase.

Legislation to Regulate Drugs

Exhibit 5.3 summarizes the main pieces of legislation that regulate drugs and medical devices. The regulatory functions of the FDA have evolved over time. Under the Food and Drugs Act of 1906, the Bureau of Chemistry (predecessor of the FDA) was authorized to take action only after drugs had been marketed to consumers. It was assumed that the manufacturer would conduct safety tests before marketing the product. If innocent consumers were harmed, only then could the FDA take action (Bronzino et al., 1990, p. 198). The drug law was strengthened by the passage of the Federal Food, Drug, and Cosmetic Act of 1938 in response to the infamous Elixir Sulfanilamide

Exhibit 5.3   Summary of FDA Legislation

1906	Food and Drugs Act: FDA is authorized to take action only after drugs sold to consumers cause harm.
1938	Federal Food, Drug, and Cosmetic Act: Evidence of safety is required before new drugs or devices can be marketed.
1962	Drug Amendments: FDA takes charge of reviewing efficacy and safety of new drugs, which can be marketed only once approval is granted.
1976	Medical Devices Amendments: Premarket review of medical devices is authorized; devices are grouped into three classes.
1983	Orphan Drug Act: Drug manufacturers are given incentives to produce new drugs for rare diseases.
1990	Safe Medical Devices Act: Health care facilities must report device-related injuries or illness of patients or employees to the manufacturer of the device and, if death is involved, the incident must also be reported to the FDA.
1992	Prescription Drug User Fee Act: FDA receives the authority to collect application fees from drug companies to provide additional resources to shorten the drug approval process.
1997	Food and Drug Administration Modernization Act: Fast-track approvals for life-saving drugs are permitted when their expected benefits exceed those of existing therapies.

disaster, which caused more than 100 deaths because of poisoning from a toxic solvent used in the liquid preparation (Flannery, 1986). Under the revised law, drug manufacturers were required to provide scientific evidence about the safety of new products before putting them on the market.

The drug approval system was further transformed by the 1962 Drug Amendments (Kefauver-Harris Amendments) to the Federal Food, Drug, and Cosmetic Act. The approval system authorized by these amendments remains in place today for most new drugs. The law was tightened after the thalidomide tragedy. In the United States, thalidomide was a sleeping pill distributed as an experimental drug, but in Europe, it had been widely marketed to pregnant women as a means of preventing "morning sickness." Thousands of deformed infants were born to mothers who had used this new drug. The 1962 Drug Amendments essentially stated that premarket notification was not sufficient. This legislation established a premarket approval system, giving the FDA authority to review the safety as well as the effectiveness of a new drug before it could be marketed. Its consumer protection role now enabled the FDA to prevent harm before it occurred. The new rule, however, was criticized for slowing down the introduction of new drugs and, consequently, denying patients the early benefit of the latest treatments.

In the late 1980s, pressure on the FDA from those wanting rapid access to new drugs for the treatment of HIV infection called for a reconsideration of the drug review process (Rakich et al., 1992, p. 186). The Orphan Drug Act of 1983 and subsequent amendments were passed to provide incentives, such as grant funding, for pharmaceutical firms to develop new drugs for rare diseases and conditions. As a result, certain new drug therapies, called *orphan drugs*, have become available for conditions that affect fewer than 200,000 people in the United States.

In 1992, Congress passed the Prescription Drug User Fee Act, which authorized the FDA to collect fees from pharmaceutical companies to review their drug applications. According to the U.S. General Accounting Office, these fees have allowed the FDA to make new drugs available more quickly by shortening the time it takes for approvals to be issued. On the flip side, the percentage of drugs that have had to be withdrawn from the market after approval because of safety-related concerns has increased ("New Leadership for the FDA," 2002). There is clearly a tradeoff between accelerating the review process and potential safety risks.

In 1997, Congress passed the Food and Drug Administration Modernization Act. This law provides for increased patient access to experimental drugs and medical devices. It also permits "fast-track" approvals when the potential benefits of new drugs for serious or life-threatening conditions are considered significantly greater than those for currently available therapies.

The FDA's drug approval process remains far from perfect, however. The agency does not carry out its own testing of new drugs, but instead evaluates the drug studies conducted by pharmaceutical companies. Many times drug recalls are issued by the FDA years after a drug has been on the market and further research has shown the drug to be ineffective and/or unsafe.

Legislation to Regulate Devices

Medical devices include a wide range of products. They can be as simple as tongue depressors and bedpans, and as complex as pacemakers and laser surgical equipment. Medical devices include general-purpose lab equipment, reagents, and test kits. Other examples include diagnostic ultrasound equipment, x-ray machines, and other imaging technology.

The FDA was first given jurisdiction over medical devices under the Federal Food, Drug, and Cosmetic Act of 1938. Initially, such jurisdiction was confined to the sale of products that were believed to be unsafe or that made misleading claims of effectiveness (Merrill, 1994). In the 1970s, however, several deaths and miscarriages were attributed to the Dalkon Shield, which had been marketed as a safe and effective contraceptive device (Flannery, 1986). The Medical Devices Amendments of 1976 extended the FDA's authority to include premarket review of medical devices divided into three classes:

- Class I: Devices that pose the lowest risk and are generally simple in design. These devices are subject to general controls regarding misbranding—that is, fraudulent claims regarding their therapeutic effects. Examples of Class I devices include enema kits and elastic bandages.

- Class II: Devices subject to requirements for labeling, performance standards, and postmarket surveillance. Examples include powered wheelchairs and some pregnancy test kits.

- Class III: Devices that come under the most stringent requirements of premarket approval regarding safety and effectiveness. Devices in this class support life, prevent health impairment, or present a potential risk of illness or injury (Rakich et al., 1992). Examples include implantable pacemakers and breast implants.

The Safe Medical Devices Act of 1990 has particular relevance for health care providers, who are required by law to report to the manufacturer and, in some cases to the FDA as well, all injuries and deaths caused by medical devices. Requirements under this Act serve as an early warning system for any serious device-related problems that could potentially become widespread.

Research on Technology

The Agency for Healthcare Research and Quality (AHRQ), a division of the DHHS, is the lead federal agency charged with supporting research to improve the quality of health care, reduce health care costs, and improve access to essential services. The agency's reports on technology assessment are made available to medical practitioners, consumers, and other health care purchasers.

The federal government is also a major provider of financial support to private and public institutions for biomedical research. The AHRQ and the National Institutes of Health (NIH) support both basic and applied biomedical research in the United States.

IMPACT OF MEDICAL TECHNOLOGY

The effects of advances in scientific knowledge and medical technology have been far-reaching and pervasive. The effects often overlap, making it difficult to pinpoint accurately the impact of technology on the delivery of health care.

Impact on Quality of Care

Americans generally equate high-technology medicine to high-quality care, but such an association is not always accurate. Quality is enhanced only when new procedures can prevent or delay the onset of serious disease, provide better diagnosis, make quicker and more complete cures possible, increase safety of medical treatment, minimize undesirable side effects, promote faster recovery from surgery, increase life expectancy, and add to quality of life (**Exhibit 5.4**). Improvements in diagnostic capabilities increase the likelihood that timely and more appropriate treatments will be provided. Technology can provide new remedies where none existed before. It also

Exhibit 5.4   Criteria for Quality of Care

• Prevent or delay disease onset	• Increase safety of treatment
• Provide a more accurate diagnosis than is possible with currently available options	• Minimize side effects
	• Provide for faster recovery from surgery
• Provide a quicker cure	• Increase life expectancy
• Provide a more complete cure	• Add to quality of life

offers improved remedies that are more effective, less invasive, or safer. The outcomes in such cases can include increased longevity and decreased morbidity, both of which are indicators of better quality of health care.

Numerous examples illustrate the role of technology in enhancing the quality of care. Tiny cardiac pacemakers and implantable cardioverter defibrillators (ICDs) can be placed in the human body to prevent sudden cardiac death. New imaging technologies such as positron emission tomography (PET) and single-photon emission computed tomography (SPECT) are available as advanced diagnostic tools to study brain function and identify the sources of both physical and mental disorders. Laser technology permits surgery to be performed with less trauma, better precision, and quicker postsurgical recovery. Advanced lasers are used for high-precision eye surgery. New blood screening methods, such as nucleic acid testing, have made the U.S. blood supply far safer than it was a few years ago. Molecular and cell biology are being employed to screen for genetic disorders and provide gene therapy. Major pharmaceutical breakthroughs enable Americans suffering from heart disease, cancer, AIDS, and preterm birth to have much longer life expectancies and improved health status (Kleinke, 2001).

Amid all the enthusiasm that emerging technologies might garner, some degree of caution must prevail. Past experience shows that greater proliferation of technology may not necessarily lead to higher quality of care. Unless the effect of each individual technology is appropriately assessed, some innovations may actually be wasteful, and others may possibly be harmful.

Impact on Quality of Life

Quality of life indicates a patient's overall satisfaction with life during and after medical treatment. For example, quality of life is enhanced when technology enables people to live normal lives despite disabling conditions affecting speech, hearing, vision, and movement. Major technological advances have furnished the clinical ability to help patients cope with diabetes, heart disease, end-stage renal disease, and HIV/AIDS. Thanks to modern treatments, HIV/AIDS has become a chronic disease, not a death sentence (Komaroff, 2005). New categories of drugs are also instrumental in relieving pain and suffering. For example, for cancer pain management, new opioids have been developed for transdermal, nasal, and nebulized administration that allow needleless means of controlling pain (Davis, 2006). Finally, minimally invasive surgical procedures, such as lithotripsy, which crushes kidney and bile stones by using shock waves, have improved quality of life by reducing pain and suffering and allowing a quicker return to normal life. Similarly, procedures such as coronary artery bypass graft (CABG) surgery—an open-heart surgical procedure to correct blockage of coronary arteries—has made it possible for people with severe heart disease to return to normal activity within a few weeks after surgery. Previously, such patients would have required lifelong medication and suffered prolonged disability (Nitzkin, 1996).

Impact on Health Care Costs

Technological innovations have been the single most important factor in medical cost inflation (Institute of Medicine, 2002). In fact, they may have accounted for as much as half of the total rise in health care spending in recent years (Congressional Budget Office [CBO], 2008). Unlike other industries, in which new technology often reduces labor force and production costs, the addition of new technology in health care usually increases both labor and capital costs (Iglehart, 1982). **Exhibit 5.5** summarizes the

Exhibit 5.5   Cost Increases Associated with New Medical Technology

• Capital costs: Acquisition costs are often high because of R&D and precision manufacturing   • Training or hiring of technicians with special skills   • Facilities: May require refurbishing or expansion to accommodate the new technology   • Utilization when covered by insurance (moral hazard and provider-induced demand)

main factors underlying technology-driven cost escalation. First, there is the cost of acquiring the new technology and equipment. Second, special training for physicians and technicians to operate the equipment and to analyze the results often leads to increases in labor costs. Third, new technology may require special space and facilities (McGregor, 1989). Finally, the utilization of new technology is assured when it is covered by insurance. From a systems perspective, costs associated with utilization of technology after it becomes available are more important than the purchase price.

Although it is true that many new technologies increase costs, others actually reduce costs when they replace treatments that are more expensive. **Exhibit 5.6** shows the three main areas in which technology has saved health care costs. Cost-saving technologies include peripheral vascular angioplasty, lithotripsy, endoscopic lasers, valvuloplasty, and automated clinical chemistry analyzers (Stripp, 1989). Minimally invasive technologies have reduced costs indirectly by eliminating the need for overnight hospital stays. Technology should also be credited for an overall reduction in the need for hospitalization. For example, antiretroviral therapies have been largely credited with the dramatic reduction in the hospitalization of AIDS patients (Centers for Disease Control and Prevention [CDC], 1999). In addition, breakthroughs in antidepressants and antipsychotics have been instrumental in reducing admissions for inpatient psychiatric care.

Impact on Access

Geographic access to health care can be improved for many people by providing mobile equipment or by using new communications technologies that allow remote access to centralized equipment and specialized personnel. Mobile equipment can be transported to rural and remote sites, making it accessible to those populations. Mobile cardiac catheterization laboratories, for example, can make the benefits of high technology available in rural settings.

Exhibit 5.6   Cost-Saving Medical Technology

- Replacement of earlier, more expensive procedures
- Minimally invasive procedures that eliminate the need for overnight hospital stays
- Technologies that shorten hospital stays

Impact on the Structure and Processes of Health Care Delivery

Medical technology has transformed large urban hospitals into medical centers where the latest diagnostic and therapeutic remedies are offered, but technology also takes modern medicine to outpatient services and patients' own homes. This trend has led to reduced costs where similar technology was previously available only in hospitals. Without technological innovations, extensive adaptations of modern treatments in outpatient and home care would not have been possible. For example, monitoring devices can permit cardiac implants to transmit vital information over telephone lines, respirators can maintain breathing in the home, and kidney dialyzers are being used for some patients at home. Surgical procedures now commonly performed on an outpatient basis include hernia repair, surgery for kidney and gallbladder stones, cataract removal, tonsillectomy, carpal tunnel release, left heart catheterization, knee arthroscopy, and much gynecological surgery. Numerous diagnostic procedures, including some of the latest imaging procedures, are also performed in outpatient settings.

Impact on Global Medical Practice

The United States leads the world in R&D spending and development of new medical technology. For example, the United States spends more per capita on pharmaceutical R&D than either Europe or Japan (Hay, 2006). Many nations wait for the United States to develop new technologies that can then be introduced into their health care systems in a more controlled and manageable fashion. As a result of this practice, European and other economies get a free ride on U.S. biomedical R&D and obtain nearly all of the benefits of U.S. medical technology at much lower health care costs (Hay, 2006). If technology development was slowed by a modest amount in the United States, it would likely have serious health consequences globally (Massaro, 1990). Telemedicine has also made clinical care, distance education, and medical research possible in parts of the world traditionally unexposed to such advancements (Umar, 2003).

Impact on Bioethics

Increasingly, technological change is raising serious ethical and moral issues. Gene mapping of humans, genetic cloning, stem cell research, genetic engineering, genetic testing, and so forth may hold potential benefits, but they also present serious ethical dilemmas. For example, research on embryonic stem cells may lead one day to the discovery of treatments and cures for diseases and other long-term degenerative illnesses such as cardiac failure, Parkinson's disease, spinal cord injury, and diabetes. However, the use of human embryos for research is highly controversial. Life support technology also raises serious ethical issues in medical decisions, including whether life support should continue when a patient may simply exist in a permanent vegetative state or whether life support should be discontinued, and if so, at what point.

ASSESSMENT OF MEDICAL TECHNOLOGY

Health technology assessment (HTA) refers to the evaluation of medical technology to determine its efficacy, safety, and cost-effectiveness. Assessment can go beyond examining the direct effects of technology to include its social, economic, and ethical consequences (Institute of Medicine, 1985). The objective of HTA is to establish the appropriateness of medical technology for widespread use. Hence, HTA should govern decisions to adopt and disseminate new technology.

Efficacy and safety are the basic starting points in evaluating the overall usefulness of medical technology. *Cost-effectiveness* goes a step further in evaluating the safety and efficacy of a technology in relation to its cost. Efficacy and safety are evaluated through clinical trials. A *clinical trial* is a carefully designed research study in which human subjects participate under controlled observations. Cost-effectiveness is determined by using economic models that compare the benefits of a treatment to its costs.

In the United States, it is primarily the private sector that conducts HTA; in contrast, nations such as Sweden, the Netherlands, and Canada have centralized technology assessment agencies that perform this task (Neumann & Sandberg, 1998). Hence, much of the talent needed to assess medical technology is also located, organized, and financed in the private sector.

Efficacy

Efficacy may be defined simply as the health benefit to be derived from the use of technology, or how effective a given technology is in diagnosing or treating a condition. If a product or service actually produces some health benefits, it can be considered efficacious or effective. Decisions about efficacy require that the right questions be asked. For example, is the current diagnosis satisfactory? What is the likelihood that a different procedure would result in a better diagnosis? If the problem is more accurately diagnosed, what is the likelihood of a better cure? Apart from evaluating the effects on mortality and morbidity, issues related to quality of life are important.

Safety

Safety refers to protection against unnecessary harm from the use of technology. As a primary benchmark, the benefits of any intervention must outweigh any negative consequences. After safety has been experimentally determined, the outcomes from the wider use of a certain technology are closely monitored over time to identify any problems.

Cost-Effectiveness

Cost-effectiveness, or cost-efficiency, goes a step beyond the determination of efficacy and safety by weighing benefits against costs. When a medical treatment is first introduced in caring for a patient, the benefits generally exceed the costs, and the use of technology is regarded as cost-effective. Over time, additional treatments then begin to lower the benefits in relation to rising costs. At some point along a timeline, continued medical interventions yield benefits that are roughly equal to the additional costs. Optimal cost-effectiveness is achieved when additional benefits equal the additional cost of treatment. Beyond the optimal point, additional interventions either deliver no further benefits or the cost of providing additional care begins to exceed the benefits. In these cases, additional care becomes wasteful. In cost-effectiveness analysis, the potential risk from medical treatment can also be incorporated as a type of cost, recognizing that most medical procedures are associated with varying degrees of risk or potential harm.

Experts believe that much of the medical care delivered in the United States is wasteful because, after a certain point, additional care adds little or no health benefits while the costs continue to accumulate. One of the problems is that little is known about the cost-effectiveness of even well-established health care technologies. As the overall health care cost burden continues to mount, HTA will play a considerable role in future health care planning, policy, financing, and delivery. Establishing the cost-effectiveness of various treatments (called comparative effectiveness study) can potentially relieve physicians and insurers of the responsibility of making certain treatment decisions that might otherwise become controversial and lead to conflict and legal battles.

BENEFITS OF TECHNOLOGY ASSESSMENT

From the previous section, some of the main benefits of HTA become obvious. For example, establishing the safety and efficacy of new technology is essential to prevent potential harm to patients. Other beneficial effects discussed earlier, such as improved quality of care, better quality of life, better access, and control of costs, are all based on the use of technologies that pass rigorous examination of their safety, efficacy, and cost-effectiveness.

Delivering Value

Possibilities regarding what technology can achieve are potentially limitless. However, health services decision making is increasingly being governed by the answer to the question "What is appropriate?" rather than "What is possible?" (Abele, 1995). The concept of *value*—improved benefits at lower costs and health risks—is becoming important to those who finance health care, including private employers, the government, and managed care organizations. Value can be increased by improving quality, reducing cost, or doing both. The problem is that insured patients often want to use all available medical resources, regardless of how little health benefit is received in relation to their cost. Physicians often find themselves in a precarious situation when they are required to withhold treatment because of its cost-inefficiency. Payers generally get blamed as uncaring profit mongers when they intervene in the delivery of medical care based on costs. Eventually the government may find itself in a central position of issuing practice guidelines based on cost-efficiency.

Cost-Containment

Simply pointing to technology as the culprit for cost escalations and putting arbitrary restraints on technology development and dissemination would be a misdirected strategy. As stated earlier, technology has the potential to not only enhance health benefits but also reduce costs. Demands for reducing costs without sacrificing quality must influence technological change. Also, a greater emphasis should be placed on developing technology specifically for reducing costs.

Standardized Practice Protocols

Medical practice guidelines (or clinical practice guidelines) are systematically developed protocols to assist practitioners in delivering appropriate health care for specific clinical circumstances (Field & Lohr, 1990). HTA plays a significant role in the development of clinical protocols. Unlike in some other countries, however, cost-effectiveness has not taken central stage in health care delivery in the United States. Rising health care costs and excessive spending remain a top concern in the United States.

CONCLUSION

Medical technology includes drugs, devices, procedures, facilities, information systems, and organizational systems. Several factors have engendered the mindset among Americans that all available medical technology must be used regardless of its cost. The United States has the world's foremost position in both the production and the utilization of medical technology. Other countries may then adopt the technology developed in the United States, thereby avoiding the high R&D costs necessary to create the technology in the first place. In addition, these nations use supply-side rationing to contain the diffusion and use of technology. Such an approach has been deemed unacceptable by most Americans. Consequently, medical technology has been one of the primary factors in the growth of health care expenditures in the United States. In the United States, the FDA regulates the introduction of new drugs and devices based on their efficacy and safety, but without evaluating their cost-effectiveness. Experts believe that much of the medical care delivered in America is actually wasteful, but at this point, no one is quite sure how to contain Americans' insatiable demand for the almost indiscriminate use of technology.

REFERENCES

Abele J. Health reform and technology: What does it mean for us? *Biomed Instrument Tech.* 1995;29(6):476–478.

Anderson G, Hussey PS. Comparing health system performance in OECD countries. *Health Affairs.* 2001;20(3):219–232.

Blumenthal D. Doctors in a wired world: Can professionalism survive connectivity? *Milbank Quarterly.* 2002;80(3):525–546.

Bronzino JD, et al. *Medical Technology and Society: An Interdisciplinary Perspective.* Cambridge, MA: MIT Press; 1990.

Centers for Disease Control and Prevention (CDC). New data show AIDS patients less likely to be hospitalized. 1999. http://www.cdc.gov/od/oc/media/pressrel /r990608.htm/. Accessed July 2008.

Clayton PD. Confidentiality and medical information. *Ann Emerg Med.* 2001;38(3):312–316.

Congressional Budget Office (CBO). *Technological Change and the Growth of Health Care Spending.* Washington, DC: Congressional Budget Office; 2008.

Davis MP. Management of cancer pain: Focus on new opioid analgesic formulations. *Am J Cancer.* 2006;5(3):171–182.

Dolan PL. 86% of physicians use Internet to access health information. 2010. http://www.ama-assn.org/amednews/2010/01/04/bisc0104.htm. Accessed November 2011.

Dorsey ER, et al. Funding of US biomedical research, 2003–2008. *JAMA.* 2010;303(2):137–143.

Esmail N, Walker G. *Waiting Your Turn: Hospital Waiting Lists in Canada.* 16th ed. Vancouver, British Columbia: Fraser Institute; 2006.

Evans M. Primary-care worries. *Mod Healthcare.* 2008;38(7):8–9.

Field MJ, Grigsby J. Telemedicine and remote patient monitoring. *JAMA.* 2002;288:423–425.

Field MJ, Lohr KN, eds. *Clinical Practice Guidelines: Directions for a New Agency.* Washington, DC: National Academy Press; 1990.

Flannery EJ. Should it be easier or harder to use unapproved drugs and devices? *Hastings Center Rep.* 1986;16(1):17–23.

Gelijns A, Rosenberg N. The dynamics of technological change in medicine. *Health Affairs.* 1994;13(3):28–46.

Haselkorn A, et al. The future of remote health services summary of an expert panel discussion. *Telemed J E-Health.* 2007;13(3):341–348.

Hay JW. Where's the value in health care? *Value Health.* 2006;9(3):141–143.

Hillestad R, et al. Can electronic medical record systems transform health care? Potential health benefits, savings, and costs. *Health Affairs.* 2005;24(5):1103–1117.

Iglehart JK. The cost and regulation of medical technology: Future policy directions. In: McKinlay JB, ed. *Technology and the Future of Health Care.* Cambridge, MA: MIT Press; 1982:69–103.

Institute of Medicine. *Assessing Medical Technologies.* Washington, DC: National Academy Press; 1985.

Institute of Medicine. *Medical Innovation in the Changing Healthcare Marketplace*. Washington, DC: National Academy Press; 2002.

Institute of Medicine. *Key Capabilities of an Electronic Health Records System*. Washington, DC: National Academy Press; 2003.

Kim M, et al. How interested are Americans in new medical technologies? A multicountry comparison. *Health Affairs*. 2001;20(5):194–201.

Kleinke JD. The price of progress: Prescription drugs in the health care market. *Health Affairs*. 2001;20(5):43–60.

Komaroff AL. Beyond the horizon. *Newsweek*. December 12, 2005;146:82–84.

Maheu MM, et al. *E-Health, Telehealth, and Telemedicine: A Guide to Start-Up and Success*. San Francisco: Jossey-Bass; 2001.

Massaro TA. Impact of new technologies on health care costs and on the nation's health. *Clin Chem*. 1990;36(8B):1612–1616.

McClellan M, Kessler D. A global analysis of technological change in health care: The case of heart attacks. *Health Affairs*. 1999;18(3):250–257.

McGregor M. Technology and the allocation of resources. *New Engl J Med*. 1989;320(2):118–120.

Merrill RA. Regulation of drugs and devices: An evolution. *Health Affairs*. 1994;13(3):47–69.

Morrissey J. Hospitals offer remote control. *Mod Healthcare*. 2002;32(51):32–35.

Neumann PJ, Sandberg EA. Trends in health care R & D and technology innovation. *Health Affairs*. 1998;17:111–119.

New leadership for the FDA. *Lancet*. 2002;360(9341):1183.

Nitzkin JL. Technology and health care: Driving costs up, not down. *IEEE Tech Soc Mag*. 1996;15(3):40–45.

Rakich JS, et al. *Managing Health Services Organizations*. Baltimore, MD: Health Professions Press; 1992.

Schur CL, Berk ML. Views on health care technology: Americans consider the risks and sources of information. *Health Affairs*. 2008;27(6):1654–1664.

Stripp D. A two-edged sword. *Wall Street Journal*, November 11, 1989, pp. R21–R23.

Tan JKH. *Health Management Information Systems: Theories, Methods, and Applications*. Gaithersburg, MD: Aspen; 1995.

Umar K, Office of Minority Health Resource Center. Telemedicine works: Quality, access, and cost impacts cited. In: *Closing the Gap* (January–February 2003). Washington, DC: Department of Health and Human Services; 2003.

Chapter 6

Financing and Reimbursement Methods

INTRODUCTION

Financing refers to any mechanism that gives people the ability to pay for health care services. For most people, financing is necessary to access health care. Some uncompensated or charity care, mainly provided through free clinics, community health centers, and hospital emergency departments, is delivered to those who have little or no means to finance their health care. Such services, however, are not available in all geographic locations.

The complexity of financing is one of the primary characteristics of medical care delivery in the United States. Most health insurance is privately financed. Certain categories of people, however, can become eligible for tax-supported public health insurance. Almost all Americans age 65 and older qualify for Medicare, which also covers some younger adults with disabilities. Medicaid is another major public insurance program that covers many of the poor, including children in low-income households. Expansion of Medicaid to cover an estimated 16 million additional people is one of the main features of the Patient Protection and Affordable Care Act (ACA) of 2010 (Cunningham, 2011). Other public programs, such as the Department of Veterans Affairs (VA) and the military health system, cover a relatively small number of people.

In 2010, government financing accounted for 45% of total U.S. health care expenditures (U.S. Census Bureau, 2011b). The most notable shift from the private share of national health expenditures to the government's share occurred soon after the Medicare and Medicaid programs were created in 1965. Since then, the government has continued to liberalize benefits and has added new programs in a piecemeal fashion. The ACA of 2010, if fully implemented in 2014, will have a substantial effect in shifting the burden of national health care spending to taxpayers.

Financing also includes the various methods of paying providers in exchange for the health care they deliver. Hence, the two functions encompassed in financing are purchase of health insurance and payment for the services delivered to insured patients.

The actual payments to providers of care are handled in numerous ways. In most cases, patients directly pay a relatively small portion of the total cost of the services they receive, although cost-sharing by patients has increased significantly in recent years. Various private and public insurance plans pay the bulk of the cost of health care, and they use several different types of payment mechanisms. The financing of health care through the various private and public sources ultimately aggregates into national health expenditures, which comprise the total amount of money a nation spends on health care delivery and other health-related activities. **Figure 6.1** illustrates the relationships between financing, insurance, access, payment, and total expenditures.

Private employers and the government are the primary financiers of health care in the United States. From an economic perspective, one could argue that Americans, through employment and taxes, finance their own health care and subsidize health care for those who cannot afford it. For instance, employer-paid health insurance actually represents an exchange for salary. Working Americans also have a Medicare tax deducted from their paychecks, which amounts to prepayment of certain Medicare benefits they can expect to start receiving at age 65. General taxes collected from

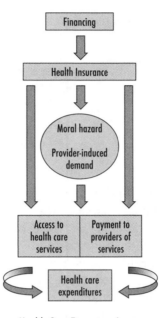

Figure 6.1 Relationships Between Health Care Financing, Insurance, Access, Payment, and Expenditures

working Americans subsidize health care delivered to Medicaid recipients. Certain Medicare benefits are also subsidized by taxpayers.

EFFECTS OF HEALTH CARE FINANCING AND INSURANCE

Health care financing produces effects that go beyond merely providing access and paying the providers of care (**Exhibit 6.1**). It also produces some undesirable effects.

Taken together, financing and insurance are instrumental in creating the demand for health care services. Health insurance enables people to pay for health care, but it also desensitizes both consumers and providers to the price of those services. First, it creates excessive demand from consumers who want to use their health insurance benefits. Consumers are driven to utilize more health care services than they would if they had to pay the

Exhibit 6.1   Health Care Financing and Its Effects

• Financing of private and public health insurance enables access to health care • Payment to providers • Moral hazard • Provider-induced demand	• Technology and services with liberal reimbursement proliferate • Total health care expenditures are greater than if the same services were to be paid by the patients

entire price out of their own pockets. Consumer behavior that leads to a higher utilization of health care services when the services are covered by insurance is referred to as *moral hazard* (Feldstein, 1993, p. 125).

Second, financing exerts powerful influences on supply-side factors, such as how much health care is delivered. Financing also indirectly affects the growth of medical technology, in that technology and services that are subject to more liberal reimbursement tend to proliferate rapidly. Conversely, when reimbursement is constrained, the supply of services is curtailed accordingly. Moreover, health insurance desensitizes the providers against the price of services, with the result that providers deliver additional and more expensive services. Again, if consumers had to pay for these services out of their own pockets, many of them would not be used. The providers' ability to create demand is referred to as *provider-induced demand*. These additional services often deliver little or no additional health benefits, however.

Financing eventually affects the total health care expenditures (also referred to as health care costs or health care spending) incurred by a health care delivery system. Both moral hazard and provider-induced demand waste health care resources and add to the rising cost of health care. To counter these effects, countries with national health insurance implement *supply-side rationing*, which focuses on restricting the availability of expensive medical technology and specialty care. Otherwise, the health care expenditures in these countries would be astronomical. Without a centrally managed health care system, the United States cannot ration health care directly. However, utilization of services is curtailed to some extent because not all Americans have health insurance coverage. This indirect type of rationing is called *demand-side rationing*. When they lack insurance, people face barriers to obtaining health care that they would have the desire to use if they were insured. If health insurance is extended to everyone, without other restrictions, total health care expenditures will rise at a much faster rate than they now do.

INSURANCE: ITS NATURE AND PURPOSE

Basic Insurance Concepts

Insurance is a mechanism for protection against risk. In the context of insurance, *risk* refers to the possibility of a substantial financial loss from some event. In health care, illnesses requiring expensive treatments and hospitalization pose substantial financial risk to most people. Similarly, the cost of most surgeries and subsequent treatment would be beyond the means of many people to pay out of pocket. Insurance, in a general sense, is primarily designed to protect people against such eventualities. Health care providers are also subject to substantial risk when they are required to treat the sick and injured who cannot pay.

An individual who is protected by insurance against the possible risk of financial loss is called the *insured*. The insured may also be referred to as the *enrollee* or the *beneficiary*. The insuring agency that assumes risk is called the insurer or underwriter. *Underwriting* is a systematic technique for evaluating, selecting (or rejecting), classifying, and rating risks. Four fundamental principles underlie the concept of insurance (Health Insurance Institute, 1969, p. 9; Vaughn & Elliott, 1987, p. 17):

- Risk is unpredictable for the individual insured.
- Risk can be predicted with a reasonable degree of accuracy for a group or a population.
- Insurance provides a mechanism for transferring or shifting risk from the individual to the group through the pooling of resources.
- Actual losses are shared on some equitable basis by all members of the insured group.

Based on underwriting, the insurer determines a fair price to insure against specified risks. The amount charged for insurance coverage is called a *premium*, which is usually paid every month. Including both the employer's and employee's share, the average monthly cost of health insurance premiums in 2011 was $452 for a single plan and $1,256 for a family plan (Claxton et al., 2011).

Cost Sharing

Insurance requires some type of *cost sharing* so that the insured assumes at least part of the risk. The purpose of cost sharing is to reduce the misuse of insurance benefits. Three main types of cost sharing are utilized in private health insurance: premium cost sharing, deductibles, and copayments.

In employer-sponsored health insurance, the employee is generally required to share in the total cost of the premium. Of the premium costs given previously, insured workers on an average paid 18% of the cost for single (individual) plans and 28% of the cost for family plans (Claxton et al., 2011). In addition to paying a share of the cost of premiums through payroll deductions, insured individuals also pay a portion of the actual cost of medical services out of their own pockets. These out-of-pocket expenses take the form of deductibles and copayments and are incurred only if and when medical care is used.

A *deductible* is the amount the insured must first pay before any benefits by the plan are payable. In most cases, the deductible must be paid on an annual basis. For example, suppose a plan requires the insured to pay a $675 deductible. When the insured receives medical care, the plan starts paying for benefits only after the cost of medical services received by the insured has exceeded $675 in a given year. In many managed care plans, preventive care is exempt from the deductible, but separate deductibles often apply for hospitalization and outpatient surgery.

Another type of shared cost is the *copayment*—the amount that the insured has to pay out of pocket each time health services are received after the deductible amount has been paid. For example, a plan may require a copayment of $25 for a primary care visit and $35 for a visit to a specialist. Copayment is cost sharing in the form of a dollar amount; cost sharing in the form of a percent amount is called *coinsurance*. Suppose a plan requires a $675 deductible and 80:20 coinsurance. After the deductible requirement has been met, the plan starts paying 80% of all covered medical expenses; the insured pays the remaining 20%. Most plans include a *stop-loss* provision, which is the maximum out-of-pocket liability an insured would incur in a given year. In case of a catastrophic illness or injury, the copayment amount can add up to a substantial sum. The purpose of the stop-loss provision is to limit the total out-of-pocket costs to a certain amount—for example, $2,500. Thus, after the deductible and copayments have totaled $2,500 in a given year, no further copayments are required and the plan pays 100% of any additional expenses.

Previously, lifetime limits on benefits of $1 to $2 million were common. Under the ACA of 2010, lifetime limits are prohibited for all health plans sold or renewed on or after September 23, 2010.

The rationale for cost sharing is to control the utilization of health care services. Because insurance creates moral hazard by insulating the insured against the cost of health care, making the insured pay part of the cost promotes more responsible behavior in health care utilization. A comprehensive study employing a controlled experimental design conducted in the 1970s, known as the Rand Health Insurance Experiment, demonstrated that cost sharing had a material impact on lowering utilization without any significant negative health consequences.

PRIVATE INSURANCE

Private health insurance is also referred to as voluntary health insurance because it is not mandatory. The modern health insurance industry is pluralistic; that is, private insurance includes many different types of health plan providers, such as commercial insurance companies (e.g., Aetna, Cigna, Metropolitan Life, Prudential), Blue Cross/Blue Shield, self-insured employers, and managed care organizations (MCOs). The nonprofit Blue Cross and Blue Shield Associations function much like private health insurance companies.

Private insurance is generally available in the form of single or family plans. A family plan covers the spouse and children of the subscriber in addition to the subscriber. In contrast, government programs such as Medicare and Medicaid do not offer family plans; each individual is an independent beneficiary. Five main types of private insurance are available: group insurance, self-insurance, individual private insurance, managed care plans, and high-deductible health plans (HDHPs). Managed care plans and HDHPs can be group insurance or self-insurance plans. Managed care plans are also available to individuals. In 2011, 90% of employer-based health plans were managed care plans (Claxton et al., 2011).

Private insurance is mostly employer based. Health insurance offer rates vary quite significantly according to employer characteristics (**Exhibit 6.2**). In 2011, 60% of all employers in the United States offered

Exhibit 6.2   Employer Characteristics Associated with Health Insurance Rates

- Large employers versus small employers
- Greater number of high-wage earners versus low-wage earners
- Full-time workers versus part-time workers
- Unionized versus nonunionized employers
- Smaller percentage of young workers versus older workers

health insurance benefits, but the offer rates varied significantly between large and small employers. Whereas 99% of large employers (200 or more workers) offered health insurance in 2011, only 59% of small employers (3 to 199 workers) did so. A large number of small employers believe that their workers prefer higher wages in lieu of health insurance. The offer rate among the smallest employers (3 to 9 workers) was 48%. The offer rate is also lower among employers that employ a large percentage of low-wage earners. Also, only 16% of employers offered health insurance to part-time workers. Large employers are more likely than small employers to offer health insurance benefits to part-time workers. Health insurance offer rates are higher among workplaces that are unionized. Offer rates are lower among employers that employ a large percentage of young workers aged 26 years and younger (Claxton et al., 2011).

Among employers that offer health insurance, 79% of the workers are eligible for health insurance but only 65% decide to take the coverage. The main reasons for not taking one's own employer's health insurance include coverage under a spouse's plan, low wages, and young age (Claxton et al., 2011).

Group Insurance

Group insurance can be obtained through an organization such as an employer, a union, or a professional organization. A group insurance program anticipates that a substantial number of people in the group will participate in purchasing insurance through its sponsor. Risk and often the cost of insurance are shared by the members of the group.

Earlier health insurance plans were designed to protect the insured against financial hardships that could occur because of the high cost of hospitalization, extended illness, and expensive surgery. These plans were referred to as "major medical plans." Since the 1970s, health insurance plans have commonly combined major medical coverage with all-inclusive comprehensive coverage that includes basic and routine physician office visits and diagnostic services.

Self-Insurance

A large employer often has a workforce that is big enough and sufficiently well diversified in terms of risk to warrant offering its own insurance. Rather than pay insurers a dividend to bear the risk, large employers can simply assume the risk by budgeting funds to pay medical claims incurred by their employees. This practice, which is referred to as *self-insurance,* gives employers better control over the health plan. Self-insured employers can protect themselves against any potential risk of high losses by purchasing *reinsurance* from a private insurance company.

Individual Private Insurance

Although most Americans obtain health insurance coverage through employer-sponsored group plans or government programs, individually purchased private health insurance is an important source of coverage for many Americans. In 2009, approximately 5% of Americans were covered under private nongroup plans (Henry J. Kaiser Family Foundation, 2009). The family farmer, the early retiree, the employee of a business that does not offer health insurance, and the self-employed make up the bulk of the people who rely on private nonemployer-related health insurance. Unlike with group insurance, in which risk is spread over the entire group, insurers that offer individual private insurance determine the premium price and eligibility based on the risk indicated by each individual's health status and demographics (U.S. General Accounting Office, 1996). Consequently, high-risk individuals are often unable to obtain privately purchased health insurance.

Managed Care Plans

Managed care plans are offered mainly by health maintenance organizations (HMOs) and preferred provider organizations (PPOs). Such plans are a type of health insurance because they assume risk in exchange for an insurance premium. Unlike traditional insurance companies, however, MCOs assume the responsibility for obtaining health care services for their enrollees by contracting with a network of providers. MCOs also use a variety of mechanisms to monitor utilization and a variety of methods to reimburse providers for the services rendered.

High-Deductible Health Plans

HDHPs have grown in popularity because of their low premium costs. In 2011, 17% of employer-based health coverage was through an HDHP.

Generally, health plans that carry at least $1,000 deductible for single coverage or $2,000 for family coverage are considered HDHPs. Two types of HDHP arrangements are widely used, both of which link a savings account to high-deductible insurance. The savings accounts give consumers greater control over how to use the funds. Hence, these plans are also referred to as *consumer-driven health plans.*

The first type includes a health reimbursement arrangement (HRA—hence HDHP/HRA for the combination). The HRA is funded by the employer; employees are prohibited from contributing to it. The funds are used to reimburse the insured for qualified medical expenses, which include payment of HDHP premiums and premiums for long-term care insurance. Employees do not pay taxes on the payments made to them from HRAs. Although participants in an HRA are not required to have an HDHP, the arrangement commonly includes both. When coupled with an HDHP, the employee first pays for health care from the HRA and then pays for care on an out-of-pocket basis until the health plan deductible is met. Subsequently, HDHP kicks in. Unused HRA funds can generally be carried forward to the next year.

The second type of arrangement combines a health savings account (HSA) with an HDHP (HDHP/HSA) that meets federal standards. For example, federal regulations require caps on the amounts contributed to an HSA ($3,050 for single coverage and $6,150 for family coverage in 2011). Out-of-pocket expenses are also capped at a maximum. Also, the HDHP deductible amounts are indexed annually (e.g., $1,200 and $2,400 for single and family plans, respectively, in 2011). HSAs were authorized under the Medicare Prescription Drug, Improvement, and Modernization Act, 2003. Under this law, HSA holders must have an HDHP. Employers may contribute to the account, but are not required to do so; more than half of the employers currently make contributions to HSAs. The funds belong to the account holder and can accumulate without limit. HSAs have significant tax advantages—namely, contributions are tax deductible, withdrawals used to pay for medical expenses are exempt from federal income taxes, and account earnings are tax exempt.

PUBLIC INSURANCE

This section discusses the financing, eligibility requirements, and covered services for the major public health insurance programs. According to the U.S. Census Bureau, in 2010, 64% of Americans were covered by private health insurance (55.3% were covered through their employers) and 31% were covered by public insurance (15.9% were covered by Medicaid) (U.S. Census Bureau, 2011a).

Public financing supports *categorical programs*, each of which is designed to provide benefits to a certain category of people who meet the eligibility criteria to become beneficiaries. The United States does not have publicly financed health insurance specifically for the unemployed. Even though public insurance is financed by the government, services are purchased from providers in the private sector, for the most part. One notable exception involves the Department of Veterans Affairs (VA), which runs its own health care system to provide most of the services to its beneficiaries.

Medicare

The Medicare program, also referred to as Title 18 of the Social Security Act, finances medical care for three categories of people:

- Persons 65 years and older
- Disabled individuals of any age who are entitled to Social Security benefits
- People of any age who have permanent kidney failure (end-stage renal disease)

Medicare is a federal program administered by the Centers for Medicare and Medicaid Services (CMS), an agency under the U.S. Department of Health and Human Services (DHHS). In 1966, shortly after the program was created, it had 19.1 million enrollees. According to the 2011 annual report of the Medicare's boards of trustees, in 2010, the program had grown to 47.5 million Medicare enrollees (39.6 million elderly and 7.9 million nonelderly). Although the program was initially created for the elderly population, almost 17% of the enrollees are now persons younger than 65 years of age who qualify on the basis of their disability. With the aging of the population, this program is expected to grow to 63.9 million enrollees by the year 2020 and to 80.8 million by 2030 (CMS, 2011a). Of all government programs, Medicare poses the single greatest future challenge to taxpayers.

Deductibles, copayments, premiums, and noncovered services can leave Medicare beneficiaries with substantial out-of-pocket costs. Noncovered services include vision care, eyeglasses, dental care, hearing aids, and many long-term care services.

In 2009, Medicare beneficiaries devoted roughly 15% of their household spending to health care, even though most beneficiaries carry some form of supplemental insurance. Employer-sponsored plans provide supplemental coverage to more than one-third of the beneficiaries. Medicaid helps pay for Medicare's premiums and cost sharing for 21% of the Medicare beneficiaries with low incomes. Approximately 20% of Medicare participants privately purchase supplemental insurance policies from insurance companies (Henry J. Kaiser Family Foundation, 2011b). These policies, referred to as *Medigap* policies, cover all or a portion of Medicare deductibles and copayments and may pay for services not covered by Medicare.

For almost 30 years after its inception, Medicare had a dual structure comprising two separate insurance programs referred to as Part A and Part B. Now Medicare has a four-part structure.

Hospital Insurance (Part A)

Part A, the hospital insurance (HI) portion of Medicare, is financed by special payroll taxes paid equally by employers and employees. These mandatory taxes are paid by all working individuals, including those who are self-employed. All earnings are subject to the Medicare tax.

Part A is designed to cover hospitalization, short-term convalescence and rehabilitation in a skilled nursing facility (SNF), and home health care. For terminally ill patients, Medicare pays for care provided by a Medicare-certified hospice. **Figure 6.2** shows the distribution of Part A payments for various services. Since the year 2003, hospice expenditures by Medicare have exceeded payments for home health services. (Note the managed care expenditures are for Medicare Advantage, which is discussed later.)

The structure of Part A benefits is rather complex. For hospital and nursing home stays, the timing of benefits is determined by what is referred to as a *benefit period*. It begins on the day a beneficiary is hospitalized, and ends when the beneficiary has not been in a hospital or an SNF for 60 consecutive days. If after 60 days the beneficiary is hospitalized again, a new benefit period begins. The number of benefit periods a beneficiary can have over his or her lifetime is unlimited. The following is a brief description of acute care, postacute skilled nursing care, home health, and hospice benefits under Part A.

Services received during a hospital stay are fully paid for the first 60 days in a benefit period after a deductible ($1,156 in 2012) has been met.

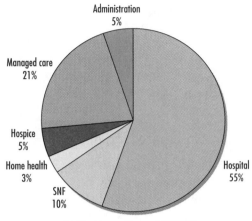

Total Part A expenditures = $235.6 billion

Figure 6.2 Medicare Part A Expenditures, 2008 (Estimates)
Data from National Center for Health Statistics. *Health, United States,* 2010. Hyattsville, MD: U.S. Department of Health and Human Services; 2010:402.

Part A deductible applies to each benefit period. If ongoing hospitalization beyond 60 days is necessary, a copayment ($289 per day in 2012) must be paid from days 61 through 90. A benefit period has 90 days of maximum coverage. Beyond the 90 days, there is a lifetime reserve of 60 additional hospital inpatient days to which a higher copayment applies ($578 per day in 2012). Benefits for medical care in a psychiatric hospital are limited to 190 days in the beneficiary's lifetime.

For postacute care, Medicare pays for up to 100 days in a Medicare-certified SNF subsequent to inpatient hospitalization for at least 3 consecutive days, not including the day of discharge. Admission to the SNF must occur within 30 days of hospital discharge, and it must be related to the same condition for which the beneficiary was hospitalized. All covered services are fully paid for the first 20 days in the SNF. Beyond that, a copayment ($144.50 per day in 2012) must be paid from days 21 through 100.

Medicare pays for home health care when a person is homebound and requires intermittent or part-time skilled nursing care or rehabilitation therapy determined necessary by a physician. Services must be obtained from a Medicare-certified home health agency. Durable medical equipment

(DME), such as wheelchairs, hospital beds, walkers, and medical supplies, is also covered. Home health visits do not have a deductible, but a 20% coinsurance applies to DME.

For terminally ill patients, Medicare pays for care provided by a Medicare-certified hospice. A small copayment of up to $5 applies for prescription drugs for these patients.

Supplementary Medical Insurance (Part B)

Part B, the supplementary medical insurance (SMI) portion of Medicare, is a voluntary program, financed partly by general tax revenues and partly by required premium contributions. Almost all persons entitled to hospital insurance also choose to enroll in SMI because they cannot get similar coverage at that price from private insurers. Coverage includes physician, ambulance, outpatient rehabilitation, and limited preventive services; hospital outpatient services such as outpatient surgery, diagnostic tests, radiology, and pathology; emergency department visits; renal dialysis; prostheses; and medical equipment and supplies. Part B also covers limited home health services that are not associated with a hospital or SNF stay.

Preventive services covered under Part B include Pap smears, mammography, screening for colorectal and prostate cancer, glaucoma screening, flu shots, and vaccinations against pneumonia. Under the ACA of 2010, an annual physical exam, called a Wellness Exam, was made available to all Part B enrollees as of January 2011. No deductible or copayments apply to this benefit.

Participation in Part B requires the beneficiaries to pay a monthly premium. As of 2007, the premium became income based. The standard premium for 2012 is $99.90 per month. For those persons earning more than $85,000 and filing individual tax returns (or earning more than $170,000 and filing joint tax returns), 2012 premiums range between $139.40 and $319.70 depending on income. Part B also carries an annual deductible ($140 in 2012), and an 80:20 coinsurance applies to most services.

Medicare Advantage (Part C)

In reality, Part C is not a special program that offers specifically defined medical services. The program was formerly called Medicare+Choice, which took effect on January 1, 1998, and was mandated by the Balanced

Budget Act of 1997. The law expanded the role of private managed care health plans such as HMO and PPO plans. The beneficiaries, however, do have the choice to remain in the original Medicare fee-for-service program. Medicare+Choice was revamped and renamed Medicare Advantage under the Medicare Prescription Drug, Improvement, and Modernization Act (MMA) of 2003, which authorized higher payments to MCOs to reverse declining enrollments and MCO withdrawals from the program.

By enrolling in Medicare Advantage, the beneficiary receives all Part A, Part B, and Part D services through an MCO. Medicare pays a set capitated amount of money each month to the participating managed care plans on behalf of each beneficiary. In turn, the plan manages Medicare benefits for its members. To attract Medicare enrollees, MCOs may offer extra benefits, such as basic dental and vision benefits, that may lower the beneficiaries' out-of-pocket costs. Part C also eliminates the need for Medigap coverage. Beginning in 2012, the ACA of 2010 requires bonus payments to Medicare Advantage plans based on quality of services.

For many seniors, navigating through the Medicare choices available to them is a daunting task. They must decide whether to remain in the original Medicare program or enroll in Part C. If the original program is chosen, separate enrollment in Part D and choosing a stand-alone prescription drug plan are required. If Part C is chosen, the enrollee must choose from a number of available Medicare Advantage plans. The numerous variations are accompanied by substantial differences in premium costs and out-of-pocket costs.

Prescription Drug Coverage (Part D)

Part D was added to the existing Medicare program under the MMA of 2003 and was fully implemented in January 2006. The program is available to anyone, regardless of income, who has coverage under Part A or Part B. Coverage is offered through two types of private plans approved by Medicare. Stand-alone prescription drug plans (PDPs) that offer only drug coverage are available to those who want to stay in the original Medicare fee-for-service program. Alternatively, Medicare Advantage prescription drug plans (MA-PDs) are available to those who want to obtain all health care services through MCOs participating in Part C.

Like Part B, the Part D program is voluntary because it requires payment of a monthly premium. For 2012, the base premium was estimated to

• •

Table 6.1 Medicare Part D Benefits and Individual Out-of-Pocket Costs, 2012

	Drug Costs	Medicare Pays	Beneficiary Pays
Deductible	$320	None	$320
Initial coverage	$321–2,930	75% up to $1,957.50	25% up to $652.50
Gap or "doughnut hole"	$2,931–6,657.50	None	100% up to $3,727.50 (up to 50% discount on drugs)
Catastrophic coverage	Over $6,657.50	Approximately 95%	Approximately 5%

Notes: (1) The beneficiary must pay a total of $4,700 ($320 + $652.50 + $3,727.50) before catastrophic coverage begins. (2) Some minor details have been left out.
Source: Data from Centers for Medicare and Medicaid Services. http://www.cms.gov/Medicare/Health-Plans /MedicareAdvtgSpecRateStats/downloads//Announcement2012.pdf. Accessed May 2012.

• •

be $31.08 per month (Spitalnic, 2011), which is adjusted upward according to income and type of plan selected by the beneficiary. After an annual deductible ($320 in 2012), benefits are paid according to three layers of personal out-of-pocket spending on prescription drugs (see **Table 6.1**). The program is designed to help everyone at a basic threshold level of spending and, beyond that, those who have excessive needs for prescription drugs. For example, in 2012, the program pays 95% of the cost of prescription drugs after a beneficiary incurs $4,700 in out-of-pocket costs.

Medicaid

Also referred to as Title 19 of the Social Security Act, Medicaid is the United States' public health insurance program for the indigent. Each state has established its own criteria for determining eligibility according to income and other resources such as bank accounts, real property, and other assets. Federal law specifies coverage for low-income elderly, the blind, the disabled receiving Supplemental Security Income (SSI), and some pregnant women. Medicaid is also instrumental in providing health insurance to children in low-income families (**Figure 6.3**). In addition, most states, at their discretion, have defined other "medically needy" categories. Most

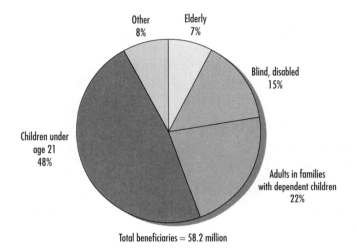

Total beneficiaries = 58.2 million

Figure 6.3 Medicaid Recipient Categories, 2008
Data from National Center for Health Statistics. *Health, United States,* 2010. Hyattsville, MD: U.S. Department of Health and Human Services; 2010:407.

important among these are individuals who are institutionalized in nursing or psychiatric facilities and individuals who are receiving community-based services but would otherwise be eligible for Medicaid if institutionalized. All of these people have to qualify based on assets and income, which must be below the threshold levels established by each state. Hence, Medicaid is a *means-tested program.*

The Medicaid program is jointly financed by the federal and state governments. The federal government provides matching funds to the states based on the per capita income in each state. Wealthier states have a smaller share of their costs reimbursed by the federal government.

Each state administers its own Medicaid program. Hence, eligibility criteria, covered services, and payments to providers vary considerably from state to state. However, for a state to receive federal matching funds, the state must provide some specific health services (see **Table 6.2**).

Children's Health Insurance Program

The Children's Health Insurance Program (CHIP), codified as Title 21 of the Social Security Act, was enacted under the Balanced Budget Act of 1997. Initially specified to last 10 years, the program has been extended

Table 6.2 Federally Mandated Services for State Medicaid Programs

- Inpatient hospital services
- Hospital outpatient services
- Physician services
- Federally qualified health center services
- Rural health clinic services
- Outpatient laboratory and x-ray services
- Nursing facility services for beneficiaries age 21 and older
- Home health services for those eligible for nursing facility services, including medical supplies and equipment
- Certified pediatric and family nurse practitioner services (when licensed to practice under state law)
- Nurse-midwife services
- Medical and surgical services of a dentist
- Preventive, diagnosis, and treatment services (including vaccinations) for children
- Family planning services and supplies
- Pregnancy-related services, including postpartum care for 60 days

Source: Adapted from Smith GA. 2007. *A primer on how to use Medicaid to assist persons who are homeless to access medical, behavioral health, and support services.* Baltimore, MD: Centers for Medicare and Medicaid Services.

without interruption. Most recently, the ACA of 2010 authorized the extension of CHIP through September 30, 2015.

When the program was created, nearly one-fourth of the children in low-income families were uninsured. CHIP offers additional federal matching funds to states to expand Medicaid eligibility to enroll children up to 19 years of age who otherwise would not qualify for coverage because their families' incomes exceed the Medicaid threshold levels. Certain adults, such as pregnant women, parents, and caretaker relatives, may also be covered under CHIP.

In most states, CHIP is available to families with incomes up to 200% of the federal poverty level, or about $44,700 (higher in Alaska and Hawaii) for a family of four in 2011–2012, and if they are not covered under a private insurance plan. CHIP offers participating states three options: (1) expansion of Medicaid, (2) establishment of a special child-health assistance program, or (3) a combination of the two approaches. States are required to screen applicants for Medicaid eligibility and to enroll eligible children in Medicaid rather than in the CHIP program. In December 2010, 5.2 million children were enrolled in CHIP (Henry J. Kaiser Family Foundation, 2011a).

THE PATIENT PROTECTION AND AFFORDABLE CARE ACT

As of this book's writing, the final fate of the ACA of 2010 was to be decided in 2012. Some provisions of the Act have already gone into effect, as pointed out previously in this chapter. Assuming that the Act survives the challenges it faces, the expansion of health insurance to cover a large number of the uninsured will take effect in 2014.

Insurance expansion under this law mainly covers six aspects of health care financing:

1. Individuals are mandated to have health insurance, and tax penalties are levied for not having health insurance.

2. Employers with 50 or more employees are mandated to offer insurance coverage or pay a "free rider" tax.

3. Medicaid is expanded to cover all people at or below 133% of the federal poverty level (FPL).[*] People with incomes up to 400% of FPL will get premium subsidies from the government.

4. States are mandated to establish health insurance exchanges through which small groups and individuals can purchase health insurance.

5. A sliding-scale tax credit is allowed for small businesses with fewer than 25 workers.

6. It is illegal to deny health insurance to people with preexisting medical conditions.

---

[*]Medicaid currently covers only children younger than the age of 6 and pregnant women whose family income is at or below 133 percent of FPL. Eligibility for others is decided by each state based on people's assets and income.

Ironically, despite these provisions of the ACA, approximately 21 million people will remain uninsured according to estimates by the Congressional Budget Office (CBO, 2010). When President Bill Clinton proposed a national health care program in 1994, increases in national health expenditures were estimated to range between $16.3 billion and $24.8 billion (Short et al., 1997). The ACA of 2010 carries a much higher price tag. The Office of the Actuary estimated the cost of health insurance alone to be $150 billion in 2016, after the coverage provisions of the Act are planned to be fully implemented (Foster, 2010).

REIMBURSEMENT METHODS

Insurance companies, MCOs, Blue Cross/Blue Shield, and the government (for Medicare and Medicaid) are referred to as *third-party payers*, with the other two parties in the arrangement being the patient and the provider (Wilson & Neuhauser, 1985, p. 118). Payment made by third-party payers to the providers of services is called *reimbursement*.

A variety of methods are currently in use for determining how much providers should be paid. Traditionally, providers have preferred the fee-for-service method, which has fallen into disfavor with payers because of cost escalations. Private payers as well as the government have devised various methods aimed at limiting the amount of reimbursement.

Fee for Service

Fee-for-service reimbursement is based on the assumption that services are provided in a set of identifiable and individually distinct units of services. For example, physician services may include units such as an examination, x-ray, urinalysis, and a tetanus shot. For surgery, individual services may include an admission kit, numerous medical supplies (each accounted for separately), surgeon's fees, anesthesia, anesthesiologist's fees, recovery room charges, and so forth. Each of these services is separately billed.

Initially, fee-for-service charges were set by providers, and insurers passively paid the claims. Later, insurers started to limit reimbursement to a "usual, customary, and reasonable" (UCR) amount that was determined by each payer. In this case, providers would *balance bill*—that is, ask the patients to pay the difference between the actual charges and the payments received from insurers.

The main problem under fee-for-service arrangements is that providers have an incentive to induce demand and deliver additional services that are nonessential. Although other methods of reimbursement have been widely in use for some time now, modified versions of fee-for-service reimbursements are still used.

Package Pricing

In package pricing, also referred to as *bundled charges*, a number of related services are included in one price. For example, normal vaginal delivery may have one set fee that includes predelivery and postdelivery care (Williams, 1995, p. 114). Optometrists sometimes advertise package prices that include the charges for eye exams, frames for eyeglasses, and corrective lenses.

Resource-Based Relative Value Scale

In 1989, Medicare developed the resource-based relative value scale (RBRVS)—a method to reimburse physicians according to a "relative value" assigned to each physician service. Relative values are based on the time, skill, and intensity it takes to provide a service, and the actual reimbursement is derived using a complex formula. Each year, Medicare publishes the Medicare Fee Schedule, which gives the reimbursement amount for each of the services and procedures identified by a current procedural terminology (CPT) code. The reimbursement amounts are adjusted for the geographic area in which the practice is located.

Reimbursement Under Managed Care

Three distinct approaches are used by MCOs. PPOs use a variation of the fee-for-service method, in which the PPO establishes fee schedules based on discounts negotiated with providers participating in its network. HMOs sometimes have physicians on their staff who are paid a salary. *Capitation* is another mechanism used by HMOs. Under this reimbursement scheme, a provider is paid a set monthly fee per enrollee (sometimes referred to as per member per month [PMPM] rate), regardless of whether an enrollee sees the provider or not, and regardless of how often an enrollee sees the provider. Capitation removes the incentive for provider-induced demand. It makes providers prudent and encourages them to provide only necessary services.

From Retrospective to Prospective Reimbursement

Traditionally, Medicare and Medicaid established *per diem* (daily) rates for reimbursing hospitals, nursing homes, and other inpatient facilities. The per diem rates were based on the actual costs the providers had incurred during the previous year. Because rates were set after evaluating the costs retrospectively, the method was referred to as *retrospective reimbursement*. Home health was also reimbursed on the basis of cost.

Because the retrospective method was based on costs that were directly related to length of stay, services rendered, and the cost of providing the services, providers had no incentive to control costs. Services were rendered indiscriminately because health care institutions could increase their profits by increasing costs. Because of the perverse financial incentives inherent in retrospective cost-based reimbursement, it has been largely replaced by prospective methods of reimbursement.

In contrast to retrospective reimbursement, where historical costs are used to determine the amount paid to providers, *prospective reimbursement* uses certain pre-established criteria to determine in advance the amount of reimbursement. Medicare has been using the prospective payment system (PPS) to reimburse inpatient hospital acute care services under Medicare Part A since 1983.

The Balanced Budget Act of 1997 mandated implementation of a PPS for hospital outpatient services and postacute care providers such as SNFs, home health agencies, and inpatient rehabilitation facilities. Depending on the type of service setting, the four main prospective reimbursement methods currently in use are based on diagnosis-related groups (DRGs), ambulatory payment classifications (APCs), resource utilization groups (RUGs), and home health resource groups (HHRGs).

Diagnosis-Related Groups

The DRG method is used to pay for hospital inpatient services. Medicare has established approximately 500 DRGs corresponding to the most prevalent diagnoses among patients using inpatient services. Instead of a per diem rate, the reimbursement method based on DRGs prospectively sets a bundled price according to the principal diagnosis at the time of admission. The hospital receives the predetermined fixed rate for that particular DRG classification.

The primary factor governing the amount of reimbursement is the main clinical diagnosis, but additional factors can create differences in reimbursement for the same DRG. Such factors include differences in wage levels between geographic areas, an urban versus a rural hospital location, whether the institution is a teaching hospital (i.e., it has residency programs for medical graduates; adjustments in reimbursement are based on the intensity of teaching), and an adjustment related to treating a disproportionately large share of low-income patients (Health Care Financing Administration [HCFA], 1996).

The DRG-based prospective reimbursement has forced hospitals to control their costs. To keep the cost of services below the fixed reimbursement amount, this reimbursement method has also forced hospitals to minimize the length of inpatient stay. If the total cost of services is less than the DRG-based reimbursement amount, a hospital gets to keep the difference as profit. Conversely, a hospital loses money when its costs exceed the prospective reimbursement rate. As an example, if the prospective reimbursement rate for a given DRG is $3,500 and the costs associated with each day of hospital stay are as shown in **Table 6.3**, a patient admitted under this DRG should be hospitalized for no more than 4 days when the cumulative costs will equal $3,400. If the hospital discharges this patient after 3 days, it will make a profit of $700 ($3,500 − $2,800). If the patient is discharged after 5 days, the hospital will suffer a loss of $500 ($3,500 − $4,000).

Ambulatory Payment Classifications

The prospective payment method based on APCs, implemented in August 2000, is associated with Medicare's Outpatient Prospective Payment System (OPPS) for services provided by hospital outpatient departments. The APC divides all outpatient services into more than 300 procedural groups. Reimbursement rates are associated with each APC group.

Table 6.3 Hospital Days of Stay and Costs for a Given DRG

Days of stay	1	2	3	4	5	6
Cost per day	$1,200	$900	$700	$600	$600	$600

The rates are also adjusted for geographic variations in wages. APC reimbursement includes services such as anesthesia, certain drugs, supplies, and recovery room charges in a package price established by Medicare.

In January 2008, Medicare implemented the OPPS to pay for facility services—such as nursing, recovery care, anesthetics, drugs, and other supplies—in freestanding (i.e., nonhospital) ambulatory surgery centers. The most common procedures performed in these centers are cataract removal and lens replacement, colonoscopy, and other eye procedures. Physician services are reimbursed separately under the physician fee schedule based on RBRVS (MedPAC, 2009).

Resource Utilization Groups

Medicare pays SNFs on the basis of RUGs, but the method differs from the way in which DRG-based payments are used for hospitals. Whereas a fixed amount of reimbursement is associated with each DRG, RUG categories are used for determining an SNF's overall intensity of health conditions requiring medical and nursing intervention. The overall acuity level in a facility, as determined by the severity of the patients' condition, is referred to as its *case mix*. It is determined by first evaluating each patient's medical and nursing care needs. Based on this evaluation, each patient is classified into one of 66 RUGs (according to RUG-IV classifications). The case-mix composite of an institution is then used to determine a fixed per diem amount associated with that case mix. The higher the case mix score, the higher the reimbursement. Adjustments to the PPS rate are made for differences in wages prevailing in various geographic areas and for facility location in urban as opposed to rural areas.

Home Health Resource Groups

Implemented in October 2000, the PPS for home health care pays a fixed, predetermined rate for each 60-day episode of care, regardless of the specific services delivered. Thus all services provided by a home health agency are bundled under one payment made on a per-patient basis. An assessment instrument called the Outcomes and Assessment Information Set (OASIS) is used to rate each patient's functional status and clinical severity level. The assessment measures translate into "points"; the points are totaled to determine the patient's HHRG. Payment is based on the patient's specific HHRG category. The HHRG classification uses 153 distinct groups in which patients can be classified according to clinical severity, functional status, and the need for rehabilitation therapies.

NATIONAL HEALTH EXPENDITURES

National health expenditures (also called national health spending or national health care costs) are an estimate of the amount spent for all health services and supplies and health-related research and construction activities in the United States during a calendar year. In 2010, national health expenditures in the United States amounted to $2.6 trillion. To put some meaning into such large expenditures, it is common to compare the total health care expenditures to the total economic consumption. The gross domestic product (GDP) measures the total value of goods and services produced and consumed in a country. In 2010, the U.S. GDP was $14.5 trillion. Hence, 17.9% of the total economic output in the United States in 2010 was consumed by health care. Another way to look at health care expenditures is in terms of the average per capita spending, which controls for changes in the size of the population. In 2010, the average per capita spending for health care amounted to $8,402 for each American (CMS, 2011b). National health expenditures from 1960 to 2010 are presented in **Table 6.4**.

Table 6.4 National Health Expenditures, Selected Years

Year	Amount ($ billions)	Percentage of GDP	Amount per Capita
1960	27.3	5.2	$147
1970	74.8	7.2	356
1980	255.7	9.2	1,110
1990	724.0	12.5	2,853
2000	1,378.0	13.8	4,878
2010	2,593.6	17.9	8,402

Source: Data from National Center for Health Statistics. *Health, United States,* 2007, pp. 375, 378; CMS, Office of the Actuary. National Health Expenditures 1960–2010 (Table 1). https://www.cms.gov /NationalHealthExpendData/downloads/tables.pdf. Accessed January 2012.

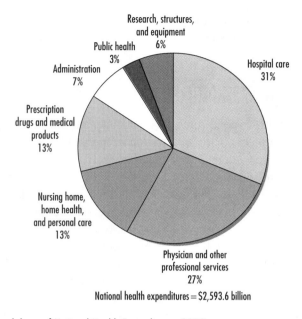

National health expenditures = $2,593.6 billion

Figure 6.4   Breakdown of National Health Expenditures, 2010
Data from Centers for Medicare and Medicaid Services, *National Health Expenditure Projections: 2010–2020.*

Figure 6.4 shows the breakdown of how 2010 national health dollars were used. Approximately 84% of total national health expenditures were devoted to personal health services and products, which include hospital care, physician and clinical services, dental care, other professional services, nursing home care, home health care, prescription drugs, medical supplies, durable medical equipment (DME), and other personal health care products and services. The remaining 16% of national expenditures were accounted for by public health services, research, investment in structures and equipment, costs related to administration of government programs, and administrative costs of private insurance.

The annual growth in health care spending, or health care cost inflation, is a matter of concern for almost all developed nations because health care spending has been rising faster than people's incomes. Cost inflation in health care is evaluated by comparing it to the growth of the GDP as well as to the *consumer price index* (CPI), which measures inflation in the general economy. As **Table 6.5** shows, in the United States, health care cost inflation has exceeded the growth in the GDP and CPI.

Table 6.5 Growth Comparisons of National Health Expenditures to the GDP and CPI, 2000–2010

	2000	2010
National health expenditures	$1,352.9 billion	$2,593.6 billion
Average annual increase		6.7%
GDP	$9,952.0 billion	$14,527.0 billion
Average annual increase		3.9%
CPI	172.4	218.0
Average annual increase		2.4%

Sources: Data from Centers for Medicare and Medicaid Services (http://www.cms.gov/Research-Statistics-Data-and-Systems/Statistics-Trends-and Reports/NationalHealthExpendData/downloads//tables.pdf) and the Bureau of Labor Statistics (ftp://ftp.bls.gov/pub/special.requests/cpi/cpiai.txt). Accessed March 2012.

CONCLUSION

Financing plays a critical role in health care delivery. For consumers, it pays for insurance coverage, which enables them to obtain health care services. For providers, it reimburses them for the services they deliver.

For most services, the methods of reimbursement were changed from retrospective to prospective mechanisms after it became widely known that cost-based methods and fee-for-service reimbursement contained perverse incentives for providers to increase the cost of health care delivery. Prospective payment methods, now widely in use, and capitation, used by health maintenance organizations, contain incentives for the delivery of cost-effective health care. Comprehensive health insurance also contains perverse incentives for consumers to use more health care than needed, a phenomenon known as moral hazard. Deductibles and copayments were instituted after payers realized that these methods of cost sharing reduce the excessive use of health care.

The financing of health care is shared between private and public sources. Contrary to what many people might think, the government incurs a sizable proportion of total health care expenditures, estimated to be 45% of all health care spending in the United States. Hence, at least from a financing standpoint, the United States has a quasi-national health care system. The share of public expenditures in the future is expected to grow substantially if the ACA of 2010 is implemented in 2014.

REFERENCES

Centers for Medicare and Medicaid Services (CMS). 2011 Annual report of the boards of trustees of the Federal Hospital Insurance and Federal Supplementary Medical Insurance Trust Funds. 2011a. https://www.cms.gov /ReportsTrustFunds/downloads/tr2011.pdf. Accessed December 2011.

Centers for Medicare and Medicaid Services (CMS). National health expenditure data: 1960–2010. 2011b. https://www.cms.gov/NationalHealthExpendData /downloads/tables.pdf. Accessed March 2012.

Claxton G, et al. *The Kaiser Family Foundation and Health Research and Educational Trust Employer Health Benefits 2011 Annual Survey.* Menlo Park, CA: Henry J. Kaiser Family Foundation/Chicago, IL: Health Research and Educational Trust; 2011.

Congressional Budget Office (CBO). Payments of penalties for being uninsured under the Patient Protection and Affordable Care Act—revised April 30, 2010. 2010. http://www.cbo.gov/ftpdocs/113xx/doc11379/Individual_ Mandate_Penalties-04-30.pdf. Accessed December 2011.

Cunningham PJ. State variation in primary care physician supply: Implications for health reform Medicaid expansions. Research Brief No. 19. Washington, DC: Center for Studying Health System Change; 2011.

Feldstein PJ. *Health Care Economics*, 4th ed. New York: Delmar Publishers; 1993.

Foster RS. Estimated financial effects of the "Patient Protection and Affordable Care Act," as passed by the Senate on December 24, 2009. Memo from Richard S. Foster, Office of the Actuary, January 8, 2010. https://www.cms .gov/ActuarialStudies/Downloads/S_PPACA_2010-01-08.pdf. Accessed November 2011.

Health Care Financing Administration (HCFA). *Medicare and Medicaid Statistical Supplement, 1996*. Pub. No. 03386. Baltimore, MD: U.S. Department of Health and Human Services; 1996.

Health Insurance Institute. *Modern Health Insurance*. New York: Health Insurance Institute; 1969.

Henry J. Kaiser Family Foundation. United States: Health insurance coverage of the total population, states 2008–2009. 2009. http://www.statehealthfacts .org/profileind.jsp?ind=125&cat=3&rgn=1. Accessed November 2011.

Henry J. Kaiser Family Foundation. CHIP enrollment: December 2010 data snapshot. 2011a. http://www.kff.org/medicaid/upload/7642-06.pdf. Accessed December 2011.

Henry J. Kaiser Family Foundation. Medicare at a glance, November 2011. 2011b. http://kff.org/medicare/upload/1066-14.pdf. Accessed December 2011.

MedPAC. *Ambulatory surgical centers payment system*. Washington, DC: Medicare Payment Advisory Commission; 2009. http://www.medpac.gov /documents/MedPAC_Payment_Basics_09_ASC.pdf. Accessed December 2011.

Short PF, et al. The effect of universal coverage on health expenditures for the uninsured. *Med Care*. 1997;35(2):95–113.

Smith GA. *A Primer on How to Use Medicaid to Assist Persons Who Are Homeless to Access Medical, Behavioral Health and Support Services*. Baltimore, MD: Centers for Medicare and Medicaid Services; 2007.

Spitalnic P. Annual release of Part D national average bid amount and other Part C & D bid related information (Memo dated August 3, 2011). Centers for Medicare and Medicaid Services; 2011. https://www.cms.gov /MedicareAdvtgSpecRateStats/Downloads/PartDandMABenchmarks2012 .pdf. Accessed December 2011.

U.S. Census Bureau. Income, poverty and health insurance coverage in the United States: 2010. 2011a. http://www.census.gov/newsroom/releases/archives /income_wealth/cb11-157.html. Accessed December 2011.

U.S. Census Bureau. *Statistical Abstract of the United States: 2012*. Washington, DC: U.S. Census Bureau; 2011b.

U.S. General Accounting Office. *Private Health Insurance: Millions Relying on Individual Market Coverage Face Cost and Coverage Trade-Offs*. Washington, DC: U.S. General Accounting Office; 1996.

Vaughn EJ, Elliott CM. *Fundamentals of Risk and Insurance*. New York: John Wiley & Sons; 1987.

Williams SJ. *Essentials of Health Services*. Albany, NY: Delmar Publishers; 1995.

Wilson FA, Neuhauser D. *Health Services in the United States*, 2nd ed. Cambridge, MA: Ballinger Publishing; 1985.

Chapter 7

Outpatient Services and Primary Care

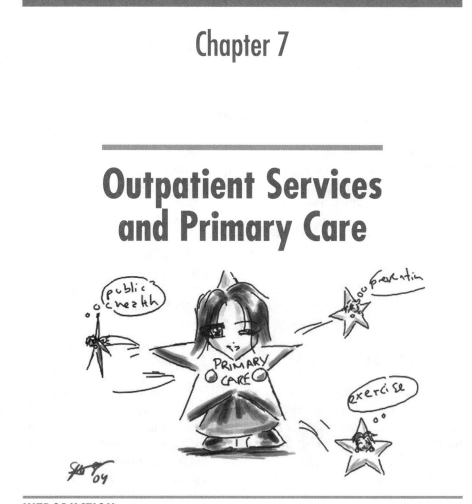

INTRODUCTION

Historically, outpatient care has been independent of most services provided in health care institutions. In earlier days, most physicians made home visits to treat patients, in addition to seeing patients in their clinics. Physicians generally provided a full spectrum of medical services, including diagnosis, treatment, surgery, and dispensing of medications. With modern advancements in medical science, the locus of health care delivery became concentrated in community hospitals. As the range of services that could be provided on an outpatient basis continued to expand, hospitals gradually became the dominant players in providing the vast majority of outpatient care, with the exception of cognitive and basic diagnostic care provided in physicians' offices (Barr & Breindel, 1995). During the past three decades, health care delivery has increasingly shifted away from expensive stays in acute care hospitals, and many intensive procedures are increasingly performed on an outpatient basis in various community health care settings. Unlike hospitals, independent providers face capital constraints and competitive pressures in the health care marketplace; thus, most solo practitioners have joined group practices, in which multiple providers consolidate their services under a single umbrella.

State and local government agencies have also actively sponsored limited outpatient services to meet the needs of underserved populations, mainly indigent patients who lack the personal resources to obtain health care in the private sector. Community health centers, which primarily depend on federal and state funds, serve a number of rural and inner-city areas, and provide a wide array of outpatient services.

WHAT IS OUTPATIENT CARE?

The terms "outpatient" and "ambulatory" are used interchangeably, although the term "outpatient" is more comprehensive. Strictly speaking, *ambulatory care* consists of diagnostic and therapeutic services and treatments provided to the "walking" (ambulatory) patient. Based on this definition, it follows that ambulatory care includes care rendered to patients who come to physicians' offices, outpatient departments of hospitals, and health centers to receive care. However, patients do not always ambulate to health service centers to receive ambulatory care. For example, in a hospital emergency department (ED), patients may arrive by land or air ambulance. In other instances, such as with mobile diagnostic units and home health care, services are transported to the patient, rather than the patient coming to receive the services. The terms "outpatient" and "inpatient" are more precise ways to describe health care; the term *outpatient services* refers to any health care services that do not require an overnight stay in an institution of health care delivery. Some outpatient services may be offered by a hospital or long-term care facility. For instance, in addition to EDs, many hospitals have other outpatient service centers such as outpatient surgery, rehabilitation, and specialized clinics.

In recent years, extraordinary growth in the volume of outpatient services has occurred, with the emergence of new types of settings where outpatient services are delivered. The most basic outpatient services, such as

Exhibit 7.1   Outpatient Settings and Services

- Private practice
- Hospitals Outpatient Clinics
- Freestanding facilities
- Mobile facilities for medical, diagnostic, and screening services
- Telephone triage

- Home care
- Hospice care
- Outpatient long-term care services
- Public health services
- Community health centers and free clinics
- Alternative medicine clinics

physical exams and minor treatments, are still delivered in a physician's office. Advanced outpatient care has traditionally been provided in hospital-based facilities, generally in various building complexes surrounding the main hospital. In recent years, there has also been explosive growth in the type and ownership of nonhospital-based facilities offering ambulatory care (see **Exhibit 7.1**).

SCOPE OF OUTPATIENT SERVICES

In 2008, according to the National Ambulatory Medical Care Survey, Americans made approximately 960 million visits, or more than 3 visits per person, to office-based physicians. Physicians in general and family practice accounted for the largest share of these visits (23.5%), followed by physicians in internal medicine (16.0%), pediatrics (12.5%), and obstetrics and gynecology (8.6%). Doctors of osteopathy accounted for 7.3% of all visits. The South led the nation in share of physician visits (37.4%), followed by the West (22.0%), the Northeast (20.6%), and the Midwest (20.0%). Ambulatory visits per person were highest in the Northeast (3.6 visits) and lowest in the Midwest (2.9 visits). Most physician office visits (91.5%) took place in metropolitan areas. Visits per person were also higher in metropolitan areas (3.5) than in rural areas (1.6), reflecting poorer access to primary care in rural areas of the United States. Access to care remains problematic for some individuals, especially for the uninsured and racial/ethnic minorities (see **Exhibit 7.2**).

Exhibit 7.2   Access to Primary Care

Did Not Get or Delayed Medical Care due to Cost, 2009 (%)

Younger than 18 years	5.2
18–64 years	15.1
65 years and older	5.1
White	15.2
Black	16.7
Hispanic	16.4
Insured	9.5
Uninsured	36.5

Did Not Get Prescription Drugs due to Cost, 2009 (%)

Younger than 18 years	3.2
18–64 years	3.7
65 years and older	4.2
White	10.9
Black	14.5
Hispanic	14.3
Insured	7.0
Uninsured	26.7

Did Not Get Dental Care due to Cost, 2009 (%)

Younger than 18 years	7.1
18–64 years	16.8
65 years and older	6.2
White	16.7
Black	19.0
Hispanic	22.2
Insured	10.8
Uninsured	39.0

Source: Data from U.S. Department of Health and Human Services, *Health, United States 2010*, pp. 276–277.

Outpatient care now includes much more than primary care services. For example, most surgeries are now performed in outpatient settings, whereas many of these same procedures could previously be performed only in hospitals. This shift toward outpatient care is expected to continue. Hospital occupancy rates have declined for more than two decades, and hospital executives have increasingly viewed outpatient care as an essential portion of their health care business (Barr & Breindel, 1995). Establishing a firm position in the outpatient care market has become critical to continued hospital survival, as has expanding into services not previously considered part of these organizations' core business.

On the one hand, the growth of nonhospital-based outpatient services has intensified competition for outpatient medical services between hospitals and community-based providers. Examples of such competition include home health care, ambulatory clinics for routine and urgent care, and outpatient surgery. On the other hand, several other services, such as dental care and optometric services, continue to be office based. Financing is the main reason that dental and optometric services have not been integrated with other outpatient medical services. Medical insurance plans have traditionally been separate from dental and vision care plans. Philosophical and technical differences account for other variations. For example, chiropractic care is generally covered by most health plans, yet remains isolated from the mainstream practice of medicine. Other services, such as alternative therapies and self-care, are not covered by insurance but have experienced remarkable growth in recent years.

Several key changes have been instrumental in shifting the balance between inpatient and outpatient services. These factors can be broadly classified as reimbursement, technologic factors, utilization control factors, and social factors.

Reimbursement

Today, both private and public payers have a clear preference for outpatient treatment because it costs less than inpatient care. Quicker discharge of patients from hospital beds under prospective and capitated reimbursement methods created a substantial market for outpatient services. In response to changes in financial incentives for reimbursement of outpatient care, hospitals aggressively developed outpatient services to offset declining inpatient income. These financial factors have provided a major impetus for the unprecedented growth of home health care.

Technologic Factors

The development of new diagnostic and treatment procedures and less invasive surgical methods has made it possible to provide some services in outpatient settings that had previously required inpatient hospital stays. Shorter-acting anesthetics and the proliferation of minimally invasive technologies have made many surgical procedures less traumatic and led to much shorter recovery times. Many office-based physicians have expanded their capacity to perform outpatient diagnostic, treatment, and surgical services because the acquisition of necessary technology has become more feasible and cost-effective.

Utilization Control Factors

Inpatient hospital stays are strongly discouraged by various payers. Prior authorization for inpatient admission and close monitoring during hospitalization have been actively pursued with the objective of minimizing a patient's length of stay.

Social Factors

In addition to financial, technologic, and utilization control factors, social factors have contributed to the growth of outpatient services. Patients generally have a strong preference for receiving health care in home- and community-based settings. Indeed, most people do not want to be institutionalized unless absolutely necessary. Remaining in their own homes gives individuals a strong sense of independence and control over their lives—elements considered important for quality of life.

OUTPATIENT CARE SETTINGS AND METHODS OF DELIVERY

The myriad outpatient care and community-based services that currently exist sometimes make it difficult to adequately differentiate between the structural settings in which these services are provided (see **Exhibit 7.1**). For example, agencies providing home health services may be freestanding, hospital based, or nursing home based. In many instances, physician group practices are merging with hospitals, and hospitals and freestanding surgical clinics often compete for various types of surgical procedures. Therefore, the classifications used in this section are merely illustrative—there are many exceptions to the arrangements presented here. Furthermore, in this constantly evolving system, new settings and methods are likely to emerge. The various settings for outpatient services found in the U.S. health care delivery system can be grouped as described in the following subsections.

Private Practice

Physicians, as office-based practitioners, form the backbone of ambulatory care and constitute the majority of primary care services. Most visits entail relatively limited examination and testing, and encounters with physicians are generally of a relatively short duration. The waiting time in the office is typically longer than the actual time spent with the physician.

In the past, the solo practice of medicine and small partnership arrangements attracted the most practitioners. Self-employment offered a degree of independence not generally available in large organizational settings. Now, group practices and institutional affiliations, such as employment by a managed care organization (MCO), have become the norm. Today, relatively few graduates of residency programs are entering solo practice. Several factors account for this shift: uncertainties created by rapid changes in the health care delivery system, contracting by MCOs with consolidated rather than solo entities, competition from large health care delivery organizations, the high cost of establishing a new practice, complexity of billings and collections in a multipayer system, and increased external controls over the private practice of medicine. Group practice and other organizational arrangements offer several benefits to providers, including patient-referral networks, negotiating leverage with MCOs, sharing of overhead expenses, ease of obtaining coverage from colleagues for personal time off, and attractive starting salaries along with benefits and profit-sharing plans. Most young physicians find that these advantages far outweigh the allure of being an independent solo practitioner.

Hospital Outpatient Clinics

Many hospital outpatient clinics, particularly those in inner-city areas, function as the community's safety net, providing primary care to the medically indigent and uninsured populations. On the other hand, outpatient services now constitute a key source of profits for many hospitals. Consequently, hospitals have expanded their outpatient departments, and utilization of these entities has grown. This trend is the result of fierce competition in the health care industry, in which MCOs emphasizing preventive and outpatient care have relentlessly strived to cut costs. As hospitals have seen their inpatient revenues steadily erode, they have begun improving and expanding their outpatient services. A hospital providing both inpatient and outpatient services can enhance its revenues by, for example, referring postsurgical cases to its affiliated units for rehabilitation and home care follow-up. Patients receiving various types of hospital-affiliated outpatient services become an important source of referrals back to the hospitals for inpatient care, thereby allowing a hospital to expand its patient base.

Hospital-based outpatient services can be broadly classified into five main types: clinical (typically for the uninsured or those in research studies), surgical (patients are discharged on the day of surgery), home health care (postacute care and rehabilitation), women's health, and traditional emergency care.

Freestanding Facilities

Various types of proprietary, community-based, freestanding medical facilities have opened across the country. These settings are known as walk-in clinics, urgent care centers, and surgical centers. *Walk-in clinics* provide outpatient services ranging from basic primary care to urgent care, and are generally used on a nonroutine, episodic basis. *Urgent care centers* generally offer a wide range of routine services for basic and acute conditions. The main advantages of walk-in clinics and urgent care centers are convenience of location, evening and weekend hours, and availability of services on a walk-in, no-appointment basis. *Surgicenters* are freestanding outpatient surgery centers that operate independently of hospitals. They usually provide a full range of services for the types of surgery that can be performed on an outpatient basis and do not require overnight hospitalization. Other types of outpatient facilities include outpatient rehabilitation centers, optometric centers, and dental clinics. Walmart and Walgreens in-store medical clinics represent an emerging trend.

Mobile Facilities for Medical, Diagnostic, and Screening Services

Mobile health care services are transported to patients and constitute an efficient and convenient means for providing certain types of routine health services. These services include mammography and magnetic resonance imaging. Such mobile units take advanced diagnostic services to small towns and rural communities. Screening vans, staffed by volunteers who are trained professionals, are generally operated by various nonprofit organizations and are often seen at malls and fairgrounds. Various types of health education and health promotion services, and screening checks such as blood pressure and cholesterol screening, are commonly performed for anyone who walks in.

Telephone Triage

Telephone access, referred to as telephone triage, is a means of bringing expert opinion and advice on health care to the patient, especially during hours when physicians' offices are generally closed. Such a system is staffed by specially trained nurses who have access to patient medical records and provide guidance with the use of standardized protocols. They can consult with primary care physicians when necessary or refer patients to an urgent care facility or ED (Appleby, 1995).

Home Care

In home health care, services are brought to patients in their own homes. Without home services, the only alternative for such patients would be institutionalization in a hospital or nursing home. Home health care is consistent with the philosophy of maintaining people in the least restrictive environment possible. Most people express a strong preference for receiving health services at home. Home health services typically include nursing care, such as changing dressings, monitoring medications, and help with bathing; short-term rehabilitation, such as physical therapy, occupational therapy, and speech therapy; homemaker services, such as meal preparation, shopping, transportation, and some specific household chores; and certain medical supplies and equipment, such as ostomy supplies, hospital beds, oxygen tanks, and walkers and wheelchairs (the latter are referred to as durable medical equipment).

Hospice Care

The term *hospice* refers to a cluster of comprehensive services for terminally ill patients who have a life expectancy of six months or less. Hospice programs provide services that address the special needs of dying persons and their families. Hospice is a method of care, not a location, and services are taken to patients and their families wherever they are located. Hospice services include medical, psychologic, and social services provided in a holistic context. The two primary areas of emphasis in hospice care are (1) pain and symptom management, which is referred to as *palliative care*, and (2) psychosocial and spiritual support.

Outpatient Long-term Care Services

Long-term care (LTC) has typically been associated with care provided in nursing homes, but a number of alternative settings are also now available to address a variety of needs. Two types of ambulatory LTC services are *case management* and *adult day care*. Case management provides coordination and referral among a variety of health care services; the objective is to find the most appropriate setting in which to meet a patient's health care needs. Adult day care complements informal care provided at home by family members, with professional services available in adult day care centers during the day.

Public Health Services

Public health services in the United States are typically provided by local health departments, and the range of services offered varies greatly by locality. Generally, public health programs are limited in scope. They include well-baby care, venereal disease clinics, family planning services, screening and treatment for tuberculosis, and outpatient mental health care. States vary in the range and extent of public health services offered.

Community Health Centers and Free Clinics

The federal government authorized the creation of community health centers during the 1960s, primarily to reach medically underserved regions of the United States. Community health centers are supported by grant funding administered by the Bureau of Primary Health Care (BPHC), within the Department of Health and Human Services (DHHS). These centers are required by law to be located in medically underserved areas and to provide services to anyone seeking care, regardless of insurance status or ability to pay (McAlearney, 2002).

Community health centers provide family-oriented preventive care, primary care, and dental care, and serve as a primary care safety net. According to the BPHC, in 2010, 1,124 of these centers were funded through the program and provided care to approximately 19.5 million people through more than 77 million medical, dental, mental health, and substance abuse visits across the United States. Approximately 37.5% of these patients were uninsured, and an additional 38.5% were covered under Medicaid. The vast majority (92.8%) of patients who visited community health centers had incomes less than 200% of the federal poverty level, and more than 1 million were homeless.

Other health centers developed through federal funding include migrant health centers, serving transient farm workers in agricultural communities (approximately 860,000 patients were seen in 2010), and rural health centers located in isolated, underserved rural areas. One example is the Community Mental Health Center Program, which was established to provide outpatient mental health services in underserved areas.

Alternative Medicine Clinics

Complementary and alternative medicine (CAM) refers to the broad domain of all health care resources, other than those intrinsic to biomedicine, to which people have recourse (CAM Research Methodology Conference, 1997). The 2007 National Health Interview Survey defined CAM as treatment that "covers a heterogeneous spectrum of ancient to new-age approaches that purport to prevent or treat disease…complementary interventions are used together with conventional treatments, whereas alternative interventions are used instead of conventional medicine." Alternative therapies are regarded as nontraditional forms of care and include a wide range of treatments such as homeopathy, herbal remedies, natural products used as preventive and treatment agents, acupuncture, meditation, yoga exercises, biofeedback, and spiritual guidance or prayer (Barnes et al. 2008). A significant number of adults in the United States use alternative medicine exclusively; one-fourth of all adults with no medical practitioner visits reported using CAM therapy in 2007. Patients also reported the alternative use of CAM when conventional therapy was too costly. Alternative medicine is not yet a system of healing endorsed by most practitioners of conventional Western medicine, although interest in the efficacy of these treatments has been growing among the traditional medical establishment.

No single health care delivery setting is specifically involved in alternative treatments. Furthermore, many of the therapies are self-administered or at least require active patient participation.

PRIMARY CARE

Primary care is the conceptual foundation for outpatient services, but not all outpatient care is primary care. For example, hospital ED services are usually intended to provide acute, episodic care, rather than primary care. In addition, services beyond primary health care have become an integral part of outpatient services. As the supply and use of specialist services increase, specialist physicians have become more integrated into the primary care system. Nevertheless, approximately 46.3% of specialist visits from 2002 to 2004 involved services deemed primary follow-up or preventive, and little care coordination existed between specialists and primary providers (Valderas et al., 2009). Primary care practice must evolve and adapt to recent changes in the health care system; this is particularly important in light of research predicting a shortage of as many as 200,000 primary care physicians by 2025 (Macinko et al., 2007).

What Is Primary Care?

Primary care plays a central role in the health care delivery system. Other essential levels of care include secondary and tertiary care. Primary care is distinguished from secondary and tertiary care by its duration, frequency, and level of intensity. *Secondary care* is usually short term in nature, involving sporadic consultation from a specialist to provide expert opinions and/or surgical or other advanced interventions that primary care physicians are not equipped to perform. Secondary care includes hospitalization, routine surgery, specialty consultation, and rehabilitation. *Tertiary care* is the most complex level of care and is required for conditions that are relatively uncommon. Typically, tertiary care is institution based, highly specialized, and technology driven. Much of it is rendered in large teaching hospitals, especially university hospitals. Examples include trauma care, burn treatment, neonatal intensive care, tissue transplants, and open-heart surgery. In some instances, tertiary treatment may be long term in nature, and the tertiary care physician may assume long-term responsibility for the bulk of the patient's care.

In defining primary care, the focus is often on the type or level of services, such as prevention, diagnostic and therapeutic services, health education and counseling, and minor surgery. Although primary care specifically emphasizes these services, many specialists also provide the same spectrum of services; therefore, primary care should be viewed as an approach to providing health care rather than as a set of specific services (Starfield, 1994). The World Health Organization (WHO) and the Institute of Medicine (IOM) offer useful definitions of primary care that differentiate primary health care from primary care. Primary health care focuses on its function as the point of entry into the health service system and its coordination of the delivery of health services, whereas primary care is more involved in the integration of health care services and the accountability of clinicians and patients to the health care system.

WHO Definition

According to WHO, primary health care is essential health care that is based on practical, scientifically sound, and socially acceptable methods and technology. Such care is universally accessible to individuals and families in the community by means acceptable to them, and at a cost that the community and the country can afford to maintain at every stage of their development in a spirit of self-reliance and self-determination. Primary health care serves as the foundation of ambulatory services, characterized by the first level of contact between individuals, the family, and the community on the one hand and the health care delivery system on the other hand, bringing health care as close as possible to where people live and work. It constitutes the first element of a continuing health care process (WHO, 1978, p. 25).

IOM Definition

The IOM Committee on the Future of Primary Care recommended that *primary care* be the usual and preferred route of entry, although not the only route of entry, into the health care system. The IOM defined primary care as follows:

> The provision of integrated, accessible health care services by clinicians who are accountable for addressing a majority of personal health care needs, developing a sustained partnership with patients, and practicing in the context of family and community. (Vanselow et al., 1995, p. 192)

Domains of Primary Care

The WHO and IOM definitions highlight several important domains, which are critical to understanding primary care. Three elements in the WHO

Exhibit 7.3   Domains of Primary Care

- Point of entry
- Coordination of care
- Essential care

- Integrated care
- Accountability

definition and two elements in the IOM definition are particularly noteworthy for an understanding of primary care, as summarized in **Exhibit 7.3**.

Point of Entry

Primary care is the point of entry into a health services system in which health care delivery is organized around primary care (Starfield, 1992, p. vii); that is, it is the first contact a patient makes with the health care delivery system. This first contact feature is closely associated with the gatekeeper role of the primary care practitioner. *Gatekeeping* implies that patients do not visit specialists and are not admitted to a hospital without being referred for such care by their primary care physicians. On the surface, gatekeeping may appear to be a controlling mechanism for denying needed care. In reality, in most cases, primary care protects patients from unnecessary procedures and overtreatment (Franks et al., 1992) because specialists use medical tests and procedures to a much greater extent than do primary care providers, and such interventions carry a definite risk of iatrogenic (i.e., caused by the process of health care) complications (Starfield, 1994).

One of the goals of primary care is to bring health care as close as possible to where people live and work. In other words, true primary care is community based; it is characterized by convenience and easy accessibility. To make such services widely available to communities in urban, suburban, and rural areas, the nature of primary care services must remain basic, routine, and inexpensive. At the same time, appropriate technology must be incorporated into the delivery of primary care so that costly referrals to other components of the health delivery system are made only when necessary.

Coordination of Care

One of the main functions of primary care is to coordinate the delivery of health services between the patient and the myriad components of the system. Hence, in addition to providing basic services, primary care professionals serve as patient advisors and advocates. In this coordinating role, the provider refers patients to sources of specialized care, gives advice regarding various diagnoses and therapies, discusses treatment options, and provides continuing care for chronic conditions (Williams, 1993). Coordination of an individual's total health care needs is meant to ensure continuity and comprehensiveness. These desirable goals of primary care are best achieved when the patient and the provider have formed a close relationship over time. Primary care can be regarded as the hub of the health care delivery system wheel. The various components of the health care delivery system are located around the rim, with the spokes of the wheel signifying the coordination of continuous and comprehensive care (see **Figure 7.1**).

Countries whose health systems are more oriented toward primary care achieve better health levels, higher satisfaction with health services among their populations, and lower expenditures in the overall delivery of health care (Starfield, 1994). By comparison, countries with weak primary care infrastructures have poorer health outcomes and higher health care costs. Even in the United States, those states with higher ratios of primary care physicians to patients show better health outcomes associated with the availability of better primary care (Shi, 1992, 1994). Higher ratios of

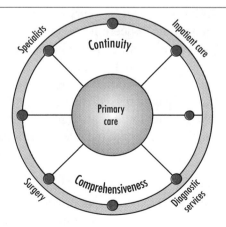

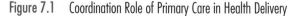

Figure 7.1   Coordination Role of Primary Care in Health Delivery

family and general practice physicians in the population are also associated with lower hospitalization rates for conditions treatable with good primary care (Parchman & Culler, 1994). Adults who have primary care physicians as their regular source of care subsequently experience lower death rates and incur lower health care costs (Franks & Fiscella, 1998).

An ideal system of health care delivery is based on primary care, but is closely linked with adequate and timely specialized services. Continuous and coordinated care requires that secondary and tertiary services be integrated with primary care through appropriate interaction and consultation among physicians. Coordination of health care has certain advantages. Studies have shown that both the appropriateness and the outcomes of health care interventions are better when primary care physicians refer patients to specialists, rather than when patients engage in self-referral (Bakwin, 1945; Roos, 1979).

Essential Care

Primary health care is regarded as essential health care. As such, the goal of the health care delivery system is to optimize population health, not just the health of individuals who have the means to access health services. Achievement of this goal requires that disparities across population subgroups be minimized to ensure equal access to care. Because financing of health care is a key element in determining access, the goal of optimizing population health is better achieved under a national health care program. For this reason, the lack of access to primary care for countless millions of its residents remains a nagging concern in the United States.

In the United States, the mixture of public and private financing has created a fragmented system in which primary care does not form the organizing hub for continuous and coordinated health services. Although the primary care model has gained increased popularity under the managed care system, its current role appears to be limited to low-cost general medicine and gatekeeping, controlling access to the rest of the health care system.

Integrated Care

Integrated care embodies the concepts of comprehensive, coordinated, and continuous services that provide a seamless process of care. Primary care is comprehensive because it addresses any health problem at any given stage of a patient's life cycle. The coordinating function ensures the provision of a combination of health services to best meet the patient's needs. Continuity refers to care delivered over time by a single provider or a team of health care professionals. The IOM definition goes further to emphasize accessibility and accountability as key characteristics of primary care. Accessibility refers to the ease with which a patient can initiate an interaction with a clinician for any health problem. It includes efforts to eliminate barriers such as those posed by geography, financing, culture, race, and language.

Accountability

The IOM Committee recognizes that both clinicians and patients have accountability. On the one hand, the clinical system is accountable for providing quality care, producing patient satisfaction, using resources efficiently, and behaving in an ethical manner. On the other hand, patients are responsible for their own health to the extent that they are capable of influencing it. Patients also have the responsibility to be judicious in their use of resources when they need health care. Partnership between a patient and a clinician does not necessarily imply an equal role for each party. The role played by each party will vary both over time and on a case-by-case basis. Mutual trust, respect, and responsibility are the hallmarks of this partnership. The IOM Committee has proposed that primary care clinicians must possess the knowledge and skills necessary to manage most of the physical, mental, social, and emotional concerns that affect the functioning of patients. Primary care clinicians must use their best judgment to involve other practitioners in diagnosis, treatment, or both when it is appropriate to do so (Vanselow et al., 1995).

Community-Oriented Primary Care

The 1978 International Conference on Primary Health Care (held in Alma Ata, USSR, under the auspices of the WHO) concluded that people throughout the world had very little control over their own health care and that emphasis should be placed on attaining health through a response from the community to their health problems (WHO, 1978). More positive outcomes occur when people have a greater sense of ownership of health programs that address their needs. Achieving this goal requires a partnership between health care providers and the communities they serve. It has been suggested that collective action by a community may enhance its competence in mitigating risk factors, thereby reducing the community's vulnerability to social problems and disease (Minkler, 1992).

Community-oriented primary care incorporates the elements of good primary care delivery and adds a population-based approach to identifying and addressing community health problems. Current thoughts about primary care delivery have extended beyond the traditional biomedical paradigm, which focuses on medical care for the individual in an encounter-based system. The broader biopsychosocial paradigm emphasizes the health of the population as well as that of the individual (Lee, 1994).

Primary Care Effectiveness

Although preventive interventions might be better performed by specialists if the interventions are in the specialists' area of expertise, it is in primary care that preventive interventions unrelated to any one disease or organ system are best carried out. For example, rates of cholesterol testing might be highest among cardiologists, who are more likely to follow patients with cardiovascular disease; however, immunizations and the encouragement of healthy personal behavior are best carried out by primary care physicians, given their focus on the entire person rather than a particular body system or disease and their reach to a broad cross-section of the population.

U.S. states with higher ratios of primary care physicians to the total population have lower smoking rates, less obesity, and higher seatbelt use than states with lower primary care physician-to-population ratios (Shi, 1994; Shi & Starfield, 2000). Continuity of care with a single provider was also positively associated with primary preventive care, including smoking cessation and influenza immunization, in a large, ongoing 60-community study in the United States (Saver, 2002). Studies have shown that an increase of one primary care physician per 10,000 population is linked to a reduction of 1.44 deaths per 10,000 population, a 2.5% reduction in infant mortality, and a 3.2% reduction in low-birth-weight infants on average. Similarly, population subgroups with a good primary care source have better birth-weight distributions than comparable populations without good primary care. In 2000, it was shown that among white and black populations in both urban and rural areas of the United States, birth weights were higher when the source of care was a community health center designed to provide good primary care than they were in the comparable population as a whole (Politzer et al., 2001). The likelihood that disadvantaged children will have preventive care visits is much greater when their source of care is a good primary care practitioner (Gadomski et al., 1998). Early detection of breast cancer is also enhanced when the supply of primary care physicians (at least relative to specialists) is adequate, while a one-third increase in the supply of family physicians correlates to a 20% decrease in the mortality rates of cervical cancer in a population (Ferrante et al., 2000; Macinko et al., 2007). Additionally, studies have suggested that as many as 127,617 deaths per year in the United States might be prevented with an increase of one primary care physician per 10,000 population (Macinko et al., 2007).

Secondary Prevention

To the extent that most secondary preventive activities are disease focused, better quality for primary care (compared with specialty care) would not necessarily be expected; however, the evidence suggests otherwise for those conditions that are common and that fall within the realm of primary care. For example, several studies have demonstrated positive associations among the cardinal features of primary care and improved access to care and health outcomes (Bertakis et al., 1998; Bindman et al., 1996; Flocke et al., 1998; Greenfield et al., 1992).

Disease Management

Following the line of reasoning just established, it might be expected that specialists would perform better than generalists and achieve better outcomes for those conditions within their purview. Even when considering care for many specific common diseases, primary care physicians perform at least as well as specialists. For uncommon conditions, appropriate specialist care is undoubtedly better because primary care physicians do not see patients with such diseases frequently enough to maintain competence in managing them (Bartter & Pratter, 1996; Donohoe, 1998; Grumbach et al., 1999; Harrold et al., 1999; Hirth et al., 1996; Kaag et al., 1996; Starfield et al., 2003).

Hospitalizations and Use of Emergency Care

Strong evidence in the literature shows that lower rates of hospitalization for ambulatory care-sensitive conditions (i.e., hospitalizations that could be prevented with good primary care) are strongly associated with receiving primary care. Children receiving their care from a good primary care source have lower hospitalization rates for these conditions as well as lower hospitalization rates overall; these findings are associated with better receipt of preventive care from primary care providers (Gadomski et al., 1998). Rates of hospital admission are lower in U.S. communities in which primary care physicians are more widely involved in the care of children both before and during hospitalization (Perrin et al., 1996). Adolescents with the same regular source of care for preventive and illness care (i.e., a source of primary care) are much more likely to receive indicated preventive care and less likely to seek care in emergency rooms (Ryan et al., 2001). Thus strong and consistent evidence indicates that hospitalizations—and especially hospitalizations for ambulatory care-sensitive conditions—are less frequent when primary care is strong.

The geographic distribution of primary care physicians has also been found to be an important factor in determining the level of health for the local population. As an example, Parchman and Culler (1994, p. 45) demonstrated that geographic areas with more family and general care physicians per population had lower hospitalization rates for conditions that could be preventable with good primary care (including diabetes mellitus and pneumonia in children and congestive heart failure, hypertension, pneumonia, and diabetes mellitus in adults). Another study found that poor primary care resources were independently associated with higher rates of hospitalization for conditions that could be prevented by adequate primary care.

Cost of Care

Areas in which the emphasis on primary care is stronger, as measured by primary care physician-to-population ratios, have much lower total health care costs than other areas. This relationship has been demonstrated to hold among elderly in the United States who live in metropolitan areas, both for total costs (i.e., inpatient and outpatient) (Mark et al., 1996; Welch et al., 1993) and for the total population in the United States (Franks & Fiscella, 1998), as well as in international comparisons of industrialized countries (Starfield & Shi, 2002). Care for illnesses common in the population (e.g., community-acquired pneumonia) is more expensive if provided by specialists than if provided by generalists, with no difference in outcomes being noted based on the type of provider (Rosser, 1996; Whittle et al., 1998).

Morbidity

The supply of primary care physicians has been associated with lower rates of self-reported poor health in 60 representative U.S. communities, after controlling for a wide range of sociodemographic and socioeconomic characteristics (Shi & Starfield, 2000). Data from this same survey confirmed the positive impact of primary care by showing that those persons who actually experienced better primary care reported better health (Shi et al., 2002). Birth weight and infant mortality were also associated with primary care physician supply in U.S. states. Higher primary care physician supply has been associated with lower low-birth-weight percentages and lower infant mortality, even after controlling for educational levels, unemployment, racial/ethnic composition, income inequality, and urban–rural differences (Shi et al., 2004).

One population-based study (Roetzheim et al., 1999) in an entire U.S. state found that detection of colorectal cancer at earlier stages was better in areas that had a greater supply of primary care physicians. Conversely, diagnosis tended to be delayed in areas with more specialist physicians. The nature of their findings led the authors to conclude that a lower supply of specialists enhances the likelihood that primary care physicians will screen their patients for such cancers.

Several studies have shown the importance of primary care as an entry point to the health care system for a majority of conditions. For example, one study demonstrated that entry-level access is associated with better outcomes for 16 common conditions in children and youth (Starfield, 1985). Another study, conducted only among males, showed that men who lack a primary care provider were at greater risk for severe uncontrolled hypertension than those who lacked medical insurance or had alcohol-related problems (Shea et al., 1992).

Mortality

Perhaps the most frequent demonstration of the benefits of primary care has been with regard to mortality (i.e., death rates). One line of evidence comes from ecological studies of the relationship between primary care personnel-to-population ratios and various types of health outcomes in the United States. Two separate studies found better health outcomes in states with higher primary care physician-to-population ratios after controlling for sociodemographic measures (i.e., percentage of elderly, percentage of urban residents, percentage of minority individuals, education, income, unemployment, pollution) and lifestyle factors (i.e., seatbelt use, obesity, and smoking) (Shi, 1992, 1994). The supply of primary care physicians has also been shown to exert a strong and significant direct influence on life expectancy, stroke, and postnatal and total mortality (Shi et al., 1999).

Studies using multiple years of data have also identified a relationship between primary care physician supply and mortality outcomes, where increases in the supply of primary care physicians are associated with decreases in overall and cause-specific population mortality rates (Shi et al., 2003; Villalbi et al., 1999). There is a significant positive association between life expectancy and higher numbers of primary care physicians. The greater the ratio of physicians per population, the greater the life expectancy of the population (Shi et al., 1999).

The Medical-Home Strategy

As health care delivery becomes increasingly complex, a renewed proposal for coordinating care in a system termed *medical home* has gained support. In 2006, the American College of Physicians (ACP) recommended this care model as an improved fundamental change in the provision and financing of primary care. In its "Advanced Medical Home" ideal, the ACP advocates for practices that "provide patient-centered care based on the principles of the Chronic Care Model; use evidence-based guidelines; apply appropriate health information technology; and demonstrate the use of 'best practices' to consistently and reliably meet the needs of patients while being accountable for the quality and value of care provided" (ACP, 2006). With one "personal physician" as their primary, continual medical contact, patients are wholly cared for by a directed team with coordination across all areas of the health system. The medical-home model is being implemented on a small scale in certain systems; studies have found that it improves patient health outcomes and satisfaction; quality measures, such as reduction in medical errors; and value measures, such as cost savings per capita without worse health outcomes (Rosenthal, 2008). As care for individuals with chronic conditions becomes more central to primary care providers, this new vision of "patient-centered, physician-guided, cost-efficient, longitudinal care" by a team of experts working together to deliver consistently better health outcomes offers a long-term vision of reform that could help improve and revolutionize the primary care system.

CONCLUSION

Outpatient services now transcend basic and routine primary care services. Many general medical and surgical interventions are provided in ambulatory care settings. In response to changing economic incentives in the health care delivery system, numerous types of ambulatory services have emerged, and a variety of settings for the delivery of services have developed. In most settings, patients visit delivery sites to receive services. In other cases, services are brought to the patients.

Primary care is the point of entry into a health services system in which health care delivery is organized around primary care. It is regarded as essential health care. One of the main functions of primary care is to coordinate the delivery of health services between the patient and the myriad delivery components of the system so as to maintain long-term health for patients. Continuity of care over a period of time is essential—not just for individuals, but also for the community as a whole. Primary care is comprehensive because it addresses any health problem at any given stage of a patient's life cycle. It plays a central role in a health care delivery system because it is linked to both improved patient health status and cost-effectiveness.

REFERENCES

American College of Physicians (ACP). The advanced medical home: A patient-centered, physician-guided model of health care. 2006. http://www.acponline.org/.

Appleby C. Boxed in? *Hosp Health Networks.* 1995;69(18):28–34.

Bakwin H. *Pseudodoxia pediatrica. N Engl J Med.* 1945;232:691–697.

Barnes PM, Bloom B, Nahin RL. Complementary and alternative medicine use among adults and children: United States, 2007. *Natl Health Statistics Rep.* 2008;12:1–23.

Barr KW, Breindel CL. Ambulatory care. In *Health Care Administration: Principles, Practices, Structure, and Delivery*, 2nd ed., edited by Wolper LF. Gaithersburg, MD: Aspen Publishers; 1995:547–573.

Bartter T, Pratter MR. Asthma: Better outcome at lower cost? The role of the expert in the care system. *Chest.* 1996;110(6):1589–1596.

Bertakis KD, Callahan EJ, Helms LJ, et al. Physician practice styles and patient outcomes: Differences between family practice and general internal medicine. *Med Care*. 1998;36(6):879–891.

Bindman AB, Grumbach K, Osmond D, et al. Primary care and receipt of preventive services. *J Gen Intern Med*. 1996;11(5):269–276.

Complementary and Alternative Medicine (CAM) Research Methodology Conference. Defining and describing complementary and alternative medicine. *Altern Therap*. 1997;3(2):49–56.

Donohoe MT. Comparing generalist and specialty care: Discrepancies, deficiencies, and excesses. *Arch Intern Med*. 1998;158(15):1596–1608.

Ferrante JM, Gonzalez EC, Pal N, Roetzheim RG. Effects of physician supply on early detection of breast cancer. *J Am Board Family Pract*. 2000;13(6):408–414.

Flocke SA, Stange KC, Zyzanski SJ. The association of attributes of primary care with the delivery of clinical preventive services. *Med Care*. 1998;36 (8 suppl):AS21–AS30.

Franks P, Fiscella K. Primary care physicians and specialists as personal physicians: Health care expenditures and mortality experience. *J Family Pract*. 1998;47(2):105–109.

Franks P, et al. Gatekeeping revisited: Protecting patients from overtreatment. *N Engl J Med*. 1992;327(4):424–429.

Gadomski A, Jenkins P, Nichols M. Impact of a Medicaid primary care provider and preventive care on pediatric hospitalization. *Pediatrics*. 1998;101(3):E1. http://www.pediatrics.org/cgi/content/full/101/3/e1.

Greenfield S, et al. Variations in resource utilization among medical specialties and systems of care: Results from the medical outcomes study. *JAMA*. 1992;267(12):1624–1630.

Grumbach K, Selby JV, Schmittdiel JA, Quesenberry CP Jr. Quality of primary care practice in a large HMO according to physician specialty. *Health Serv Res*. 1999;34(2):485–502.

Harrold LR, Field TS, Gurwitz JH. Knowledge, patterns of care, and outcomes of care for generalists and specialists. *J Gen Intern Med*. 1999;14(8):499–511.

Hirth RA, Fendrick AM, Chernew ME. Specialist and generalist physicians' adoption of antibiotic therapy to eradicate *Helicobacter pylori* infection. *Med Care*. 1996;34(12):1199–1204.

Kaag ME, Wijkel D, de Jong D. Primary health care replacing hospital care: The effect on quality of care. *Int J Qual Health Care*. 1996;8(4):367–373.

Lee PR. Models of excellence. *Lancet*. 1994;344(8935):1484–1486.

Macinko J, Starfield B, Shi L. Quantifying the health benefits of primary care physician supply in the United States. *Int J Health Serv.* 2007;37(1):111–126.

Mark DH, Gottlieb MS, Zellner BB, et al. Medicare costs in urban areas and the supply of primary care physicians. *J Family Pract.* 1996;43(1):33–39.

McAlearney JS. The financial performance of community health centers, 1996–1999. *Health Affairs.* 2001;21(2):219–225.

Minkler M. Community organizing among the elderly poor in the United States. *Int J Health Serv.* 1992;22(2):303–316.

Parchman ML, Culler S. Primary care physicians and avoidable hospitalizations. *J Family Pract.* 1994;39(2):123–128.

Perrin JM, et al. Primary care involvement among hospitalized children. *Arch Pediatr Adolesc Med.* 1996;150(5):479–486.

Politzer RM, Yoon J, Shi L, et al. Inequality in America: The contribution of health centers in reducing and eliminating disparities in access to care. *Med Care Res Rev.* 2001;58(2):234–248.

Roetzheim RG, et al. The effects of physician supply on the early detection of colorectal cancer. *J Family Pract.* 1999;48(11):850–858.

Roos N. Who should do the surgery? Tonsillectomy and adenoidectomy in one Canadian province. *Inquiry.* 1979;16(1):73–83.

Rosenthal TC. The medical home: Growing evidence to support a new approach to primary care." *J Am Board Family Med.* 2008;21:427–440.

Rosser WW. Approach to diagnosis by primary care clinicians and specialists: Is there a difference? *J Family Pract.* 1996;42(2):139–144.

Ryan A, Riley A, Kang M, Starfield B. The effects of regular source of care and health need on medical care use among rural adolescents. *Arch Pediatr Adolesc Med.* 2001;155(2):184–190.

Saver B. Financing and organization findings brief. *Acad Res Health Care Policy.* 2002;5(1):1–2.

Shea S, Misra D, Ehrlich MH, et al. Predisposing factors for severe, uncontrolled hypertension in an inner-city minority population. *N Engl J Med.* 1992;327(11):776–781.

Shi L. The relation between primary care and life chances. *J Health Care Poor Underserved.* 1992;3:321–335.

Shi L. Primary care, specialty care, and life chances. *Int J Health Serv.* 1994;24(3):431–458.

Shi L, Starfield B. Primary care, income inequality, and self-rated health in the United States: A mixed-level analysis. *Int J Health Serv.* 2000;30:541–555.

Shi L, et al. Income inequality, primary care, and health indicators. *J Family Pract.* 1999;48:275–284.

Shi L, et al. Primary care, self-rated health, and reductions in social disparities in health. *Health Serv Res.* 2002;37:529–550.

Shi L, Macinko J, Starfield B, et al. Primary care, infant mortality, and low birthweight in US states. *J Epidemiol Community Health.* 2004;58(5):374–380.

Starfield B. Motherhood and apple pie: The effectiveness of medical care for children. *Milbank Memorial Fund Quarterly: Health and Society.* 1985;63(3):523–546.

Starfield B. *Primary Care: Concept, Evaluation, and Policy.* New York: Oxford University Press; 1992.

Starfield B. Is primary care essential? *Lancet.* 1994;344(8930):1129–1133.

Starfield B, Shi L. Policy relevant determinants of health: An international perspective. *Health Policy.* 2002;60:201–218.

Starfield B, Lemke KW, Bernhard T, et al. Comorbidity: Implications for the importance of primary care in "case" management. *Ann Family Med.* 2003;1:8–14.

Valderas JM, Starfield B, Forrest CB, et al. Ambulatory care provided by office-based specialists in the United States." *Ann Family Med.* 2009;7(2):104–111.

Vanselow NA, et al. From the Institute of Medicine. *JAMA.* 1995;273(3):192.

Villalbi JR, et al. An evaluation of the impact of primary care reform on health. *Aten Primaria.* 1999;24(8):468–474.

Welch WP, Miller ME, Welch HG, et al. Geographic variation in expenditures for physicians' services in the United States. *N Engl J Med.* 1993;328(9):621–627.

Whittle JC, et al. Relationship of provider characteristics to outcomes, process, and costs of care for community-acquired pneumonia. *Med Care.* 1998;36(7):977–987.

Williams SJ. Ambulatory health care services. In *Introduction to Health Services,* 4th ed., edited by Williams SJ, Torrens PR. Albany, NY: Delmar Publishers; 1993.

World Health Organization (WHO). *Primary Health Care.* Geneva: WHO; 1978.

Chapter 8

Hospitals

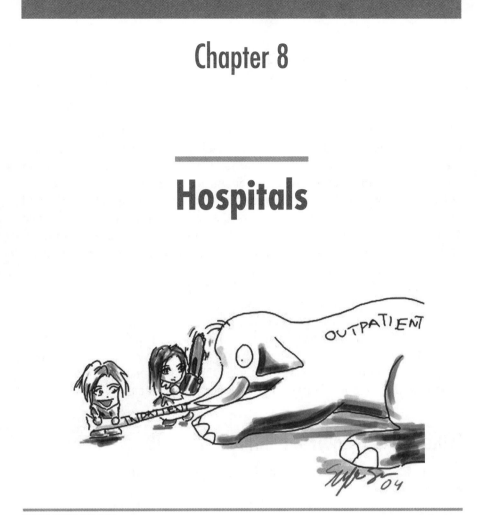

INTRODUCTION

The term *inpatient* refers to an overnight stay in a health care facility, such as a hospital or a nursing home, when the patient is formally admitted with a physician's order. *Outpatient* (described in Chapter 7), in contrast, refers to services provided while the patient is not lodged in the hospital or some other health care institution. This chapter describes what a hospital is, its evolution, and its current role in health care delivery.

The American Hospital Association (AHA) defines a hospital as an institution with at least six beds whose primary function is "to deliver patient services, diagnostic and therapeutic, for particular or general medical conditions" (AHA, 1994). In addition, a hospital must be licensed, it must have an organized physician staff, and it must provide continuous nursing services under the supervision of registered nurses (RNs). A hospital must appoint a governing body or board that is legally responsible for the conduct of the hospital. It must also appoint a full-time chief executive officer (CEO) to be responsible for the hospital's operations. The hospital must maintain medical records on each patient, have pharmacy services available within the institution, and provide food services to meet the nutritional and therapeutic requirements of the patients (Health Forum, 2001). The construction and operation of the modern hospital is governed by federal laws, state health regulations, city ordinances, standards of The Joint Commission (formerly the Joint Commission on Accreditation of Healthcare Organizations [JCAHO]), and national codes for building, fire protection, and sanitation.

In the past 200 years or so, hospitals have gradually evolved from ordinary institutions of refuge for the homeless and poor to ultramodern facilities providing the latest medical services to the critically ill and injured. The term *medical center* is used by some hospitals, reflecting their high level of specialization and wide scope of services. Medical centers often engage in teaching and research. Since the 1980s, many hospitals have expanded their scope of services to include outpatient care.

EVOLUTION OF THE HOSPITAL IN THE UNITED STATES

The six major stages of hospital evolution in the United States are listed in **Exhibit 8.1**.

Stage 1

Before 1850 or so, only a few hospitals existed, all of which were found in major U.S. cities. The main health care institutions were the almshouses (also called poorhouses) run by local governments. Pesthouses were operated

Exhibit 8.1   Major Stages of Hospital Evolution

1. Almshouses as primarily institutions of social welfare
2. Community-owned private hospitals as charitable institutions supported by affluent donors
3. Institutions of medical practice and training serving the needs of all members of society, and able to make a profit
4. Emergence of a relatively small number of physician-owned proprietary hospitals
5. University-based centers of medical research
6. Emergence of medical systems providing a large array of health services

to confine people with contagious diseases. Services in these institutions were more akin to social welfare than to medicine, consisting mainly of providing food and shelter to the destitute and some nursing care to the sick. Medicine and nursing as the professions we know today had not emerged. People generally stayed in these institutions for months rather than days.

Stage 2

During the latter half of the 1800s, hospitals evolved from the almshouses and pesthouses, but continued to serve mainly the poor. At this time, hospitals began to transition from being primarily government-run institutions to community-owned institutions supported mainly through private charitable donations. Influential donors exercised control over the hospital as members of the board of trustees. Since this period, private (rather than government-owned) nonprofit hospitals have dominated the hospital landscape in America.

Stage 3

Medical discoveries during the latter half of the 1800s were instrumental in transforming hospitals into true institutions of medical practice. Discoveries that had a profound impact on hospital care included anesthesia, which aided significantly in advancing new surgical techniques, and the development of the germ theory of disease, which led to the subsequent discovery of antiseptic and sterilization techniques (Haglund & Dowling, 1993). From around 1850 onward, technological progress led to the development of advanced equipment, facilities, and personnel training, which became centered in the hospital. Hospitals established laboratories and x-ray units so that physicians could have convenient access to diagnostic technology. These advances made it necessary for community-based physicians to treat acute illnesses in hospitals, which also became centers where physicians received their practical training. From this point onward, hospitals came to be regarded as a necessity, because the superior medical services and surgical procedures offered there could not be obtained at home.

Stage 4

With advances in sanitation, nursing care, and medical services, hospitals began to attract well-to-do patients who could afford to pay for their care on an out-of-pocket basis. As these wealthier individuals began to use their services, hospitals found that they no longer had to depend totally on charitable contributions. They could now generate a profit. At this stage, some physicians started opening their own small hospitals, thereby laying the foundation for proprietary (for-profit) hospitals in the United States.

Stage 5

Many hospitals established formal affiliations with university-based medical schools and became centers of medical research where new discoveries were made. Even today medical research plays a critical role in finding better cures and in disseminating research findings through publications in medical journals to advance new medical knowledge throughout the world.

During this stage, hospitals became complex organizations, and the field of hospital administration became a discipline in its own right. To manage hospitals, administrators needed expertise in financial management and good organizational and human relations skills. Also, departments such as food service, pharmacy, x-ray imaging, and the laboratory required well-trained professional staff to manage the delivery of services.

Stage 6

Since the 1990s, local market pressures have prompted many hospitals to merge or enter into formal affiliations with other hospitals. In urban areas, *medical systems* (or health systems) have formed. These systems are large organizations that may include more than one hospital to serve a large geographical area. They also provide a full array of health care services, including outpatient clinics, same-day surgery, outpatient imaging services, outpatient rehabilitation therapies, nursing home care, home health services, and hospice care. Many health systems have also opened special women's health centers and fitness centers. Increasingly, community services such as health education, promotion of healthy lifestyles, and prevention of disease have become an important part of a hospital's mission.

EXPANSION AND DOWNSIZING OF HOSPITALS IN THE UNITED STATES

The number of hospital beds in the United States grew from 35,604 in 1872 to 907,133 in 1929 (Haglund & Dowling, 1993). This phenomenal growth started once hospitals became institutions of medical practice, serving the needs of all members of society and making a profit (Stage 4 in the six-stage model). Technological advances increased the volume of surgical work, which at that time could be done only in hospitals. As new facilities with additional beds were built, they were quickly filled by patients needing acute treatment or surgery. Advances in medical science, as well as professional training of nurses and other health care professionals, played an important role in creating a demand for more beds. Additional factors contributing to the growth of hospitals from the preindustrial era to around 1980 are listed in **Exhibit 8.2**.

After 1930, the wider availability of private health insurance enabled more and more people to pay for hospital services, which became increasingly more costly and unaffordable. Once people had health insurance, that fact in itself generated new demand. Early insurance plans provided generous coverage for inpatient care, and few restrictions were placed on the use of hospital based services.

In the 1940s, the U.S. government recognized that a severe shortage of hospitals existed in the country. In response, Congress passed the Hospital Survey and Construction Act of 1946, commonly known as the Hill-Burton Act. It provided federal grants to the states for the construction of new hospital beds. The objective of the Hill-Burton Act was to increase the United States' hospital capacity to 4.5 beds per 1,000 population (Teisberg et al., 1991). Indeed, the Hill-Burton program has been regarded as the greatest single factor in increasing the nation's bed supply. This building program made it possible for even small and remote communities to establish their own hospitals (Wolfson & Hopes, 1994).

The creation of Medicaid and Medicare in 1965 made public health insurance available to a large segment of the U.S. population. Hospital demand, in turn, continued to grow. Between 1965 and 1980, the number of community hospitals in the United States increased from 5,736 (741,000 beds) to 5,830 (988,000 beds) (AHA, 1990). By 1980, the United States had also

Exhibit 8.2   Factors Contributing to the Growth of Hospitals

* Broad appeal, once hospitals evolved into institutions of medical practice as a result of technological advances and professional training of health care professionals
* Private health insurance
* Hill-Burton Act
* Medicaid and Medicare

reached its goal of 4.5 community hospital beds per 1,000 civilian population (National Center for Health Statistics, 2002).

In 1983, the U.S. government decided it needed to contain the exploding cost of hospital care, mostly because of its impact on the rising cost of Medicare (**Figure 8.1** shows the rise in costs that occurred between 1970 and 1980). This goal of cost containment was achieved through the enactment of the Social Security Amendments of 1983. The law required Medicare to stop paying hospitals per diem rates established on the basis of their costs of operation (retrospective reimbursement). Instead, a prospective payment system (PPS) was established to reimburse hospitals on the basis of diagnosis-related groups (DRGs). Under this method, hospitals received a pre-established fixed rate per admission. To ensure that they would not lose money, hospitals had to cut their costs of operation. They also had to discharge patients more quickly than before because keeping patients in the hospital longer than necessary cut into the hospital's profits. Many hospitals were forced to close when they had difficulty coping with the new method of reimbursement. Other hospitals

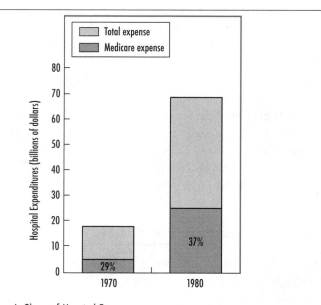

Figure 8.1   Medicare's Share of Hospital Expenses
Data from Department of Health and Human Services. *Health, United States,* 2003, p. 342; Table C-5: Selected data on community hospital expenses, 1965-95. http://aspe.os.dhhs.gov/96gb/cappend.txt.

Exhibit 8.3   Factors Contributing to the Downsizing of Hospitals

- Change in Medicare reimbursement to hospitals from a retrospective to a prospective method, leading to shorter hospital stays
- Hospital closings
- Managed care's emphasis on cost containment and use of services such as outpatient, home health, and skilled nursing care

continued to operate but had to take unused beds out of service. PPS triggered the downsizing phase in the U.S. hospital industry.

During the 1990s, the growth of managed care played a significant role in curtailing inpatient utilization even further. Managed care emphasized cost containment and efficient delivery of care through early discharge from hospitals, and, if necessary, continuity of care through home health agencies and skilled-care nursing homes. In other instances, the emphasis has been on using outpatient services whenever appropriate instead of admitting patients to hospitals.

The three main factors just discussed (and summarized in **Exhibit 8.3**) were largely successful in reducing the growth of national spending on hospital care. **Figure 8.2** illustrates the growth of spending on hospital inpatient

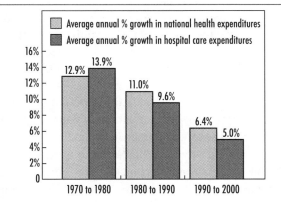

Figure 8.2   Comparison of Growth in Hospital and National Health Expenditures
Data from National Center for Health Statistics. *Health, United States, 2002.* Hyattsville, MD: Department of Health and Human Services; 2002: 291.

care compared with the growth of national health expenditures. Notice the slower rates of growth after the implementation of the PPS between 1980 and 1990, and a further slowdown between 1990 and 2000 resulting from the advent of managed care.

ACCESS AND UTILIZATION MEASURES

Measures of Access

The total number of patient discharges per 1,000 population is an indicator of the level of access to hospital inpatient services. Because newborn infants are not included in admissions, discharges provide a more accurate measure of the number of people served by a hospital. *Discharges* refer to the total number of patients released from a hospital's acute care beds during a given period, including those patients who die while in the hospital. Discharges measure the number of patients who received hospital inpatient services.

Measures of Utilization

An *inpatient day* (also referred to as a patient-day or a hospital-day) is a night spent in the hospital by a patient. The average number of days a patient spends in the hospital is called the *average length of stay* (ALOS). The total number of inpatient days incurred by a population over a given period of time is referred to as *days of care*. Mathematically,

$$\text{Days of care} = \text{discharges} \times \text{ALOS}$$

National data on days of care per 1,000 population show that elderly individuals spend more time in hospitals than do younger people. Even after adjusting for childbearing among women 18 years of age and older, women are admitted to hospitals more often than men, but men incur longer stays. Hospital utilization is higher among blacks than whites and is also higher among the poor than the nonpoor. Various factors (e.g., education, socioeconomic status, behaviors, lifestyles, heredity, access to primary care) interact to produce differences in health status and onset of acute conditions for the various population groups; hence, some groups incur more frequent hospitalizations and require longer stays once admitted. From this information, it can be concluded that overall hospital utilization is higher among Medicare and Medicaid recipients compared to the rest of the population.

Since 2003, the ALOS for community hospitals in the United States has been 4.8 days, the lowest ever recorded. The PPS, as noted earlier, had a marked influence on the decline in the ALOS, as did the introduction of managed care during the 1990s. The sharp decline in ALOS during the 1990s became possible with the growth of alternative services, such as home health and subacute long-term care, which enabled people to be discharged earlier than was previously possible. Thanks to the development of these substitute sites of care and more advanced technology, there has been no evidence that quicker discharges of patients from hospitals under the PPS or managed care payment systems resulted in medical harm to patients.

Utilization of Hospital Capacity

Capacity refers to the number of beds set up, staffed, and made available by a hospital for inpatient use. Eighty-four percent of all community hospitals in the United States have fewer than 300 beds. The average size of a community hospital was approximately 161 beds in 2008 (Department of Health and Human Services [DHHS], 2011).

The term *census* refers to the number of patients in a hospital on a given day or the number of beds occupied on a given day. The cumulative census over a given period of time is called *patient days* or *days of care*. The average census over a period of time is called the *average daily census* (see **Table 8.1**). Mathematically,

$$\text{Average daily census} =$$
$$\text{patient-days over a given period} \div \text{number of days in the period}$$

The *occupancy rate* is the percentage of capacity used during a given period of time. It is calculated by dividing the average daily census for that period by the capacity (see **Table 8.1**). The fraction is expressed as a percentage (percent beds occupied). An individual hospital's performance in capacity utilization can be meaningfully compared with local and national composite occupancy rates. In 2008, the occupancy rate for all U.S. community hospitals was 66.4% (DHHS, 2011).

. . . .

Table 8.1 Relationship Between the Selected Measures of Capacity Utilization

Day Number	Census	Patient-Days
1	100	100
2	104	204
3	101	305
4	99	404
5	98	502
6	102	604
7	103	707

Patient-days for this week: 707. Average daily census: 707 ÷ 7 = 101. If hospital capacity is 153, the occupancy rate is 66% [(101 ÷ 153) × 100].

. . . .

HOSPITAL EMPLOYMENT

In 2010, the U.S. health care sector employed approximately 16.4 million workers. Of these individuals, 4.7 million, or approximately 29%, were employed in hospitals. Between 2000 and 2010, hospital employment grew by 18.5%. Between 2008 and 2018, hospital employment is expected to expand by 12% (U.S. Census Bureau, 2011).

TYPES OF HOSPITALS

The United States supports a variety of institutional forms, including both private and government-owned hospitals. A hospital can be classified under more than one category.

Community Hospitals

Approximately 85% of all U.S. hospitals are classified as community hospitals. The identifying characteristics of these hospitals are listed in **Exhibit 8.4**. By definition, a *community hospital* is a nonfederal, short-stay

Exhibit 8.4   Characteristics of a Community Hospital

- Nonfederal: hospitals operated by local and state governments can be community hospitals
- Short stay: average length of stay must be ≤ 25 days
- Open to the general public
- Private for-profit or nonprofit; general or specialty

hospital whose services are available to the general public. This definition excludes federal hospitals, such as those operated by the Department of Veterans Affairs (VA) and military systems, and hospital units of some institutions, such as prisons and infirmaries in colleges and universities, because their services are not available to the general public. In contrast, most hospitals operated by local and state governments are community hospitals. Also excluded from the definition of a community hospital are long-stay hospitals, such as psychiatric facilities, tuberculosis hospitals, and other chronic disease hospitals. In long-stay hospitals, the average length of stay is more than 25 days.

Public Hospitals

In health care, the word "public" connotes government ownership. *Public hospitals*, therefore, are hospitals owned by agencies of federal, state, or local governments. An estimated 25% of the U.S. hospitals are in the public sector (**Figure 8.3**).

A public hospital is not necessarily a hospital that is open to the general public. For example, because they are government owned, federal hospitals are classified as public hospitals, even though they do not serve the general public. Federal hospitals are maintained primarily for special groups of federal beneficiaries such as Native Americans, military personnel, and veterans. In 2009, there were 211 federal hospitals in operation, down from 337 in 1990 (U.S. Census Bureau, 2011). VA hospitals constitute the largest group among federal hospitals; the VA system operates approximately 150 medical centers across the country.

State governments have generally limited themselves to the operation of mental and tuberculosis hospitals, reflecting the government's early role

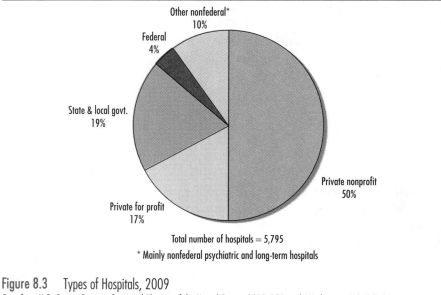

Total number of hospitals = 5,795
* Mainly nonfederal psychiatric and long-term hospitals

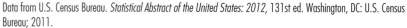

Figure 8.3   Types of Hospitals, 2009
Data from U.S. Census Bureau. *Statistical Abstract of the United States: 2012*, 131st ed. Washington, DC: U.S. Census Bureau; 2011.

in protecting communities by isolating the mentally ill and persons with contagious diseases.

Local governments, such as counties and cities, operate hospitals that are open to the general public. Hence, these hospitals are also classified as community hospitals. Government-owned community hospitals are often located in large urban areas where they serve mainly the inner-city indigent and disadvantaged populations. Due to the generally poor health status of these populations and inner-city violence, these hospitals incur higher utilization than hospitals located in suburban areas. Most of these hospitals are of small to moderate size (the average size is approximately 115 beds). Some large public hospitals are affiliated with medical schools, and they play a significant role in training physicians and other health care professionals. Medicare, Medicaid, and state and local tax dollars finance most of the services these hospitals provide. These hospitals also provide a substantial amount of charity care and often suffer financial losses that are covered by funneling tax dollars into the operations. Because of increasing financial pressures, many public hospitals have undergone privatization or had to close in recent years. Consequently, the number of state and local government-owned community hospitals has steadily declined, from 1,444 in 1990 to 1,092 in 2009 (U.S. Census Bureau. 2011).

Private Nonprofit Hospitals

Private nonprofit hospitals are also called *voluntary hospitals*. About half of the hospitals in the United States are under private nonprofit ownership (see **Figure 8.3**). The majority of these hospitals are operated by community associations, but other nongovernment organizations, such as philanthropic foundations and fraternal orders and societies, operate a few such institutions. The primary mission of these hospitals is to benefit the communities in which they are located. Their operating expenses are covered from patient fees, third-party reimbursement, donations, and endowments.

Church-owned hospitals also play a significant role in delivering hospital services in the United States. For example, the Catholic Church operates 620 hospitals across the United States and delivers care to one-sixth of all hospital patients each year (Filteau, 2010). Some Protestant denominations and Jewish philanthropic organizations also operate several community hospitals. Jewish hospitals were first established so that Jewish patients could observe their dietary laws more faithfully and so that Jewish physicians could find sites for training and work opportunities (Raffel, 1980, p. 241). These hospitals are not discriminatory in terms of access to care; however, they are generally sensitive to the special spiritual or dietary needs of the sponsoring denomination (Raffel & Raffel, 1994, pp. 131–132).

Lay people make a common assumption that nonprofit (sometimes referred to as not-for-profit) organizations do not make a profit. The fact is that every corporation, regardless of whether it is for profit or nonprofit, has to make a profit (a surplus of revenues over expenses) to survive over the long term. No business can survive for long if it continually spends more than it takes in. This statement is as true for nonprofit organizations as it is for the for-profit sector. The Internal Revenue Code, Section 501(c)(3), grants tax-exempt status to nonprofit organizations. As such, these institutions are exempt from federal, state, and local taxes such as income, sales, and property taxes. In exchange for the tax benefit these organizations receive, they must (1) provide some defined public good, such as service, education, or community welfare, and (2) not distribute any of the profits to any individual.

The rationale behind tax exemption is that these facilities provide an essential community benefit, principally for charitable, training, or research purposes. Discussions in the U.S. Congress over the years have suggested that benefits received by a community should at least be equal to the benefit of tax exemption enjoyed by the organization (Wolfson & Hopes, 1994).

In reality, nonprofit hospitals, in many instances, compete head-on with for-profit hospitals. Competition commonly occurs in the same communities, for the same patients, with revenues coming from the same public and private third-party sources, and often the same physician providers have admitting privileges at more than one hospital. Moreover, many nonprofit hospitals engage in the same kinds of aggressive marketplace behaviors that for-profit hospitals pursue. Research has shown that for-profit and nonprofit hospitals provide similar levels of charity and uncompensated care. Hence, whether nonprofit hospitals are indeed charitable institutions remains controversial. Many nonprofit entities must redefine their missions to differentiate themselves and provide tangible evidence of the benefits received by the communities in which these hospitals operate.

Private For-Profit Hospitals

Private for-profit hospitals, also referred to as *proprietary hospitals* or investor-owned hospitals, are owned by individuals, partnerships, or corporations. They are operated for the financial benefit of the entity that owns the institution—that is, the stockholders. At the beginning of the 20th century, more than half of all hospitals in the United States were proprietary. Most of these hospitals were small and were established by physicians who wanted a place to hospitalize their own patients (Stewart, 1973). Later, most of these institutions were closed or acquired by community organizations or hospital corporations because of population shifts, increased costs, and the necessities of modern clinical practice (Raffel & Raffel, 1994, p. 133).

For-profit corporations operate some of the largest multihospital chains in the United States. The largest among them are Hospital Corporation of America (156 hospitals), Community Health Systems (120 hospitals), and Tenet Health System (50 hospitals). A significant trend over the past few years has been the building or acquisition of a substantial number of hospitals by large investor-owned corporations. Even so, most multihospital health care systems today are operated by nonprofit corporations. Although a major goal for a for-profit organization is to provide a return on investment to its shareholders, it achieves this goal primarily by excelling at accomplishing its basic mission. The basic mission of any health services provider is to deliver the highest quality of care possible at the most reasonable price possible.

General Hospitals

A *general hospital* provides diagnostic, treatment, and surgical services for patients with a variety of acute medical conditions. Its services may include general and specialized medicine, general and specialized surgery, and obstetrics. Most hospitals in the United States are general hospitals, but they are not all community hospitals because most federal hospitals are general hospitals, too.

The term "general hospital" does not imply that these hospitals are less specialized or that their care is inferior to that of specialty hospitals. The difference lies in the nature of services, not the quality. General hospitals provide a broader range of services for a larger variety of conditions, whereas specialty hospitals provide a narrow range of services for specific medical conditions or patient populations.

Specialty Hospitals

Specialty hospitals admit only certain types of patients or those with specified illnesses or conditions (Rakich et al., 1992, p. 261). Specialty hospitals have traditionally included tuberculosis, psychiatric, rehabilitation, and children's hospitals. With increasing competition, other types of specialty hospitals have emerged to provide treatments that are also available in many general hospitals. Examples include hospitals specializing in orthopedic surgery and cardiology. Specialty hospitals forge a distinct service niche in a given market. These hospitals are also considered community hospitals as long as they meet the criteria discussed in that section.

In the entire nation, only a handful of tuberculosis hospitals are now left. Brief discussions of the other three categories of specialty hospitals follow.

Psychiatric Hospitals

The primary function of a psychiatric hospital is to provide diagnostic and treatment services for patients who have mental illnesses. Specifically, such an institution must have facilities to provide psychiatric, psychological, and social work services. A psychiatric hospital must also have a written agreement with a general hospital for the transfer of patients who may require medical, obstetric, or surgical care (Health Forum, 2001, p. A3). Historically, state governments took the primary responsibility for establishing facilities to care for the mentally ill, but as new therapies have become available to treat mental illness, private psychiatric facilities and outpatient treatment centers have assumed the task of delivering most mental health services.

Rehabilitation Hospitals

Rehabilitation hospitals specialize in therapeutic services to restore the maximum level of functioning in patients who have suffered recent disability due to illness or accident. Such hospitals serve patients who generally cannot be cured but whose functioning can be improved. These patients include amputees, patients who have sustained spinal cord or sports injuries, stroke victims, and others (Raffel & Raffel, 1989, p. 160). Patients often transfer to such facilities after undergoing orthopedic surgery or receiving trauma care in a general hospital. Facilities and staff are available to provide physical, occupational, and speech and language therapy.

Children's Hospitals

Children's hospitals are community hospitals that typically have special facilities and trained staff to deal with the unique medical problems of children, particularly those with complex and rare conditions. Roughly three-fourths of the inpatients in children's hospitals are treated for chronic or congenital conditions. The remaining patients require intensive care for a variety of needs, such as cancer treatment, treatment of cystic fibrosis, and tissue transplants.

Children's hospitals have equipment and furnishings that are specially designed for children—from newborn babies requiring intensive care to teens with chronic illness. They also maintain a nurse staffing ratio that is higher than that in general hospitals because children require more nursing care than adults.

Rural Hospitals

A *rural hospital* is one that is located in a county that is not part of a metropolitan statistical area (MSA). The U.S. Bureau of the Census has defined an MSA as a geographical area that includes at least (1) one city with a population of 50,000 or more or (2) an urbanized area of at least 50,000 inhabitants and a total MSA population of at least 100,000. Compared with other hospitals, rural hospitals generally treat a larger percentage of poor and elderly patients. Remote geographic location, small size, and limited workforce along with physician shortages and inadequate financial resources pose a unique set of challenges for rural hospitals (AHA, 2011).

To save some of the very small rural hospitals from having to close, the Balanced Budget Act of 1997 allowed certain rural hospitals to operate as *critical access hospitals* (CAHs). According to Medicare rules, a CAH should have no more than 25 beds and must provide 24-hour emergency medical services. An additional 10 beds may be operated for psychiatric and/or rehabilitation services. CAHs are reimbursed according to the retrospective cost-plus method, instead of the PPS method.

Teaching Hospitals

To be designated as a *teaching hospital*, a hospital must offer one or more graduate residency programs approved by the American Medical Association (AMA). Hence, the primary role of a teaching hospital is to train physicians. Although these hospitals may also be actively involved in training nurses and other health professionals, such as therapists and dietitians, unless they train physicians, they cannot be called teaching hospitals.

Depending on the type and number of residency programs offered, a hospital can be classified as either a major or a minor teaching institution. To be a full teaching hospital, it should offer, at a minimum, residencies in general medicine, surgery, obstetrics and gynecology, and pediatrics. Many teaching hospitals offer residencies in every subspecialty of medicine and surgery in addition to pathology, anesthesiology, family practice, and other programs (Wolper & Peña, 1995).

Most major teaching hospitals are affiliated with medical schools of universities. The term *academic medical center* (AMC) applies to an organization in which there is active collaboration among the university, medical school, hospital/health system, and health care professionals. An AMC is uniquely capable of conducting basic and applied clinical research, providing health care services, and offering medical education (Daniels & Carson, 2011).

In addition to fulfilling a substantial teaching and research mission, teaching hospitals deliver specialized care for a variety of complex medical problems. These institutions often operate several intensive care units, possess the latest medical technologies, and attract a diverse group of physicians representing most specialties and many subspecialties. Major teaching hospitals also offer many unique tertiary care services not generally found in other institutions, such as burn care, trauma care, and organ transplantation.

Osteopathic Hospitals

Osteopathic medicine represents an approach to medical practice that employs all the methods traditionally associated with allopathic medicine, such as pharmaceuticals, laboratory tests, x-ray diagnostics, and surgery. Osteopathic medicine, however, takes a holistic approach and goes a step further in advocating treatment that involves correction of the position of the joints or tissues and in emphasizing diet and environment as factors that prevent disease and improve health. For many years after osteopathy was established as a separate branch of medicine in 1874, osteopaths had to develop their own hospitals because of antagonism toward their profession demonstrated by the established allopathic medical practitioners. In 1970, osteopathic hospitals became eligible to apply for registration with the AHA (AHA, 1994). Since then, allopathic and osteopathic physicians have been practicing side by side in the same clinics and hospitals.

For all practical purposes, osteopathic hospitals are community general hospitals. However, with the integration of medical practice, having separate hospitals has become economically unnecessary. Also, the operation of osteopathic hospitals has been found to be more costly and less productive in comparison to their counterparts (Sinay, 2005). Hence, a large number of osteopathic hospitals have closed.

LICENSURE, CERTIFICATION, AND ACCREDITATION

A hospital is legally required to have a *license* from the state in which it operates. The licensure function is usually carried out by each state's department of health. State licensure standards strongly emphasize compliance with building codes, fire safety, climate control, space allocations, and sanitation. States have also established minimum standards for equipment and personnel that health care organizations must meet to be licensed.

Certification by the federal government gives a hospital the authority to participate in the Medicare and Medicaid programs. The DHHS has developed health, safety, and quality standards referred to as *conditions of participation*, and has the authority to enforce those standards. Hospitals accredited by The Joint Commission or the American Osteopathic Association (AOA) have been automatically "deemed" to meet all the health and safety requirements for participation in Medicare and Medicaid.

The Joint Commission, a private nonprofit body, was formed in 1951 with the approval of the various medical and hospital organizations. Upon compliance with its standards, The Joint Commission accredits most of the nation's general hospitals, as well as many of the long-term care facilities, psychiatric hospitals, substance abuse programs, outpatient surgery centers, urgent care clinics, group practices, community health centers, hospices, and home health agencies. Different sets of standards apply to each category of health care organization. Over the years, The Joint Commission has refined its accreditation standards and process of verifying compliance to put greater emphasis on quality of care. Seeking accreditation is voluntary, but Medicare regulations confer *deemed status* on accredited hospitals, allowing these hospitals to participate in Medicare and Medicaid without having to be certified.

THE MAGNET RECOGNITION PROGRAM*

Since 1994, the American Nurses Association has conferred Magnet status on hospitals that have met strict standards on quality of patient care and leadership in creating healthy work environments through nursing excellence and innovations in professional nursing practice. Research has shown that such an environment attracts and promotes retention of well-qualified nurses, as well as leads to quality patient care. Hospitals that meet those criteria are labeled as *Magnet hospitals*. Approximately 7% (400) of U.S. hospitals have Magnet status.

---

*The Magnet Recognition Program® is a registered trademark of the American Nurses Credentialing Center of the American Nurses Association.

HOSPITAL ORGANIZATION

Hospitals are complex organizations. A hospital is generally responsible to numerous external stakeholders, such as the community, the government, managed care organizations, and accreditation agencies. Internally, hospital governance involves three major sources of power, whose motivations are sometimes at odds. The organizational structure of a hospital also differs substantially from that of other large organizations. The CEO receives delegated authority from the governing body (board) and is responsible for managing the organization with the help of senior executives. In large hospitals, these senior executives often carry the title of senior vice president or vice president responsible for various key service areas, such as nursing services, rehabilitation services, human resources, finance, and so forth. Most physicians belong to a separate organizational structure that operates in parallel to the administrative structure (**Figure 8.4**). Such a dual structure is rarely seen in other types of businesses and presents numerous opportunities for conflict to arise between the CEO and the medical staff. Sometimes matters can be further complicated because most physicians are not employed by the hospital, yet they must be closely involved in its operations. Also, the

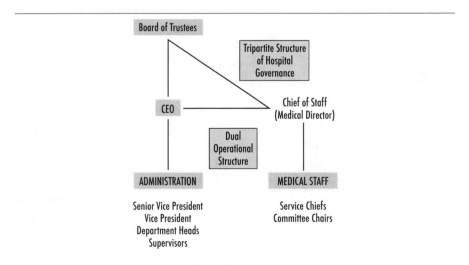

Figure 8.4   Hospital Governance and Operational Structure

nursing staff, pharmacists, diagnostic technicians, dietitians, and others are administratively accountable to the CEO but professionally accountable to the medical staff (Raffel & Raffel, 1994, p. 139).

One major exception to the medical staff organization described here occurs with employment of physicians on salary in organizations such as VA hospitals. Other hospitals employ a small number of salaried hospitalists.

ETHICS AND PUBLIC TRUST

Ethical issues arise in all types of health services organizations, but the most significant ones occur in acute care hospitals. Advanced technologies create situations requiring decision making under complex circumstances. Constraints on reimbursement often make it essential to cut costs or eliminate unprofitable services, which also can raise ethical concerns. Many physicians must deal with issues such as legalized abortion, physician-assisted suicide, artificial prolongation of life, and experimentation.

Ethical Challenges

Physicians and other caregivers have moral responsibilities when delivering clinical care. These professionals are guided by the principles of beneficence and non-maleficence. *Beneficence* means that a health services organization has an ethical obligation to do all it can to alleviate suffering caused by ill health and injury. This obligation includes providing essential services, such as emergency care, to needy individuals who do not have the ability to pay. Closely related to beneficence, *non-maleficence* means that health services personnel have a moral obligation not to harm the patients. This principle requires physicians to use their best professional judgment in choosing interventions that maximize the potential health benefits at minimum risk.

No less challenging is the ethical issue surrounding the definition of extraordinary or heroic measures to sustain a person's life. Medical and legal experts differ on the controversial issue of withdrawing nutrition and other means of life support for dying patients (Bresnohan & Drane, 1986). The questions raised in such cases do not have easy answers, and most of the time physicians must follow their own consciences and apply their own personal ethical values. Other legal and ethical standards in medical treatment require the patient's consent before treatment is rendered, a discussion of the various treatment alternatives, and patient's participation in decision making and the selection of treatment options. Health care providers are also duty bound to hold all patient information in strict confidence. Likewise, fairness, equality, and nondiscrimination are essential in the delivery of health care.

Addressing Ethical Issues

Many health care organizations, especially large acute care hospitals, now have ethics committees. The *ethics committee* is charged with the responsibility of developing guidelines and standards for ethical decision making in the delivery of health care (Paris, 1995). Ethics committees are also responsible for resolving issues related to medical ethics. Such committees are interdisciplinary, involving physicians, nurses, clergy, social workers, legal experts, ethicists, and administrators.

Certain legal mechanisms are also available to help deal with difficult decisions about life and death. The Patient Self-Determination Act of 1990 applies to all health care facilities participating in Medicare or Medicaid. This law requires hospitals and other facilities to provide all patients, on admission, with information on patients' rights.

Informed consent is a basic patient right. Every patient has the right to make an informed choice regarding his or her medical treatment, including the choice to refuse treatment. For a patient who is mentally capable, physicians must provide all the information the patient asks for or should have to make a properly informed decision.

Patients also have the right to formulate *advance directives*, allowing the patient to express in advance his or her wishes regarding continuation or withdrawal of treatment in the event that he or she becomes incompetent. When advance directives are not available, the burden of ethical decision making falls squarely on the shoulders of those responsible for providing health care services. In actual practice, however, discussions between physicians and patients about the prognosis at the end of life are infrequent and limited in scope (Bradley et al., 2001). Hence, relatively few people use advance directives. Physicians can play an important role by engaging their patients in discussions about the patients' preferences regarding end-of-life decisions.

Public Trust

Communities must place a high degree of trust in their hospitals, but occasionally the behavior of some hospitals has called this trust into question. Hospital administrators have a fiduciary responsibility. They are responsible for acting prudently in managing the affairs of the organization. Because a hospital's mission is to benefit the community, the hospital should be viewed as a community asset regardless of whether it is an investor-owned or nonprofit institution. When such a viewpoint is lost, and a hospital's board and its executives start placing other priorities ahead of their main responsibility to serve the community, a breach of public trust can occur. Although hospitals must maintain their financial and operational integrity, a real danger arises when financial concerns are put above a genuine concern for the welfare of the patients and the community. Because hospitals form the institutional hub of health care delivery, their integrity within the system is crucial. Hospitals are increasingly being held accountable for enhancing the health status of the communities they are supposed to serve. A growing emphasis on wellness and health promotion is part of this mandate.

CONCLUSION

Any facility that treats patients on the basis of an overnight stay is called an inpatient facility. The most common types of inpatient facilities are hospitals and nursing homes. Both of these institutions trace their beginnings to the almshouses of the eighteenth and nineteenth centuries, but as medical science advanced, hospitals emerged as institutions specializing in acute care and surgical services. In many parts of the United States, medical systems serve large geographical areas, delivering a full array of health care services.

Hospitals in the United States went through an expansion and then a contraction phase, both of which were triggered primarily by government policy. Hospital employment has steadily risen over time, and this trend is expected to continue.

Hospitals can be classified in a number of different ways. The majority of hospitals in the United States are private, nonprofit facilities. These hospitals have a legal obligation to provide benefits, such as education and charity care. Most hospitals are community hospitals, meaning that they are nonfederal, short stay, and open to the public. Licensure of hospitals is a legal requirement. Accreditation by The Joint Commission confers deemed status that enables a hospital to admit Medicare and Medicaid patients. Hospitals confront numerous ethical challenges, and must operate in a way that strengthens public trust.

REFERENCES

American Hospital Association (AHA). *Hospital Statistics 1990–1991 Edition.* Chicago: AHA; 1990.

American Hospital Association (AHA). *AHA Guide to the Health Care Field 1994 Edition.* Chicago: AHA; 1994.

American Hospital Association (AHA). Section for small or rural hospitals: Annual report for 2010. 2011. http://www.aha.org/content/11/2010-SRsectionAnnual-Report.pdf. Accessed January 2012.

Bradley EH, et al. Documentation of discussions about prognosis with terminally ill patients. *Am J Med.* 2001;111(3): 218–23.

Bresnohan JF, Drane JF. A challenge to examine the meaning of living and dying. *Health Prog.* 1986;67:32–37, 98.

Daniels RJ, Carson LD. Academic medical centers: Organizational integration and discipline through contractual and firm models. *JAMA.* 2011;306(17):1912–1913.

Department of Health and Human Services (DHHS). *Health, United States, 2010.* 2011. Hyattsville, MD: DHHS; 2011.

Filteau J. Catholic hospitals serve one in six patients in the United States. *Natl Catholic Rep.* 2010. http://ncronline.org/news/catholic-hospitals-serve-one-six-patients-united-states. Accessed January 2012.

Haglund CL, Dowling WL. The hospital. In *Introduction to Health Services.* 4th ed., edited by Williams SJ, Torrens PR. Albany, NY: Delmar Publishers; 1993:135–176.

Health Forum. *AHA Guide to the Health Care Field. 2001–2002 Edition.* Chicago: Health Forum; 2001.

National Center for Health Statistics. *Health, United States, 2002.* Hyattsville, MD: Department of Health and Human Services; 2002.

Paris M. The medical staff. In *Health Care Administration: Principles, Practices, Structure, and Delivery.* 2nd ed., edited by Wolper LF. Gaithersburg, MD: Aspen Publishers; 1995:32–46.

Raffel MW. *The U.S. Health System: Origins and Functions.* New York: John Wiley and Sons; 1980.

Raffel MW, Raffel NK. *The U.S. Health System: Origins and Functions,* 3rd ed. Albany, NY: Delmar Publishers; 1989.

Raffel MW, Raffel NK. *The U.S. Health System: Origins and Functions,* 4th ed. Albany, NY: Delmar Publishers; 1994.

Rakich JS, et al. *Managing Health Services Organizations,* 3rd ed. Baltimore, MD: Health Professions Press; 1992.

Sinay T. Cost structure of osteopathic hospitals and their local counterparts in the USA: Are they any different? *Soc Sci Med.* 2005;60(8):1805–1814.

Stewart DA. *The History and Status of Proprietary Hospitals. Blue Cross Reports—Research Series 9.* Chicago: Blue Cross Association; 1973.

Teisberg ED, et al. *The Hospital Sector in 1992.* Boston: Harvard Business School; 1991.

U.S. Census Bureau. *Statistical Abstract of the United States: 2012,* 131st ed. Washington, DC: U.S. Census Bureau; 2011.

Wolfson J, Hopes SL. What makes tax-exempt hospitals special? *Healthcare Financ Manage.* July 1994: 56–60.

Wolper LF, Peña JJ. History of hospitals. In *Health Care Administration: Principles, Practices, Structure, and Delivery,* 2nd ed., edited by Wolper LF. Gaithersburg, MD: Aspen Publishers; 1995:3–15.

Chapter 9

Managed Care and Integrated Systems

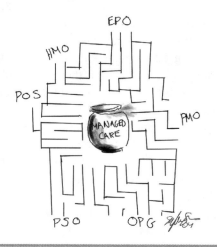

INTRODUCTION

Since around 1990, managed care has been the single most dominant force to fundamentally transform the delivery of health care in the United States. At first, some observers viewed the managed care phenomenon as an aberration. However, as private employers began to realize cost savings and public policy makers and administrators saw the opportunity to slow down the growth of Medicare and Medicaid expenditures, they increasingly turned to managed care. For now, managed care has become firmly entrenched in the United States, and some other countries have adopted its features to reform their own traditional systems of health care delivery.

Shortly after the start of health insurance in the United States, Blue Cross/Blue Shield and then other commercial insurance companies started to dominate the health insurance market. Health insurance became employer based, but neither the employers nor the insurance companies had any incentive to manage the delivery of services or payments made to providers. Providers showed a strong preference to be paid on a fee-for-service basis. Thus both the delivery of health care and payments for care got out of control. Managed care was designed to limit both the quantity of health care delivered and the amount of reimbursement to providers.

Managed care has experienced unprecedented success. For example, only 27% of all employees insured through employer-sponsored health insurance were enrolled in managed care plans in 1988. By 2002, however, 95% were enrolled in managed care. This growth occurred despite attacks on managed care from both physicians and consumers. In 2011, only 1% of workers were enrolled in employer-sponsored conventional health insurance plans (Claxton et al., 2011). Given their success, many conventional insurance companies and Blue Cross/Blue Shield have been offering managed care plans.

By enrolling a large segment of the insured U.S. population and taking responsibility to procure cost-effective health care for the enrollees, managed care organizations (MCOs) garnered enormous buying power. To a large extent, the organizational consolidation of providers represented a response to this growing power of MCOs. These changes have given rise to new organizational arrangements. The freestanding hospital and the solo practitioner continue to be replaced with medical systems and physicians' group practices. In many instances, physicians and hospitals also have formed partnerships. Organizational consolidation created *integrated delivery systems* or health networks in many parts of the country. These organizations are capable of providing a full array of health care services to large populations.

WHAT IS MANAGED CARE?

Managed care is a mechanism of providing health care services in which a single organization takes on the management of financing, insurance, delivery, and payment.

- Financing. Premiums are usually negotiated between employers and the MCO. Generally, a fixed premium per enrollee includes all health care services provided for in a contract.

- Insurance. The MCO collects premiums for insuring groups of enrollees. It then functions like an insurance company by assuming all risk. In other words, it takes financial responsibility if the total cost of services provided exceeds the revenue from fixed premiums. MCOs retain 15% to 25% of the premium dollar to manage risk and to cover their own administrative expenses. The remainder of the premium that is spent on health care services is called the *medical loss ratio*.

- Delivery. Unlike conventional insurance, the MCO arranges to provide health care to its enrollees. To do so, most MCOs establish contracts with physicians, clinics, hospitals, and medical systems. These providers operate independently but are linked to the MCO through legal contracts. Some very large MCOs have their own physicians on salary and operate their own clinics; in some instances, MCOs even operate their own hospitals. To keep costs under control, MCOs use various methods to manage the utilization of health care services.

- Payment. The most common methods used for reimbursing providers are capitation and discounted fees, but fee-for-service reimbursement continues to be used by health maintenance organizations (HMOs). Under *capitation*, the provider is paid a fixed monthly sum per enrollee, often called a per member per month (PMPM) payment. The provider receives the capitated fee per enrollee regardless of whether the enrollee uses health care services and regardless of the quantity of services used. The provider is responsible for providing all needed health care services determined to be medically necessary. Thus, under capitation, a portion of the risk is shifted from the MCO to the provider. When providers have to bear some of the risk, they become prudent in providing services cost-effectively—after all, they can lose money if they deliver services indiscriminately. The discounted fee arrangement uses a modified form of fee for service. After services have been delivered, the provider can bill the MCO for each service separately but is paid according to a schedule of fees. The fee schedule is prenegotiated and is based on discounts off the regular fees the provider would otherwise charge. Providers agree to discount their regular fees in exchange for the volume of patients the MCO brings them.

Exhibit 9.1   Main Characteristics of Managed Care

MCOs manage financing, insurance, delivery, and payment for providing health care:
• Premiums are usually negotiated between MCOs and employers.
• MCOs function like an insurance company and assume risk.
• MCOs arrange to provide health care, mainly through contracts with providers.
• MCOs manage the utilization of health care services.
• Commonly used payment methods are capitation and discounted fees.

The main characteristics of managed care are summarized in **Exhibit 9.1**.

Accreditation and Quality Indicators

Since 1991, MCOs have been accredited by the National Committee for Quality Assurance (NCQA). Accreditation is voluntary. The NCQA has also designed a set of standardized performance measures for MCOs. Commonly referred to as managed care report cards, the national standards and performance reports on individual MCOs are contained in the Healthcare Effectiveness Data and Information Set (HEDIS). The report cards are voluntary efforts that were begun out of concerns that controlling health care utilization could adversely affect the quality of care. HEDIS data include a number of different measures on cost and quality. Although there is no federal legislation requiring that MCOs comply with HEDIS standards, compliance is required in some states.

The Centers for Medicare and Medicaid Services (CMS) rates the relative quality of Medicare Advantage plans (Medicare Part C) on a one- to five-star scale, with five stars representing the highest quality. The star rating, which provides an overall measure of a plan's quality, is a cumulative indicator of the quality of care, access to care, responsiveness, and beneficiary satisfaction provided by the plan. Ratings are available on Medicare's website to help beneficiaries choose from among the various Medicare Advantage plans if they want to enroll in Part C of Medicare. The star rating incorporates HEDIS as one of the four measures. The Patient Protection and Affordable Care Act (ACA) of 2010 requires the use of star ratings to reward higher-quality plans with incentive payments (Henry J. Kaiser Family Foundation, 2009).

EVOLUTION AND GROWTH OF MANAGED CARE

In the early 1900s, certain railroad, mining, and lumber companies located in isolated areas employed salaried physicians to provide medical care to their workers. In other instances, such companies contracted with physicians and hospitals at a flat fee per worker. Such arrangements can be viewed as prototypes of managed care.

The first known private health insurance plan started at the Baylor University Hospital in Dallas, Texas, in 1929 was also a prepaid plan. For a predetermined fixed fee per month, Baylor, and subsequently other hospitals, provided inpatient services. Thus the financing of the first health insurance plan was based on capitation.

Later, during the 1940s, some large health plans emerged in New York, California, Washington, and St. Louis. These plans also provided comprehensive health care to enrolled populations for a capitated fee. For example, the well-known Kaiser Permanente plan started in California in 1942 when the industrialist Henry J. Kaiser was faced with the problem of providing health care to his 30,000 workers. In 1945, the Permanente Health Plan was made available to the general public; today, the Kaiser Foundation Health Plan, operated by Kaiser Permanente, is the largest HMO in the United States. In the rest of the country, however, delivery of health care typically continued to follow the fee-for-service system. Commercial insurance companies were the dominant players in the private health insurance market.

The Health Maintenance Organization Act of 1973 was passed out of concern for escalating health care expenditures. Subsequent to the creation of Medicare and Medicaid, national health expenditures rose at more than double the rate of growth in the consumer price index during the five-year period from 1966 to 1971 (**Figure 9.1**). The 1973 law was designed to provide an alternative to the traditional fee-for-service practice of medicine; it aimed to stimulate the growth of HMOs by providing federal funds to establish new HMOs (Wilson & Neuhauser, 1985, p. 206). The reasoning behind promoting HMO growth was that medical care delivery under capitation would reduce costs, which would stimulate competition among health plans, increase efficiency, and slow the rate of growth in health care expenditures. The law's objective was to create 1,700 HMOs to serve 40 million members by 1976 (Iglehart, 1994). By the end of the 1970s, however, HMOs had enrolled fewer than 10 million members.

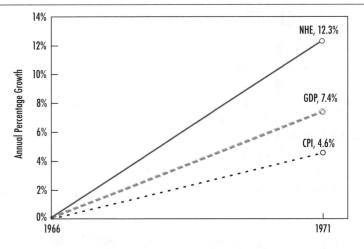

Figure 9.1   Average Annual Rates of Increase in National Health Expenditures (NHE), Gross Domestic Product (GDP), and Consumer Price Index (CPI), 1966–1971
Data from Bureau of Labor Statistics, National Center for Health Statistics. *Health, United States*, 1995, p. 239. http://stats .bls.gov/cpi.

During the 1980s, managed care experienced relatively slow growth, but in states such as California and Minnesota, growth was faster than in most parts of the United States. Health care costs continued to rise uncontrollably, and private businesses were increasingly threatened by the erosion of profits resulting from double-digit increases in the cost of health care premiums. As health insurance became less affordable, employers started switching from traditional health insurance to managed care plans during the 1980s. It was not until the early 1990s, however, that a veritable managed care revolution got under way when private employers experienced a total increase of 217% (12.2% average annual increase) in the cost of health insurance between 1980 and 1990. **Figure 9.2** illustrates the growth of enrollment in managed care plans between 1988 and 2003.

As the market for managed care grew, competition among MCOs gave rise to new forms of managed care plans. To differentiate among themselves, some new organizations adopted variations in payment. Preferred provider organizations (PPOs), for example, differentiated themselves by using discounted fee payments instead of capitation. Other MCOs

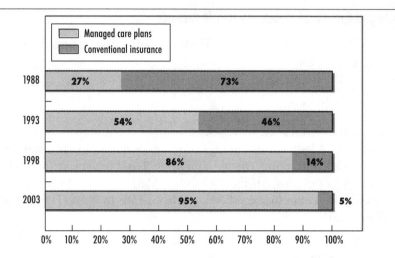

Figure 9.2   Enrollment of Workers in Employer-Sponsored Health Plans, Selected Years
Data from Claxton G., et al. 2007. The Kaiser Family Foundation and Health Research and Educational Trust Employer Health Benefits 2007 Annual Survey. Menlo Park, CA: Henry J. Kaiser Family Foundation and Chicago, IL: Health Research and Educational Trust, p. 65.

differentiated themselves according to how the medical care providers were organized. Still others offered their enrollees a choice between providers who were contractually affiliated with the organization and those who were not. MCOs also adopted various methods to control health care costs by actively monitoring utilization.

Managed Care and Private Health Insurance

Managed care has become the primary vehicle for delivering health care to the vast majority of Americans and is now a mature industry in the United States. In essence, private health insurance can now be equated with managed care, whether it is obtained through a small or large employer. High-deductible health plans are also commonly offered in the form of managed care plans. Many employers offer their workers a choice of plans with level-dollar employer contributions, meaning workers pay more themselves—in premium contributions as well as deductibles and copayments—if they choose a more expensive conventional insurance plan.

Managed Care and Public Health Insurance

Enrollments of Medicare and Medicaid beneficiaries have continued to grow in recent years.

Medicare Enrollment

Medicare beneficiaries have the choice of enrolling in a managed care plan under the Medicare Advantage program or remaining in the traditional fee-for-service program. The latter option has been more popular with Medicare beneficiaries. Of the 49 million Medicare beneficiaries in 2011, 25% were enrolled in managed care, up from 15% in 2001 (Henry J. Kaiser Family Foundation, 2011).

Medicaid Enrollment

Of the 54.6 million Medicaid recipients in July 2010, 71.5% were enrolled in managed care, up from 56.8% in 2001 (CMS, 2010). Waivers under the Social Security Act, particularly Sections 1115 and 1915(b), allowed states to enroll their Medicaid recipients in managed care plans. Later, the Balanced Budget Act of 1997 gave states the authority to implement mandatory managed care enrollments without federal waivers (Moscovice et al., 1998). As a result, enrollment in managed care has grown at a rapid pace. This growth has been realized particularly as MCOs were able to expand their markets into rural areas. Almost half the states now have at least 80% of their Medicaid recipients enrolled in managed care (Sanofi-Aventis, 2011c), and this trend is accelerating across the country.

MANAGED CARE TODAY

Managed care made significant headway during the decade of the 1990s and achieved notable success in slowing down the growth of national health care expenditures. Toward the latter half of the 1990s, however, it drew a backlash from consumers, providers, and politicians. The American media also played a role in shaping public opinion against managed care by presenting, in many instances, one-sided and subjective "news" stories focusing on denial of services.

For consumers, dissatisfaction with managed care was associated mainly with the erosion of choice resulting from the limited number of providers associated with the plans and some restrictions in direct access to specialized services. Dissatisfaction on the part of physicians, hospitals, and other providers was related to the control that MCOs exerted over utilization and limits on reimbursement. Risk sharing under capitation became particularly controversial. Politicians responded by passing laws to contain some of the perceived excesses of managed care. In the process, however, all parties had to accept certain compromises.

In response to the backlash, HMOs moved away from tight management of health care services but without totally abandoning utilization controls. They also incorporated fee-for-service reimbursement, along with capitation for certain services, within their payment schemes. PPOs emerged, offering greater choice of access to providers. Both consumers and providers welcomed these changes. In the end, enrollees had to give up unconditional freedom over choice, providers had to accept some controls over how they would practice medicine and settle for lower rates of reimbursement than what they were getting under fee-for-service arrangements, and MCOs had to relax tight management of health care utilization. Even though some differences between individual plans still exist, relaxed controls and flexibility have become common features of all plans. Managed care today is quite different from what it was initially intended to be: an organizational mechanism that would tightly control the financing and delivery of health care. At the same time, because of these compromises, managed care has been enormously successful—practically replacing traditional health insurance in the United States.

UTILIZATION CONTROL METHODS IN MANAGED CARE

MCOs use three main approaches to monitor and control the utilization of services:

- Expert evaluation of which services are medically necessary in a given case. Such an evaluation ensures that only medically necessary services are actually provided.
- Determination of how services can be provided most inexpensively while maintaining acceptable standards of quality. For example, often

similar services can be obtained as an outpatient or as an inpatient; outpatient services cost less. Similarly, generic drugs cost less than brand-name drugs.

* Review of the process of care and changes in the patient's condition to revise the course of medical treatment if necessary.

Utilization management of inpatient services takes priority because such services account for 40% or more of the total expenses in a managed care plan (Kongstvedt, 1995). The methods most commonly used for utilization monitoring and control are gatekeeping and utilization review. Generally, HMOs employ tighter utilization controls than other types of managed care plans, which are discussed later in this chapter.

Gatekeeping

Commonly used by HMOs, *gatekeeping* is an arrangement that requires a primary care physician to coordinate all health care services needed by an enrollee. The physicians have contracts with the HMO as in-network providers. Gatekeeping also emphasizes preventive care, routine physical examinations, and other primary care services that are delivered by the primary care gatekeeper. Secondary care services, such as diagnostic testing, consultation from specialists, and admission to a hospital, are provided only on referral from the gatekeeper. In this way, the gatekeeper controls access to costly medical services.

Utilization Review

Utilization review is the process of evaluating the appropriateness of services provided. It is sometimes misunderstood to be a mechanism for denying services, but its main objective is actually to review each case and to determine the most appropriate level of services. Three main types of utilization review are employed: prospective, concurrent, and retrospective.

Prospective Utilization Review

Under this method, the medical necessity for certain treatments is determined before the care is actually delivered. An example of prospective utilization review is the decision by a primary care gatekeeper to refer or not refer a patient to a specialist. However, not all managed care plans use gatekeepers. Some plans require the enrollee or the provider to call the plan administrators for *precertification*—that is, approval before certain services are provided. Most plans use established clinical guidelines to determine the appropriateness of services. Preauthorization of hospital admissions and second opinions for surgical procedures are examples of precertification. In case of an emergency admission to an inpatient facility, plans generally require notification within 24 hours. One of the main objectives of prospective review is to prevent unnecessary or inappropriate institutionalization or other courses of treatment such as surgery.

Concurrent Utilization Review

Concurrent utilization review occurs when decisions regarding appropriateness are made during the course of health care utilization. The most common examples of this type of review involve monitoring the length of inpatient stays. When a patient is hospitalized, a certain number of inpatient days are generally preapproved. A trained nurse then monitors the patient's status and reviews the case with a physician if a longer stay is necessary. A decision is made to authorize or deny additional days.

Discharge planning is an important component of concurrent utilization review. A patient's prognosis for recovery, expected outcomes, and anticipated day of discharge are critical elements of concurrent review. Discharge planning deals with the patient's ongoing care and evaluates any special requirements that are necessary after discharge. For example, if a patient is admitted with a fractured hip, it is important to decide whether home health care or a skilled nursing facility would be more appropriate for convalescent care. If the patient requires care in a skilled nursing facility, then discharge planning must find out whether the appropriate level of rehabilitation services would be available and for how long insurance will pay for rehabilitation therapy in a long-term care setting.

Retrospective Utilization Review

Retrospective utilization review determines the appropriateness of utilization after services have already been delivered. Such review is based on an examination of medical records to assess the appropriateness of care. It may involve an assessment of individual cases. Large claims may be reviewed for billing accuracy. Retrospective review may also involve an analysis of data to examine patterns of excessive utilization or underutilization. *Underutilization* occurs when medically necessary care is not delivered. *Overutilization* occurs when medical services that are not necessary are delivered.

TYPES OF MANAGED CARE PLANS

Three main factors led to the development of different types of managed care plans. The first and most important involved the choice of providers. HMOs were the most common type of MCOs in the 1970s, but HMO plans had inherent weaknesses, especially with regard to choice of providers. Other types of MCO plans that offered greater choice were developed mainly to compete with the more restrictive HMO plans. Second, different ways of arranging the delivery of services led to different forms of MCOs because there is no single way to arrange providers into a delivery network. Payment and risk sharing make up the third major factor. The main differences between the three different types of managed care plans discussed in this section are presented in **Exhibit 9.2**.

HMO Plans

HMOs were the first type of managed care plans to appear on the market. An HMO is distinguished from other types of plans by its focus on wellness care. Such an organization not only provides medical care during illness but also offers a variety of services to help people maintain their health—hence the name "health maintenance" organization. HMOs place considerable emphasis on preventive and screening services through routine checkups and tests. Prevention of disease and early detection and treatment save health care costs in the long run when the course of a disease is checked before it turns into a more complex case. As an incentive to the enrollees to seek wellness care, HMO plans typically do not have annual deductibles, and they also have lower copayments than do other types of plans.

Initially, HMOs used only capitation to reimburse providers, but providers disliked the risk-sharing feature of capitation. HMOs, therefore, had to compromise by raising PMPM rates and, in many instances, switching to fee-for-service reimbursement. In 2010, fee for service was used by 60% of HMO plans (Sanofi-Aventis, 2011a).

Exhibit 9.2   Differences Between the Three Main Types of Managed Care Plans

Main Distinguishing Factors

1. Choice of providers
2. Delivery of services
3. Payment and risk sharing

HMO Plans	PPO Plans	POS Plans
• Use of only in-network providers is permitted	• Use of both in-network and out-of-network providers is permitted	• Use of both in-network and out-of-network providers is permitted
• Providers on staff and/or contracted providers	• Contracted providers only	• Contracted providers only
• Use of gatekeeping	• No gatekeeping	
• Focus on prevention and primary care		
• Specialty services are obtained upon referral	• Unrestricted use of specialty services	• Unrestricted use of specialty services
• Providers are paid mostly under capitation	• Providers are paid according to discounted fee schedules	• Combination of capitation and fee for service
• Some fee for service		
• Risk sharing with providers under capitation	• No risk sharing	• Some risk sharing

Note: There may be some variations to the above for individual plans.

HMO plans require that enrollees use in-network providers. The utilization of services is coordinated and managed by the HMO, mainly through primary care gatekeepers. Enrollees must obtain services from in-network hospitals, physicians, and other health care providers. Specialty services, such as mental health and substance abuse treatment, are frequently carved out. A *carve-out* is a special contract outside regular capitation, which is funded separately by the HMO.

The four most widely used HMO models differ from each other according to the arrangements they make with participating physicians. These models are the staff, group, network, and independent practice association models.

Staff Model HMO

A staff model HMO employs its own salaried physicians. The physicians are typically paid fixed salaries, and at the end of the year, a pool of money is distributed among the physicians in the form of bonuses based on each physician's productivity and the HMO's profitability. Physicians work only for their employer HMO and provide services to that HMO's enrollees (Rakich et al., 1992, p. 281). Staff model HMOs must employ physicians in all of the common specialties to provide for the health care needs of their members. In addition, contracts with selected subspecialties are established for less-frequently needed services. The HMO operates one or more outpatient clinics, which contain physicians' offices, support staff, and sometimes ancillary support facilities, such as laboratory and radiology departments. In most instances, the HMO contracts with area hospitals for inpatient services (Wagner, 1995).

Compared with other HMO models, staff model HMOs are able to exercise a greater degree of control over the practice patterns of their physicians. Hence, it is easier to monitor utilization. Even so, the fixed salary expense can be high, which requires that these HMOs have a large number of members to support the operating expenses. Enrollees generally have a limited choice of physicians. Because of its disadvantages, the staff model has been the least popular type of HMO. Nationwide, the number of staff model HMOs has continued to decline.

Group Model HMO

A group model HMO contracts with a multispecialty group practice and separately with one or more hospitals to provide comprehensive services to its members. The group practice is an independent practice, employing its own physicians who can treat non-HMO patients as well. The HMO generally pays an all-inclusive capitation fee to the group practice to provide physician services to its members. Under a different scenario, the HMO may own the group practice, which is organized as a separate corporation but one that is administratively tied to the HMO. In this case, the group practice may provide services exclusively to the HMO's members. Ownership or an exclusive contract enables the HMO to exercise better control over utilization. Even when it is not an exclusive contract, the HMO brings a block of business to the group practice, which gives the HMO a fair amount of leverage regarding financial terms and utilization controls.

Network Model HMO

Under the network model, the HMO contracts with more than one medical group practice. This model is particularly well suited for operations in large metropolitan areas and across widespread geographic regions where group practices are located. Each group practice is paid a capitation fee based on the number of enrollees. The group is responsible for providing all physician services. It can make referrals to specialists but is financially responsible for reimbursing them for any referrals it makes. The network model is generally able to offer enrollees a wider choice of physicians than the staff or group models. The main disadvantage is the dilution of utilization control.

Independent Practice Association Model HMO

Of the four HMO models, the independent practice association (IPA) model has been the most successful in terms of the largest share of enrollments. The IPA model became popular with both providers and enrollees. IPAs gave small groups and individual physicians the opportunity to participate in managed care and, therefore, were preferred by physicians. The enrollees generally have the greatest choice of providers under the IPA model.

An IPA is a legal entity separate from the HMO. The IPA, not the HMO, establishes contracts with both independent solo practitioners and group practices. The HMO, in turn, contracts with the IPA for physician services. Physicians do not have a contract with the HMO, but with the IPA. Hence, the IPA functions as an intermediary representing a large number of physicians. The IPA is generally paid a capitation amount by the HMO. The IPA retains administrative control over how it pays its physicians. It may reimburse physicians through capitation or some other mechanism, such as modified fee for service. The IPA often shares risk with the physicians and assumes the responsibility for utilization management and quality assessment.

Under the IPA model, the HMO is still responsible for providing health care services to its enrollees, but the logistics of arranging physician services are shifted to the IPA. As a consequence, the HMO is relieved of the administrative burden of establishing contracts with numerous providers and controlling utilization. Financial risk is also shared with the IPA.

IPAs may be independently established by community physicians, or the HMO may create an IPA and invite community physicians to participate in it. An IPA may also be hospital based and structured so that only physicians from one or two hospitals are eligible to participate in it (Wagner, 1995). One major disadvantage of the IPA model is that if a contract is lost, the HMO loses a large number of participating physicians.

PPO Plans

PPO plans were created by insurance companies in response to the growth of HMOs. PPOs differentiated themselves by offering out-of-network options for enrollees. By early 1990s, PPOs became more popular and their market share began to exceed that of HMOs.

PPO enrollees can either choose in-network preferred providers with whom the PPO has established contracts, or use physicians and hospitals outside the network. Higher copayments apply for using nonpreferred providers. The additional out-of-pocket expenses largely act as a deterrent to going outside the network for care.

PPOs make discounted fee arrangements with providers. The discounts typically range between 25% and 35% off the providers' regular fees. Negotiated payment arrangements with hospitals can take a variety of forms, such as payments based on diagnosis-related groups, bundled charges for certain services, and discounts. Hence, no direct risk sharing with providers is involved. PPOs also apply fewer restrictions to the care-seeking behavior of enrollees. In most instances, they do not use gatekeeping, which allows enrollees to see specialists without being referred by a primary care physician. Precertification (prospective utilization review) is generally employed only for hospitalization and high-cost outpatient procedures (Robinson, 2002).

Point-of-Service Plans

Point-of-service (POS) plans combine features of classic HMOs with some of the characteristics of patient choice found in PPOs. Through this combination, POS plans overcome the drawback of restricted provider choice but retain the benefits of tight utilization management. Many POS plans are actually offered by HMOs to offer members an optional plan that allows utilization of out-of-network providers. From the consumer's perspective, free choice of providers was a major selling point for POS plans, but after reaching a peak in popularity in 1998–1999, enrollment in POS plans gradually declined mainly because of the high out-of-pocket costs associated with them.

IMPACT ON COST, ACCESS, AND QUALITY

Influence on Cost Containment

Other countries assign the task of cost containment to the government, which controls health care expenditures by budgeting systemwide expenditures (global budgets) and imposing limits on services (supply-side rationing) and payments to providers. In the United States, the primary responsibility for cost containment falls on the private sector, but the government also has pioneered various approaches, mostly aimed at controlling Medicaid and Medicare costs. The private-sector approach to cost containment has involved the expansion of managed care, which has been widely credited for slowing down the rate of growth in health care expenditures during the 1990s. Because of the backlash against managed care, however, between 2001 and 2004, health insurance premiums rose at double-digit annual rates. Since then, growth in premiums has declined consistently each year. This slower growth has been achieved at least partly by shifting costs to the insured through higher cost sharing. Lower costs have also been achieved through MCOs' negotiation of prices with providers and the utilization control measures discussed earlier in this chapter.

Experience with cost containment in public insurance programs has been controversial. Recent studies, for example, do not show any cost savings from such approaches. The Medicare Advantage program has cost more than the traditional fee-for-service Medicare (McGuire et al., 2011). Shifting Medicaid recipients from fee for service into managed care also did not reduce Medicaid spending in the typical state (Duggan & Hayford, 2011).

Impact on Access

Managed care enrollees generally have good access to primary care, preventive services, and health promotion activities (Udvarhelyi et al., 1991). Compared to traditional fee for service, HMO enrollees also experience fewer disparities in health care access and utilization with regard to income, race, and ethnicity (Cook, 2007; DeFrancesco, 2002). Behavioral health carve-outs have also been instrumental in addressing long-standing challenges in access and utilization of behavioral health care (Frank & Garfield, 2007). Some evidence indicates that Medicaid managed care has improved access to health care relative to fee-for-service Medicaid (Coughlin et al., 2008–2009). The elderly and the disabled enrolled in Medicaid managed care are more likely to report being "very satisfied" with their benefits than those in the fee-for-service plan, even though differences in access to care may not be significant (Graham et al., 2011).

Influence on Quality of Care

Despite anecdotes, individual perceptions, and isolated stories propagated by the news media, no comprehensive research to date has clearly demonstrated that the growth of managed care has come at the expense of the quality of care delivered to Americans. Actually, the available evidence points to the opposite conclusion: The quality of health care provided by MCOs has improved over time (Hofmann, 2002). Early detection and treatment are more likely in a managed care plan than in a traditional fee-for-service plan (Riley et al., 1999). Financial pressures do not lead to significant changes in physician behavior because under capitation a physician takes full responsibility for the patient's overall care (Eikel, 2002).

A comprehensive review of the literature by Miller and Luft (2002) concluded that HMO and non-HMO plans provide roughly equal quality of care as measured by a wide range of conditions, diseases, and interventions. At the same time, HMOs lower the use of hospital and other expensive resources. Hence, medical care delivered through managed care plans has been cost-effective. Evidence also suggests that the race, ethnicity, and socioeconomic status of managed care enrollees have little or no effect on the quality of care they receive (Balsa et al., 2007; Brown et al., 2005). Conversely, evaluation of the existing literature does point to lower access and lower enrollee satisfaction ratings for HMO plans compared with non-HMO plans (Miller & Luft, 2002). Also, quality of care may be lower in for-profit health plans compared to nonprofit plans (Himmelstein et al., 1999; Schneider et al., 2005). In addition, quality may not be consistent across all managed care plans. Quality of care may be lower in some managed care plans compared to commercial plans (Landon et al., 2007).

INTEGRATED SYSTEMS

With the rapid growth of managed care, MCOs acquired enormous power. On the other side, the bargaining power of independent health delivery organizations, such as hospitals and clinics, was eroded. Health care organizations also came under growing pressure to reduce costs and deliver services efficiently to populations spread over large geographic areas. It became increasingly more difficult for smaller organizations, such as solo physician practices and small clinics and hospitals, to cope with external pressures and stay profitable. For many health care delivery organizations, integration into networks has been a rational choice for survival. For example, even some large multispecialty physician groups often do not have adequate financial reserves. When managed care contracts are changed, huge blocks of patients may come and go in such practices. Such fluctuations can result in a wild financial roller-coaster ride. Joining an integrated system may help minimize such financial uncertainties (Goldfarb, 1993). Organizational integration occurred in such an environment of uncertainty that accompanied the growth of managed care.

An *integrated delivery system* (IDS) or health network includes several organizations under the same ownership that provide an array of health care services to large communities. Some of these organizations may have alliances with the IDS through formal contracts. A fully integrated health network typically includes the following (DeLuca & Cagan, 1998):

- One or more acute care hospitals
- Outpatient clinics and surgical facilities
- One or more physician group practices
- One or more long-term care facilities
- Home health and hospice services
- Ownership or contract with one or more MCOs

In some communities, IDSs have added women's health centers, specialized cardiac care clinics, and rehabilitation clinics. Cancer centers are a growing area of specialization. Sometimes satellite service centers are opened or mobile delivery programs are instituted to serve smaller communities located outside the IDS's primary market base. In other instances, these large full-service organizations have created their own managed care plans or have directly contracted with large employers to provide one-stop health care services to their employees.

On the one hand, health networks help achieve cost savings through resource sharing and elimination of duplication. On the other hand, these organizational networks tend to become complex and, therefore, difficult to manage. Physician relations, for instance, is one area that many networks are still trying to figure out. In 2010, there were approximately 800 small and large IDSs operating in the United States (Sanofi-Aventis, 2011b).

Accountable Care Organizations

The ACA of 2010 authorized the CMS to implement a national program that involves care delivery to Medicare patients through *accountable care organizations* (ACOs). ACOs are integrated groups of providers—including hospitals, physician group practices, and others—who take responsibility for improving the overall health status, efficiency, and satisfaction with care for a defined population (DeVore & Champion, 2011). The idea of ACOs has been tested in demonstration projects conducted by the CMS. As yet, however, little is known how these organizations might work in actual practice. Nevertheless, the CMS has crafted extensive and complex regulations to promote the formation of ACOs.

The ACA of 2010 also authorized the CMS to develop reimbursement methods that include incentives for reducing cost and improving quality. These regulations have been criticized by the American Hospital Association and the American Medical Association as too burdensome and costly considering the limited incentives that the program offers (Correia, 2011).

TYPES OF INTEGRATION

Integration Based on Major Participants

Physicians and hospitals have been two key participants in the formation of integrated organizations because, in almost all instances, one entity cannot function without the other. Hence, a *physician–hospital organization* (PHO) has been a common type of integrated organization. A PHO is a legal entity that represents an alliance between a hospital and local physicians and combines their services under the aegis of a single organization. It allows both entities to have greater bargaining power in contract negotiations with MCOs. PHO formation is often initiated by the hospital, but it is unlikely to succeed without the participation of the medical staff leaders. PHOs provide the benefits of integration while preserving the independence and autonomy of physicians.

Between 1998 and 2000, the number of hospitals associated with PHOs more than doubled, but the number of PHOs has since shrunk by one-third. The percentage of hospitals with PHOs dropped from 32% in 1995 to less than 23% in 2004 (Taylor, 2006). Many such liaisons failed because of poor management, undercapitalization, and federal scrutiny. However, other models of physician–hospital collaboration appear to be emerging. The ACO (discussed earlier) is one such model.

Integration Based on Type of Ownership or Affiliation

The objectives of organizational integration can be accomplished in ways other than outright ownership. For example, relatively simple cooperative arrangements, sharing of resources, and joint responsibilities through contracts can be established.

Acquisitions and Mergers

Acquisition refers to the purchase of one organization by another. The acquired company ceases to exist as a separate entity and is absorbed under the name of the purchasing corporation. A *merger* involves a mutual agreement to unify two or more organizations into a single entity. The separate assets of two organizations are brought together, typically under a new name. Both former entities cease to exist, and a new corporation is formed.

Small hospitals may merge to gain efficiencies by eliminating the duplication of services. Acquisitions and mergers can also help an organization expand into new geographic markets. A large hospital may acquire smaller hospitals to serve as satellites in a large metropolitan area with sprawling suburbs. A regional health care system may be formed after a large hospital has acquired other hospitals and diversified into services such as outpatient care, long-term care, and rehabilitation.

Joint Ventures

A *joint venture* results when two or more institutions share resources to create a new organization to pursue a common purpose (Pelfrey & Theisen, 1989).

Each of the participants in a joint venture continues to conduct business independently. The new company created by the participants also remains independent. Joint ventures are often used to diversify into new services when the participants can benefit by joining hands rather than competing against each other. For example, hospitals in a given region may engage in a joint venture to form a home health agency that benefits all partners. An acute care hospital, a multispecialty physician group practice, a skilled nursing facility, and an insurer may join to offer a managed care plan (Carson et al., 1995, p. 209). In this scenario, each of the participants would continue to operate its own business, and all would have a common stake in the new HMO or PPO.

Alliances

In one respect, the health care industry is unique because organizations often develop cooperative arrangements with rival providers. Cooperation instead of competition, in some situations, eliminates duplication of services while ensuring that all the health needs of the community are fulfilled (Carson et al., 1995, p. 217). An *alliance* is an agreement between two organizations to share their resources without joint ownership of assets. For example, a hospital may form an alliance with a physician group practice to conduct community health assessments, jointly create programs to minimize health risks, and work to improve the community's health.

Alliances are relatively simpler to form than mergers. An alliance may be a first step that gives both organizations the opportunity to evaluate the advantages of a potential merger. Alliances require little financial commitment and can be easily dissolved if the anticipated benefits do not materialize.

Virtual Organizations

When contractual arrangements between two or more organizations form a new organization, the resulting entity is referred to as a *virtual organization*, or an organization without walls. The formation of a health network based on contractual arrangements is called *virtual integration*. IPAs are a prime example of virtual organizations; a PHO may also be a virtual organization. The main advantage of virtual organizations is that they require less capital to enter new geographic or service markets

(Gabel, 1997). They also help bring together scattered entities under one mutually cooperative arrangement.

Integration Based on Service Consolidation

Horizontal Integration

Horizontal integration is a growth strategy in which a health care organization extends its core product or service. For example, an acute care hospital that adds coronary bypass surgery to its existing surgical services or that builds a suburban acute care facility is integrating horizontally (Rakich et al., 1992, p. 326). Multihospital chains, nursing facility chains, or a chain of drugstores, all under the same management with member facilities offering the same core services or products, are other examples of horizontal integration. The main objective of horizontal integration is to achieve geographic expansion. Diversification into new products or services is not achieved through horizontal integration.

Vertical Integration

Vertical integration links services that are at different stages in the production process of health care—for example, organization of preventive services, primary care, acute care, and postacute service delivery around a hospital. The intended purpose of vertical integration is to increase the comprehensiveness and continuity of care. Vertical integration is a diversification strategy. It may be achieved through acquisitions, mergers, joint ventures, or alliances. Health networks are formed through vertical integration. Vertically integrated regional health systems may be the best-positioned organizations to become the providers of choice for managed care or for direct contracting with self-insured employers (Brown, 1996).

CONCLUSION

Most insured Americans today receive health care through a managed care organization. MCOs have been credited with cost containment in health care, and enrollment in managed care plans has continued to grow in both private and public insurance programs. Remarkably, cost containment has been achieved while the overall quality of health care has been maintained.

Integrated delivery systems emerged as hospitals and physicians, in particular, faced growing pressures from managed care to deliver services at reduced costs. Integration has enabled large health care organizations to win sizable managed care contracts and, in some instances, to offer their own health insurance plans. However, the delivery of health care has become complex from the standpoint of providers and consumers. Integration of physicians into these large organizations has proved particularly challenging. It remains to be seen whether accountable care organizations—a format proposed under the ACA of 2010—will flourish as a new type of organizational entity.

REFERENCES

Balsa A, et al. Does managed health care reduce health care disparities between minorities and whites? *J Health Econ.* 2007;26(1):101–121.

Brown AF, et al. Race, ethnicity, socioeconomic position, and quality of care for adults with diabetes enrolled in managed care. *Diab Care.* 2005;28(12):2864–2870.

Brown M. Mergers, networking, and vertical integration: Managed care and investor-owned hospitals. *Health Care Manage Rev.* 1996;21(1):29–37.

Carson KD, et al. *Management of Healthcare Organizations.* Cincinnati, OH: South-Western College Publishing; 1995.

Centers for Medicare and Medicaid Services (CMS). Managed care trends. 2010. http://www.cms.gov/MedicaidDataSourcesGenInfo/downloads/2010Trends .pdf. Accessed December 2011.

Claxton G, et al. *The Kaiser Family Foundation and Health Research and Educational Trust Employer Health Benefits 2011 Annual Survey.* Menlo Park, CA: Henry J. Kaiser Family Foundation/Chicago, IL: Health Research and Educational Trust; 2011.

Cook BL. Effect of Medicaid managed care on racial disparities in health care access. *Health Serv Res.* 2007;42(1 Pt 1):124–145.

Correia EW. Accountable care organizations: The proposed regulations and the prospects for success. *Am J Managed Care.* 2011;17(8):560–568.

Coughlin TA, et al. Does managed care improve access to care for Medicaid beneficiaries with disabilities? A national study. *Inquiry.* 2008–2009;45(4):395–407.

DeFrancesco LB. HMO enrollees experience fewer disparities than older insured populations. *Findings Brief: Health Care Financing & Organization.* 2002;5(2):1–2.

DeLuca JM, Cagan RE. The integrated delivery system. In *CEO's Guide to Health Care Information Systems.* Chicago: Health Forum; 1998:35–46.

DeVore S, Champion RW. Driving population health through accountable care organizations. *Health Affairs.* 2011;30(1):41–50.

Duggan M, Hayford T. *Has the Shift to Managed Care Reduced Medicaid Expenditures? Evidence from State and Local-Level Mandates.* Working Paper No. 17236. National Bureau of Economic Research; 2011.

Eikel CV. Fewer patient visits under capitation offset by improved quality of care: Study brings evidence to debate over physician payment methods. *Findings Brief: Health Care Financing & Organization.* 2002;5(3):1–2.

Frank RG, Garfield RL. Managed behavioral health care carve-outs: Past performance and future prospects. *Ann Rev Public Health.* 2007;28(1):303–320.

Gabel J. Ten ways HMOs have changed during the 1990s. *Health Affairs.* 1997;16(3):134–145.

Goldfarb B. Corporate health care mergers. *Med World News.* 1993;34(2):26–34.

Graham CL, et al. Fee-for-service and managed care for seniors and people with disabilities on Medicaid: Implications for the managed care mandate in California. *J Health Care Poor Underserved.* 2011;22(4):1413–1423.

Henry J. Kaiser Family Foundation. What's in the starts? Quality ratings of Medicare Advantage Plans, 2010. 2009. http://www.kff.org/medicare/upload/8025.pdf. Accessed January 2012.

Henry J. Kaiser Family Foundation. Fact sheet: Medicare Advantage. 2011. http://www.kff.org/medicare/upload/2052-15.pdf. Accessed January 2012.

Himmelstein D, et al. Quality of care in investor-owned vs not-for-profit HMOs. *JAMA.* 1999;282(2):159–163.

Hofmann MA. Quality of health care improving. *Bus Insurance.* 2002;36(38):1–2.

Iglehart JK. The American health care system: Managed care. *The Nation's Health,* 4th ed., edited by Lee PR, Estes CL. Sudbury, MA: Jones and Bartlett; 1994:231–237.

Kongstvedt PR. Managing hospital utilization. In *Essentials of Managed Health Care,* edited by Kongstvedt PR. Gaithersburg, MD: Aspen Publishers; 1995:121–135.

Landon BE, et al. Quality of care in Medicaid managed care and commercial health plans. *JAMA.* 2007;298(14):1674–1681.

McGuire TG, et al. An economic history of Medicare Part C. *Milbank Quarterly.* 2011;89(2):289–332.

Miller RH, Luft HS. HMO plan performance update: An analysis of the literature, 1997–2001. *Health Affairs.* 2002;21(4):63–86.

Moscovice I, et al. Expanding rural managed care: Enrollment patterns and perspectives. *Health Affairs.* 1998;17(1):172–179.

Pelfrey S, Theisen BA. Joint venture in health care. *J Nurs Admin.* 1989;19(4):39–42.

Rakich JS, et al. *Managing Health Services Organizations*, 3rd ed. Baltimore, MD: Health Professions Press; 1992.

Riley GF, et al. Stage at diagnosis and treatment patterns among older women with breast cancer. *JAMA.* 1999;281:720–726.

Robinson JC. Renewed emphasis on consumer cost sharing in health insurance benefit design. *Health Affairs Web Exclusives.* 2002;W139–W154.

Sanofi-Aventis. *Managed Care Digest Series, 2011–2012: HMO-PPO Digest.* Bridgewater, NJ: Sanofi-Aventis US; 2011a.

Sanofi-Aventis. *Managed Care Digest Series, 2011–2012: Hospitals/Systems Digest.* Bridgewater, NJ: Sanofi-Aventis US; 2011b.

Sanofi-Aventis. *Managed Care Digest Series, 2011–2012: Public Payer Digest.* Bridgewater, NJ: Sanofi-Aventis US; 2011c.

Schneider EC, et al. Quality of care in for-profit and not-for-profit health plans enrolling Medicare beneficiaries. *Am J Med.* 2005;118(12):1392–1400.

Taylor M. Revival of the fittest. *Mod Healthcare.* 2006;36(26):24–26.

Udvarhelyi IS, et al. Comparison of the quality of ambulatory care for fee-for-service and prepaid patients. *Ann Intern Med.* 1991;115(5):394–400.

Wagner ER. Types of managed care organizations. In *Essentials of Managed Health Care,* edited by Kongstvedt PR. Gaithersburg, MD: Aspen Publishers; 1995:24–34.

Wilson FA, Neuhauser D. *Health Services in the United States*, 2nd ed. Cambridge, MA: Ballinger Publishing; 1985.

Chapter 10

Long-term Care Services

INTRODUCTION

Long-term care (LTC) is often associated with the care provided in
nursing homes (skilled nursing facilities, subacute care facilities, and specialized care facilities). That is actually a rather narrow view, because
LTC services are also provided in a variety of community-based settings.
Indeed, most LTC in the United States is provided informally by family
and friends, who receive no payment for their time and effort. Perhaps
more than 7 million Americans provide informal care to more than 4 million elderly persons with functional limitations. The economic value of
such care may be as high as $96 billion per year (O'Keeffe & Siebenaler,
2006). It is also estimated that two of five elderly LTC users rely solely on
informal care (Alecxih, 2001). Also, older people who have close access to
family or surrogates (such as neighbors, friends, and church or other community organizations) often continue to live in the community much longer

than those who do not have such support. Social support networks have a positive effect on physical and mental functioning status and forestall institutionalization (Wan & Weissert, 1981).

LTC includes a variety of services, such as care provided in a nursing home, home health care brought to a person's own home, home-delivered meals, and minimal assistance provided in residential settings such as foster care homes and board-and-care facilities. Also, contrary to common belief, LTC is not confined to the elderly, although the elderly are the predominant users of these services, and this chapter focuses on the elderly as the primary clients of LTC. Most older adults, however, do not need LTC services. In fact, most elderly persons are physically and mentally healthy enough to live independently. In 2009, only 24% of elderly Americans assessed their own health status as fair to poor, down from 26.9% in 2000 (Department of Health and Human Services, 2011, pp. 225).

Nevertheless, the aging process leads to chronic, degenerative conditions that resist cure. Hence, older people collectively use a disproportionately large share of total health care services. Although people older than age 65 represent only about 13% of the U.S. population, this group accounts for one-third of all national health care spending and occupies one-half of all physician time. Hence, utilization of health care services is much higher among older adults than among younger persons. This means that as people grow older, the odds increase that they will require LTC. It also means that LTC cannot be an isolated component of the health care delivery system, but rather non-LTC services must be closely integrated with those of LTC. To address the total health care needs of LTC patients, the delivery system must allow ease of transition among various types of health care settings and services.

Chronic conditions are the leading cause of illness, disability, and death in the United States today. *Chronic conditions* are characterized by persistent and recurring health consequences lasting over a long period, which are generally irreversible. Arthritis, diabetes, asthma, heart disease, and dementia are some examples of chronic conditions, but a person's age or the mere presence of a chronic condition does not predict the need for LTC. However, as a person ages, chronic ailments, *comorbidity* (multiple health problems), disability, and dependency tend to follow each other, depending on the individual's lifestyle and compliance with medical directives. This progression increases the probability that a person will need LTC (**Figure 10.1**).

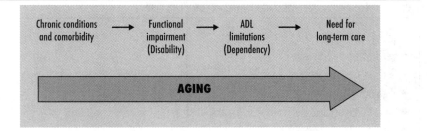

Figure 10.1   Progressive Steps Toward the Need for Long-term Care Among the Elderly. ADL: activity of daily living; LTC: long-term care.
Adapted from Singh DA. *Effective Management of Long-Term Care Facilities.* 2nd ed. Sudbury, MA: Jones and Bartlett; 2010: 13.

The elderly population in the United States continues to grow, and between 2000 and 2020 the number of Americans with chronic conditions is projected to increase from 125 million (45% of the population) to 157 million (48% of the population) [Partnership for Solutions, 2002]. The number of Americans who suffer from multiple chronic conditions is projected to rise to 81 million (25% of the population) by 2020 (Anderson, 2003). In addition, with the aging of the baby boom generation, the number of people 70 years of age and older needing LTC is expected to increase from 10 million in 2000 to 15 million in 2020 and then to 21 million in 2030 (National Academy on an Aging Society, 2000). Although the rate of institutionalization among the elderly has been falling, this trend is likely to reverse itself within the next decade. Rising levels of obesity and diabetes suggest that the need for nursing home care will increase in the future (Lakdawalla et al., 2003). The rest of the developed world also faces aging-related problems and challenges in providing adequate LTC services very similar to those in the United States.

WHAT IS LTC?

LTC can be defined as a variety of individualized, well-coordinated services that promote the maximum possible independence for people with functional limitations and are provided over an extended period of time in accordance with a holistic approach, while maximizing their quality of life.

Exhibit 10.1   Seven Essential Characteristics of Long-term Care

- It includes a variety of health care services.
- Services are individualized.
- Services must be well coordinated.
- The goal is to promote maximum possible functional independence.
- Services are needed over an extended period of time.
- Patients' physical, mental, social, and spiritual needs must be met.
- Patients' quality of life must be maximized.

The seven essential characteristics of LTC are summarized in **Exhibit 10.1** and are explained in this section.

A Variety of Health Care Services

LTC clients need a variety of services for two main reasons:

- A variety of services is necessary because the need for services varies greatly from individual to individual. Even the elderly, who are the predominant users of LTC services, are not a homogeneous group. For example, some people just require supportive housing, whereas others require intensive treatments. Hence, LTC includes services such as housing programs, transportation, case management, recreation, nutrition, and various types of social support services.

- Even for the same individual, the need for the various types of services generally changes over time. Such change is not necessarily progressive, developing from lighter to more intensive levels of care. Depending on the change in condition and functioning, the individual may shift back and forth between the various levels and types of LTC services. For example, after hip surgery, a patient may require extensive rehabilitation therapy in a nursing facility for 2 or 3 weeks before returning home, where he or she receives continuing care from a home health agency. After that, the individual may continue to live independently but require a daily meal from Meals on Wheels. Later, this same person may suffer a stroke and after hospitalization have to stay indefinitely in an LTC facility.

LTC clients often require non-LTC services, such as primary care and acute care. Hence, LTC is not a self-contained system of comprehensive health care services, nor can it function independently of primary, acute, mental health, and ancillary services such as pharmaceuticals and diagnostics.

LTC must also include both therapeutic and preventive services. The primary goal of preventive services is to prevent or delay the need for institutionalization in LTC facilities. Preventive measures call for ensuring that the elderly receive good nutrition and have access to preventive medical care. For example, older adults must have access to services such as vaccination against pneumonia, annual flu shots, glaucoma screening, diabetes screening, and cancer screening.

For those elderly persons who live independently, certain social support programs also serve a preventive function. Programs such as homemaker, chore, and handyman services can assist with a variety of tasks that older adults may no longer be able to perform. Examples include shopping, light cleaning, general errands, lawn maintenance, and minor home repairs.

Individualized Services

An assessment of the patient's physical, mental, and emotional condition and past medical and social history, former occupation, leisure activities, and cultural factors is used to determine which services would be most suitable for the individual. An individualized plan of care is developed, and services are rendered according to that plan.

Coordination of Services

The mere availability of a spectrum of services may not be sufficient to meet the varied and changing needs of LTC clients unless those services are well coordinated. As it is, many people find the health care delivery system difficult to navigate. Such difficulties are often compounded in the case of elderly and disabled individuals. For example, acute episodes, such as pneumonia, bone fracture, or stroke, require admission to a general hospital. Many acute care services are now delivered in a variety of outpatient settings instead of hospitals. After acute care delivery, a patient may be transferred to a hospital-based transitional care unit for intensive rehabilitation. The patient may subsequently have to be moved to an LTC facility for ongoing care. Depression may create a need to visit an outpatient mental health clinic. The same individual may also require dental or optometric care.

Maximum Possible Functional Independence

LTC becomes necessary when there is a noticeable decline in an individual's ability to perform certain common tasks of daily living. Among children, disabilities requiring LTC can result from birth defects, brain damage, or mental retardation. Younger adults may lose functional capacity as a result of an accident or a crippling disease such as multiple sclerosis. Among the elderly, complications from chronic disease or acute episodes can lead to functional impairment and, therefore, the need for LTC. Adaptive devices, such as walkers, wheelchairs, special utensils, and many other types of equipment and modification of the living environment with safety features such as grab bars, can enable many individuals to continue to live independently. However, as dependency increases, the need for LTC services also increases (see Figure 10.1).

Two standard measures are used to determine a person's level of dependency. The first one is the activities of daily living (ADL) scale, which is used to assess a person's ability to perform certain common tasks referred to as *activities of daily living* (see **Exhibit 10.2**). Severe ADL limitations often indicate the need for institutional care. The second measure is the *instrumental activities of daily living* (IADL) scale. It incorporates activities that are necessary for living independently in the community, such as using the telephone, driving a car or traveling alone by bus or taxi, shopping, preparing meals, doing light housework, taking medicine, and handling money.

Exhibit 10.2   Activities of Daily Living

The classic ADL scale includes six basic activities:
- Eating
- Bathing
- Dressing
- Using a toilet
- Maintaining bowel and bladder control
- Transferring, such as getting out of bed and moving into a chair
Sometimes grooming and walking a distance of 8 feet are also included in the scale.

Exhibit 10.3   Progression of Long-term Care Intensity

- Independent living
- Decline in IADLs
  - Informal care for those who have adequate social support
  - Informal care supplemented by paid community-based services
- Decline in ADLs
  - For light ADLs (eating, dressing, using a toilet), informal care with supplemental services may continue
  - Institutionalization

IADLs are not generally used in institutional settings because institutionalized persons are not required to perform many IADLs (Ostir et al., 1999). It is estimated that approximately 40% of the elderly have some functional limitations associated with ADLs or IADLs (National Academy on an Aging Society, 2000). The progression of LTC intensity is illustrated in **Exhibit 10.3**.

The main goal of LTC is to enable the individual to maintain functional independence to the maximum level that is practicable. Restoration of function may be possible to some extent through appropriate rehabilitation therapy, but in most cases a full restoration of normal functioning is an unrealistic expectation. Caregivers must render care and assistance wherever the patient is either unable to do things for himself or herself or absolutely refuses to do so. The focus should be on maintaining whatever functional ability the patient still has and on preventing further decline of that ability. Caregivers should motivate and help patients do as much as possible for themselves.

Extended Period of Time

Compared to acute care, LTC is sustained over a longer period of time. The period of care and institutional stays, when needed, generally extend to weeks, months, and years instead of days. Even when institutional LTC is indicated for a short period (90 or fewer days), LTC services may continue in the patient's own home after the patient has been discharged from a long-term care facility. At other times, long-range confinement to a nursing home may be necessary.

Holistic Approach

The holistic model of health focuses not merely on a person's physical and mental needs, but also emphasizes well-being in every aspect of what makes a person whole and complete. A patient's physical, mental, social, and spiritual needs and preferences are incorporated into medical care delivery and the living environment. The following are brief descriptions of the four aspects of holistic caregiving:

1. Physical. The physical aspect refers to the technical aspects of care, such as medical examination, nursing care, medications, diet, and rehabilitation treatments. It also includes comfort factors such as appropriate temperature and cozy furnishings, cleanliness, and safety in home and institutional environments.

2. Mental. The emphasis with mental care is on the total mental and emotional well-being of each individual. Such care may include treatment of mental and behavioral problems, if necessary. Maintaining mental health goes beyond diagnosis and treatment of mental conditions, however. In an institutional setting, it includes appropriate layout, décor, and techniques that help overcome disorientation and confusion; mental stimulation to help overcome boredom and depression; and an environment that promotes positive feelings. For example, the living atmosphere can be enhanced through live plants, flowers, moving water, pleasant aromas, and soothing music. Pet animals, fish in aquariums, and birds create a vibrant living environment.

3. Social. Almost everyone enjoys warm friendships and social relationships. Visits from family, friends, or volunteers provide numerous opportunities for socializing. Many nursing homes have created indoor and outdoor spaces such as game rooms, alcoves, balconies, and patios where people can sit and enjoy one another's company.

4. Spiritual. The spiritual dimension operates at an individual level. It includes personal beliefs, values, and commitments in a religious and faith context. Spirituality and spiritual pursuits are very personal matters, but for most people, they also require continuing interaction with other members of their faith community.

Quality of Life

Quality of life refers to the total living experience that results in overall satisfaction with one's life. It is particularly relevant to LTC facilities because people typically reside there for an extended period. Quality of life factors include lifestyle pursuits, living environment, clinical palliation, and human factors:

- Lifestyle factors are associated with personal enrichment and making one's life meaningful through enjoyable activities. For example, many older people still enjoy pursuing their former leisure activities, such as woodworking, crocheting, knitting, gardening, and fishing.

- The living environment must be comfortable, safe, and appealing to the senses. Cleanliness, décor, furnishings, and other aesthetic features are important.

- Clinical *palliation* should be available to provide relief from unpleasant symptoms such as pain or nausea, for instance, when a patient is undergoing chemotherapy.

- Human factors refer to caregiver attitudes and practices that emphasize caring, compassion, and the preservation of human dignity for the patient. Institutionalized patients generally find it disconcerting to have lost their autonomy and independence. Quality of life is enhanced when residents have some latitude to govern their own lives. Residents in long-term care facilities also desire an environment that gives them adequate privacy.

COMMUNITY-BASED LONG-TERM CARE SERVICES

Community-based LTC services have four objectives: (1) to deliver LTC in the most economical and least restrictive setting whenever appropriate for the patient's health care needs, (2) to supplement informal caregiving when more advanced skills are needed to address the patient's needs, (3) to provide temporary respite to family members from caregiving stress, and (4) to delay or prevent institutionalization. These goals are accomplished through an administrative network that includes the Federal Administration on Aging, State Units on Aging, and Area Agencies on Aging. Nationally, more than 600 Area Agencies on Aging administer funds appropriated by the U.S. federal government under the Older Americans Act of 1965.

For the financially needy, Title III of the Older Americans Act may finance such community-based services as adult day care, home maintenance, health promotion and disease prevention (e.g., medication management, nutrition, and health screening), telephone reassurance, and transportation services. States may also have some federal funds available under Title XX Social Services Block Grants. In addition, community-based LTC services have grown under the Home and Community Based Services waiver program that was enacted under Section 1915(c) of the Social Security Act. Medicare and Medicaid may partially cover certain LTC services; the remainder must be covered by individual savings and private donations.

Home Health Care

Home health care refers to health care provided in the home of the patient by health care professionals. The organizational setup commonly requires a hospital-based or freestanding home health agency that sends health care professionals and paraprofessionals (such as home care aides) to patients' homes to deliver services approved by a physician. In 2009, more than 10,500 Medicare-certified home health agencies were in operation in the United States. Of these, 13% were affiliated with an institution such as a hospital or nursing facility (National Association of Home Care and Hospice, 2010).

Home health services typically include nursing care, such as changing dressings, monitoring medications, and providing help with bathing; short-term rehabilitation, such as physical, occupational, and speech therapy; homemaker services, such as meal preparation, shopping, transportation, and some specific household chores; and certain medical supplies and equipment, such as ostomy supplies, hospital beds, oxygen tanks, walkers, and wheelchairs. Not all home health agencies provide all of these services, however.

As the largest single payer for home health services, Medicare paid for 41% of home health expenditures in the United States in 2008 (National Center for Health Statistics, 2011). To qualify for home care under the Medicare program, patients must (1) be homebound, (2) have a plan of treatment that is periodically reviewed by a physician, and (3) require intermittent or part-time skilled nursing and/or rehabilitation therapies.

Medicaid payments for home care are divided into three main categories: the traditional home health benefit, which is a federally mandated service provided by all states, and two optional programs, the personal care option and home- and community-based waivers. Together, services under these three programs represent a relatively small but growing portion of total Medicaid payments. In 2008, Medicaid paid for 35% of home health expenditures (Department of Health and Human Services, 2011).

Adult Day Care

Adult day care is a daytime, community-based, group program that is designed to meet the needs of functionally and/or cognitively impaired adults and to provide a partial respite to family caregivers. Such care is designed for people who live with their families, but because of physical or mental conditions cannot remain alone during the day when the family members are working.

Three main types of adult day centers have emerged: (1) social, which provide meals, recreation, and some health-related services; (2) medical/health, which provide social activities as well as more intensive clinical and therapeutic services; and (3) specialized, which provide specialized services such as dementia care or care for those persons with developmental disabilities (dysfunctions that begin in early childhood and are often accompanied by diminished mental capacity). According to the National Adult Day Services Association, nearly 50% of adult day care participants have some level of dementia. In 2009, there were 4,600 adult day care centers across the United States, a 35% increase since 2002 (MetLife Mature Market Institute, 2010).

Adult Foster Care

Adult foster care is defined as a service characterized by small, family-run homes providing room, board, oversight, and personal care to nonrelated adults who are unable to care for themselves ("AARP Studies Adult Foster Care," 1996). Foster care generally provides services in a community-based dwelling in an environment that promotes the feeling of being part of a family unit (Stahl, 1997). Participants in these programs are elderly or disabled individuals who require assistance with one or two ADLs, and many of the residents have a psychiatric diagnosis.

Typically, the caregiving family resides in part of the home. To maintain the family environment, most states license fewer than 10 beds per family unit. Each state has established its own standards for licensing foster care homes. As states have continued to shift Medicaid funds from institutional to community-based services, adult foster care use has grown. Medicare does not pay for services provided by the adult foster care home, but may cover rehabilitation services.

Senior Centers

Senior centers are local community centers for older adults where seniors can congregate and socialize. Many centers serve a noon meal daily. Others sponsor wellness programs, health education, counseling services, recreational activities, information and referral, and some limited health care services. Health care services typically offered at senior centers include health screening, especially for glaucoma and hypertension.

Approximately 11,000 senior centers have been established across the United States, serving 1 million older adults every day. To maintain operations, senior centers rely on a variety of public and private sources of funding from various branches of government, businesses, donations, and volunteer hours (National Council on Aging, 2011).

Home-delivered and Congregate Meals

The Elderly Nutrition Program operates under the U.S. Administration on Aging and serves congregate meals in senior centers and home-delivered meals to those elderly persons who want to stay at home. The main goal of this program is to improve the dietary intake of older Americans. The program generally provides one hot noon meal for 5 days a week to people aged 60 and older (and their spouses) who are unable to prepare a nutritionally balanced noon meal for themselves.

Home-delivered meals for homebound persons are commonly referred to as Meals on Wheels. With this service, meals are prepared by local institutions and delivered by volunteers. The volunteers also offer an important opportunity to check on the welfare of homebound elderly and are encouraged to report any health or other problems that they may notice during their visits.

Homemaker and Handyman Services

Some older adults are relatively healthy but cannot carry out a few simple tasks necessary for independent living. These tasks may be as urgent as repairing a burst plumbing pipe or as mundane as cleaning the house. Some tasks, such as grocery shopping, must be performed often, whereas others, such as replacing storm windows, require attention just once or twice a year. Homemaker, household chore, and handyman services can assist older adults with a variety of such tasks, including shopping, light cleaning, general errands, and minor home repairs. Homemaker programs may be staffed largely or entirely by volunteers.

Emergency Response Systems

A personal emergency response system (PERS), also called a medical emergency response system, consists of an electronic device that enables people to summon help in an emergency. This kind of system is specifically designed for disabled or elderly people who live alone and may not otherwise need ongoing medical or supportive care. Other patients, after returning home from hospitals and nursing homes, are plagued by anxiety about relapses or accidents because they are often unprepared for self-management after returning home. Usually they either wear or carry a transmitter unit that enables them to send a medical alert to a 24-hour monitoring and response center. The system is available for a reasonable fee.

Case Management

In the LTC context, *case management* refers to a method of linking, managing, and coordinating services to meet the varied and changing health care needs of elderly clients (Zawadski & Eng, 1988). Case management services assess the special needs of older adults, formulate a care plan to address those needs, identify which services are most appropriate, determine eligibility for services, make referrals and coordinate delivery of care, arrange for financing, and ensure that clients are receiving services in accordance with the plan of care. Case managers often assist the adult children of disabled elderly persons who may be living far from each other.

INSTITUTIONAL LONG-TERM CARE

Generally, institutional LTC is more appropriate for patients whose needs cannot be adequately met in a less clinical, community-based setting. However, a variety of institutional options are available to meet the

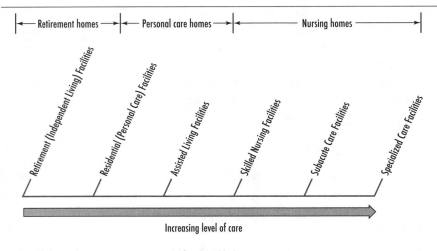

Figure 10.2   Long-term Care Institutions for the Elderly

varying needs of the elderly who no longer can live alone safely. Available options today include retirement centers, residential or personal care facilities, assisted living facilities, and nursing homes. These facilities provide varying levels of assistance.

An evaluation of the extent of functional impairment often determines which services are best suited to the individual, but personal preferences, and often the availability of financing, also play a significant role. Most people prefer to receive care in their own home, and when institutionalization becomes necessary, they prefer a home-like, nonclinical setting. Nevertheless, medical needs must often override personal preferences, especially when severe physical or mental problems develop. **Figure 10.2** illustrates, on a continuum, six types of elder care institutions that can be classified under three general categories: retirement homes, personal care homes, and nursing homes. Continuing-care retirement communities (CCRCs) offer all three options within one campus-like setting. Based on the concept of aging-in-place, CCRCs can address people's changing needs.

Retirement Facilities

Retirement facilities do not deliver nursing care services but emphasize privacy, security, independence, and active lifestyles. Some basic personal care such as assistance with bathing may be available in some retirement facilities, but in most instances, when additional nursing or rehabilitation services are needed, arrangements are made with a local home health agency.

The special features and amenities in retirement facilities are designed to create a physically supportive environment that promotes independence. For example, the living quarters are equipped with emergency call systems. Many facilities provide monthly blood pressure and vision screenings. Most organize programs for socializing, physical fitness, recreation, and local outings for shopping and entertainment. Some basic hotel services, such as one meal a day and periodic housekeeping, are generally provided. Apartment units or detached cottages equipped with kitchenettes and private baths are the most common types of retirement facilities. Common laundry rooms are often shared with other residents. Many upscale retirement centers abound, in which one can expect to pay a fairly substantial entrance fee plus a monthly rental or maintenance fee. At the other end of the income scale, many communities have government-subsidized housing units for the low-income elderly and disabled individuals.

Personal Care Facilities

Personal care can be defined as nonmedical custodial care. *Custodial care* is confined to basic assistance provided in a protected environment and does not include active medical or rehabilitative treatments.

Facilities providing personal care may be called by different names, such as domiciliary care facilities, board-and-care homes, foster care homes, residential care facilities, or personal care facilities. These facilities provide physically supportive dwelling units, monitoring and/or assistance with medications, oversight, and light assistance with certain ADLs such as bathing and grooming. To maintain a residential rather than an institutional environment, many such facilities limit the admission of residents who use wheelchairs. Most of these facilities are relatively small and can be viewed as community-based alternatives rather than institutions. Staff members are mostly nursing paraprofessionals, such as personal care aides, who do not require a license or professional certification to deliver care. Similar workers employed in nursing homes must be certified by the state.

Assisted Living Facilities

An assisted living facility is generally described as a residential setting that provides personal care services, 24-hour supervision, scheduled and unscheduled assistance, social activities, and some nursing care services (Citro & Hermanson, 1999). The most common areas of assistance with ADLs are bathing, dressing, and toileting. The majority of residents also require help with medications. Some facilities maintain a skeleton staff of licensed nurses, generally licensed practical nurses (LPNs; referred to as licensed vocational nurses [LVNs] in some states), to do admission assessments and deliver basic nursing care. Hence, these facilities can be classified on the LTC continuum somewhere between personal care homes and nursing homes. Advanced nursing care and rehabilitation therapies can be arranged through a home health agency. Approximately one-third of the residents are discharged because their functional status has declined to the extent that they need a higher level of services, which are provided in skilled nursing facilities (National Center for Assisted Living, 2006).

Skilled Nursing Facilities

A skilled nursing facility provides a full range of clinical LTC services, from skilled nursing care to rehabilitation to assistance with all ADLs. *Skilled nursing care* is medically oriented care provided by a licensed nurse. The plan of treatment is authorized by a physician. The majority of direct care with ADLs is delivered by paraprofessionals, such as certified nursing assistants and therapy assistants, but under the supervision of licensed nurses and therapists.

A variety of disabilities, including problems with ambulation, incontinence, and behavior, often coexist among a relatively large number of patients in need of skilled care. Compared to other types of facilities, these nursing homes have a significant number of patients who are cognitively impaired because of confusion, delirium, or dementia. The social functioning of many of the patients in such facilities is also in severe decline.

Licensed professionals who work in skilled care facilities include registered nurses (RNs), licensed practical/vocational nurses (LPNs/LVNs), and registered therapists (physical therapists, occupational therapists, respiratory therapists, and speech/language pathologists). Rehabilitation is often an important component of skilled care, as are therapeutic diets and nutritional supplements. The patient's assessment requires multidisciplinary input from various health care professionals, and the plan of care is highly individualized.

Subacute Care Facilities

Subacute care is a blend of intensive medical, nursing, and other services that are technically complex and provided in an LTC setting. Examples include wound care, intravenous therapy, blood transfusion, ventilator support, and AIDS care. Subacute care is a substitute for services that were previously provided in acute care hospitals; its popularity has grown because it represents a cheaper alternative to a hospital stay. The severity of a patient's condition often requires active physician contact, professional nursing care, rehabilitative services, and the involvement of a multidisciplinary team of caregivers (National Subacute Care Association, 1996).

Subacute care generally follows hospitalization and is required for a relatively short period of time, such as between 20 and 90 days. Services are available in three main settings:

1. Long-term care hospitals (LTCHs), according to federal regulations, must be certified as acute care hospitals and must have an average length of stay greater than 25 days.
2. Many skilled nursing facilities have opened subacute care units by raising the staff skill mix by hiring additional RNs and having therapists on staff.
3. Some subacute-type services are rendered by community-based home health agencies. Thanks to new technology, certain subacute services can be provided in a patient's own home.

Specialized Care Facilities

By their very nature, both subacute care and specialized care place high emphasis on medical and nursing services. Some skilled nursing facilities have opened specialized care units for patients requiring ventilator care, wound care, services for Alzheimer's disease, intensive rehabilitation, or closed head trauma care. Other freestanding facilities have chosen a niche, specializing only in Alzheimer's care, rehabilitation, or AIDS care.

LICENSING AND CERTIFICATION OF NURSING HOMES

Nursing homes are heavily regulated through licensure and certification requirements. In the United States, it is illegal to operate a nursing facility without a license. To serve Medicare and/or Medicaid beneficiaries, a facility must be certified by the federal government.

Licensing

Every state requires nursing homes to be licensed by the state. Annual renewal of a license is required for existing nursing homes. To keep their licenses in good standing, it is essential that facilities comply with the state's standards for nursing homes. These standards vary from state to state, except for national fire safety regulations. The Life Safety Code, published by the National Fire Protection Association, encompasses national building and fire safety rules that have become a part of licensure standards. In addition, each state has crafted basic standards for nursing care and other services. Compliance with standards is verified through periodic inspections, generally once a year. A state's department (board or division) of health or department of human services generally has nursing home licensing and oversight responsibilities.

Certification

The Centers for Medicare and Medicaid Services (CMS), an agency of the U.S. Department of Health and Human Services, is responsible for certifying a nursing home that wants to serve Medicaid and/or Medicare clients. To be certified, a nursing home must first be licensed by the state. Thus, licensure and certification serve different purposes. A license allows a facility to operate and do business, whereas certification allows a nursing home to admit patients who are on public assistance. It is possible for a facility to have only a license, but in that case, it cannot receive payments from Medicaid or Medicare.

Three distinct federal certification categories exist, and facilities in all three categories are generically referred to as nursing homes:

1. SNF certification allows a facility to admit patients whose care is financed by Medicare; Medicare pays for postacute skilled care only after a patient has stayed in a hospital for a minimum of 3 days, not

counting the day of discharge. The maximum coverage in an SNF-certified facility is 100 days, but in actual practice the average length of stay is much shorter. This is due to complex Medicare rules that the facility must use for determining length of stay. Also, Medicare pays the full cost of skilled nursing care only for the first 20 days; the beneficiary must pay a substantial copayment ($144.50 per day in 2012) for days 21 through 100.

2. NF certification allows a facility to admit patients whose care is financed by Medicaid. Unlike Medicare, Medicaid is a comprehensive health care program that allows patients to stay in an NF-certified nursing home indefinitely as long as the patient's physician authorizes the need for nursing care and the patient qualifies for Medicaid assistance. The beneficiary is required to turn over most of his or her monthly income to the facility; Medicaid pays the remaining costs. Many patients are initially admitted to a facility with a private-pay source of funding. When their private funds are exhausted, these patients generally become eligible for Medicaid assistance.

3. Intermediate care facility for the mentally retarded (ICF/MR) certification allows a nursing facility to serve patients who are mentally retarded/developmentally disabled. Developmental disability is a physical incapacity that generally accompanies mental retardation and often arises at birth or in early childhood. These institutions provide specialized programming and care modules for patients suffering from mental retardation and associated disabilities. The reimbursement is derived mostly from Medicaid.

Certification is granted on the basis of compliance with federal standards. The same standards apply to both SNF and NF certifications, but different standards apply to ICF/MR certification. A facility may be dually certified as both an SNF and an NF. Facilities having dual certification can admit Medicare and/or Medicaid patients to any part of the facility.

The small number of facilities that have elected not to be certified can admit only those patients who have a private source of funding for nursing home care. Such private-pay patients—those not covered by either Medicare or Medicaid for long-term nursing home care—are not restricted to noncertified facilities, however. In most certified nursing homes, private-pay patients are placed alongside those who depend on Medicare and Medicaid.

OTHER LONG-TERM CARE SERVICES

Respite Care

Family caregivers often experience physical and emotional problems. Caregiving responsibilities can ignite family conflicts and encroach on caregivers' employment and leisure activities. Under these circumstances, many caregivers experience stress and burnout. *Respite care* enables family caregivers to take some time off to deal with their feelings of stress and ease their burden. Virtually any kind of LTC service—adult day care, home health care, and temporary institutionalization—can be viewed as respite care as long as the focus is on giving informal caregivers some time off while meeting disabled persons' needs for assistance (Doty et al., 1996).

Restorative Care

Restorative care or rehabilitation refers to therapeutic interventions designed to help patients regain or improve function. Restorative rehabilitation involves intensive short-term treatments rendered by physical therapists, occupational therapists, and speech/language pathologists. Example of persons requiring rehabilitation therapy include individuals who have experienced orthopedic surgery, stroke, limb amputation, and prolonged illness. Rehabilitation is based on the philosophy of caregiving in which patients are viewed as participants who can reach their maximum potential in physical and mental functioning.

Hospice Care

Approaches to terminal illness and death with the objective of maintaining the patient's dignity and comfort have received increased attention in the delivery of health care. Roughly 75% of all deaths occur at age 65 or older. Among the elderly, 35% of all deaths are related to heart disease, and 22% are related to cancer. Other diseases that are often fatal to the elderly are cerebrovascular disease (stroke), chronic obstructive pulmonary disease, diabetes, pneumonia, and influenza (Sahyoun et al., 2001). Hence, dealing with death and dying is very much a part of LTC.

End-of-life care is commonly associated with *hospice*, a cluster of comprehensive services for terminally ill persons who have a life expectancy of six months or less. Hospice is a method of care, not a location, although some freestanding hospice facilities have been established. Hospice can be a part of home health care when the services are provided in the patient's home. In other instances, hospice services are taken to patients in nursing homes, retirement centers, or hospitals.

NURSING HOME INDUSTRY AND EXPENDITURES

During the past several years, the number of nursing homes, bed capacity, and the number of residents in U.S. nursing homes have continued to decline (**Table 10.1**). This downward trend largely reflects the growth of community-based LTC alternatives and other institutional options. For example, home health care and assisted living facilities have experienced remarkable growth and popularity. The need for various types of LTC services will continue to increase given a growing population with chronic conditions, comorbidities, and subsequent disability, but with increased life span.

The nursing home industry in the United States is dominated by private for-profit nursing home chains. Chain nursing homes are members of a group of nursing homes operated under a corporate ownership. According to the last National Nursing Home Survey (2004), approximately 54% of

Table 10.1 Nursing Home Trends (Selected Years).

	2000	2005	2009
Number of nursing homes	16,886	15,995	15,700
Number of beds	1,795,388	1,724,582	1,705,808
Average beds per nursing home	106	108	109
Number of residents	1,480,076	1,436,442	1,401,718
Occupancy rate*	82.4%	83.3%	82.2%

*Percentage of beds occupied (number of residents per 100 beds). These data do not include long-term care facilities that are not classified as nursing homes (Figure 10.2).
Data from National Center for Health Statistics. *Health, United States, 2007* (pp. 370–371); *Health, United States, 2010* (pp. 358–359).

all nursing home beds in the United States were chain affiliated, reflecting consolidation within the industry as chains have acquired an increasing number of independent facilities. Approximately 62% of all nursing home beds were operated by proprietary (for-profit) nursing homes, and 29% were operated by private nonprofit entities. Only about 9% were government owned, and most of these are owned and operated by local counties (U.S. Census Bureau, 2010). The average-size nursing home has 109 beds (see Table 10.1).

Nursing home expenditures are shown in **Table 10.2**. In 2008, 62% of U.S. nursing home expenditures were attributed to government sources. Medicaid is the largest single source of financing for nursing home care. Medicare pays for eligible beneficiaries under Part A, but the coverage is for a short duration. Out-of-pocket payments constitute a substantial source of financing for nursing home care. Only 7% of nursing home services are paid through private insurance. LTC insurance policies are generally expensive; hence, few people purchase them. Less than 10% of people age 50 and older have purchased private insurance policies for LTC coverage (Seff, 2003).

Table 10.2 Sources of National Nursing Home Expenditures, 2008

	Billions of Dollars	Percent	
Total expenditures	138.4		
Medicare	25.7	18.6	
Medicaid	56.8	41.0	
Veterans Administration	3.6	2.6	
Total public sources			**62%**
Out of pocket	37.0	26.7	
Private health insurance	10.3	7.4	
Total private sources			**34%**
Other sources	**5.0**	**3.6**	**4%**

Source: Data from U.S. Census Bureau. 2010. *Statistical Abstract of the United States: 2011.* Washington, D.C.

CONCLUSION

LTC should be viewed not as an isolated component of the health care delivery system, but rather as a continuum of both community-based and institution-based services that are rationally linked to the rest of the health care delivery system. LTC includes medical care, social services, and housing alternatives. Hence, it involves a range of services that can vary according to individual needs. Chronic conditions and comorbidities can lead to physical or mental disability, which in turn may impair the performance of ADLs and IADLs. LTC services often complement what people with impaired functioning can do for themselves. Informal caregivers provide the bulk of these services. Respite care can provide family members temporary relief from the burden of caregiving.

When the required intensity of care exceeds the capabilities of informal caregivers, available alternatives include professional community-based services to supplement informal care or admission to a long-term care facility. Services offered at these facilities range from basic personal assistance to more complex skilled nursing care and subacute care. Specialized facilities caring for patients with Alzheimer's disease, AIDS, or head trauma have also proliferated in recent years. Some LTC patients may require long-range custodial care without the prognosis of a cure; others may require short-term postacute convalescence and therapy. Still others may need end-of-life care through a hospice program. With the aging of the baby boom population, both demand and supply for LTC services are expected to grow at a rapid rate in the future.

REFERENCES

AARP studies adult foster care for the elderly. *Public Health Rep.* 1996;111(4):295.

Alecxih L. 2001. The impact of sociodemographic change on the future of long-term care. *Generations.* 2001;25(1):7–11.

Anderson GF. Physician, public, and policymaker perspectives on chronic conditions. *Arch Intern Med.* 2003;163(4):437–442.

Citro J, Hermanson S. *Fact Sheet: Assisted Living in the United States.* Washington, DC: AARP; 1999.

Department of Health and Human Services. *Health, United States, 2010.* Hyattsville, MD: U.S. Department of Health and Human Services; 2011.

Doty P, et al. Informal caregiving. In *The Continuum of Long-Term Care: An Integrated Systems Approach,* edited by Evashwick CJ. Albany, NY: Delmar Publishers; 1996:125–141.

Lakdawalla D, et al. Forecasting the nursing home population. *Med Care.* 2003;41(1):8–20.

MetLife Mature Market Institute. *The MetLife National Study of Adult Day Services.* Westport, CT: Metropolitan Life Insurance Company; 2010.

National Academy on an Aging Society. 2000. *Caregiving: Helping the Elderly with Activity Limitations.* Washington, DC: National Academy on an Aging Society.

National Association of Home Care and Hospice. Basic statistics about home care. 2010. http://www.nahc.org/facts/10HC_Stats.pdf. Accessed January 2012.

National Center for Assisted Living. Assisted living resident profile. 2006. http://www.ncal.org/about/resident.cfm. Accessed August 2008.

National Council on Aging. Fact sheet: Senior centers. 2011. http://www.ncoa .org/assets/files/pdf/FactSheet_SeniorCenters.pdf. Accessed January 2012.

National Subacute Care Association. Definition of subacute care as developed and approved by the NSCA board of directors. June 27, 1996. http://www .nsca.net/info/definition.htm.

O'Keeffe J, Siebenaler K. *Adult Day Services: A Key Community Service for Older Adults.* Washington, DC: U.S. Department of Health and Human Services; 2006.

Ostir GV, et al. Disability in older adults 1: Prevalence, causes, and consequences. *Behav Med.* 1999;24(4):147–156.

Partnership for Solutions. *Chronic Conditions: Making the Case for Ongoing Care.* Baltimore, MD: Johns Hopkins University; 2002.

Sahyoun NR, et al. Trends in causes of death among the elderly. In *Aging Trends.* Hyattsville, MD: National Center for Health Statistics; March 2001.

Seff MK. Clearing up health care myths. *Golden Lifestyles.* January–March 2003:7.

Stahl C. Adult foster care: An alternative to SNFs? *ADVANCE for Occupational Therapists.* September 29, 1997.

U.S. Census Bureau. *Statistical Abstract of the United States, 2010.* Washington, DC: Government Printing Office; 2010.

Wan T, Weissert WB. Social support networks, patient status, and institutionalization. *Res Aging.* 1981;3:240–256.

Zawadski RT, Eng C. Case management in capitated long-term care. *Health Care Financing Review Annual Supplement.* December 1988:75–81.

Chapter 11

Populations with Special Health Needs

INTRODUCTION

Certain population groups in the United States face greater challenges than the general population in accessing timely and needed health care services and financing of health care, putting them at greater risk of poor physical, psychological, and social health (Aday, 1994). Various terms are used to describe these populations, such as "underserved populations," "medically underserved," "medically disadvantaged," "underprivileged," and "American underclasses." The causes of their vulnerability are largely attributable to unequal social, economic, health, and geographic conditions. These population groups encompass racial and ethnic minorities, uninsured women and children, persons living in rural areas, the homeless, the mentally ill, the chronically ill and disabled, and individuals with HIV/AIDS. These groups also experience greater barriers to racial or cultural acceptance. This chapter defines these population groups, describes their health needs, and summarizes the major challenges that they typically face in the United States.

FRAMEWORK TO STUDY VULNERABLE POPULATIONS

The vulnerability model (see **Figure 11.1**) is an integrated approach to studying vulnerability. *Vulnerability* denotes susceptibility to negative events. From a health perspective, vulnerability refers to the likelihood of experiencing poor health or illness. Poor health can be manifested physically, psychologically, and socially. Health needs are greater for those individuals who experience problems along multiple dimensions, because poor health along one dimension is often compounded by poor health along others. Vulnerability does not represent a personal deficiency inherent to certain populations, but rather the effects of interactions between multiple factors over which individuals have little or no control (Aday, 1999). This characterization of vulnerability also justifies the role and responsibility of society as a whole to address the concerns of vulnerable populations.

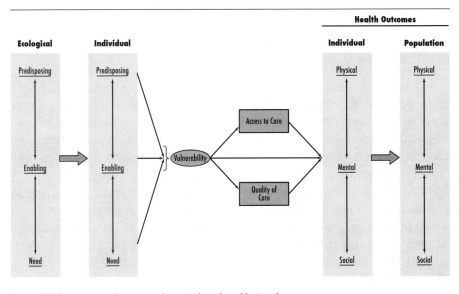

Figure 11.1   A General Framework to Study Vulnerable Populations

Exhibit 11.1   Predisposing, Enabling, and Need Characteristics of Vulnerability

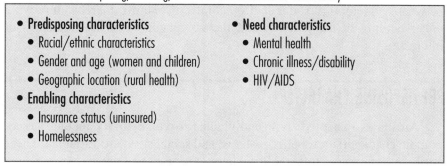

- **Predisposing characteristics**
  - Racial/ethnic characteristics
  - Gender and age (women and children)
  - Geographic location (rural health)
- **Enabling characteristics**
  - Insurance status (uninsured)
  - Homelessness

- **Need characteristics**
  - Mental health
  - Chronic illness/disability
  - HIV/AIDS

Vulnerability is determined by a convergence of (1) predisposing, (2) enabling, and (3) need characteristics at both individual and ecological (contextual) levels (**Exhibit 11.1**). Not only do these predisposing, enabling, and need characteristics converge and determine individuals' access to health care, but they also ultimately influence individuals' risk of contracting illness or, for those who are already sick, recovering from illness. Individuals with multiple risks (i.e., a combination of two or more vulnerability traits) typically experience worse access to care, care of lesser quality, and inferior health status than those with fewer vulnerability traits.

Understanding vulnerability as a combination or convergence of disparate factors is preferred over studying individual factors separately because vulnerability, when defined as a convergence of risks, best captures reality. Furthermore, this approach reflects the co-occurrence of risk factors and underscores the belief that it is difficult to address disparities in one risk factor without addressing others.

The vulnerability model presented here has a number of distinctive characteristics. First, it is a comprehensive model, including both individual and ecological attributes of risk. Second, it is a general model, focusing on the attributes of vulnerability for the total population rather than vulnerable traits of subpopulations. Although there are certainly individual differences in exposure to risks, a number of common, crosscutting traits affect all vulnerable populations. Third, a major distinguishing factor of this model is the emphasis on the convergence of vulnerability; that is, the effects of experiencing multiple vulnerability traits may lead to cumulative vulnerability that is additive or even multiplicative. Examining vulnerability as a multidimensional construct can also demonstrate gradient relationships between vulnerability status and outcomes of interest, thereby improving understanding of the patterns and factors related to health outcomes of interest.

PREDISPOSING CHARACTERISTICS

Attributes that predispose individuals to vulnerability include demographic characteristics, belief systems, and social structure variables. These attributes influence vulnerability status because they are associated with social position, access to resources, health behaviors, and variations in health status. Individuals have relatively little control over predisposing attributes, which are difficult to change. Predisposing attributes are often sources of discrimination. Patients may be discriminated against by health care providers and the health care delivery system because of their race, gender, financial status, or sexual preference. The following subsections discuss some of these predisposing characteristics, including race and ethnicity, gender, age, and geographic distribution.

Racial/Ethnic Minorities

The U.S. Office of Management and Budget (OMB) periodically revises standards for federal data on race and ethnicity to better reflect the growing diversity in the country (U.S. Census Bureau, 2000). In the 2010 census, the minimum categories for race in the U.S. population were white, black or African American, American Indian or Alaska Native, Asian, and Native Hawaiian or other Pacific Islander. The Census Bureau is also permitted to use the additional category "some other race." Multiple-race reporting is also accepted.

Two categories for ethnicity also exist: "Hispanic or Latino" and "not Hispanic or Latino." Hispanic or Latino Americans include Mexicans, Puerto Ricans, Central or South Americans, Cubans, and persons from other Spanish cultures or origins. The categories of race and ethnicity are separate; that is, those who identify as either ethnicity can be any race (Mackun & Wilson, 2011).

"Asian" refers to persons originating from the Far East, Southeast Asia, or the Indian subcontinent, including those from Cambodia, China, India, Japan, Korea, Malaysia, Pakistan, the Philippine Islands, Thailand, and Vietnam.

"Native Hawaiians or other Pacific Islanders" include persons originating from Hawaii, Guam, Samoa, or other Pacific Islands. "American Indian or Alaska Natives" include persons originating from North and South America (including Central America) who maintain tribal affiliation or community attachment. Nearly 30% of the U.S. population is made up of minorities: black or African American (12.3%), Hispanics or Latinos (16.3%), Asians (4.4%), Native Hawaiian and other Pacific Islanders (0.1%), American Indian and Alaska Natives (0.9%), or some other race (5.5%). In addition, 2.4% of the U.S. population identify themselves as being of two or more races (Mackun & Wilson, 2011).

Significant differences exist across the various racial/ethnic groups on health. Minority race and ethnicity often serves as a proxy for other factors such as socioeconomic status, language ability, or cultural behaviors that are correlated with health status and health care experiences. The available evidence suggests that racial/ethnic minorities generally have poorer access to health care, receive poorer-quality care, and experience worse health outcomes (see **Exhibit 11.2**).

One of the most consistent findings across decades of research is that minorities have poor access to health services compared with their white counterparts, even after taking into account insurance, socioeconomic, and health status. A variety of studies have documented that minority Americans experience higher rates of illness and mortality than white Americans. Disparities in health exist between white and nonwhite Americans in terms of perceived health status as well as in traditional indicators of health such as the infant mortality rate, general population mortality rate, and birth weight.

The most commonly used measure of access to care is whether a person has a regular or usual source of care. In most research studies, a *usual source of care* is defined as a single provider or place where patients obtain, or can obtain, the majority of their health care. Having a usual source of care is associated with greater coordination of care.

The majority of federal initiatives have primarily served to draw national attention to racial disparities in health care (see **Exhibit 11.3**). The creation of the Office of Minority Health was particularly important in this regard because it plays a coordinating role for other federal agencies and the minority health initiatives they support. The programs developed at both the federal and state levels provide extensive services that address some of the key pathways leading to racial disparities in Hispanic and Indian health and health care.

Exhibit 11.2   Racial and Ethnic Disparities

Black Americans
- More likely than whites to be economically disadvantaged
- Shorter life expectancies than whites
- Higher age-adjusted death rates for leading causes of death
- Higher neonatal, infant, and postneonatal mortality rates
- More likely than whites to report fair or poor health status
- Males more likely than white males to smoke cigarettes (U.S. Department of Health and Human Services, 1990)

Hispanic Americans
- Nearly one-third have less than ninth-grade education
- More than one-fourth of families live below the poverty line (U.S. Census Bureau, 2007)
- More likely to be uninsured and underinsured than non-Hispanic whites
- AIDS is the leading cause of death
- Homicide rate remains the second leading cause of death for young males (National Center for Health Statistics, 2002)
- Among individuals 18 years or older, a higher proportion of Hispanics are overweight or obese
- Alcoholism rate is 30.3% in Hispanics versus 7.9% in all races (National Center for Health Statistics, 1995)
- Among individuals age 18–25 years, 28% of Hispanics smoke versus 24% of non-Hispanic blacks (National Center for Health Statistics, 2002)

Asian Americans
- Bipolar distribution of education, income, and health status
- Asian/Pacific Islander category is extremely heterogeneous, encompassing 21 subgroups with different health profiles
- In 1999, median family income was $35,353; a higher percentage (11.9%) live in poverty than non-Hispanic whites (10.3%) (U.S. Census Bureau, 2002)
- Cambodian refugees have extremely high rates of post-traumatic stress disorder, dissociation, depression, and anxiety
- As a whole, Asian/Pacific Islanders have the lowest smoking rates in the United States, but certain groups have higher smoking rates:
  - 92% of Laotians
  - 71% of Cambodians
  - 65% of Vietnamese (Yoon & Chien, 1996)
- Korean Americans have a fivefold incidence of stomach cancer and eightfold incidence of liver cancer compared with whites

American Indians and Alaska Natives
- At the bottom of the socioeconomic strata
- Poverty is associated with high injury-related mortality rate among these children
- The rate of death due to alcohol is 7 times greater and the suicide rate is 3.5 times greater than the national averages (Pleasant, 2003)

Exhibit 11.3   Selected Federal Programs to Eliminate Racial and Ethnic Disparities

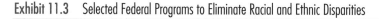

U.S. Department of Health and Human Services Initiative to Eliminate Racial and Ethnic Disparities in Health (1998)

- To reduce disparities in six key areas: infant mortality, cancer screening and management, cardiovascular disease, diabetes, HIV/AIDS, immunizations

U.S. Office of Minority Health (1985)

- Mission is to "improve the health of racial and ethnic minority populations through the development of effective health policies and programs that help eliminate disparities in health" (*Racial and Ethnic Approaches to Community Health,* 2010)
- Program launched by the Centers for Disease Control and Prevention in 1999
- Aimed to support the goals of *Healthy People 2010* to eliminate racial disparities in health and health care

Minority Health Initiative (1992)

- Launched by the Office for Research on Minority Health at the National Institutes of Health to improve the national research agenda on minority health issues and strengthen the national commitment and responsiveness to the health and training needs of minority Americans

Indian Health Service

- An agency within the U.S. Department of Health and Human Services with the mission to be the principal advocate and provider of health services to American Indians and Alaska Natives

Migrant Health Center Program

- Was established by the Migrant Health Act (1962) to provide medical and support services to migrant farm workers and their families

Although these programs are designed to address specific needs of the minorities in their target populations, they nonetheless reflect a somewhat fragmented approach to addressing disparities in minority health and health care. The creation of the Federal Office of Minority Health may overcome this problem by facilitating the coordination of future efforts to improve health, access to health care, and quality of health services. In any event, it will remain important to balance national efforts to improve racial/ethnic equity in health and health services delivery with the ability to address the specific cultural barriers and unique needs of each racial and minority group.

Women and Children

Although women in the United States now enjoy a life expectancy almost eight years longer than that of men, they suffer greater morbidity

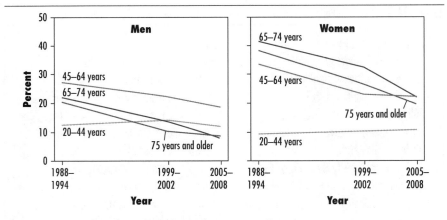

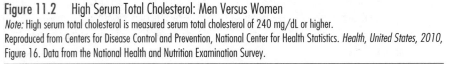

Figure 11.2   High Serum Total Cholesterol: Men Versus Women

Note: High serum total cholesterol is measured serum total cholesterol of 240 mg/dL or higher.
Reproduced from Centers for Disease Control and Prevention, National Center for Health Statistics. *Health, United States, 2010,*
Figure 16. Data from the National Health and Nutrition Examination Survey.

and poorer health outcomes than their male counterparts. Women also have a higher prevalence of certain health problems than men over the course of their lifetimes (Sechzer et al., 1996). Compared with men of comparable age, women develop more acute and chronic illnesses, resulting in a greater number of short- and long-term disabilities (National Institutes of Health [NIH], 1992). For example, heart disease and stroke account for a higher percentage of deaths among women than among men at all stages of life. For example, 49% of women who have heart attacks die within one year, compared to 31% of men who suffer this fate. Similarly, women have higher cholesterol level than men at all ages (see **Figure 11.2**). Finally, women represent the fastest-growing population diagnosed with AIDS.

The differences between men and women are equally pronounced regarding mental illness. For example, anxiety disorders and major depression affect twice as many women as men (Rodin & Ikovics, 1990). Approximately 90% of all cases occur in young women, and eating disorders—which affect mostly women—account for the highest mortality rates among all mental disorders (Weissman & Klerman, 1977).

The mission of the Office of Research on Women's Health (ORWH), under the NIH (within the U.S. Department of Health and Human Services), is to stimulate, coordinate, and implement a comprehensive women's health agenda on research, service delivery, and education across agencies of the U.S. Department of Health and Human Services, as well as other government agencies.

Children's health has certain unique aspects in terms of the delivery of health care, reflecting children's developmental vulnerability, dependency, and differential patterns of morbidity and mortality. *Developmental vulnerability* refers to the rapid and cumulative physical and emotional changes that characterize childhood, and the potential effects that illness, injury, or untoward family and social circumstances can have on a child's life-course trajectory. *Dependency* refers to the special circumstances that children face that require others to recognize and respond to their health needs. Children depend on their parents, school officials, caregivers, and sometimes neighbors to discover their need for health care, seek health care services on their behalf, authorize treatment, and comply with recommended treatment regimens. These relationships can affect the utilization of health services by children.

Children are increasingly affected by a broad and complex array of conditions that were not very prevalent among older generations, collectively referred to as "new morbidities." *New morbidities* include drug and alcohol abuse, obesity, family and neighborhood violence, emotional disorders, and learning problems (see **Figure 11.3** for data on obesity among children). Addressing such conditions requires a continuum of comprehensive services that includes multidisciplinary assessment, treatment, rehabilitation, and community-based prevention strategies.

Geographic Distribution: Rural Health

Poverty is a common dimension of life in rural areas; rural residents earn, on average, $7,417 less than their urban counterparts, and 24% of rural children live in poverty (National Rural Health Association, 2011). Poor economic conditions are often reflected in diminished access to health care and poor health outcomes among rural citizens (Cohen et al., 1994). Rural communities face an increased burden of heart disease, stroke, diabetes, mental health disorders, tobacco usage, and substance abuse (Gamm et al., 2003).

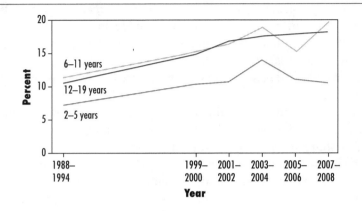

Figure 11.3   Obesity Among Children
Note: Obesity is body mass index (BMI) for age and sex at or above the 95th percentile of the CDC growth charts.
Reproduced from Centers for Disease Control and Prevention, National Center for Health Statistics. *Health, United States, 2010,*
Figure 13. Data from the National Health and Nutrition Examination Survey.

One dimension of the barriers to health care access among rural residents is geographic maldistribution of health care professionals. An estimated 51 million Americans (approximately one-fifth of the total U.S. population) live in places classified as nonmetropolitan, and more than 20 million of these nonmetropolitan residents live in areas designated as having primary health care provider shortages. According to the National Rural Health Association, just 10% of all practicing physicians are based in rural areas. Low population density makes it difficult for such communities to attract physicians and for physicians to establish financially viable practices. Rural residents have particularly low access to specialist physicians.

As a result, rural populations face greater barriers in access to care. In fact, 73% of national- and state-level rural health experts recently named "access to health care" as a rural health priority.

Various measures have been undertaken to improve access to care in rural America, including the promotion of the National Health Service Corps (defined in a later section), the designation of Health Professional Shortage Areas (HPSAs) and Medically Underserved Areas, the development of community and migrant health centers, and the enactment of the Rural Health Clinics Act.

ENABLING CHARACTERISTICS

Enabling characteristics include socioeconomic status, individual assets, and various mediating factors. *Socioeconomic status* is associated with social position, access to resources, and variations in health status (e.g., income, education, employment status, and occupation). Individual assets (i.e., human capital) contribute to an individual's ability to be economically self-sufficient (e.g., possessing inheritance, wealth, or certain skills). *Mediating factors* are associated with the use of health care services (e.g., health insurance, access to health care, quality of health care). The following section discusses enabling characteristics such as insurance status and homelessness.

Uninsured

According to recent estimates, slightly more than 17.5% of civilian non-institutionalized Americans lack health care coverage (National Center for Health Statistics, Health, United States, 2010). In general, the uninsured are likely to be poorer and less educated than insured populations, and tend to work in part-time jobs and/or be employed by small firms. The uninsured also tend to be younger (25 to 40 years old) because most of the elderly (age 65 and older) are covered by Medicare. Ethnic minorities are also more likely to lack health insurance.

The uninsured face greater barriers to accessing needed health care, and are more likely to report delays in seeking needed medical care or dental care (see **Figure 11.4** and **Figure 11.5**). The plight of the uninsured also affects those who have insurance. For example, community hospitals provide uncompensated care to the uninsured through emergency health care; the cost of such care was estimated at $31 billion in 2009 (American Hospital Association, 2010). Much of this cost is currently shared by Medicaid, federal grants to nonprofit hospitals, and charitable organizations, although these costs are likely to be (at least partly) passed on to the U.S. public at large if the level of uncompensated care remains the same in the future.

The Patient Protection and Affordable Care Act of 2010 (ACA of 2010) was a landmark health care reform legislation, aimed at reducing the number of uninsured Americans and promoting health care access. Various provisions of the law are intended to extend coverage to previously uninsured

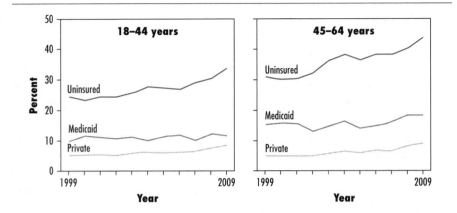

Figure 11.4   Delay in Seeking Needed Medical Care by Insurance Status
Reproduced from Centers for Disease Control and Prevention, National Center for Health Statistics. *Health, United States, 2010,* Figure 19. Data from the National Health Interview Survey.

groups. For example, health exchanges (i.e., insurance markets for individuals and small businesses) are expected to cover 24 million formerly uninsured people when fully implemented. Similarly, expansion of Medicaid coverage to all individuals and families at or below 133% of the federal poverty level is expected to cover an additional 16 million people (Healthcare.gov).

Homelessness

Across the United States, approximately 3.5 million people experience homelessness each year (1% of the total U.S. population); nearly one-third of this population consists of families with children. Some 40% of all homeless men have served in the armed forces. Single women account for about 17% of the U.S. homeless adult population. Approximately 26% of all homeless persons have a severe mental illness, yet just 5 to 7% require institutionalization; the rest can live in the community with appropriate help (National Coalition for the Homeless, 2009a, 2009b).

The homeless face several barriers to adequate and appropriate health care. They have financial barriers and problems in satisfying eligibility requirements for health insurance. Accessible transportation to medical facilities is often unavailable to this population. The homeless usually suffer from a lack of proper sanitation, do not have a stable place to store

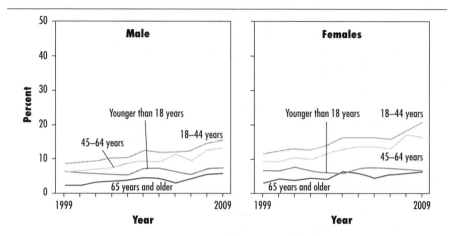

Figure 11.5   Delay in Seeking Needed Dental Care by Insurance Status
Reproduced from Centers for Disease Control and Prevention, National Center for Health Statistics. *Health, United States, 2010,*
Figure 20. Data from the National Health Interview Survey.

medications safely, and are unable to obtain the proper food for a medically indicated diet necessary for conditions such as diabetes mellitus or
hypertension. The homeless population suffers from a high prevalence of
untreated acute and chronic medical, mental health, and substance abuse
problems. Such persons are also at a greater risk of assault and victimiza-
tion, as well as exposure to harsh environmental elements.

Federal Initiatives to Eliminate Socioeconomic Disparities

Several federal programs have been established to help eliminate socioeconomic differences that jeopardize health:

- The Community Health Center Program was established in 1969 to
  improve access to health care services for low-income families in
  high-need communities.
- The National Health Service Corps (NHSC), established in 1972,
  works with communities and health care clinics in federally designated Health Profession Shortage Areas to provide primary medical
  care to individuals living in these underserved areas. There are currently more than 10,000 NHSC members providing care to more than
  10.5 million underserved people.

- The Public Housing Primary Care Program is administered by the Bureau of Primary Health Care and supports health centers and other community providers in delivering care to nearly 134,000 residents of public housing, individuals living near public housing, and anyone benefiting from public rent subsidies.

- The Healthy Schools, Healthy Communities Program, established in 1994, was the first federal program to encourage the development of comprehensive full-time school-based health centers that serve vulnerable youth.

- The Health Care for the Homeless Program, administered by the Bureau of Primary Health Care, supports grantees from community health centers, local health departments, community coalitions, and other nonprofit organizations to provide services to homeless individuals.

NEED CHARACTERISTICS

Need attributes of individuals include their self-perceived or professionally evaluated health status and quality-of-life indicators. "Self-perceived or professionally evaluated health status" refers to self-perceived physical and mental health status and diagnoses of disease and illness from health professionals. *Quality-of-life indicators* include such factors as the ability to perform activities of daily living (ADLs) and instrumental activities of daily living (IADLs); social limitations; cognitive limitations; and limitations in work, housework, or school.

Certain subpopulation groups are known to be at higher health risks. These potential threats include risks to physical health (e.g., high-risk mothers and infants, chronically ill and disabled individuals, and persons with HIV/AIDS), mental health (e.g., the mentally ill and disabled, alcohol or substance abusers, those who are suicide- or homicide-prone), and social well-being (e.g., abusive families, the homeless, and immigrants and refugees).

Mental Health

Mental disorders are common psychiatric illnesses affecting both adults and children, and they represent a serious public health problem in the United States. National studies have concluded that the most common mental disorders include phobias, substance abuse (including alcohol and drug dependence), and affective disorders (including depression). Schizophrenia is considerably less common, affecting approximately 1.1% of the population.

Mental illness ranks second, after ischemic heart disease, as a nationwide burden on health and productivity. An estimated 26.2% of the U.S. adult population has at least one diagnosable mental disorder in any given year, with 22.3% of those individuals (5.8% of the total population) facing a severe mental illness. Only 41% of those persons with a disorder receive any treatment (National Institute of Mental Health [NIMH], 2005). In 2006, 36.2 million people received $57.5 billion of mental health services, at an average cost of $1,591 per person (NIMH, 2006). Mental illness is a risk factor for death from suicide, cardiovascular disease, and cancer.

Most mental health services are provided in the general medicine sector—a concept first described by Regier et al. (1988) as the de facto mental health service system—rather than through formal mental health specialist services. The de facto system combines specialty mental health services with general counseling services, such as those provided in primary care settings, nursing homes, and community health centers by ministers, counselors, self-help groups, families, and friends. The nation's mental health system is composed of two subsystems—one primarily for individuals with insurance coverage or private funds and the other for those without private means of coverage.

Chronic Illness/Disability

Every person is vulnerable to *chronic illness* and disability during his or her lifetime. Overall, chronic diseases are responsible for 7 of 10 deaths in the United States every year. Almost half of all Americans have at least one chronic condition. Chronic disease deaths are largely attributable to preventable illnesses. Tobacco use, a lack of physical activity, poor nutrition, and excessive alcohol consumption contribute to the major chronic disease killers: cardiovascular disease, cancer, diabetes, and chronic obstructive pulmonary disease (Centers for Disease Control and Prevention [CDC], 2010a) (see **Figure 11.6** for diabetes prevalence in the United States). An illness is considered chronic if a disease or injury with long-term (i.e., noticed for three months or more) conditions or symptoms is present. Other illnesses—namely, congenital anomalies, asthma, diabetes, and heart disease—have been specifically classified as chronic by the

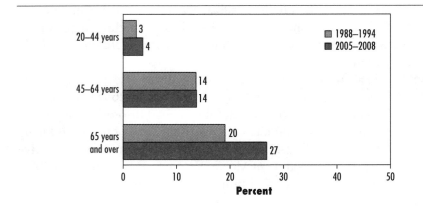

Figure 11.6   Diabetes Prevalence in the United States
Reproduced from Centers for Disease Control and Prevention, National Center for Health Statistics. *Health, United States, 2010,* Figure 5. Data from the National Health and Nutrition Examination Survey.

National Center for Health Statistics, regardless of their duration (National Center for Health Statistics, 1999b, p. 5). Chronic illness and disability also pose unique challenges to a health care system that is primarily oriented toward treating acute illness.

HIV/AIDS

Acquired immunodeficiency syndrome (AIDS) is caused by infection with the human immunodeficiency virus (HIV). HIV is an unusual type of virus, called a retrovirus, that causes immune system suppression leading to AIDS. Certain widely recognized risk factors promote the transmission of HIV, including male-to-male sexual contact, male-to-female sexual contact, drug use by injection, exposure to contaminated blood products, and perinatal transmission from mother to infant (during pregnancy, delivery, or breastfeeding).

The CDC estimates that more than 1 million adults and adolescents are currently living with HIV in the United States. Efforts at reporting and surveillance have been more successful in recent years, with data showing that more people infected with HIV know their positive status and that higher numbers of cases are being reported to the CDC—this trend is particularly due to increased and more widespread HIV testing (CDC, 2010b).

In addition, with the advent of combination antiretroviral therapy, AIDS surveillance data no longer reflect trends in HIV transmission because such therapy has been effective in delaying the progression of HIV to AIDS (CDC, 1999). Advancements in diagnosis and treatment have led to an increase in the number of people living with HIV/AIDS, although the incidence of new cases has remained relatively stable (CDC, 2010b).

The average cost of antiretroviral therapy is at least $15,000 per year, making such treatment difficult for many patients in the United States to obtain, and keeping it out of reach in developing countries where more than 90% of the new HIV infections occur (Long, 2010). Some patients temporarily stop treatment, because the complicated drug regimen requires coordination of many pills and doses, making it easier to skip medications or doses. Other problems associated with HIV in the United States include issues of urban home health care; HIV infection in rural communities, children, and women; lack of HIV prevention programs; late diagnosis; discrimination; and the need for more HIV/AIDS-related research and health care provider training.

CONCLUSION

This chapter has examined the major characteristics of certain vulnerable U.S. population groups that face challenges and barriers in accessing health care services. These population groups may be organized along predisposing, enabling, and need characteristics and include racial/ethnic minorities, children and women, persons living in rural areas, the homeless, the mentally ill, and individuals with HIV/AIDS. The gaps that currently exist between these population groups and the rest of the population indicate the need for significant efforts to address the unique health concerns of vulnerable U.S. subpopulation groups.

REFERENCES

Aday LA. Health status of vulnerable populations. *Ann Rev Public Health.* 1994;15:487–509.

Aday LA. Vulnerable populations: A community-oriented perspective. In *Special Populations in the Community,* ed. Sebastian JG, Bushy A. Gaithersburg, MD: Aspen; 1999;313–330.

American Hospital Association. Uncompensated hospital care cost fact sheet: Health Forum, AHA annual survey data, 1980–2009. 2010. www.aha.org/content/00-10/10uncompensatedcare.pdf.

Centers for Disease Control and Prevention (CDC). Guidelines for national human immunodeficiency virus case surveillance, including monitoring for human immunodeficiency virus infection and acquired immunodeficiency syndrome. *MMWR.* 1999;48(RR-13):2–7.

Centers for Disease Control and Prevention (CDC). Chronic diseases and health promotion. 2010a. http://www.cdc.gov/chronicdisease/overview/index.htm.

Centers for Disease Control and Prevention. 2010b. "HIV in the United States: An Overview." http://www.cdc.gov/hiv/resources/factsheets/us.htm.

Cohen SE, et al. The geography of AIDS: Patterns of urban and rural migration. *Southern Med J.* 1994;85(6):599.

Gamm LD, et al. *Rural healthy people 2010: A companion document to healthy people 2010.* Vol. 1. College Station, Texas: Texas A&M University System Health Science Center, School of Rural Public Health; 2003.

Long EF, Brandeau ML, Owens DK. The cost-effectiveness and population outcomes of expanded HIV screening and antiretroviral treatment in the United States. *Ann Intern Med.* 2010;153:778–789.

Mackun P, Wilson S. Population distribution and change: 2000 to 2010. In *2010 census briefs.* U.S. Census Bureau; 2011.

National Center for Health Statistics. *Healthy people 2000 review, 1998–99.* Hyattsville, MD: Public Health Series; 1999b:163–167.

National Center for Health Statistics. *Health, United States, 2002.* Hyattsville, MD: U.S. Department of Health and Human Services; 2002.

National Center for Health Statistics. *Health, United States, 2010.* Hyattsville, MD: U.S. Department of Health and Human Services; 2010.

National Coalition for the Homeless. NCH fact sheet #2: How many people experience homelessness? 2009a. http://www.nationalhomeless.org/publications/facts/How_Many.pdf.

National Coalition for the Homeless. NCH fact sheet #3: Who is homeless? 2009b. http://www.nationalhomeless.org/publications/facts/Whois.pdf.

National Institute of Mental Health. Statistics: Prevalence: Any disorder: Adults. 2005. http://www.nimh.nih.gov/statistics/index.shtml.

National Institute of Mental Health. Statistics: Cost: Mental healthcare cost data for all Americans. 2006. http://www.nimh.nih.gov/statistics/index.shtml.

National Institutes of Health, Office of Research on Women's Health. *Report of the National Institutes of Health: Opportunities for research on women's health* (NIH Publ. No. 92–3457). Washington, DC: Government Printing Office; 1992.

National Rural Health Association, 2011. What's Different about Rural Health Care? http://www.ruralhealthweb.org/go/left/about-rural-health. Accessed December 20, 2011.

Pleasant R. Minority health. In *The Department of Health and Human Services: 50 years of service.* U.S. Department of Health and Human Services; 2003:92–95.

Regier DA, et al. One month prevalence of mental disorders in the United States: Based on five epidemiologic catchment area sites. *Arch Gen Psychiatr.* 1988;45(11):977–986.

Rodin J, Ikovics J. Women's health: Review and research agenda as we approach the 21st century. *Am Psychol.* 1990;45:1018–1034.

Sechzer JA, et al. *Women and mental health.* New York: New York Academy of Sciences; 1996.

U.S. Census Bureau. *Racial and ethnic classifications used in Census 2000 and beyond.* Washington, DC: Government Printing Office; 2000.

U.S. Census Bureau. *Statistical abstract of the United States, 2002: The national data book.* Washington, DC: Government Printing Office; 2002.

U.S. Census Bureau. *Statistical abstract of the United States, 2007: The national data book.* Washington, DC: Government Printing Office; 2007.

U.S. Department of Health and Human Services. *Health status of the disadvantaged.* Department of Health and Human Services Publication No. (HRSA) HRS-P-DV 90–1. Washington, DC: Government Printing Office; 1990.

U.S. Office of Minority Health. 2010. Racial and Ethnic Approaches to Community Health, Author.

Weissman MM, Klerman GL. Sex differences and the epidemiology of depression. *Arch Gen Psychiatr.* 1977;34(1):98–111.

Yoon E, Chien F. Asian American and Pacific Islander health: A paradigm for minority health. *JAMA.* 1996;275(9):736–737.

Chapter 12

Cost, Access, and Quality

INTRODUCTION

Cost, access, and quality are the three cornerstones of health care delivery (Al-Assaf, 1993a). For many years, employers and third-party payers in the United States have been preoccupied with controlling the growth of health care expenditures. One reason that past attempts to adopt universal health insurance in the United States have failed is the concern that such a move would be extremely costly in terms of national health care expenditures. Such a fear is based on the premise that cost and access go hand in hand. While cost and access remain the primary concerns within the U.S. health care delivery system, the quality of health care is increasingly taking center stage. At the same time, rising systemwide costs will remain the focus of attention for many years to come.

An interactive relationship exists between the cost of health care, people's ability to obtain health care when needed, and the quality of services delivered.

From a macroperspective, costs are commonly viewed in terms of national expenditures for health care. A widely used measure for national health expenditures is the proportion of the gross domestic product (GDP) that a country spends on the delivery of health care services. In simple terms, it refers to the proportion of a country's national income that is spent on health care. From a microperspective, health care costs refer to both costs incurred by employers to purchase health insurance and out-of-pocket costs incurred by individuals when they receive health care services. Improvements in access to health care and equal access to quality health care are contingent on expenditures at both the macro and micro levels. High-quality care should also be the most cost-effective care. Hence, cost is an important factor in the evaluation of quality. Conversely, quality is achieved when accessible services are provided in an efficient, cost-effective, and acceptable manner (Al-Assaf, 1993a).

This chapter discusses some of the major reasons for the dramatic rise in health care expenditures in recent decades. Costs of health care in the United States are compared with those of other countries, and the impact of various cost-containment measures is examined. The government has played a significant role in cost containment and quality improvement, but health insurance for all Americans has remained an elusive dream.

COST OF HEALTH CARE

"Cost" can carry different meanings in the delivery of health care. The meaning depends on the perspective one takes. Three different meanings are presented here.

1. When consumers and financiers speak of the cost of health care, they are usually referring to the "price" of health care, such as the physician's bill or the premiums that both employers and employees pay for purchasing health insurance.

2. From a national perspective, health care costs refer to how much a nation spends on health care services, commonly referred to as "health care expenditures" or "health care spending." These terms primarily reflect the consumption of economic resources in the delivery of health care. Such economic resources include health insurance, the skills of health care professionals, organizations and institutions of health care

delivery, pharmaceuticals, medical equipment and supplies, public health functions, and new medical discoveries. Because expenditures equal price times quantity, $E = (P)(Q)$, growth in health care spending can be accounted for by growth in the prices charged by providers of health services as well as by increases in the utilization of services.

3. A third perspective is that of the providers, where the notion of cost refers to staff salaries, capital costs for building and equipment, rental of space, purchase of supplies, and other costs of production.

Regardless of the perspective taken, it is useful to understand which factors drive costs in the health care delivery system. This understanding enables one to identify which costs can be controlled to ensure that health care is delivered at an optimal value.

THE HIGH COST OF U.S. HEALTH CARE

Health care spending spiraled upward at double-digit rates during the 1970s after a massive growth in access created by the Medicare and Medicaid programs in 1965. By 1970, U.S. government expenditures for health care services and supplies had grown by 140%, from $7.9 billion to $18.9 billion (National Center for Health Statistics [NCHS], 1996). During the 1980s, the rate of increase began slowing down. In the 1990s, medical inflation was finally brought under control to a single-digit rate of growth, mostly because medical care costs and utilization were controlled through managed care. The average annual rate of growth in health spending slowed to 5.7% between 1993 and 2000 as managed care proliferated; however, the rate of growth then started to accelerate again. Annual growth in 2001, at 8.7%, was the fastest since 1991, with the main culprits for this rise in expenditures being hospital services, prescription drugs, and physician services (Levit et al., 2003). Growth continued at 8.0% in 2005, 6.5% in 2006, and 6.1% in 2007 (Martin et al., 2011). After that point, the economic recession slowed healthcare spending growth substantially, with only a 4.1% increase occurring in 2008 and a 4.0% increase in 2009—the slowest growth rate in more than 50 years. The recession led to less private health care spending, both in insurance premiums and out-of-pocket payments, although spending as a proportion of GDP continued to increase. Simultaneously, federal health spending increased as more people became eligible for benefits and government revenues declined, increasing spending from 37.6% of federal revenue in 2008 to 54.2% in 2009 (Martin et al., 2011).

Trends in national health expenditures are commonly evaluated by comparing medical inflation to general inflation in the economy (measured by annual changes in the consumer price index [CPI]) and by comparing changes in national health spending to changes in the GDP. Typically, the rates of change in medical inflation have remained consistently above the rates of change in the CPI, and health care spending growth rates have consistently surpassed growth rates in the general economy. When spending on health care grows at a faster rate than the GDP, it means that a growing share of total economic resources is devoted to the delivery of health care.

Table 12.1 compares U.S. health spending with that of 30 other developed countries. In 2005, the United States spent $6,401 per capita on health—approximately $1,500 more per capita than the country with the second highest per capita spending, Luxembourg. National health care expenditures were projected to reach $2.8 trillion in 2011 (Heffler et al., 2002), and to surpass 18% of the GDP. These data suggest that the health care sector will remain one of the fastest-growing components of the U.S. economy. In addition to an increased demand for services that will expand job opportunities, we can expect to see policy debates and new initiatives to keep costs from spiraling out of control in the future.

REASONS FOR HIGH HEALTH CARE COSTS

The rising health care expenditures have been attributed to the complex interaction of numerous factors. General inflation in the economy is a highly visible cause of health care spending because it affects the cost of producing health care services through such tangibles as higher wages and costs of supplies. Apart from the effects of general inflation, nine major areas influence medical cost inflation (see **Exhibit 12.1**).

Third-Party Payment

Health care is among the few services for which a third party—not the consumer—pays the lion's share for most of the services used. Whether the government or a private insurance company foots the bill, individual patients pay a price that is far lower than the actual cost of the service

Table 12.1 Health Spending in Organization for Economic Cooperation and Development Countries

	Total Health Spending per Capita, 2009			GDP per Capita, 2009			Health Spending as a Percentage of GDP, 2009	
	U.S. $ PP	% of U.S. Level	AAG, 2000–2009 (5)	U.S. $ PPP	% of U.S. Level	AAG, 2000–2009 (%)	% of GDP	% of U.S. Level
United States	7,960	100.0	3.3	45,797	100.0	0.6	17.4	100.0
Luxembourg	4,808	60.4	0.7	85,521	186.7	1.6	7.8	44.8
Norway	5,352	67.2	2.4	55,730	121.7	0.9	9.6	55.2
Switzerland	5,114	64.2	2.0	45,150	98.6	0.7	11.4	65.5
Austria	4,289	53.9	2.2	38,823	84.8	1.0	11.0	63.2
Iceland	3,538	44.4	1.6	36,655	79.2	1.4	9.7	55.7
Belgium	3,946	49.6	4.0	36,278	79.2	0.7	10.9	62.6
France	3,978	50.0	2.2	33,763	73.7	0.5	11.8	67.8
Canada	4,363	54.8	3.7	38,230	83.5	0.8	11.4	65.5
Germany	4,218	53.0	2.0	36,328	79.3	0.6	11.6	66.7
Australia	3,445	43.3	2.8	39,409	86.1	1.7	9.1	52.3
Denmark	4,348	54.6	3.3	37,706	82.3	0.1	11.5	66.1

(continues)

Table 12.1 Health Spending in Organization for Economic Cooperation and Development Countries (continued)

	Total Health Spending per Capita, 2009			GDP per Capita, 2009			Health Spending as a Percentage of GDP, 2009	
	U.S. $ PP	% of U.S. Level	AAG, 2000–2009 (5)	U.S. $ PP	% of U.S. Level	AAG, 2000–2009 (%)	% of GDP	% of U.S. Level
The Netherlands	4,914	61.7	4.4	41,085	89.7	1.6	12.0	69.0
Greece	2,724	34.2	6.9	28,251	61.7	3.9	10.1	58.0
Ireland	3,781	47.5	6.1	39,652	86.6	1.1	9.5	54.6
Sweden	3,722	46.8	3.4	37,155	81.1	1.1	10.0	57.5
United Kingdom	3,487	43.8	4.8	35,656	77.8	1.0	9.8	56.3
Italy	3,137	39.4	1.6	33,105	72.3	-0.2	9.5	54.6
Japan	2,878	36.2	2.4	33,854	73.9	1.1	8.5	48.9
New Zealand	2,983	37.5	4.8	28,985	63.3	1.4	10.3	59.2
Finland	3,226	40.5	4.0	35,237	76.9	1.3	9.2	52.9
Spain	3,067	38.5	4.0	32,254	70.4	0.8	9.5	54.6
Portugal	2,508	31.5	1.5	24,953	54.5	0.5	10.2	58.6
Czech Republic	2,108	26.5	5.7	25,568	55.8	3.0	8.2	47.1

Hungary	1,511	19.0	2.8	20,280	44.3	2.2	7.4	42.5
Korea	1,879	23.6	8.6	27,150	59.2	3.5	6.9	39.7
Slovak Republic	2,084	26.2	10.9	22,868	49.9	4.8	9.1	52.3
Poland	1,394	17.5	7.3	18,929	41.3	3.9	7.4	42.5
Mexico	918	11.5	3.1	14,322	31.3	0.4	6.4	36.8
Turkey	902	11.3	6.3	14,848	32.4	3.6	7.6	43.7
Organization for Economic Cooperation and Development Median	3,233	40.6	4.0	33,320	72.8	1.6	9.6	55.2

Sources: Data from *OECD health at a glance 2011, Annex A* (pp. 190–197). Paris: Organization for Economic Cooperation and Development.

Exhibit 12.1   Main Reasons for the High Cost of Health Care

• Third-party payment	• Multipayer system and administrative costs
• Imperfect market	• Defensive medicine
• Growth of technology	• Waste and abuse
• Increase in the elderly population	• Practice variations
• Medical model of health care delivery	

(Altman & Wallack, 1996). As a result, moral hazard and provider-induced demand (discussed in earlier chapters) often lead to excessive utilization of health care services. The patient and provider have little incentive to be cost conscious when someone else is paying the bill.

Imperfect Market

Prices charged by providers for health care services are likely to be much closer to the cost of producing the services in a highly regulated market or in a highly competitive market (Altman & Wallack, 1996); the U.S. health care market is neither. Because the U.S. health care delivery system does not consist of a national health care program, it is not as highly regulated as are single-payer systems in other countries. Furthermore, health care delivery in the United States does not constitute a highly competitive market because of the various market imperfections discussed earlier in this text. In an imperfect market, the use of health care is driven by need rather than by economic demand. The quantity of health care services produced and delivered is likely to be much higher than in a competitive market, and the prices charged for health care services are permanently higher than the true economic costs of production (Altman & Wallack, 1996).

Growth of Technology

In the adoption and diffusion of intensive procedures, the United States follows an early-start, fast-growth pattern (TECH Research Network, 2001). The introduction and intensive use of technology have a direct impact on the escalation of health care costs. New technology is expensive to develop, and costs incurred in its research and development are included in the total health care expenditures. Once technology is developed, it creates demand for its use. The development of new technology raises the expectations of consumers about what medical science can do to diagnose and treat disease and prolong life. Unsurprisingly, attempts to limit the diffusion of certain expensive technologies in the United States have proved largely unsuccessful.

Increase in the Elderly Population

During the past 100 years, life expectancy in the United States has increased significantly. Life expectancy at birth increased by almost 30 years from 47.3 years in 1900 to nearly 78 years in 2007 (NCHS, 2010). Owing to this increased life expectancy combined with the aging of the baby boom generation, the United States is experiencing a notable increase in its elderly population. The number of elderly residents is projected to continue to rise through the middle of the twenty-first century. The elderly consume more health care compared to other age groups, and they incur costs that are nearly three times as high as the general population. In 2007, the average medical expenses for a person 65 years or older amounted to $9,696 per person, compared with $3,499 per person for individuals younger than the age of 65 (NCHS, 2010, p. 377).

Medical Model of Health Care Delivery

The *medical model* emphasizes medical intervention after a person has become sick. Prevention and lifestyle/behavior changes to promote health are de-emphasized in this model. Although health promotion and disease prevention are not the answer to every health problem, these principles have not been accorded their rightful place in the U.S. health care delivery system. Consequently, more costly health care resources must be employed to treat many health problems that could have been prevented.

Multipayer System and Administrative Costs

Administrative costs are those costs associated with the management of the financing, insurance, delivery, and payment functions. They include expenditures for management of the enrollment process, setting up contracts with providers, claims processing, utilization monitoring, denials and appeals, and marketing and promotional expenses. Because of the complexity of a multipayer system, costs are often duplicated and may account for as much as 24% to 25% of total health care expenditures in the United States. A single-payer health care system might cut health care administrative costs by half (Hellander et al., 1994).

Defensive Medicine

The U.S. health care delivery system is riddled with legal risks for providers that promote defensive medicine. The practice of *defensive medicine* leads to tests and services that are not medically justified but rather are performed by physicians to protect themselves against potential malpractice lawsuits. Unrestrained malpractice awards by the courts and increased malpractice insurance premiums for physicians significantly add to the cost of health care.

Waste and Abuse

In general terms, *fraud* involves a knowing disregard of the truth and typically occurs when billing claims or cost reports are intentionally falsified. Health care fraud has been identified as a major problem in the Medicare and Medicaid programs. It may also occur when more services are provided than are medically necessary or when services not provided are billed to third-party payers. The latter practice may include billing for a higher-priced service when a lower-priced service is actually delivered.

Practice Variations

The work of John Wennberg and others brought to light a disturbing aspect of physician behavior accounting for wide variations in treatment patterns for similar patients. These practice variations are referred to as *small-area variations,* in recognition of the fact that the observed differences in practice patterns have been associated only with certain geographic areas of the country. Such a variation in practice intensity, which can be as great as twofold, cannot be explained by age, gender, race, pricing variations, demand inducements, or health status (Baucus & Fowler, 2003). Small-area variations signal gross inefficiencies in the U.S. health care delivery system because they increase costs without appreciably better outcomes.

COST CONTAINMENT

Even though rising health care expenditures may seem innocuous to some, they must be controlled for several reasons. First, rising health care costs mean that Americans have to forgo other goods and services when more is spent on health care. Second, economic resources should be directed to their highest-valued uses, even though consumers decide how much should be spent on purchasing a product or service based on their perception of the value they expect to receive (Feldstein, 1994, p. 13).

The United States has made many attempts to control health care spending, using a combination of government regulation and market-based competition. Most of these undertakings have met with limited success, mainly because implementing a systemwide cost-control initiative has not been feasible in such a fragmented system. In contrast, national health care programs in other countries have *all-payer systems* in which centralized controls allow cost-containment efforts to sweep through the entire health care delivery system. Cost-containment measures in the United States can be applied only in a piecemeal fashion and can affect only certain targeted sectors of the health care delivery system at one time.

Another reason that cost-control efforts in the United States have not proved very successful is because of cost shifting between programs and sectors. *Cost shifting* refers to the ability of providers to make up for lost revenues in one area by increasing utilization or charging higher prices in other areas that are free of controls. Providers are able to shift costs when cost-control measures are not applied on a systemwide basis. Regulatory approaches to cost containment typically control the capacity of the supply side, through what is referred to as health planning, and the demand side, in the form of price and utilization control.

Health Planning

Health planning refers to an undertaking by the government to align and distribute health care resources in a manner that, in the eyes of the government, would achieve desired health outcomes for all people. Health planning employs supply-side rationing to control health care expenditures. The central planning function does not fit well in a system that is largely private because of the absence of a central administrative agency to monitor the system. Instead, market forces are allowed to govern the system.

The types of health care services, their geographic distribution, access to these services, and the prices charged by providers develop independently of any pre-formulated plans.

Price Controls

In 1971, President Richard Nixon imposed the Economic Stabilization Program (ESP), which placed limits on the amount that hospitals could raise their prices from year to year (Williams & Torrens, 1993). The ESP controls did generate a moderating influence on price increases for most medical services; however, the program placed no limits on the quantity of services or costs of production (Altman & Eichenholz, 1976). After the controls were lifted, inflation returned to its pre-control levels (Altman & Eichenholz, 1976).

Perhaps the most important undertaking to control prices for inpatient hospital care was the conversion of hospital Medicare reimbursement from a retrospective plan to a prospective system based on diagnosis-related groups (DRGs) as authorized under the Social Security Amendments of 1983. This change reduced the growth in inpatient hospital spending, but had little impact on total per capita Medicare cost inflation; costs mainly shifted from the inpatient to the outpatient sector.

Another rate-setting mechanism was the Omnibus Budget Reconciliation Act (OBRA) of 1989, which helped establish a national Medicare fee schedule. With this fee schedule, known as the *resource-based relative value scale (RBRVS)*, physicians are paid according to relative value units established for more than 7,000 covered services, and a volume performance standard was implemented to contain the annual rate of growth in Medicare physician payments.

Peer Review

The term *peer review* refers to the general process of medical review of utilization and quality carried out directly by, or under the supervision of, physicians (Wilson & Neuhauser, 1985, p. 270). Under the Medicare program, peer review organizations (PROs) were established in 1984 to determine whether care is reasonable, necessary, of adequate quality, and provided in the most appropriate setting. These organizations are now called quality improvement organizations (QIOs). They are statewide private organizations composed of practicing physicians and other health care professionals who are paid by the federal government to review the care provided to Medicare beneficiaries. They can deny payment if care does not meet certain standards.

Competitive Approaches

Competition refers to rivalry among sellers for customers (Dranove, 1993). In health care delivery, it means that providers of health care services try to attract patients who have the ability to choose from several different providers. Although competition more commonly refers to price competition, it may also be based on technical quality, amenities, access, or other factors (Dranove, 1993). In the United States, competitive reforms were given preference because of the growing interest in market-oriented approaches across many sectors of the economy during the Ronald Reagan presidency in the 1980s. Market-oriented reforms were accompanied by mounting cost-containment efforts in the private sector and the growth of managed care. Competitive strategies can be classified into four broad types: demand-side incentives, supply-side regulation, payer-driven price competition, and utilization controls.

Demand-side incentives refer to cost-sharing mechanisms that place a larger cost burden on consumers, thereby encouraging consumers to be more cost conscious in selecting the insurance plan that best serves their needs, and more judicious in their utilization of services. *Supply-side regulation* typically refers to the antitrust laws passed in the United States, which prohibit business practices that stifle competition among providers, such as price fixing, price discrimination, exclusive contracting arrangements, and mergers deemed anticompetitive by the Department of Justice. Such restrictions force health care organizations to be cost-efficient to survive. *Payer-driven price competition* occurs when employers shop for the best value in terms of the cost of premiums and the benefits package (competition among insurers), and when MCOs shop for the best value from providers of health services (competition among providers). The *utilization controls* used in managed care have eliminated some of the unnecessary or inappropriate services provided to consumers by intervening in the decisions made by providers, in an effort to ensure that only appropriate and necessary services are provided in an efficient manner.

Electronic Health Records

Electronic health records (EHRs) comprise patients' medical records stored in a digital format that can be accessed over a computer on a network. Policy makers have strongly supported efforts to convert paper-based health records to electronic versions due to the associated cost-containment benefits. Paper records force health care personnel to engage in photocopying, faxing, and transporting of records so as to share information between providers—processes that take both time and money and may lead to missing paperwork because information may be stored at different locations. These costs and problems can be eliminated by interoperable EHRs that can be shared easily among providers, and that contain a patient's complete history in the health care system, thereby eliminating the problem of missing records or paperwork. Widespread adoption of EHRs will result in better cost efficiencies through improved care coordination that can reduce clinicians' prescription of unnecessary tests and treatments.

Chronic Disease Prevention and Management

The delivery of health care in the United States is inefficient in regard to chronic conditions such as diabetes and cardiovascular disease. The system often fails to deliver preventive programs to patients who are headed toward development of such conditions, as well as interventions to maintain health and avoid hospitalizations. Approximately 70% of all U.S. health care costs are generated by 10% of patients, who typically have one or more chronic diseases; thus there is enormous potential for cost containment through the improvement of the delivery of care for chronic conditions. So far, it has proved difficult to implement more preventive programs in the currently fragmented system of independent practitioners.

UNEQUAL IN ACCESS

In broad terms, *access* to care can be defined as the ability to obtain needed, affordable, convenient, acceptable, and effective personal health services in a timely manner. Access is one of the key determinants of health status, along with environment, lifestyle, and heredity factors. It also helps to benchmark the effectiveness of the medical care delivery system and is increasingly linked to quality of care and the efficient use of needed services.

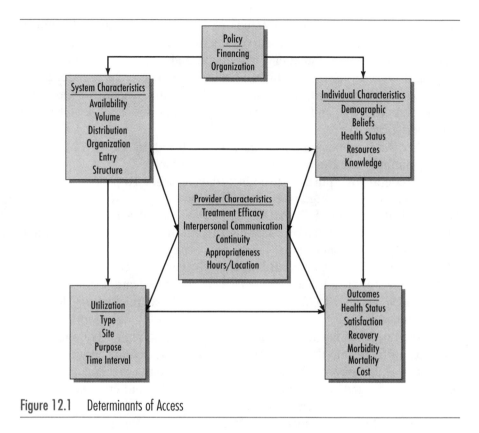

Figure 12.1   Determinants of Access

Although "access" is a familiar term used by both popular and academic media, it is associated with numerous and differing concepts. It may refer to the availability (or not) of a usual source of care for an individual, the actual utilization of health services, or the acceptability of particular services. **Figure 12.1** illustrates the system, provider, and individual characteristics that influence access to care.

Data on Access

Population-based surveys supported by federal statistical agencies are the major data sources for conducting analyses on access to care. Large national surveys such as the National Health Interview Survey (NHIS) and the Medical Expenditure Panel Survey (MEPS) are the leading data sources used to monitor access trends as well as other issues of interest. The latter comprises a series of surveys that gather data on health care use and expenditures (e.g., inpatient, outpatient, and office-based care; dental care; and prescription medications), health insurance coverage, access to care, sources of payment, health status and disability, medical conditions, health care quality, and measures of socioeconomic and demographic characteristics.

Other well-known national surveys are listed in **Table 12.2**. They include national surveys and surveys on special topics.

The federal government also collects data on special topics such as community health centers (e.g., Bureau of Common Reporting Requirement and Uniform Data System), HIV/AIDS (e.g., HIV Cost and Services Utilization Study 1994–1998), managed care (e.g., Consumer Assessment of Health Plans Study 1996), and mental health (e.g., Mental Health Care Services Study). The Medicare Current Beneficiary Survey, the Medicare Statistical System, the Medicaid Data System, and the Medicaid Demonstration Projects (1983–1984, 1992–1996) have collected data relevant to Medicare and Medicaid.

States, associations, and research institutions also regularly collect data on topics of interest to them. Examples include state health services utilization data (e.g., all-payer hospital discharge data systems), state managed care data (e.g., managed care encounter data), state Medicaid enrollee satisfaction data (e.g., Medicaid enrollee satisfaction surveys), physician data from the American Medical Association's Physician Masterfile, and hospital data from the American Hospital Association's Annual Survey of Hospitals 1946 to present. Examples of research institution-based initiatives include collection of data on the health care delivery system (e.g., Center for Evaluative Clinical Sciences: Dartmouth Atlas of Health Care in the U.S.), women's health (e.g., Commonwealth Fund: Women's Health Survey 1993), minority health (e.g., Commonwealth Fund: Health Care Services and Minority Groups: A Comparative Survey of Whites, African Americans, Hispanics, and Asian Americans 1994), health insurance (e.g., Mathematica Policy Research/Robert Wood Johnson Foundation: Family Survey on Health Insurance 1993–1994), and access to care (e.g., Robert Wood Johnson Foundation National Access Surveys, Mathematica Policy Research: Access to Care Pilot Survey of Medicaid Beneficiaries 1994).

With the growth of managed care, encounter databases have become increasingly critical in recording and evaluating access to health care.

Table 12.2   Selected National Surveys of Health Care

Survey Title	Survey Author	Survey Function
Current Population Survey and Survey of Income and Program Participation	U.S. Census Bureau	Information on population characteristics
Area Resource File	Bureau of Health Professions	Pools information on characteristics of population and health care delivery system
National Health and Nutrition Examination Survey	NCHS	Information on demographics, prevalence of selected diseases, nutrition, and behavioral risk factors
National Hospital Discharge Survey	NCHS	Data on short-stay hospital discharges and utilization
Ambulatory Medical Care Survey	NCHS	Data on ambulatory medical encounters
National Hospital Ambulatory Medical Care Survey	NCHS	Data on ambulatory hospital encounters
National Nursing Home Survey	NCHS	Data on nursing homes and utilization, nursing home residents, and nursing home staff
Behavioral Risk Factor Survey	CDC	Data on health practices and behavioral risks of illness
National Health Provider Inventory	CDC	Data on inpatient facilities
Longitudinal Survey on Aging	CDC	Data on older individuals
National Nursing Home Survey Follow-Up	CDC	Data on nursing homes
National Employer Health Insurance Survey	CDC	Data on insurance
Vital Statistics of the United States	CDC	Vital statistics information

CDC, Centers for Disease Control and Prevention; NCHS, National Center for Health Statistics.

In addition to the federal government, private nonprofit research centers collect information on managed care. Examples include the National Health Maintenance Organization Census (1977 to the present, sponsored by Interstudy) and the Healthcare Effectiveness Data and Information Set (sponsored by the National Committee for Quality Assurance).

Access Disparities

In the United States, both low socioeconomic status and minority group membership are associated with lower overall health care usage and access. Data from the 2010 National Health Interview Survey (NHIS) reveal that nonwhite persons younger than the age of 65 years were 3 to 30% less likely than their white counterparts to be insured. Among nonelderly middle- to high income individuals, only 10.7% reported being uninsured, compared with their near-poor (34%) and poor (32.8%) counterparts (NCHS, 2011). These differences are particularly significant given the predominant role of insurance in the U.S. health care delivery system.

According to NHIS measures of primary care access, racial/ethnic minorities are less likely than their white counterparts to have a specific source of ongoing care. A similar trend is observed among lower-income individuals and their higher-income counterparts. Among those persons who have a usual source of care, blacks and Hispanics are more likely than whites to have hospital-based (as opposed to office-based) care. Hispanics, in particular, are less likely to have a usual primary care provider than their non-Hispanic white counterparts (36% versus 21%). Similar trends are observed among Medicare beneficiaries, for whom many preventive services (e.g., flu shots, cancer screenings) require no cost sharing. Nonwhite beneficiaries have fewer cancer screenings, flu shots, and ambulatory and physician visits than their white counterparts (Gornick, 2000).

Geographic disparities in access are also present, and individuals from rural areas face greater access barriers than those residing in urban areas. Rural Americans have higher mortality and morbidity and shorter life expectancy than their urban counterparts (Cordes, 1989; DeFriese & Ricketts, 1989; Rowland & Lyons, 1989; Sherman, 1991). Rural Americans are more likely to be poor, to suffer from chronic impairment, to be uninsured if younger than 65 years, and to be elderly than their urban counterparts (Norton & McManus, 1989). The health care system available to address these problems, however, faces severe limitations, including maldistribution of physicians, lack of sufficient primary care services, and lack of access to care for geographic, financial, or discrimination/cultural reasons (Freeman et al., 1982; Sardell, 1988).

Reasons for Unequal Access

In the United States, significant barriers to health care access still exist at both the individual and system levels. Individually, it is those persons with minority origins, low income, less education, special needs defined by disability and chronic illness, and no health insurance coverage who continue to face greater barriers to access than the rest of the population. Access is best predicted by race, income, and occupation. These three factors are interrelated: Those individuals belonging to minority groups tend to be poorer, less educated, and more likely to work in job environments that pose greater health risks.

Access Initiatives

Access to care has been incrementally addressed by the U.S. government through a variety of public programs. Although a preventive and chronic care model of health care delivery in the United States is an evolving departure from the traditional acute care system, the concepts of prevention and comprehensive primary care are clearly established in legislative history. The Sheppard-Towner Act of 1921 exemplifies early federal attempts to provide direct primary care health services to economically disadvantaged mothers and children. Screening and other preventive care programs followed suit in subsequent Social Security amendments. Government interest in assuring access to other lower-income populations grew during World War II, when comprehensive care was extended to the wives and children of low-grade armed forces personnel. The issue of health care access among disadvantaged populations paved the way for the Great Society programs of the 1960s. During that era, rising health care costs, along with disproportionately high individual cost-sharing among the elderly, prompted Congress to create the Medicare program (which later expanded coverage to people with disabilities and end-stage renal disease) and Medicaid for the poor.

In the latter portion of the twentieth century, services such as cancer screening and immunizations were added to the Medicare program, and $24 million was allocated to states in 1997 to create the Children's Health Insurance Programs (CHIP) for low-income children in families who did not otherwise qualify for Medicaid. The 2010 Patient Protection and Affordable Care Act (ACA of 2010), signed into law by President Barack Obama on March 23 of that year, comprises comprehensive reform legislation designed to increase Americans' access to health care. Provisions of the law seek to expand insurance coverage, such as through an individual mandate to purchase insurance or face a financial penalty, Medicaid expansion to cover all adults with incomes up to 133% of the federal poverty level (FPL), and elimination of denial of coverage due to preexisting medical conditions (Connors & Gostin, 2010). Overall, these provisions should greatly reduce the number of uninsured and increase access to health care for all Americans.

Critique and Prospect

It is society's duty to ensure equitable access to an adequate level of health care for all. According to one view, economic scarcity is a relative measure. Scarcity in the U.S. medical delivery system is largely the result of distributive practices that limit access for those who are poor and those who live in rural areas. In the overall system, a surplus exists—for example, a surplus of hospital beds and physicians practicing in urban areas. The problem is that these surpluses are not generally shifted to respond to need (Brown, 1992).

Earlier chapters discussed the lack of access for the uninsured. Access, however, is also limited because of underinsurance and, for a few people, because of lifetime caps on health insurance. For years, these lifetime caps have been arbitrarily set at around $1 million or $2 million. Americans who are otherwise insured may be affected by lifetime caps because of a costly catastrophic injury or illness. For example, the average lifetime cost of care for a person with a spinal cord injury who is dependent on a ventilator can be more than $5 million. After the cap is reached, insurance companies stop coverage, even though the need for medical care continues.

Access to health care has considerable influence on population health. The prospects of universal access in the United States are contingent on drastic reductions in health care expenditures. Without significant improvements in access, the U.S. health care delivery system will continue to be rated behind most others in the developed world. From a systems standpoint, this situation is a predicament. The problem requires national policy initiatives, but it does not diminish the need to pursue quality improvements at the microlevel at which practitioners, ancillary workers, and health care managers have more control.

Exhibit 12.2   Selected Quality Indicators

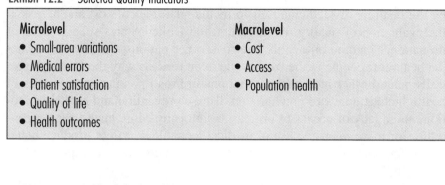

Microlevel	Macrolevel
• Small-area variations	• Cost
• Medical errors	• Access
• Patient satisfaction	• Population health
• Quality of life	
• Health outcomes	

AVERAGE IN QUALITY

Quality can be appreciated from both microperspectives and macroperspectives. **Exhibit 12.2** provides examples of micro- and macrolevel quality indicators. The microview focuses on services at the point of delivery and their subsequent effects; it is associated with the performance of individual caregivers and health care organizations. The macroview looks at quality from the standpoint of populations; it reflects the performance of the entire health care delivery system.

The Institute of Medicine has defined *quality* as "the degree to which health services for individuals and populations increase the likelihood of desired health outcomes and are consistent with current professional knowledge" (McGlynn, 1997). This definition has several implications:

1. Quality performance occurs on a continuum, theoretically ranging from unacceptable to excellent.

2. The focus is on services provided by the health care delivery system (as opposed to individual behaviors).

3. Quality may be evaluated from the perspective of individuals and populations or communities.

4. The emphasis is on desired health outcomes; research evidence must be used to identify the services that improve health outcomes.

5. In the absence of scientific evidence regarding appropriateness of care, professional consensus can be used to develop criteria for the definition and measurement of quality (McGlynn, 1997).

Although complete in many respects, the definition of quality proposed by the Institute of Medicine fails to include the roles of cost and access in the evaluation of quality. Even though the United States spends more of its national income on health care than other nations, Americans are not the healthiest people in the world. The main reasons why the United States trails behind other industrialized nations in broad population measures of health include a lack of emphasis on disease prevention and health promotion, and a lack of access to primary health care. More health care expenditures or more intensive use of medical technology do not produce better health. In other words, more is not better, and more does not represent better quality.

In his well-known model to help define and measure quality in health care organizations, Donabedian (1980) proposed three domains in which health care quality should be examined: structure, process, and outcomes. Donabedian noted that all three domains are important in measuring the quality of care. He also emphasized that these three approaches are complementary and should be collectively used to monitor quality of care (Al-Assaf, 1993b).

Structure, process, and outcomes are closely linked (**Figure 12.2**). The three domains are also hierarchical. Structure is the foundation of the quality of health care: Good processes require a good structure. In other words, deficiencies in structure generally have a negative effect on the processes (defined in the "Process" subsection later in this section) of health care delivery. Structure and processes together influence quality outcomes. Structure primarily influences process and has a secondary influence on outcome. This model views quality strictly from the delivery system's perspective; it does not account for social and individual lifestyle and behavioral factors that also have a significant influence on health status.

Structure

Structure has been defined as "the relatively stable characteristics of the providers of care, of the tools and resources they have at their disposal, and of the physical and organizational settings in which they work" (Donabedian, 1980, p. 81). Structural measures indicate the extent to which health care organizations are capable of providing adequate levels of care (Williams & Torrens, 1993). Hence, structure provides an indirect measure of quality under the assumption that a good structure enables health care

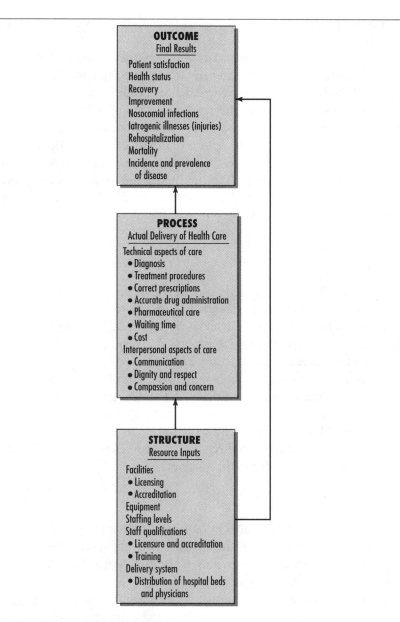

OUTCOME
Final Results

Patient satisfaction
Health status
Recovery
Improvement
Nosocomial infections
Iatrogenic illnesses (injuries)
Rehospitalization
Mortality
Incidence and prevalence
    of disease

PROCESS
Actual Delivery of Health Care

Technical aspects of care
 • Diagnosis
 • Treatment procedures
 • Correct prescriptions
 • Accurate drug administration
 • Pharmaceutical care
 • Waiting time
 • Cost
Interpersonal aspects of care
 • Communication
 • Dignity and respect
 • Compassion and concern

STRUCTURE
Resource Inputs

Facilities
 • Licensing
 • Accreditation
Equipment
Staffing levels
Staff qualifications
 • Licensure and accreditation
 • Training
Delivery system
 • Distribution of hospital beds
    and physicians

Figure 12.2   The Three Domains of Health Care Quality

delivery professionals to employ good processes that would lead to good outcomes.

A significant initiative toward improving structure are EHRs—digitally formatted medical records that, when implemented into the health care system, should reduce cost and provide greater coordination across the system. The Agency for Healthcare Research and Quality (AHRQ) is currently funding projects across the nation to implement and evaluate electronic medical and health records to determine their effects on quality, safety, efficacy, and cost of health care. One national-level analysis showed a savings to physicians of almost $10 billion when the resulting safety and efficiency improvements from EHR use were considered, whereas a study for small practices showed a net loss of $20,000 per physician per year from adoption of EHRs.

Process

Process refers to the specific way in which care is provided. Examples of process include correct diagnostic tests, correct prescriptions, accurate drug administration, pharmaceutical care, waiting time to see a physician, and interpersonal aspects of care delivery. Just as with structure, it is important to relate process to patient care outcomes. In other words, structures and processes should be employed with the objective of achieving better outcomes. Some significant initiatives toward process improvement have occurred in recent years. Some of the main developments in this area are clinical practice guidelines, cost-efficiency, critical pathways, and risk management, which are discussed in the "Developments in Process Improvement" section later in this chapter.

Outcome

Outcome refers to the effects or final results obtained from utilizing the structure and processes of health care delivery. Outcomes are viewed by many as the bottom-line measure of the effectiveness of the health care delivery system (McGlynn & Brook, 1996). Positive outcomes suggest recovery from disease and improvement in health. They also suggest an overall improvement in health status through health promotion and disease prevention efforts and adequate access to health care services. Outcome measures include postoperative infection rates, nosocomial infections, iatrogenic illnesses, rates of rehospitalization, and patient satisfaction.

DEVELOPMENTS IN PROCESS IMPROVEMENT

Clinical Practice Guidelines

In response to findings of small-area variations, various professional groups, MCOs, and the government have embarked on the development of standardized practice guidelines. *Clinical practice guidelines* (also called *medical practice guidelines*) are explicit descriptions of preferred clinical processes for managing a clinical problem based on research evidence, whenever possible, and on consensus in the absence of evidence (Larsen, 1996). Hence, clinical practice guidelines are designed to provide scientifically based protocols to guide physicians' clinical decisions; they are intended to promote lower costs and better outcomes. Currently, the National Guideline Clearinghouse (NGC) works under the Agency for Healthcare Research and Quality to compile, update, and disseminate objective, detailed clinical practice guidelines for a variety of conditions, diseases and treatments in the United States (www.guideline.gov).

Cost-Efficiency

Also referred to as cost-effectiveness, cost-efficiency (discussed earlier in this text in conjunction with technology assessment) is an important concept in quality assessment. A service is *cost-efficient* when the benefit received is greater than the cost incurred in providing the service. In economic terms, additional services beyond the optimal point produce diminishing marginal returns. This point also represents optimal quality, which serves as a point of demarcation between underutilization and overutilization. On the one hand, *underutilization* (underuse) occurs when the benefits of an intervention outweigh its risks or costs, yet the intervention is not used (Chassin, 1991). On the other hand, *overutilization* (overuse) occurs when the costs or risks of treatment outweigh the benefits, yet additional care is delivered. When health care is overused, precious resources are wasted.

Critical Pathways

Critical pathways are outcome-based and patient-centered clinical management tools that are interdisciplinary in nature and that facilitate coordination of care among multiple clinical departments and caregivers within a health care facility, such as a hospital. A critical pathway is a timeline that identifies planned medical interventions along with expected patient outcomes for a specific diagnosis or class of medical conditions, often defined by a diagnosis-related group. In addition to technical outcomes, pathways may measure factors such as patient satisfaction, self-reported health status, mental health, and activities of daily living. Use of critical pathways reduces costs and improves quality by reducing errors, improving coordination among interdisciplinary players, streamlining clinical management functions, providing systematic data for assessing care, and reducing variation in practice patterns (Giffin & Giffin, 1994).

Risk Management

Risk management consists of proactive efforts to prevent adverse events related to clinical care and facilities operations, and is especially focused on avoiding medical malpractice (Orlikoff, 1988). Initiatives undertaken by a health care organization to review clinical processes and establish protocols for the specific purpose of reducing malpractice litigation can actually enhance quality. Malpractice concerns result in defensive medicine; thus risk-management approaches should employ the principles of cost-efficiency along with standardized practice guidelines and critical pathways. Unfortunately, fear of litigation may lead to a reluctance on the part of hospitals and physicians to disclose preventable harm and actual medical errors. In this respect, fear of litigation may actually conceal problems that may compromise patient safety (Lamb et al., 2003).

New Quality Initiatives

The Centers for Medicare and Medicaid Services (CMS) has been particularly interested in promoting new quality measurements to increase accountability and health care quality for all beneficiaries. The first quality initiatives were launched in 2001, and currently encompass a wide variety of measures and reforms. These programs include the Physician Quality Reporting System, partnerships with contractual Quality Improvement Organizations to help analyze quality measurement data, the development of a standardized measurement approach for all initiatives called the Measures Management System (MMS), and specific guidelines for hospitals, nursing homes, and dialysis centers (CMS, 2011b). This information is directly available to patients.

Accountable Care Organizations

The ACA of 2010 included provisions for the creation of a new type of health care organization, designed to help increase cooperation between providers across various health care settings to improve Medicare patient outcomes. These new networks, called accountable care organizations (ACOs), were discussed in a previous chapter.

CONCLUSION

Increasing costs, lack of access, and concerns about quality pose the greatest challenges to health care delivery in the United States. To some extent, these three issues are interrelated. Increasing costs limit the system's ability to expand access; without universal coverage for all Americans, however, it is doubtful that the United States will ever match other developed countries in population health outcome.

Health care costs in the United States are the highest in the world. A move toward prospective payments and the growth of managed care can be largely credited with putting the brakes on rising health care spending during the 1990s; even so, the best current forecasts anticipate accelerated spending growth in the future, which means that a larger share of the economic resources will be devoted to the delivery of health care.

Access to medical care is one of the determinants of health status, along with environmental, lifestyle, and heredity factors. Access is also regarded as a significant benchmark in assessing the effectiveness of the medical care delivery system. Access is explained in terms of enabling and predisposing factors, as well as factors related to health policy and health care delivery.

One reason that the pursuit of quality in health care has trailed behind the emphasis on cost and access is the difficulty in defining and measuring quality. Meanwhile, growth of managed care and emphasis on cost containment have produced a heightened interest in quality because of the intuitive concern that control of costs may have a negative impact on quality; however, there is still a long way to go in specifying what constitutes good quality in medical care, how to guarantee it for patients, and how to reward providers and health plans whose outcomes indicate successes in quality improvement. One challenge in achieving such a goal is that patients, providers, and payers may all define quality differently, which translates into different expectations of the health care delivery system and, therefore, differing evaluations of its quality (McGlynn, 1997).

REFERENCES

Al-Assaf AF. Introduction and historical background. In *The Textbook of Total Quality Management,* ed. Al-Assaf AF, Schmele JA. Delray Beach, FL: St. Lucie Press; 1993a:3–12.

Al-Assaf AF. Outcome management and TQ. In *The Textbook of Total Quality Management,* ed. Al-Assaf AF, Schmele JA. Delray Beach, FL: St. Lucie Press; 1993b:221–237.

Altman SH, Eichenholz J. Inflation in the health industry: Causes and cures. In *Health: A Victim or Cause of Inflation?,* ed. Zubkoff M. New York: Milbank Memorial Fund; 1976:1–32.

Altman SH, Wallack SS. Health care spending: Can the United States control it? In *Strategic Choices for a Changing Health Care System,* ed. Altman SH, Reinhardt UE. Chicago: Health Administration Press; 1996.

Baucus M, Fowler EJ. Geographic variation in Medicare spending and the real focus of Medicare reform. *Health Affairs.* 2003 http://content.healthaffairs .org/cgi/content/abstract/hlthaff.w2.115v1.

Brown K. Death and access: Ethics in cross-cultural health care. In *Choices and Conflict: Explorations in Health Care Ethics,* ed. Friedman E. Chicago: American Hospital Publishing; 1992.

Centers for Medicare and Medicaid Services (CMS). Accountable care organizations (ACO). October 20, 2011a. https://www.cms.gov/ACO/.

Centers for Medicare and Medicaid Services (CMS). Quality initiatives: General Information. October 4, 2011b. https://www.cms.gov/QualityInitiativesGenInfo/.

Chassin MR. Quality of care: Time to act. *JAMA.* 1991;266:3472–3473.

Connors EE, Gostin LA. Health care reform: A historic moment in US social policy. *JAMA.* 2010;303(24):2521–2522.

Cordes SM. The changing rural environment and the relationship between health services and rural development. *Health Serv Res.* 1989;23(6):757–784.

DeFriese GH, Ricketts TC. Primary health care in rural areas: An agenda for research. *Health Serv Res.* 1989;23(6):931–974.

Donabedian A. *Explorations in Quality Assessment and Monitoring: The Definition of Quality and Approaches to Its Assessment.* Vol. 1. Ann Arbor, MI: Health Administration Press; 1980.

Dranove D. The case for competitive reform in health care. In *Competitive Approaches to Health Care Reform,* ed. Arnould RJ, Rich RF, White WD. (pp. 67–82). Washington, DC: Urban Institute Press; 1993:67–82.

Feldstein P. *Health Policy Issues: An Economic Perspective on Health Reform.* Ann Arbor, MI: AUPHA Press/Health Administration Press; 1994.

Freeman HE, et al. Community health centers: An initiative of enduring utility. *Milbank Mem Fund Quarterly/Health Society.* 1982;60(2):245–267.

Giffin M, Giffin RB. Market memo: Critical pathways produce tangible results. *Health Care Strat Manage.* 1994;12(7):1–6.

Gornick ME. *Vulnerable Populations and Medicare Services: Why Do Disparities Exist.* New York: Century Foundation Press; 2000.

Heffler S, et al. Health spending projections for 2001–2011: The latest outlook. *Health Affairs.* 2002;21(2):207–218.

Hellander I, et al. Health care paper chase, 1993: The cost to the nation, the states, and the District of Columbia. *Int J Health Serv.* 1994;24(1):1–9.

Lamb RM, et al. Hospital disclosure practices: Results of a national survey. *Health Affairs.* 2003;22(2):73–83.

Larsen RR. Narrowing the gray zone: How clinical practice guidelines can improve the decision-making process. *Postgrad Med.* 1996;100(2):17–24.

Levit K, et al. Trends in U.S. health care spending, 2001. *Health Affairs.* 2003;22(1):154–164.

Martin A, Lassman D, Whittle L, Catlin A, National Health Expenditure Accounts Team. Recession contributes to slowest annual rate of increase in health spending in five decades. *Health Affairs.* 2011;30(1):11–22.

McGlynn EA. Six challenges in measuring the quality of health care. *Health Affairs.* 1997;16(3):7–21.

McGlynn EA, Brook RH. Ensuring quality of care. In *Changing the U.S. Health Care System: Key Issues in Health Services, Policy, and Management,* ed. Andersen RM, Rice TH, Kominski GF. San Francisco: Jossey-Bass; 1996.

National Center for Health Statistics (NCHS). *Health, United States, 1995.* Hyattsville, MD: U.S. Department of Health and Human Services; 1996.

National Center for Health Statistics (NCHS). *Health, United States, 2010.* Hyattsville, MD: U.S. Department of Health and Human Services; 2010.

National Center for Health Statistics (NCHS). *Vital and Health Statistics* 10 (251). Atlanta, GA: Centers for Disease Control and Prevention; 2011.

Norton CH, McManus MA. Background tables on demographic characteristics. *Health Serv Res.* 1989;23(6):807–848.

Orlikoff JE. *Malpractice Prevention and Liability Control for Hospitals*, 2nd ed. Chicago: American Hospital Publishing; 1988.

Rowland D, Lyons B. Triple jeopardy: Rural, poor, and uninsured. *Health Serv Res.* 1989;23(6):975–1004.

Sardell A. *The U.S. Experiment in Social Medicine, the Community Health Center Program, 1965–1986*. Pittsburgh, PA: University of Pittsburgh Press; 1988.

Sherman A. *Falling by the Wayside: Children in Rural America*. Washington, DC: Children's Defense Fund; 1991.

TECH Research Network. Technology change around the world: Evidence from heart attack care. *Health Affairs.* 2001;20(3):25–42.

Williams SJ, Torrens PR. Influencing, regulating, and monitoring the health care system. In *Introduction to Health Services*, 4th ed., ed. Williams SJ, Torrens PR. (pp. 421–429). Albany, NY: Delmar; 1993:421–429.

Wilson FA, Neuhauser D. *Health Services in the United States*, 2nd ed. Cambridge, MA: Ballinger; 1985.

Chapter 13

Health Policy

INTRODUCTION

Although the United States does not have a centrally controlled system of health care delivery, it does have a history of federal, state, and local government involvement in health and social policy. Perhaps the most visible policy efforts were the social programs created under the Social Security legislation during Franklin Roosevelt's presidency in the 1940s. This initiative later paved the way for the creation of Medicare and Medicaid through Amendments to the Social Security Act in 1965. Even today, the government continues to find new opportunities to mold health care delivery through health policy. This chapter first defines what health policy is and explores the principal features of health policy in the United States. Next, it describes the development of legislative policy and gives examples of critical health policy issues. Finally, an outlook for the future of health policy in the United States is provided.

WHAT IS HEALTH POLICY?

Public policies are authoritative decisions made in the legislative (congressional), executive (presidential), or judicial (courts, including the Supreme Court) branches of government that are intended to direct or influence the actions, behaviors, or decisions of others (Longest, 2002). When public policies pertain to or influence the pursuit of health, they become health policies. Thus *health policy* can be defined as "the aggregate of principles, stated or unstated, that . . . characterize the distribution of resources, services, and political influences that impact on the health of the population" (Miller, 1987, p. 15).

Different Forms of Health Policies

Health policies often come as a by-product of public social policies enacted by the government. A relevant example is the expansion of health insurance coverage. In the past, policies that excluded fringe benefits from income or Social Security taxes and a U.S. Supreme Court ruling that employee benefits, including health insurance, could be legitimately included in the collective bargaining process led to important changes in the health care system. As a result of these policies, employer-provided health insurance benefits grew rapidly in the middle decades of the twentieth century (Health Insurance Association of America, 1992). In 1965, adoption of the Medicare and Medicaid legislation expanded the health sector by providing publicly subsidized health insurance to the elderly and indigent.

The American health care system has developed under extraordinarily favorable public policies. For example, the federally funded National Institutes of Health (NIH) had a budget of approximately $10 million when the agency was established in the early 1930s. Today, following exponential growth in its funding, the NIH's annual budget is approximately $10 billion. In addition, private industry spends a significant amount on biomedical research and development, encouraged by governmental policies that permit businesses to recoup their investments in research and development (NIH, 1991).

Health policies pertain to health care at all levels, including policies affecting the production, delivery, and financing of health care services. Such policies may affect groups or classes of individuals, such as physicians, the poor, the elderly, or children. They can also affect types of organizations, such as medical schools, health maintenance organizations

(HMOs), nursing homes, producers of medical technology, or employers. In the United States, each branch and level of government can influence health policy. For example, both the executive and legislative branches at the federal, state, and local levels can establish health policies, and the judicial branch can uphold, strike down, or modify existing laws affecting health and health care at any level.

Statutes or laws are also considered policies—for example, the statutory language contained in the 1983 Amendments to the Social Security Act that authorized the prospective payment system (PPS) for reimbursing hospitals for Medicare beneficiaries. Another example comprises the certificate-of-need (CON) programs through which many states seek to regulate capital expansion in their health care systems.

Regulatory Tools

Health policies can be used as *regulatory tools* (Longest, 2002). They may call upon the government to prescribe and control the behavior of a particular target group by monitoring the group and imposing sanctions if it fails to comply. Federally funded quality improvement organizations, for instance, develop and enforce standards concerning appropriate care under the Medicare program. State insurance departments across the country regulate health insurance companies in an effort to protect customers from excessive premiums, mendacious practices, and defaults on coverage in case of financial failure of an insurance company.

Some health policies are self-regulatory. For example, physicians set standards of medical practice, and schools of public health decide which courses should be part of their graduate programs in public health (Weissert & Weissert, 1996).

Allocative Tools

Health policies can also be used as *allocative tools* (Longest, 2002); that is, they may involve the direct provision of income, services, or goods to certain groups of individuals or institutions. Allocative tools in the health care arena are of two main types: distributive and redistributive. *Distributive policies* spread benefits throughout society. Typical distributive policies include funding of medical research through the NIH, the construction of facilities (e.g., hospital construction under the Hill-Burton program during the 1950s and 1960s), and the establishment of new institutions (e.g., HMOs). *Redistributive policies*, in contrast, take resources from one group and give it to another—a system that often creates visible beneficiaries and payers. As a consequence, health policy is often most visible and politically charged when it performs redistributive functions. Redistributive policies include the Medicaid program, which takes tax revenue from the public and spends it on the poor in the form of free health insurance.

PRINCIPAL FEATURES OF U.S. HEALTH POLICY

Several features characterize U.S. health policy, including the government acting as a subsidiary to the private sector; fragmented, incremental, and piecemeal reform; pluralistic (interest group) politics; a decentralized role for the states; and the impact of presidential leadership. These features often act or interact to influence the development and evolution of health policies.

Government as Subsidiary to the Private Sector

In the United States, health care is not seen as a right of citizenship or a primary responsibility of government. Instead, the private sector plays a dominant role. Much as with many other public policy issues, Americans generally prefer market solutions over government intervention in health care financing and delivery, and for this reason, they have a strong preference for minimizing the government's role in the delivery of health care. One result is that Americans have been far more reluctant than their counterparts in most industrialized democracies to develop social insurance programs. In addition, public opinion in the United States often presumes such programs to be overly generous.

Generally speaking, the role of government in U.S. health care has grown incrementally, mainly in response to perceived problems and negative consequences. Some of the most cited problems associated with government involvement include escalating costs, bureaucratic inflexibility and red tape, excessive regulation, irrational paperwork, arbitrary and sometimes conflicting public directives, inconsistent enforcement of rules and regulations, fraud and abuse, inadequate reimbursement, arbitrary denial of claims, insensitivity to local needs, consumer and provider dissatisfaction, and charges that such efforts tend to promote welfare dependence rather than a desire to seek employment (Longest, 2002).

The most credible argument for policy intervention begins with the identification of situations in which markets fail or do not function efficiently. Health care in the United States is a big industry, but certain specific characteristics and conditions of the health care market distinguish it from other types of businesses. Notably, the market for health care services in the United States violates the conditions of a competitive market in several ways.

For example, the complexity of health care services almost eliminates the ability of the consumer to make informed decisions without guidance from the sellers (providers). In addition, the entry of sellers into the health care market is heavily regulated. Widespread insurance coverage also affects the decisions of both buyers and sellers in these markets. These and other factors mean that the markets for health care services do not operate competitively, which in turn invites policy intervention to rectify perceived inequities.

Government spending for health care has largely been confined to filling the gaps in the private sector. Such interventions have, for example, included environmental protection, preventive services, communicable disease control, care of special groups, institutional care of the mentally and chronically ill, provision of medical care to the indigent, and support for research and training. With health coverage considered a privilege for those who are offered insurance through their employers, the government is left in a gap-filling role for the most vulnerable of the uninsured population.

Fragmented, Incremental, and Piecemeal Reform

The subsidiary role of the government and the attendant mixture of private and public approaches to the delivery of health care also results in a complex and fragmented pattern of health care financing in which (1) the employed are predominantly covered by voluntary insurance provided through contributions made by themselves and their employers; (2) the aged are insured through a combination of coverage financed out of Social Security tax revenues (Medicare Part A), voluntary insurance for outpatient and prescription drug coverage (Medicare Part B and Part D), and voluntary purchase of Medigap plans; (3) the poor are covered through Medicaid via federal, state, and local revenues; and (4) special population groups, such as veterans, Native Americans, and members of the armed forces, have coverage provided directly by the federal government.

Health policies in the United States have been incremental and piece-meal. An example is the gradual reforms in the Medicaid program since its establishment in 1965. In 1984, the first steps were taken to mandate coverage of pregnant women and children in two-parent families who met income eligibility requirements and to mandate coverage for all children aged 5 years or younger who met financial eligibility requirements. In 1986, states were given the option of covering pregnant women and children up to 5 years of age in families with incomes below 100% of federal poverty income guidelines. In 1988, that option was increased to cover families at 185% of the federal poverty level. In 1988, as part of the Medicaid Catastrophic Act (which remains in effect today), Congress mandated coverage for pregnant women and infants in families with incomes below 100% of federal poverty guidelines. (In 1989, this criterion was expanded to 133% of the poverty income, and coverage of children was extended to include children aged 6 years or younger.) In 1988, Congress required that Medicaid coverage be continued for 6 months for families leaving the Aid to Families with Dependent Children (AFDC) program, and allowed states the option of adding 6 months to that extension. The Children's Health Insurance Program (CHIP) allows states to use Medicaid expansion to extend insurance coverage to uninsured children who otherwise are not qualified for existing Medicaid programs.

These examples illustrate how a program may be reformed and expanded through successive legislative enactments over several years. In typical American fashion, the Medicaid program has been reformed through incremental change, but without ensuring access to medical care for all of the nation's uninsured. Among the uninsured population are millions of Americans who are not categorically eligible for services—mostly adults younger than age 65 with no dependent children. Congress has demonstrated the desire and political will to address the needs of a small number of the uninsured perceived as being the most vulnerable (e.g., pregnant women and children) but had not developed a consensus on more dramatic steps until the passage of the Patient Protection and Affordable Care Act of 2010 (ACA of 2010). This legislation greatly increases insurance options for Americans previously lacking coverage, including a Medicaid expansion for all adults with incomes up to 133% of the federal poverty level, the creation of state health insurance exchanges for better regulation of private plans, and a prohibition on insurers against denying coverage due to preexisting medical conditions.

The process of legislative health policy development offers another vivid case of institutional fragmentation. Thirty-one different congressional committees and subcommittees try to claim some fragment of jurisdiction over health legislation. The reform proposals that emerge from these committees face a daunting political challenge because proposals undergo separate consideration and passage in each chamber of Congress, are subjected to negotiations in a joint conference committee to reconcile bills passed by the two houses, and then head back to each chamber for approval. In the Senate, 41 of the 100 members can thwart the entire process at any point.

After a specific bill has passed in Congress, however, its journey is far from complete. Multiple levels of federal and state bureaucracy must interpret the legislation, and rules and regulations must be written for its implementation. During this process, political actors, interest groups, or project beneficiaries may influence the ultimate design of the program. At times, the final result may differ significantly from the initial intent of the bill's congressional sponsors. Given that many of the 2010 healthcare reform provisions will not be implemented until 2014, this implementation process could greatly affect the intended outcomes of the original ACA legislation.

This complex and seemingly anarchic process of policy formulation and implementation makes fundamental, comprehensive policy reform extremely difficult. Ideology and the organization of government reinforce the tendency toward maintaining a standstill. It usually takes a great political event—a landmark election, a mass popular upheaval, a war, or a domestic crisis—to shake off (even temporarily) the normal tilt toward inaction and the status quo. The passage of the ACA was a great accomplishment in this regard, but it remains to be seen how effectively the law actually works to reduce health care costs while increasing insurance coverage and medical care access.

Pluralistic and Interest Group Politics

Perhaps the most common explanation for health policy outcomes in the United States is one based on the role of interest groups and the incremental policies that result from compromises designed to satisfy their demands. Traditionally, the membership of the policy community has included (1) the legislative committees with jurisdiction in a policy domain, (2) the executive branch agencies responsible for implementing policies in the public domain, and (3) the interest groups in the private domain. The first two categories are the suppliers of the policies demanded by the third category.

Innovative, nonincremental policies are resisted by the established groups because such measures undermine the bargaining practices designed to reduce threats to established interests. The stability of the system is ensured because most groups are satisfied with the benefits that they receive; however, the result for any single group is less than optimal.

Interest Groups

The most effective demanders of policies are the well-organized interest groups. Interest groups' pluralism affects health policy just as it does any other policy debate in American politics. Powerful interest groups involved in health care politics are adamant about resisting any major change (Alford, 1975). Each group fights hard to protect its own interests.

By combining and concentrating the resources of their members, organized interest groups can dramatically change the ratio between the costs and benefits of participation in the political markets for policy change. Such interest groups represent a variety of individuals and entities, such as physicians in the American Medical Association, senior citizens allied with the AARP (American Association of Retired Persons), institutional providers such as hospitals belonging to the American Hospital Association, nursing homes belonging to the American Health Care Association or the American Association of Homes and Services for the Aging, and the member companies in the Pharmaceutical Research and Manufacturers of America. In recent years, physicians have often found it difficult to establish a unified voice to lobby for their interests because of the many specialty groups that exist among them.

The policy agenda of interest groups is typically reflective of their own interests. For example, AARP advocates programs to expand financing for long-term care for the elderly. Organized labor was among the staunchest supporters of national health insurance during the 1950s and again in the 1990s. Educational institutions and accrediting bodies have their primary concerns embedded in policies that would enable them to receive higher funding to educate health professionals.

Employers

The health policy concerns of American employers are mostly shaped by the degree to which employers are involved in the provision of health insurance benefits for their employees, their dependents, and their retirees. Many small business owners adamantly oppose health policies that would mandate them to provide coverage for employees because they believe they cannot afford to do so. Health policies that affect the health of workers or the health of the labor–management relations experienced by employers also attract their attention. For example, employers must comply with federal and state regulations regarding the health and well-being of their employees and engage in measures to prevent job-related illnesses and injuries. Employers are often subject to inspection by regulatory agencies to ensure that they are adhering to health and safety policies applicable to the workplace.

Consumer Groups

The interests of consumers are not uniform, nor are the policy preferences of their interest groups. Often, consumers do not have sufficient financial means to organize and advocate for their own best interests.

The health policy concerns of consumers and the groups that represent them reflect the rich diversity of the American people. African Americans and, more recently, the rapidly growing numbers of Hispanic Americans face special health problems. Both groups are underserved for many health care services and are underrepresented in all of the health professions in the United States. Their health policy interests include getting their unique health problems (e.g., higher infant mortality, higher exposure to violence among adolescents, higher levels of substance abuse among adults, and earlier deaths from cardiovascular disease and various other causes) adequately addressed.

Manufacturers of Technology

The health policy concerns of pharmaceutical and medical technology organizations include discerning changes in health policy areas and exerting influence over the formulation of policies. Health policy concerns regarding medical technology (including pharmaceuticals) are driven by three main factors: (1) Medical technology plays an important role in rising health costs, (2) medical technology often provides health benefits to people (albeit not always), and (3) the use of medical technology provides economic benefits aside from its potential to provide health benefits. These factors are likely to remain important determinants of the nation's policies toward medical technology.

Another factor driving the United States' current medical technology policy is policy makers' desire to develop cost-saving technology and to expand access to it. The government is spending an increasing amount of money on technology assessment. The goal is to identify the relative values among alternative technologies, presumably so that the government can support the best values in technology.

Alliances

To overcome pluralistic interests and maximize policy outcomes, diverse interest groups may form alliances among themselves and with members of the legislative body to protect and enhance the interests of those receiving benefits from government programs. Each member of these alliances receives some benefits from the current programs. Legislators are able to demonstrate to their constituencies the economic benefits from government spending in their districts, agencies are able to expand their programs, and interest groups are the direct recipients of benefits bestowed by government programs.

Decentralized Role of the States

In the United States, individual states play a significant role in the development and implementation of health policies. The importance of the role of individual states can be seen in programs involving the following:

- Financial support for the care and treatment of the poor and chronically disabled, which includes the primary responsibility for the administration of the federal/state Medicaid program and CHIP
- Quality assurance and oversight of health care practitioners and facilities (e.g., state licensure and regulation)
- Regulation of insurance, including health insurance
- Control of Medicaid costs
- Health personnel training (states provide the major share of the cost for the training of health care professionals)
- Authorization of local government health services

States are vested with broad legal authority to regulate almost every facet of the health care system. They license and regulate health care facilities and health professionals; restrict the content, marketing, and price of health insurance (including professional liability or malpractice insurance); set and enforce environmental quality standards; and enact a variety of controls on health care costs. All states bear a large responsibility for financing health services for the poor, primarily through the Medicaid program, for which financing is shared with the federal government. In addition, most states subsidize some of the costs of delivering health services to those persons with neither public nor private coverage. Personal health services funded or provided by states, often in cooperation with local government, include a range of services, such as public health nursing, communicable disease control, family planning and prenatal care, nutrition counseling, and home health services.

Most of the incremental policy actions of recent years originated in state governments. One action, taken by 24 states, was to create a special program called an "insurance risk pool." This measure is intended to help persons acquire private insurance who are otherwise unable to do so because of the medical risks that they pose to insurance companies. Most of these programs are financed by a combination of individual premiums and taxes on insurance carriers.

Other state-initiated programs have addressed additional vulnerable populations. New Jersey developed a program to ensure access to care for all pregnant women. Florida began a program, called Healthy Kids Corporation, that linked health insurance to schools. Massachusetts, Hawaii, and Oregon have experimented with more comprehensive programs designed to provide universal access to care within their jurisdictions.

Arguments have been made against too much state control over health policy decisions. The greater the amount of control states have, the more difficult it becomes to develop a coordinated national strategy. For example, it is difficult to plan a national disease control program if all states do not participate in the program or if they do not collect and report data in the same way. Moreover, some critics argue that disparities among states may lead to inequalities in access to health services. This factor, in turn, might lead to migration from states with poor health benefits to those with more generous programs. Finally, states may interpret federal incentives in ways that jeopardize the policy's original intent. For example, many states took advantage of federal matching grants for Medicaid programs by including a number of formerly state-funded services under an "expanded" Medicaid program. This move allowed states to gain increased federal funding while providing

exactly the same level of services as before. Although this phenomenon—
called "Medicaid maximization"—was pursued by only a few states, it had
an impact outside of those states and may have contributed to nationally rising health care costs in the early 1990s (Coughlin et al., 1999).

Impact of Presidential Leadership

Americans often look to strong presidential leadership to catalyze
major change in health policies, and presidents have important opportunities to influence congressional outcomes through their efforts to achieve
political compromises that allow bills with at least some of their preferred
agendas to be passed.

President Lyndon Johnson's role in the passage of Medicare and
Medicaid is often cited as a prime example. Johnson shepherded the passage of Medicare and Medicaid in 1965 in the context of an unusually
favorable level of political opportunity and by effectively using his leadership skills.

The major piece of health legislation that passed under Truman was
the Hill-Burton Hospital Construction Act. Two major pieces of health
legislation were passed during Richard Nixon's presidency: (1) the actions
leading to federal support of HMOs in 1973 and (2) the enactment of the
National Health Planning and Resources Development Act of 1974. Under
President Ronald Reagan, new Medicare cost-control approaches for hospitals and physicians were created, and additional Medicare coverage for the
elderly was established. Even though President Bill Clinton's comprehensive reform efforts failed, many of his incremental initiatives succeeded;
examples include the Health Insurance Portability and Accountability Act
of 1996 and CHIP.

Many political lessons can be learned from the failure of Clinton's
health care reform initiative (Litman & Robins, 1997). Presidential leadership in achieving landmark changes in health policies can be successful only when a convergence of political opportunity, political skill, and
commitment occurs. Opportunities were uniquely abundant for Johnson in
1965, and he effectively handled his legislative role. Presidents Truman,
Kennedy, and Carter might have promoted their proposals with greater
skill, but they were fundamentally thwarted by the lack of a true "window
of opportunity." Clinton enjoyed a uniquely high level of public interest in
health care reform, but failed in part because of other weaknesses related
to his level of opportunity, especially his failure to act within the first

100 days after his election. The complexity of the ever-changing details of his proposal was another major flaw and ultimately proved too much for the general public to comprehend and too easy for adversaries to distort.

The 2008 presidential race, from which Barack Obama emerged victorious, offered another opportunity for Democrats to take up health care reform. While campaigning for the presidency, Obama presented a framework for health care reform to achieve three goals: (1) modernize the health care system to improve quality and reduce costs, (2) expand coverage to all Americans, and (3) improve prevention and public health. The ACA of 2010 represents the most ambitious expansion of public health insurance since the creation of Medicare and Medicaid. Some of the most controversial provisions of this law, such as the individual mandate ordering all Americans to possess health insurance or pay a financial penalty, were constitutionally questioned in front of the Supreme Court during its 2012 session. Regardless of the outcome, passage of the ACA catalyzed a radical evolution in U.S. health policy.

DEVELOPMENT OF LEGISLATIVE HEALTH POLICY

The making of health policy in the United States is a complex process involving both private and public sectors (including multiple levels of government).

Policy Cycle

The formation and implementation of health policy occur in a policy cycle comprising five components: (1) issue raising, (2) policy design, (3) building of public support, (4) legislative decision making and building of policy support, and (5) legislative decision making and policy implementation. These activities are likely to be shared with Congress and interest groups in varying degrees.

Issue-raising activities are clearly essential in the policy formation cycle. The enactment of a new policy is generally preceded by a variety of actions that first create a widespread sense that a problem exists and needs to be addressed. The president may form policy concepts from a variety of sources, including campaign information; party ideology; recommendations from advisers, cabinet members, and agency chiefs; personal views; expert opinions; and public opinion polls.

The second component of policy-making activity involves the design of specific policy proposals. Presidents have substantial resources at their disposal for developing new policy proposals. For example, they may call on segments of the executive branch of government, such as the Centers for Medicare and Medicaid Services, or policy staffs within the U.S. Department of Health and Human Services.

In building public support, presidents can choose from a variety of strategies, including major addresses to the nation, efforts to mobilize their administrations to make public appeals, and organized attempts to increase support among interest groups.

To facilitate legislative decision making and the building of policy support, presidents, key staff, and department officials interact closely with Congress. Presidents generally meet with legislative leaders several times a month in an effort to shape the coming legislative agenda and to identify possible problems as bills move through various committees.

Legislative Process

When a bill is introduced in the House of Representatives, it is assigned to an appropriate committee by the Speaker. The committee chair forwards the bill to the appropriate subcommittee. The subcommittee then forwards proposed legislation to agencies that will be affected by the legislation, holds hearings and debates ("markup"), receives testimony, and may add amendments. The subcommittee and committee may recommend the bill, not recommend it, or recommend that it be tabled. Diverse interest groups, individuals, experts in the field, and business, labor, and professional associations often exert influence over the bill through campaign contributions and intense lobbying. The full House then hears the bill and may add amendments. The bill can be approved with or without amendments. The approved bill is sent to the Senate.

In the Senate, the bill is sent to an appropriate committee and then forwarded to an appropriate subcommittee. The subcommittee may send the bill to agencies that will be affected. It also holds hearings and receives testimony from all interested parties (e.g., private citizens, business, labor, agencies, experts). The subcommittee votes on and forwards the proposed legislation with appropriate recommendations. Amendments may or may not be added. The full Senate hears the bill and may add amendments. If the bill and House amendments are accepted, then the bill goes to the President.

If the Senate adds amendments that have not been voted on by the House, then the bill must go back to the floor of the House for a vote.

If the amendments are minor and noncontroversial, the House may vote to pass the bill. If the amendments are significant and controversial, the House may call for a conference committee to review the amendments. The conference committee consists of members from the equivalent committees of the House and Senate. If the recommendations of the conference committee are not accepted, then another conference committee is called.

After the bill has passed both the House and Senate in identical form, it is then forwarded to the President for signature. If the President signs the legislation, it becomes law. If the President does not sign it, at the end of 10 days (excluding Sundays) it becomes law unless the president vetoes it. If less than 10 days are left in the congressional session, then inaction on the part of the President results in a veto—a situation called a "pocket veto." The veto can be overturned by a two-thirds majority vote of the Congress; otherwise, the bill is dead.

After legislation has been signed into law, it is forwarded to the appropriate agency for implementation. The agency publishes proposed regulations in the Federal Register and then holds hearings regarding how the law is to be implemented. A bureaucracy only loosely controlled by either the president or Congress writes (i.e., publishes, gathers comments about, and rewrites) regulations. At that point, the program goes on to the 50 states for enabling legislation, if appropriate. There, organized interests hire local lawyers and lobbyists, and a whole new political cycle begins. Finally, all parties may adjourn to the courts to settle disputed issues, with potentially long rounds of litigation shaping the final outcome.

CRITICAL POLICY ISSUES

Government health policies have been enacted to resolve or prevent perceived deficiencies in health care delivery. Over the last four decades, most health policy initiatives and legislative efforts have focused on access to care (e.g., expanding insurance coverage, outreach programs in rural areas), cost of care (e.g., PPS, resource-based relative value scale), and quality of care (e.g., creating the Agency for Health Care Policy and Research, later renamed as the Agency for Healthcare Research and Quality, and calling for clinical practice guidelines).

Access to Care

Policies on access are aimed primarily at providers and financing mechanisms, with the purpose of expanding care to the most needy and underserved populations, including the elderly, minorities, rural residents, individuals with low incomes, and persons with AIDS. In addition to the coverage provisions included in the ACA of 2010, other programs, such as an expansion of the Community Health Center program to provide care for 268,000 additional patients, are intended to increase access to quality health care (Bureau of Primary Health Care, 2011).

Providers

Several groups of providers are involved in delivering health care. Policy issues include ensuring that there is a sufficient number of providers and that their geographic distribution is desirable. The debate over the supply of physicians is an important public policy issue because policy decisions influence the number of persons entering the medical profession; that number, in turn, has implications for other policies. The number of new entrants into the profession is influenced by programs of government assistance for individual students and by government grants given directly to educational institutions. An increasing supply of physicians may result in increased health care expenditures because of provider-induced demand. An increasing supply of physicians may also help alleviate shortages in certain regions of the country. Policy approaches to expanding access have included the National Health Service Corps, legislation supporting rural health clinics to expand geographic access, student assistance programs to expand the pool of health care workers, legislation to expand a system of emergency medical services, and establishment of community health centers in inner cities and rural areas to extend medical care services to those underserved areas.

Public Financing

Although a national health care program is seen by many people as the best means of ensuring access, the United States has historically focused instead on the needs of particular groups. Over the years, policies have been enacted to provide access to health care for specific groups otherwise unable to pay for and receive care. These groups include the elderly (Medicare), poor children (Medicaid), poor adults (Medicaid and local or state general assistance), the disabled (Medicaid and Medicare), veterans (Veterans Health Administration), Native Americans (Indian Health Service), and patients with end-stage renal disease (Medicare and Social Security benefits for kidney dialysis and transplants). Access continues to be a problem in many communities, partly because health policies enacted since 1983 have focused on narrowly defined elements of the delivery system.

Access and the Elderly

Two main concerns dominate the debate about Medicare policy. First, spending must be restrained to keep the program viable. Second, the program must be made truly comprehensive by adding services not currently covered or covered inadequately (e.g., comprehensive nursing home coverage). The two policy goals, however, are at odds.

Access and Minorities

Minorities are more likely than whites to face access problems. Hispanics, blacks, Asian Americans, and Native Americans, to name the most prevalent minorities, all experience difficulties accessing the health care delivery system. In some instances, the combination of low income and minority status creates difficulties; in others, the interaction of special cultural habits and minority status causes problems in accessing health care. Resolving the problems confronting these groups would require policies designed to encourage professional education programs sensitive to the special needs of minorities and programs to expand the delivery of services to areas populated by minorities. Many of these areas have been designated as having shortages of health care workers.

Access in Rural Areas

Delivery of health care services in rural communities has always posed the problems of how to make advanced medical care available to residents of sparsely settled areas. Purchasing high-tech equipment to serve a few people is not cost-efficient, and finding physicians who want to reside in rural areas is difficult. Thus specialists and expensive diagnostic equipment are not readily available in rural medical practices. Reimbursement systems based on average costs make it difficult for rural hospitals with few patients to survive financially.

Funding the National Health Service Corps is one step toward addressing the problem of personnel shortages in rural areas; however, the Corps affects only the percentage of graduating physicians who practice in shortage areas, and only for a limited time period for each student. Additional programs that increase the total supply of physicians and create incentives for permanent practice in rural areas are needed.

Access and Low Income

Low-income mothers and their children have problems accessing the health care system, both because they lack insurance and because they generally live in medically underserved areas. Pregnant women in low-income families are far less likely to receive prenatal care than are women in higher income categories. Limited access to health care among children creates problems of untreated chronic health conditions that lead to both increased medical expenditures and loss of productivity in society. The CHIP program, signed into law in 1997, has given states some flexibility in how they spend federal funds allocated for investment in children's health coverage ("States Face a Welcome Dilemma," 1997).

Access and Persons with AIDS

The CDC estimates that 1.2 million persons are HIV positive in the United States, one-fourth of whom are unaware of their own infection. Each year, 50,000 are newly infected with HIV, with a disproportionate burden occurring among the black and Hispanic populations. The Department of Health and Human Services supports research, prevention initiatives, and efforts to expand access to quality health care and services for those in need of them. Research initiatives include vaccine development, prevention research, clinical trials of potential therapies, and effective drugs for treatment. Prevention strategies involve funding programs for high-risk populations, promoting safety of the blood supply, monitoring the spread of AIDS/HIV, and running a national AIDS hotline. In the 2012 fiscal year budget, $28.3 billion was allocated to fight against the spread of AIDS/HIV at home and abroad, with a significant part of the budget targeted at HIV prevention and early intervention activities, as well as scientific research and development ("The President's FY 2012 Budget," 2011).

Persons with AIDS—that is, those individuals who have progressed from infection with HIV to actually having the disease and, therefore, need more expensive treatment—also have problems obtaining health care. People with AIDS experience difficulty obtaining insurance coverage, and their illness leads to catastrophic health care expenditures. Financial access can be a barrier to receiving the needed care, particularly for persons without adequate health insurance benefits. The AIDS epidemic presents a special challenge to policy makers committed to universal access to health care services. The services required are expensive, and the population in need is relatively small. Furthermore, the care is directed toward patients who are often terminally ill.

Universal Health Coverage

Universal health coverage has been a long-standing policy issue in the United States. Despite the recent enactment of the ACA of 2010, two issues remain: (1) The law faces constitutional challenges, and if it is repealed, alternative measures to cover the uninsured would become necessary; and (2) even though the ACA is expected to cover an additional 30 million uninsured, it still falls short of universal coverage (Buettgens & Hall, 2011).

Smoking and Tobacco Use

In the United States, lung cancer is the leading cancer cause of death, killing 157,000 people annually. The American Cancer Society has estimated that 87% of these deaths are a result of smoking and exposure to secondhand smoke. Overall, tobacco use causes almost 1 in 5 deaths in the United States. From 2000 to 2004, tobacco was responsible for approximately 443,000 early deaths annually. In 2007, the Institute of Medicine (IOM) released a report entitled *Ending the Tobacco Problem: A Blueprint for the Nation*, with the purpose of reducing smoking rates in the country. This goal is to be achieved through a two-pronged strategy involving strengthening and fully implementing traditional tobacco control measures and changing the regulatory landscape to permit policy innovations. The report concluded that if states maintained a comprehensive integrated tobacco control strategy at the CDC-recommended level of $15 to $20 per capita, tobacco use could be effectively reduced. Research has shown that more capital and time invested in tobacco control programs result in greater and quicker impact. For example, in California, the state with the longest-running tobacco control program, smoking rates fell from 22.7% in 1988 to 13.2% in 2008. Residents of the state now buy approximately half the number of cigarettes as the rest of the nation, and California was the first state to pass electronic tax stamp laws, making it easier to collect sales taxes and prevent tax evasion (California Tobacco Control Program, 2010). These comprehensive tobacco control programs run by the states have several goals related to reducing disease, disability, and death caused by smoking, such as preventing use among youth and young adults, promoting quitting, eliminating exposure to secondhand smoke, and identifying and eliminating tobacco-related disparities among population groups.

In addition to supporting control programs, the U.S. government teams up with national partners to run nationwide campaigns directed at smoking cessation. The American Legacy Foundation administers the "truth campaign" that supports state-based youth prevention efforts. The Americans for Nonsmokers' Rights group provides states and municipalities with assistance and guidance in the process of passing and implementing smoke-free indoor air policies. The American Cancer Society, American Heart Association, and American Lung Association provide advocacy leadership on tobacco control policy issues, while also providing support at the community level through offices across the nation.

Cost Containment

To a large extent, the strengths of the U.S. health care delivery system also contribute to its weaknesses. The United States boasts both the latest developments in medical technology and a supply of well-trained specialists, but these advances amount to the most expensive means possible to provide care to patients, making the U.S. health care system the most costly in the world. No other aspect of health care policy has received more attention during the past 20 years than efforts to contain increases in health care costs. Two major policy initiatives enacted by the federal government have targeted hospitals (PPS) and physicians' services (resource-based relative value scale) for price controls.

The National Health Planning and Resources Development Act of 1974 became law in 1975. This act marked the transition from improvement of access to cost containment as the principal theme in federal health policy.

Health planning, through certificate-of-need review, was used as a policy tool to contain hospital costs. One major change in the health policy environment was a new system of paying hospitals for Medicare clients—the PPS, which was enacted in 1983 (Mueller, 1988). The PPS method of reimbursement has proved to be the most successful tool for controlling hospital expenditures (Wennberg et al., 1984). Government programs, especially Medicare and Medicaid, federal employee benefit programs, and those of the Veterans Health Administration and armed services, face constant pressure from Congress to keep costs down.

Expenditures are a function of the price of services times the quantity of services delivered. In the past, most policies enacted have focused on the price of services. Policy makers are reluctant to consider restricting the quantity of services, fearful of intimations that they are sacrificing quality of care for cost containment. Such concerns are warranted because the media have fueled the frenzy over denial of services by managed care organizations.

Increased debate over the right to die and the value of life-extending services provides an opportunity to discuss limiting reimbursable services. So far, the federal government has been reluctant to adopt an explicit rationing strategy to contain expenditures, but state governments can be expected to experiment with various means of cost containment.

The private sector also influences the policy focus on cost containment. Major corporations are now aggressively pursuing ways to restrain the escalation of health insurance costs for their employees. Large employers have started to require their employees to undergo health screenings and to participate in programs, such as weight control and smoking cessation. These employers offer discounts toward the purchase of health insurance when employees enroll in healthy lifestyle programs and achieve certain health goals.

Recent research has shown that major factors contributing to the continued rise in health care costs include new and costly technologies and prescription drugs, increasing prevalence of chronic disease, population aging, and high administrative costs. Many solutions to these problems have been proposed and implemented, including better use of information technology (e.g., electronic medical records systems), improved quality/efficiency standards, modified provider compensation systems, more government regulation of health insurance and health care practices, greater emphasis on preventive medicine, and changes in the tax structure for employer-provided health insurance (Kimbuende et al., 2010). The ACA of 2010 authorized the implementation of programs, such as accountable care organizations and health insurance exchanges, to address at least some of these issues.

Quality of Care

Along with access and cost, quality of care is the third main concern of health care policy. The federal government began its actions to relieve the malpractice crisis and devoted greater attention to policing the quality of medical care with the Health Care Quality Act of 1986. This legislation mandated the creation of a national database within the U.S. Department of Health and Human Services to provide data on legal actions against health care providers. This information allows people recruiting physicians in one state to discover actions against those physicians in other states.

In 1989, the federal government embarked on a major effort to sponsor research to establish guidelines for medical practice. In the Omnibus Budget Reconciliation Act (OBRA) of 1989, Congress created a new agency, the National Center for Health Services Research (now called the Agency for Healthcare Research and Quality [AHRQ]), and mandated it to conduct and support research with respect to the outcomes, effectiveness, and appropriateness of health care services and procedures (U.S. House of Representatives, 1989). AHRQ has established funding for patient outcomes research teams (PORTs) that focus on particular medical conditions. The PORTs are part of a broader effort, the medical treatment effectiveness program, which "consists of four elements: medical treatment effectiveness research, development of databases for such research, development of clinical guidelines, and the dissemination of research findings and clinical guidelines" (Salive et al., 1990). The development of clinical guidelines was carried out by AHRQ from 1992 to 1996; this effort has now broadened to become the National Guidelines Clearinghouse, responsible for the analysis and dissemination of clinical guidelines across the United States (National Guidelines Clearinghouse, n.d.). AHRQ also focuses on improving quality of care through comparative-effectiveness research, health information technology initiatives, preventive medicine (through the U.S. Preventive Services Task Force in particular), and health care value analyses.

Research and Policy Development

The research community can influence the making of health policy through documentation, analysis, and prescription (Longest, 2002). The first role of research in policy making is documentation—that is, the gathering, cataloging, and correlating of facts that depict the state of the world that policy makers face. This process may help define a given public policy problem or raise its political profile.

A second way in which research informs, and thereby influences, policy making is through analysis of what does and does not work. Program evaluation and outcomes research fall under this domain. Often taking the form of demonstration projects intended to provide a factual basis for determining the feasibility, efficacy, or practicality of a possible policy intervention, analysis can help define solutions to health policy problems.

The third way in which research influences policy making is through prescription. Research demonstrating that a particular course of action being contemplated by policy makers may (or may not) lead to undesirable or unexpected consequences can make a significant contribution to policy making.

INTERNATIONAL HEALTH POLICY: COMPARISONS

Looking abroad, international analyses of health policy and health care systems show both similarities with and differences from the U.S. approach to health. One of the largest studies, the 2007 Commonwealth Fund International Health Policy Survey, sought to characterize the experience of patients in seven countries: the United States, the United Kingdom, Australia, Canada, Germany, the Netherlands, and New Zealand. All are industrialized, high-income countries, and all face challenges from rising health care costs. Nonetheless, each of these countries differs greatly in terms of issues such as insurance benefits (all except the United States have a universal coverage structure), patient referral processes (all except Germany and the United States enforce gatekeeping methods before specialist services can be obtained), cost sharing (the United Kingdom and the Netherlands have the most comprehensive programs, while the other countries use methods of cost sharing or benefit gaps in coverage), and uses of medical technology (practices in Canada and the United States are least likely to have electronic medical records) (Schoen et al., 2007).

Despite these broad differences, the United States expends vastly more for medical care both per capita ($6,697 average per person—twice as much as the average in the next-highest-cost country) and as a percentage of GDP (a total of 16.0% of the 2007 U.S. GDP went to health care spending). Additionally, all other profiled countries had uninsured rates less than 2% (versus the 2007 estimate of 16% in the United States) and significantly lower barriers to access. In light of these findings, it becomes even more important to look critically at the shortfalls of the U.S. health care system, and identify and implement fundamental changes that could work in this country to reduce costs, increase access, and improve quality.

CONCLUSION

Health policies are developed to serve the public's interests; however, public interests are diverse, and members of the public often hold conflicting views. Although the public consistently supports the goal of national health insurance, it also rejects the idea of the federal government running the health care delivery system. Similarly, although the American public wants the government to control health care costs, it also believes that the federal government already exerts too much control over Americans' daily lives. The challenge for policy makers is to find a balance between governmental provisions (i.e., control) and the private health care market to improve coverage and affordability of care. Successful health policies are more likely to be couched in terms of cost containment (a market-justice, economic, business, and middle-class concern) than in improved or expanded access and reduction or elimination of health disparities (a social-justice, liberal, labor, low-income issue); however, cost-related policies are likely to have very little impact on improving the quality of care or reducing health disparities.

REFERENCES

Agency for Healthcare Research and Quality (AHRQ). AHRQ profile: Advancing excellence in health care. n.d. http://www.ahrq.gov/about/profile.htm.

Alford RR. *Health Care Politics: Ideology and Interest Group Barriers to Reform.* Chicago: University of Chicago Press; 1975.

Buettgens M, Hall MA. *Who will be uninsured after health insurance reform?* The Urban Institute; March 2011. http://www.urban.org/UploadedPDF /1001520-Uninsured-After-Health-Insurance-Reform.pdf.

Bureau of Primary Health Care. HHS awards Affordable Care Act funds to expand access to health care. August 9, 2011. http://www.hhs.gov/news /press/2011pres/08/20110809a.html.

California Tobacco Control Program. Two decades of the California Tobacco Control Program: California tobacco survey, 1990–2008. 2010. http://www .cdph.ca.gov/programs/tobacco/Documents/CDPH_CTS2008%20sum-mary%20report_final.pdf>.

Coughlin T, et al. A conflict of strategies: Medicaid managed care and Medicaid maximization. *Health Serv Res.* 1999;34(1):281–293.

Health Insurance Association of America. *Source Book of Health Insurance Data.* Washington, DC: Health Insurance Association of America; 1992.

Institute of Medicine (IOM). *Ending the Tobacco Problem: A Blueprint for the Nation.* Washington DC: IOM; 2007.

Kimbuende E, Ranji U, Lundy J, Salganicoff A. *U.S. health care costs.* Kaiser Family Foundation; March 2010. http://www.kaiseredu.org/Issue-Modules /US-Health-Care-Costs/Background-Brief.aspx.

Litman T, Robins L. The relationship of government and politics to health and health care: A sociopolitical overview. In *Health Politics and Policy,* 3rd ed., ed. Litman T, Robins L. New York: John Wiley and Sons; 1997:3–45.

Longest BB. *Health Policymaking in the United States.* Ann Arbor, MI: Health Administration Press; 2002.

Miller CA. Child health. In *Epidemiology and Health Policy,* ed. Levine S, Lillienfeld A. New York: Tavistock; 1987.

Mueller KJ. Federal programs do expire: The case of health planning. *Public Admin Rev.* 1988;48:719–735.

National Guideline Clearinghouse. n.d. http://www.guideline.gov/about/index .aspx.

National Institutes of Health (NIH). *NIH Data Book.* Washington, DC: U.S. Department of Health and Human Services; 1991.

The President's FY 2012 budget and implementation of the national HIV/AIDS strategy. 2011. http://aids.gov/federal-resources/policies/national-hiv-aids-strategy/.

Salive ME, et al. Patient outcomes research teams and the Agency for Health Care Policy and Research. Health Serv Res. 1990;25:697–708.

Schoen C, Osborn R, Doty MM, et al. Toward higher-performance health systems: Adults' health care experiences in seven countries, 2007. *Health Affairs.* 2007;26(6);w717–w734.

States face a welcome dilemma: How to best spend $24 billion to cover nation's uninsured children. *State Health Watch.* 1997;4(8):1, 4.

U.S. House of Representatives. *Omnibus Budget Reconciliation Act of 1989: Conference Report to Accompany H.R. 3299.* Washington, DC: Government Printing Office; November 21, 1989.

Weissert C, Weissert W. *Governing Health: The Politics of Health Policy.* Baltimore, MD: Johns Hopkins University Press; 1996.

Wennberg JE, et al. Will payment based on diagnosis-related groups control hospital costs? *N Engl J Med.* 1984;311(5):295–300.

Chapter 14

The Future of Health Services Delivery

INTRODUCTION

Historical precedents and current developments can be used to predict future directions in U.S. health care delivery. Current developments are particularly significant in terms of social, demographic, and cultural changes; political will; technological innovation; economic conditions; global health issues; and ecological events, such as the emergence of new diseases and catastrophic occurrences.

In discussing the future, one key question is often raised: How close are we to having a national health care system in the United States? Since the early to mid-1900s, various plans and proposals have been put forth to move the nation toward a national health care plan, but past efforts did not succeed. One main reason why Americans have long rejected national health care is that it runs contrary to the beliefs and values that have been prevalent since the nation was founded. Americans have traditionally maintained a strong belief in capitalism and individual achievement. They have preferred relatively little government involvement in private affairs. Americans have also been disenchanted by such national programs as the public education system, which has failed to deliver on its promise of scholastic excellence for America's youth. A 1993 report by the U.S. Department of Education estimated that functional illiteracy—a person's incompetence in using such basic skills as reading, writing, and simple computations in everyday life situations—affects as many as one in four American adults (Carvin, 2000). The situation in the government-controlled educational system has not become any better. A recent survey of nearly 10,000 American global executives conducted by Harvard Business School revealed that 71% of them expected U.S. competitiveness in the world to decline, with one of the main reasons cited being the failed K–12 education system (Porter & Rivkin, 2012). Given the grim record of performance of tax-supported programs in the United States and abroad, most Americans have not been comfortable turning over critical issues of life and health to the government.

Even so, the lack of insurance for approximately 45 million Americans has remained a social concern for quite some time. Also, dependency on the government has been increasing, particularly since the prolonged period of high unemployment that began in 2008. If the U.S. economy does not significantly improve, Americans will be more prone to becoming dependent on government-run social programs. For example, in May 2011, a record 46 million people (15% of the U.S. population) relied on the country's welfare assistance program to buy food, commonly referred to as the food stamps program (Ellis, 2011). Increasing dependency on government handouts will result in a gradual erosion of the traditional American belief and value system.

At this point, any future shifts toward national health care mainly hinge on the fate of the controversial Patient Protection and Affordable Care Act of 2010 (ACA of 2010). Much will depend on the Supreme Court's decision in the summer of 2012 (to be released in June 2012) and on national elections in November 2012. Meanwhile, the majority of Americans (52%) continue to oppose the ACA, commonly referred to as "Obamacare" by its critics (McInturff & Weigel, 2011). Even if the law is implemented in 2014 as intended, the realities of cost and access problems will pose significant challenges. Conversely, if the law's implementation is blocked, coverage for the uninsured cannot be considered a dead issue because a relatively significant number of Americans will be upset at the prospect of losing the "free" health care promised under the ACA of 2010. Hence, controlling the spiraling cost of health care will probably represent the most formidable challenge in the future. While the United States is struggling to expand and pay for health care coverage, other developed nations that already have universal coverage are grappling with the dilemma of how they can keep their systems solvent without having to curtail services.

A mere expansion of health insurance will not adequately address the issue of access unless it is accompanied by a significant reform of the health delivery infrastructure. A new model of care delivery that emphasizes prevention of disease, management of chronic conditions, and individual responsibility is urgently needed. The nation also faces critical workforce challenges. Moreover, the United States must enhance the role of public health and bolster preparations to protect Americans against local, national, and global threats, both natural and human-made. Medical technology presents numerous opportunities, but its development and use must be judicious, with the goal of achieving greater cost-effectiveness in health care delivery. These daunting challenges cannot be met unless the nation gets serious about putting its financial house in order.

CONFLICTING REALITIES OF COST AND ACCESS

National health expenditures in the United States reached $2.6 trillion in 2010, accounting for 17.9% of the nation's gross domestic product (GDP). In 2014, health spending is projected to grow 8.3%, up from 5.5% growth in 2013, primarily as a result of the expansion of health insurance coverage under the ACA of 2010. **Table 14.1** shows the projected growth of health care expenditures in the United States. Under the ACA, expansion of Medicaid by liberalizing the eligibility criteria is expected to increase Medicaid enrollment by 19.5 million people and spending is projected to grow 20.3%. Medicaid, a social welfare program, already covers one-fifth of the U.S. population. The new, heavily regulated, online health insurance exchanges to be established under the ACA are expected to cover 13.9 million people in 2014, which is predicted to result in 9.4% growth in private health insurance spending (Centers for Medicare and Medicaid Services [CMS], 2011b).

Ironically, despite significant cost increases, the ACA of 2010 falls short of addressing the issue of access. Even with the enormous scope of the program, approximately 21 million people will remain uninsured according

Table 14.1 Projections of Future National Health Expenditures (NHE)

	2009	2014	2019
NHE (billions)	$2,486	$3,227	$4,346
Average annual growth		5.4%	6.1%
Average annual growth in GDP		4.7%	4.7%

Source: Data from Office of the Actuary, CMS. National health expenditure projections 2010-2020. 2011b. http://www.cms.gov/NationalHealthExpendData/downloads/proj2010.pdf. Accessed January 2012.

to estimates by the Congressional Budget Office (CBO, 2010). The legislation has other implications pertaining to access as well. The dream of *universal access*—the ability of all, or nearly all, citizens to obtain health care when needed—cannot be realized unless accompanied by supply-side rationing. The extent of rationing will depend on the cost of producing health care services.

Access also requires an adequate health delivery infrastructure. The United States already has a shortage of primary care physicians, whose effects are felt more severely in the states located in the country's southern and mountain regions. These same states will experience the most dramatic increases in Medicaid enrollments under the ACA (Grogan, 2011). The nation's graduate medical education system is inadequate to meet future needs. According to Whitcomb (2011), the combined effects of the ACA of 2010, the obesity epidemic, the increase in chronic disease prevalence, and an aging population will create a much greater demand for medical services at the same time as the relative size of the physician workforce begins to decline.

The historical relationship between Medicaid coverage and access to health care raises another issue. Currently, only about 50% of physicians accept Medicaid patients into their practices (Cunningham & May, 2006); the rate of participation in Medicaid by primary care physicians is only 36% (Grogan, 2011). The main reason for physicians' reluctance to accept Medicaid-insured patients is low reimbursement to providers and delays in receiving payment from Medicaid after services have been delivered.

With the significant expansion of Medicaid under the ACA of 2010, physicians are likely to be mandated to deliver services to Medicaid patients without favoring privately insured patients. Physicians who refuse to comply with this requirement will be charged with discrimination. Even with such mandates, access will be restricted, regardless of the source of insurance, because the delivery system will become overloaded. With an overloaded primary care system, whether the currently overtaxed emergency care system will see any relief is another lingering unanswered question.

THE FUTURE OF HEALTH CARE REFORM

In the U.S. context, *health care reform* is the term used to describe the extension of health insurance to the uninsured. For a system to remain solvent, however, expansion of coverage must be accompanied by cost control measures. To control costs materially, it is necessary to manage utilization, limit reimbursement to providers, and employ some sort of rationing for the supply of health care services. Only the government is in a position to wage war against costs on all three fronts, particularly in a single-payer national health care system. In a *single-payer system*, the government finances health care for all citizens; as a consequence, multiple programs—such as Medicare, Medicaid, CHIP, and Veterans Health Administration—are no longer needed. The government also tightly reins in the availability of services, their utilization, and payments to providers. This kind of heavy-handed government intrusion into their lives will be strongly opposed by most Americans, however, and is not seen as a practical alternative for future reforms.

The Cost Control Imperative

Some interventions to control costs are proposed in the ACA of 2010, but few provisions in the legislation address control of overall health care expenditures. In the private sector, for example, only 6% of employers believe that their company will be better off as a result of the ACA. Moreover, a report by Hewitt Associates points out that current trends, if left unchecked, will lead to an unsustainable cost burden that will severely hinder U.S. companies' ability to compete globally (Sperling & Shapira, 2011). The response of private employers so far has been to shift an increasing share of cost burden to their employees. For example, an increasing number of employers are offering consumer-driven health plans, also referred to as high-deductible health plans. Cost control measures will be necessary in both the private and public sectors.

Existing government programs—mainly Medicare and Medicaid—face severe financial challenges, particularly in an environment plagued by an escalating national debt crisis. The U.S. national debt currently exceeds $15 trillion, and most economists do not think that the nation has the capability to ever pay its ever-mounting level of debt. So far, the best "solution" that the President and Congress have been able to identify is to keep raising the debt ceiling, which will allow them to keep spending more. It seems that no one in Washington, D.C., has either the appetite or the fortitude to cut expenses or reduce the size of a bloated government. But time is running out: In the near future, politicians in the United States may be left with no choice except to take drastic "austerity measures"—a term used to describe spending cuts (including cuts in social programs) that have become urgently necessary in countries such as Greece and several European nations, despite public protests.

The financing of Medicare is essentially a generation transfer system in which current taxpayers pay for the benefits of current beneficiaries. Shortfalls in such a financing system must be paid by future generations. According to the 2011 annual report from the trustees of the Medicare and Social Security trust funds, Medicare expenditures totaled $523 billion in 2010; the program's income amounted to $486 billion in the same year, leaving a deficit of $37 billion. The Health Insurance trust fund, which covers Part A benefits, has been running annual deficits since 2008 and is projected to be exhausted in 2024, which is 5 years earlier than was projected in 2010. The Supplementary Medical Insurance trust fund for Parts B and D is expected to remain solvent. Even so, Medicare-related expenditures are projected to rise faster than growth in the U.S. economy (CMS, 2011a).

To save the Medicare program from bankruptcy, several changes to reduce costs are proposed in the ACA of 2010. These changes will save an estimated $428 billion over a 10-year period, but will also cut Medicare benefits and allow a government panel to make decisions about end-of-life care (Gitterman & Scott, 2011). States are also grappling with cost-saving measures applied to Medicaid, which is managed by the states. There is a push toward enrolling more beneficiaries in managed care and paying managed care organizations capitated monthly fees to cover all health care expenses for Medicaid beneficiaries. Such changes may be just the beginning of austerity measures, however, as states are experiencing budget deficits of their own.

Higher taxes for Americans to pay for the expanded health care program will be inevitable. Taxing just the "millionaires and billionaires," as President Obama has touted, has never been a solution to economic problems wherever in the world it has been tried, because it brings in relatively small amounts of revenues. Surprisingly, 45% of all U.S. households had to pay no federal income tax for 2010 (Sahadi, 2011). Will the government's hands finally be forced so that it has to ask these people to pay their "fair share" to save Medicare, Medicaid, and Social Security? The last of these three major social programs in the United States, Social Security, serves as a safety net for income during retirement; all working Americans pay into this system and are entitled to collect benefits as early as age 62. This program is also operating in deficit, with the shortfall amounting to $49 billion in 2010. After 2014, cash benefits delivered under the Social Security program are expected to increase rapidly as the number of beneficiaries grows at a substantially faster rate than the number of workers who pay Social Security taxes to cover benefits for current retirees (Blahous & Reischauer, 2011).

If the ACA of 2010 Fails

What if the ACA is repealed? Or if it is significantly altered? Or if funding to implement it gets slashed? These weighty questions will be decided from 2012 onward. Nevertheless, the seeds for extending health insurance have been sown. Possible alternatives for the future may come from the three bills or proposals that were introduced or proposed by the Republican legislators in 2009—namely, the Patients Choice Act of 2009, the Health Care Freedom Plan (a proposal), and the Empowering Patients First Act. The combined main features of these plans are as follows:

1. Establish state-based health care exchanges to facilitate the individual purchase of private health insurance and create a market where private health plans compete for enrollees based on price and quality. A second option is to create a national market for health insurance to allow individuals to purchase health insurance plans across state lines, which is currently prohibited.

2. Allow automatic enrollment in employer health plans. Create tax incentives for small businesses for auto-enrollment.

3. Give tax credits or vouchers to individuals to purchase health insurance. McClellan and Baicker (2002) have argued that tax credits for the purchase of health insurance would enable millions of Americans to purchase private health insurance. A variation of this approach is to issue the tax credits in advance in the form of vouchers to enable people, particularly the poor, to purchase health insurance.

4. Provide block grants to states to develop innovative models that ensure affordable health insurance coverage for Americans with pre-existing medical conditions. Approximately 35 states already have *high-risk pools* that enable hard-to-insure people to purchase subsidized coverage.

5. Replace Medicaid with a program to provide grants to states for the following expenditures: (a) acute medical care assistance to otherwise qualified blind or disabled individuals, foster care children, low-income women with breast or cervical cancer, certain tuberculosis-infected individuals, and certain individuals covered under the existing Medicaid program; and (b) long-term care services and support for qualified disabled and elderly populations. A second option is to give Medicaid beneficiaries the choice to either remain in Medicaid or purchase private health insurance by using vouchers.

6. Establish and implement a competitive bidding mechanism to promote competition among Medicare Advantage plans (Part C). Strengthen programs that help prevent Medicare fraud and abuse.

7. Supplement the cost of private health insurance for eligible low-income families through the distribution of debit cards, which may be used for costs associated with health care and provide direct support in accessing health care.

8. Repeal the CHIP program, because under the various other options this program may not be necessary.

9. Develop a national strategic plan for preventive health and for health promotion and disease prevention activities.

10. Reform the tort system by developing mechanisms for the resolution of disputes concerning injuries allegedly caused by health care providers. Reduce predatory and frivolous malpractice lawsuits.

11. Assure that consumers have access to price information prior to treatment so they can make informed decisions about their care.

FUTURE MODEL OF CARE DELIVERY

There is widespread consensus that the existing model of health care delivery in the United States must change. Several issues in the existing system, which is driven by the medical model of health, remain to be resolved:

1. There is inadequate emphasis on wellness, disease prevention, and health promotion.
2. Despite a dramatic rise in chronic conditions and ensuing disabilities, the existing health care system focuses primarily on addressing acute illnesses.
3. Inadequate access to primary care results in the overuse of costly emergency room services.
4. Undue emphasis on specialization increases the cost of health care without being accompanied by noteworthy improvements in the health status of the U.S. population.
5. The delivery of care remains fragmented, instead of continuous and coordinated.

Three emerging models of health care delivery were discussed in previous chapters—namely, the medical home model, community-oriented primary care, and accountable care organizations. In addition, two lesser known models—the teamlet model and the connected health care model—are being tested. All of these models are still in their infancy. Whichever model becomes dominant in the future is likely to incorporate the main features of all these emerging models. The ultimate test of a successful model will be its ability to deliver better access, improved health outcomes, care coordination, and continuity of care, all at reduced cost.

Teamlet Model

A teamlet refers to a two-person team consisting of a clinician—such as a primary care physician, nurse practitioner, or physician assistant—and an allied health professional who functions as a health coach. The teamlet works together collaboratively. The main function of the health coach is to assist patients with gaining the knowledge, skills, and confidence to self-manage their chronic conditions. The health coach also coordinates care by scheduling clinical visits, helping patients adopt healthy lifestyles, helping patients understand and adhere to their medication regimen, and providing other types of support (Ngo et al., 2010).

Connected Health Care Model

Connected health care incorporates the use of communication technology, patient self-management, and distant home monitoring technology. New monitoring technology has the capability of enabling just-in-time provider interventions when needed (Kvedar et al., 2011). One main objective of connected care is to keep chronically ill patients connected to necessary clinical expertise in between office visits so as to avert medical crises that might otherwise land these patients in the emergency room (Moore, 2009).

FUTURE WORKFORCE CHALLENGES

An adequate and well-trained workforce is a critical component of the health care delivery infrastructure. A shortage of health care professionals will be a major challenge to overcome. Hence, to be successful, any future model of health care delivery must be highly effective in integrating the talents and expertise of trained professionals.

According to a report produced by the National Academy of Sciences (2010), nurses should practice to the full extent of their education and training. Licensing requirements and rules governing the scope of practice across states need to be unified for advance practice nurses who have master's or doctoral degrees. Residency programs for nurses need to incorporate training in community health, public health, and geriatrics.

Primary care physicians need training so they can adequately function as "comprehensivists" to address the needs of a growing number of people with complex chronic conditions. They must be prepared to manage complex pharmacology, understand end-of-life issues and medical ethics, and lead health care teams.

Based on current trends, a shortage of health care professionals trained in geriatrics is a critical challenge with serious implications for the future. This problem is compounded by the shortage of faculty in colleges and universities who are trained in geriatrics. The elderly use the majority of home health care services and nursing home care, account for roughly half of hospital inpatient days, and represent approximately one-fourth of all ambulatory care visits. The growth of the elderly population, driven by the aging of the baby boom generation, will impose increasing challenges on a health care delivery system that has thus far ignored the need for specialized training in geriatrics. Many elderly patients suffer from chronic conditions, and their care is often complicated by the presence of comorbidities, the use of multiple prescription drugs, and an increased prevalence of mental conditions and dementia. Evidence shows that care of older adults by health care professionals prepared in geriatrics yields better physical and mental outcomes without increasing costs (H. J. Cohen et al., 2002). Current trends in the education and training of health care professionals predict that the future demand will far outstrip the supply of physicians, nurses, therapists, social workers, and pharmacists with specialized training in geriatrics.

Integration of a racially and culturally diverse workforce will also pose challenges, particularly as the U.S. health care system itself becomes more complex and taxing for both patients and workers. It is estimated that somewhere near the middle of the twenty-first century, more than half of all U.S. citizens will be nonwhite (U.S. Census Bureau, 2001). Developing skills in cultural competence will divert some resources from health care. The term *cultural competence* refers to knowledge, skills, attitudes, and behavior required of a practitioner to provide optimal health care services to persons from a wide range of cultural and ethnic backgrounds. To do so effectively, health care providers need to understand how and why different belief systems, cultural biases, ethnic origins, family structures, and many other culture-based factors influence the manner in which people experiencing illness comply with medical advice and respond to treatment. Such variations have implications for outcomes of care (J. J. Cohen et al., 2002).

GLOBAL THREATS AND INTERNATIONAL COOPERATION

The much-needed shift toward care for chronic disease and disability does not mean that infectious disease prevention and control efforts will be unnecessary in the future. In fact, intensified efforts will be required to combat emergent and resurgent infectious diseases. Immigration of people from other countries to the United States, international travel to and from the United States, and shipments coming to the United States from other countries have made it increasingly easy for deadly infections to cross international boundaries. Indeed, infectious diseases and disasters are certain to continue to affect people globally. Examples of such disasters include the earthquake and tsunami that killed thousands of people in Japan in March 2011, and industrial accidents, such as the oil rig explosion in the Gulf of Mexico in April 2010 that devastated the economies of many Gulf communities. Often, such events occur without warning. Large-scale devastation, such as that caused by the Haiti earthquake in January 2010, can severely strain a nation's capacity to deal with mass casualties and rebuilding efforts. Increasingly, disasters will require international assistance, cooperation, and joint efforts to mitigate their effects.

Increase in air travel facilitated the spread of severe acute respiratory syndrome (SARS) from China to Canada in 2003 and the spread of polio virus from India to northern Minnesota in 2005 (Milstein et al., 2006). These examples highlight the importance of early identification of infectious threats and subsequent rapid response to prevent further spread—a goal that is often difficult to achieve without international cooperation (Johns et al., 2011). Efforts to strengthen global health security include disease surveillance for outbreaks of international importance and urgency, exchange of technical information on new pathogens, and early warning and control of serious animal disease outbreaks. The importance of the last factor was amply demonstrated by the 2003–2005 outbreak of H5N1 (avian influenza) in Asia.

The International Health Regulations (IHR) represent an international legal instrument that is binding on 194 countries. IHR's aim is to help the international community prevent and respond to acute public health risks that have the potential to cross borders and threaten people worldwide. Such crises can result from emerging infections such as SARS or a new human influenza pandemic. The IHR can also apply to other public health emergencies, such as chemical spills, leaks and dumping, or nuclear meltdowns (World Health Organization [WHO], 2008).

Adequate delivery of health care to millions around the world depends on the availability of an adequate and well-trained workforce. Worldwide, there is a shortage of nearly 4.3 million health workers. Moreover, 57 countries, 39 of which are in Africa, have fewer than 23 health workers per 10,000 population. Even some of Asia's burgeoning economies, such as India and Indonesia, can face a health care crisis in the event of a major disaster. The problem in many countries is compounded by an unequal distribution of workers, lack of training, and international migration of health professionals from poor countries to rich countries. Also, in spite of the pivotal role that community health workers play in scaling up essential services, this workforce category does not receive adequate support in most nations (Chatterjee, 2011).

BIOTERRORISM AND THE TRANSFORMATION OF PUBLIC HEALTH

Historically, in the United States, the medical establishment relegated public health to a level of unimportance. The dichotomous systems of illness care and public health created two distinct cultures that have often been at odds with each other (Keck & Scutchfield, 1997). Public health, however, has always focused on protecting the population's health. More recently, emphasis on homeland security has uplifted public health to a new level of respect and recognition as an instrument to protect the public against new threats to well-being. More accurately, interest in public health in the United States has been like a seesaw, going up during times of danger to people's health and safety, but then coming down when no dangers loom. The importance of public health and deficiencies in the existing public health system received national attention during terrorism-related attempts to bring about an anthrax epidemic in October 2001, soon after the terrorist attacks and destruction of the World Trade Center in New York City on September 11, 2001. Since then, a heightened awareness of potential threats posed by chemical and biological weapons and low-grade nuclear materials has prompted public officials nationwide to review and revamp the system. Large-scale bioterrorism has not yet occurred, but global unrest amid the rise of extremism makes it a real possibility in the future.

The United States' central public health agency, the Centers for Disease Control and Prevention (CDC), will continue to play a vital role in recognizing emerging threats and developing measures to contain any unexpected outbreaks. Public health agencies at local, state, and federal levels have also been identifying infrastructure weaknesses and reevaluating plans to protect the American public (Baker & Koplan, 2002). Public health entities must prepare for threats other than those posed by "imported" infectious diseases (discussed earlier) and the possible use of chemical, biological, and nuclear agents for the purpose of inflicting harm. Safeguarding the nation's food and water supplies, for example, is equally important.

A major challenge and responsibility of public health agencies in a radically changing world is to forge partnerships with communities and all levels of government. The future effectiveness of public health initiatives will involve cooperation among public health agencies at the federal, state, and local levels; other agencies of the government such as the Department of Justice and the Food and Drug Administration; private and public organizations such as hospitals, clinics, and nursing homes; private practitioners such as physicians and nurses; volunteer agencies such as the

American Red Cross; civil defense agencies such as police and fire departments; businesses; and individuals and groups within communities.

NEW FRONTIERS IN CLINICAL TECHNOLOGY

Technological progress is currently driving much of the growth in the
health services industry. The Institute for the Future (2000) has predicted
that eight types of medical technologies will especially affect future delivery of patient care: rational drug design, advances in imaging, minimally
invasive surgery, genetic mapping and testing, gene therapy, vaccines, artificial blood, and xenotransplantation. Ongoing progress has occurred in
several of these areas, and, more recently, advances in regenerative medicine have come to the forefront. The latter deals with regenerating dam-
aged tissues and organs within the human body.

1. *Rational drug design* goes a step beyond the painstaking and costly
   random search for new pharmaceuticals, which is characterized by
   trial and error. Now scientists can study the structure and composition of a receptor or enzyme and actually design new chemicals or
   molecular entities that bind to the receptors or enzymes. Rational drug
   design will shorten the drug discovery process.

2. *Imaging technologies* have made some of the most dramatic advances
   in health care. Current research focuses on four areas: (a) finding new
   energy sources and focusing an energy beam to avoid damage to adja-
   cent tissue and minimize residual damage, (b) advances that make a
   finer detection of abnormalities, (c) faster and more accurate analysis
   of images using 3-D technology, and (d) higher-resolution displays.

3. The latest advances in *minimally invasive surgery* include image-
   guided brain surgery, minimal-access cardiac procedures, and the
   endovascular placement of grafts for abdominal aneurysms. The
   overall impact of minimally invasive procedures on cost-efficiency
   and patients' quality of life through faster recovery assures the growth
   of this technology as well as the growth of outpatient surgicenters.

4. *Genetic mapping* has enabled the identification of a wide range of
   genes that can cause complex diseases such as diabetes, cancer, heart
   disease, Huntington's disease, and Alzheimer's disease. The discovery

of genetic susceptibility to certain diseases will improve preventive techniques. The term *genometrics* is used for the association of genes with specific disease traits.

5. *Gene therapy* is a therapeutic technique in which a functioning gene is inserted into targeted cells to correct an inborn defect or to provide the cell with a new function. The future challenge in this area is to develop methods that discriminately deliver enough genetic material to the right cells. Cancer treatment is receiving much attention as a prime candidate for gene therapy because current techniques (surgery, radiation, and chemotherapy) are effective in only half of all cases.

6. *Vaccines* have traditionally been used on a preventive (prophylactic) basis for specific infectious diseases such as diphtheria, smallpox, and whooping cough. However, the therapeutic use of vaccines in the treatment of noninfectious diseases, such as cancer, has opened new fronts in medicine. At the same time, the development of new vaccines for emerging infectious diseases remains on the research agenda. Making today's vaccines safer for wide-scale preventive use against bioterrorism, in which agents such as smallpox and anthrax may be used, will also be an ongoing pursuit.

7. Research will continue on the development of fluids, including *artificial blood*, which in many instances could be used to substitute for real blood in transfusions, particularly under wartime conditions and during disasters when supplies may fall short.

8. Transplantation of organs was one of the twentieth century's greatest medical advances. Even today, however, a critical shortage of transplantable tissues remains a major concern. *Xenotransplantation*, in which animal tissues are used for transplants in humans, is a growing research area. New knowledge and methods in molecular genetics, transplantation biology, and genetic engineering look promising.

EVIDENCE-BASED HEALTH CARE

Practice variations—geographic variations in the practice of medicine without clinical justification—have both quality and cost implications. There is little evidence that high-spending providers deliver better outcomes. The goal of evidence-based medicine (EBM) is to increase the value of medical care. Even though consumers, as well as practitioners, often fear that reducing costs will translate into lower quality, this is not necessarily true. Quality of care can be improved while cutting costs— thereby increasing the value of medical care—by reducing misuse and overuse (Slawson & Shaughnessy, 2001). The tools for the practice of EBM have been developed for several years, mainly in the form of clinical practice guidelines. Evidence-based practice guidelines are intended to represent "best practices" and "proven therapies."

Nevertheless, the use of guidelines is not widespread in the medical community. Even though the research community has known about clinical variations since the 1970s, and evidence pertaining to them has mounted since then, relatively little has been done to translate this research into actual practice. Many physicians think that guidelines and protocols are either too simple or too complicated, promote "cookbook care," lack creditable authors or evidence, are biased, decrease flexibility, reduce autonomy, and are not applicable to the practice population (Oeyen, 2007).

EBM's full potential has not yet been realized, but ongoing work is seeking to improve and implement practice guidelines. At least six recommendations can be made for the future:

1. Practitioners, payers, and policy makers need to become stakeholders.

2. Computer-based models will help incorporate EBM into medical decision making. Models that are easily usable and understandable are essential.

3. Robust research designs, using clinical trials where applicable, should be the backbone of EBM.

4. Guidelines and protocols must be revised and kept current to incorporate subsequent scientific evidence.

5. Future practice guidelines must incorporate economic analysis. Mounting health care expenditures will pressure society to make rational choices about when certain types of services become unwarranted because the costs begin to exceed the expected benefits from certain treatments.

6. Financial incentives, including provider payments and patient cost sharing, must be restructured. Reimbursement methods should focus

on paying for best achievable outcomes and the most effective care over the course of treatment instead of paying for units of service (Gauthier et al., 2006).

In future, EBM will also transcend what physicians do and will incorporate all caregivers. For example, it will permeate the practice of nursing, pharmacology, and other disciplines allied with the practice of medicine. Eventually, EBM will become the standard that will govern the multidisciplinary process of health care delivery.

CONCLUSION

Health care delivery in the United States continues to change. Political factors played a major role in the passage of the ACA of 2010, but this legislation's survival will be decided in 2012. Whatever its fate, the plight of the uninsured and the nation's ability to deliver what Americans have come to expect from the health care system will continue to pose major challenges. This is particularly true in the wake of a mounting national debt that many economists think is likely to reach a point of crisis.

New models of health care delivery are now being investigated. In the end, the nation will need a model that provides better access to services, produces improved health outcomes, incorporates care coordination and continuity of care, and reduces health care costs. This model must also be highly effective in integrating the talents and expertise of trained professionals.

International threats have emerged as a result of globalization. Rapid response to deal with infectious diseases that can quickly spread around the world, natural disasters, and human-made threats of terrorism will increasingly require global assistance, cooperation, and joint efforts. The United States' public health system must prepare for these threats, in addition to safeguarding the nation's food and water supplies.

In the twenty-first century, technological innovations in the areas of advanced imaging, minimally invasive surgery, genetic mapping, regenerative medicine, information systems, and home monitoring of patients will help shape the delivery of medical care in ways never before imagined. Evidence-based medicine will proliferate as clinical practice guidelines become more firmly anchored in research-based evidence and incentives are created for caregivers to use them.

REFERENCES

Baker EL, Koplan JP. Strengthening the nation's public health infrastructure: Historic challenge, unprecedented opportunity. *Health Affairs.* 2002;21(6):15–27.

Blahous CP III, Reischauer RD. A summary of the 2011 annual reports: Social Security and Medicare boards of trustees. 2011. http://www.ssa.gov/OACT /TRSUM/index.html. Accessed January 2012.

Carvin A. Mind the gap: The digital divide as the civil rights issue of the new millennium. *Multimedia Schools.* 2000;7(1):56–58.

Centers for Medicare and Medicaid Services (CMS). *2011 Annual Report of the Boards of Trustees of the Federal Hospital Insurance and Federal Supplementary Medical Insurance Trust Funds.* Washington, D. Centers for Medicare and Medicaid Services; 2011a.

Centers for Medicare and Medicaid Services (CMS). National health expenditure projections 2010–2020. 2011b. http://www.cms.gov /NationalHealthExpendData/downloads/proj2010.pdf. Accessed January 2012.

Chatterjee P. Progress patchy on health-worker crisis. *Lancet.* 2011;377(9764):456.

Cohen HJ, et al. A controlled trial of inpatient and outpatient geriatric evaluation and management. *N Engl J Med.* 2002;346(12):906–912.

Cohen JJ, et al. The case for diversity in the health care workforce. *Health Affairs.* 2002;21(5):90–102.

Congressional Budget Office (CBO). Payments of penalties for being uninsured under the Patient Protection and Affordable Care Act—revised April 30, 2010. 2010. http://www.cbo.gov/ftpdocs/113xx/doc11379/Individual_ Mandate_Penalties-04-30.pdf. Accessed December 2011.

Cunningham PJ, May JH. *Medicaid patients increasingly concentrated among physicians.* Tracking Report No. 16. Washington, DC: Center for Studying Health System Change; 2006.

Ellis B. Food stamp use rises to record 45.8 million. *CNN Money.* August 4, 2011. http://money.cnn.com/2011/08/04/pf/food_stamps_record_high/index.htm. Accessed January 2012.

Gauthier A, et al. *Toward a High Performance Health System for the United States.* New York: Commonwealth Fund; 2006.

Gitterman DP, Scott JC. "Obama lies, grandma dies": The uncertain politics of Medicare and the Patient Protection and Affordable Care Act. *J Health Politics Policy Law.* 2011;36(3):555–563.

Grogan CM. The new Medicaid under PPACA: What will it mean for general internists? *J Gen Intern Med.* 2011;26(12):1502–1505.

Institute for the Future. *Health and Health Care 2010: The Forecast, the Challenge.* San Francisco: Jossey-Bass; 2000.

Johns MC, et al. A growing global network's role in outbreak response: AFHSC-GEIS 2008–2009. *BMC Public Health.* 2011;11(suppl 2):S3.

Keck W, Scutchfield FD. *The Future of Public Health.* Albany, NY: Delmar; 1997.

Kvedar J, et al. E-patient connectivity and the near term future. *J Gen Intern Med.* 2011;26:636–638.

McClellan M, Baicker K. Reducing uninsurance through the nongroup market: Health insurance credits and purchasing groups. *Health Affairs Web Exclusive.* October 23, 2002. http://content.healthaffairs.org/cgi/content/abstract/hlthaff.w2.363v1.

McInturff B, Weigel L. The health debate is far from over; will be cornerstone issue in 2012. *Kaiser Health News.* March 22, 2011. http://www.kaiserhealthnews.org/Stories/2011/March/23/pollsters-on-health-law-politics-mcinturff.aspx. Accessed January 2012.

Milstein JB, et al. The impact of globalization on vaccine development and availability. *Health Affairs.* 2006;25(4):1061–1069.

Moore R. Telehealth connected care. *Health Manage Technol.* 2009;30(3):39–40.

National Academy of Sciences. *The Future of Nursing: Leading Change, Advancing Health.* Washington, DC: Institute of Medicine; 2010.

Ngo V, et al. Health coaching in the teamlet model: A case study. *J Gen Intern Med.* 2010;25(12):1375–1378.

Oeyen S. About protocols and guidelines: It's time to work in harmony! *Crit Care Med.* 2007;35(1):292–293.

Porter ME, Rivkin JW. *Prosperity at Risk: Findings of Harvard Business School's Survey on U.S. Competitiveness.* Cambridge, MA: Harvard Business School; 2012.

Sahadi J. 45% don't owe U.S. income tax. *CNN Money.* April 18, 2011. http://money.cnn.com/2011/04/14/pf/taxes/who_pays_income_taxes/index.htm. Accessed January 2012.

Slawson DC, Shaughnessy AF. Using "medical poetry" to remove the inequities in health care delivery. *J Family Med.* 2001;50(1):51–65.

Sperling KL, Shapira OM. Here it comes: Defined contribution health care. *Benefits Quarterly.* 2011;27(1):42–48.

U.S. Census Bureau. *Statistical Abstract of the United States, 2001.* Washington, DC: U.S. Census Bureau; 2001.

Whitcomb ME. Commentary: Meeting future medical care needs: A perfect storm on the horizon. *J Assoc Am Med Coll.* 2011;86(12):1490–1491.

World Health Organization (WHO). What are the International Health Regulations? 2008. http://www.who.int/features/qa/39/en/index.html. Accessed December 2011.

Index